"Vande Mataran

Your book "Urb urban areas will strike a blow at the roots of the wide-spread Naxal movement in the entire country including Bastar and Chattisgarh. I am one among those thousands of young women and men, who end-up being intimidated by people from Andhra-Telangana, running a reign of terror to consolidate power, to join their gangs. I am certain your writing will help unmask these Naxal leaders, who come from outside and rule over us folk living in the jungle, and their white-collar supporters and enablers. This will be a significant contribution to bring peace to Bastar and other Naxal-affected areas."

—Kosi
Surrendered Woman Naxal Commander

"For Bastar and its people, oppressed by Naxal terror for four decades, it is great source of joy that, people outside Bastar are now beginning to feel, understand and hear our pain and are stepping forward. Better late than never. In this context, as a filmmaker, scriptwriter and author, you hold a special place. Just as you have approached any subject you have tackled, whether as a scriptwriter or as a director or as a writer, with a serious solution-oriented approach, this same sincerity and boldness shows up in your writing on the Naxal problem. Your book "Urban Naxals" is evidence of this, where you unmask the white-collar Urban Naxals sitting in the capital Delhi and other major cities of India and their violent ideology."

—Subbarao
Founding Member
Action Group for National Integrity (AGNI)
(AGNI is a leading NGO fighting Naxal terror in Bastar)

(Above letters are translated from the originals in Hindi.)

"Gripping, newsy account of a filmmaker's encounter with radicalism in urban India"

—Hindol Sengupta

Editor-at-Large, Fortune India and author of eight books.

Urban Naxals drags you into the hard, brutal and fanatical world thriving beneath the dark shadows of liberalism, free speech and tolerance. Vivek Agnihotri brings the art of storytelling and the craft of filmmaking to breathe life into an ugly phenomenon that has been setting a dangerous national agenda. This is a gripping and disturbing book that constricts your conscience and lingers within long after you've finished reading it.

—Gautam Chikermane

Vice President Observer Research Foundation and author, Tunnel of Varanavat

"Urban Naxals is a daring, if unconventional, analysis at how the far left has captured our educational institutions to produce a generation of brain-washed nihilists to wage war on the masses.

Urban Naxals is at once irreverent and introspective, moving and hard-hitting. Urban Naxals will leave you shaken and ask you to join the conversation we, as a nation, ought to be having before it is too late."

—Mayur Didolkar

Novelist

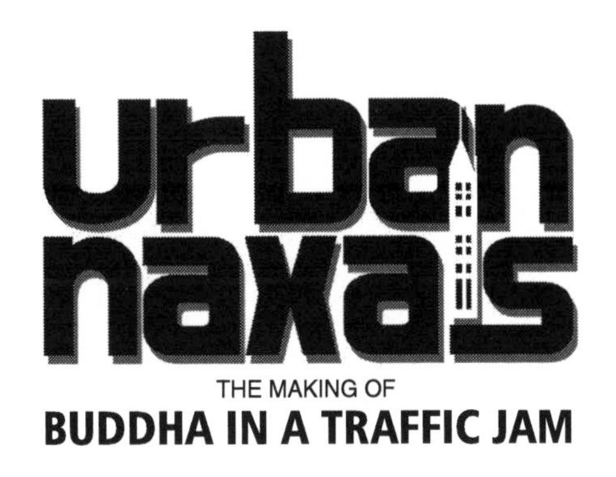

THE MAKING OF

BUDDHA IN A TRAFFIC JAM

Vivek Agnihotri

First published in India 2018

Hindi passages translated by Sankrant Sanu

ISBN: 978-1-942426-05-9

Garuda Prakashan Private Limited
Gurugram, Bharat
www.garudaprakashan.com
www.garudabooks.com

In the loving memory of my father Acharya Prabhudayalu Agnihotri, freedom fighter, Indologist and teacher who introduced me to Kalidasa and the meaning of being an Indian.

To my mother Sharda Devi Agnihotri, freedom fighter who made me understand the value of excellence.

To my wife Pallavi Joshi who did not stop my crusade even after life threats. She helped me make a better version, of this book, and me.

Everyone needs Hari. When I was seeking a new horizon, Hari found me. And sculpted me.

To the students of India.

समर शेष है
नहीं पाप का भागी केवल व्याध,
जो तटस्थ हैं
समय लिखेगा उनके भी अपराध।

–रामधारी सिंह "दिनकर"

The war still rages on
The attacker alone can't be blamed,
Those who stood aloof
In time, they also will be shamed.

-Ramdhari Singh "Dinkar"

Foreword

I don't believe in Forewords. A book should stand on its own, speak for itself. But this book is an exception. A "Bloody Fascist Brahmin" penned it, who was stopped from screening his film, Buddha in a Traffic Jam, at Jadavpur University. His car was gheraoed and damaged. He himself was injured. An angry mob of Leftist students and activists bayed for his blood.

Why such hatred? Why so much intolerance? What was Vivek Agnihotri saying or showing in his film which was so dangerous or destabilising? Why was he such a blatantly marked target of "intellectual terrorism?" Vivek is right when he says, "In India, people fight with all their might to kill an idea."

First they nearly stopped him from making his film. Then they tried to prevent him from screening it. When he took his exquisite and excruciating creation literally to the streets and to the campuses, showing it directly to target audiences, again he was heckled and blocked.

I thought to myself, whether we love or hate the film, we cannot allow this in India. In my own university, JNU, another Leftist bastion, it was blocked by the Dean of the School of Arts & Aesthetics, in whose auditorium it was originally to be screened. Instead, the students arranged an outdoor screening, which was attended by over five thousand. The film had a rousing, almost delirious reception. When I saw it, I was moved, disturbed, provoked.

It was one of the most original and unusual movies I had encountered in a long time. A political thriller, with great acting, music, and a theme of national importance. I loved it. Instantly, I became one of the "hundred owners" of the film.

What is it, I asked myself, which makes both this book, and the film whose making it recounts, exceptional?

The answer is simple and obvious. This book is a triple triumph. It not only tells the story of how this extraordinary film got to be made, but also how its auteur, Vivek Agnihotri, healed his broken spirit, snatching victory from the very brink of disaster, despair, and depression. "This film is making me reinvent myself," he realizes during the shooting, "Every day. Every moment." In addition, it is a profound reflection on the condition of India, especially on the Maoist insurgency that is gnawing at the innards of our democratic polity.

* * *

We all fail in our lives. But few of us actually recover to tell the story. Vivek is one of them.

In fact, as he confesses, Vivek "had failed four times. Like a manglik girl." In a cut-throat industry, where you're only as good as the money your last film makes, what is the future of a director who wants to tell the truth? This is every creative artist's dilemma. There is, besides, "a mindset in Bollywood that doesn't let Indic ideas flourish."

When Vivek decides to speak out against the Bollywood campaign against Narendra Modi in 2014, he finds that he has overnight become a pariah in his fraternity: "I was discriminated against by almost all my Bollywood friends, whom I used to hang around with because, like them, I also believed in a certain ideology but found it fake and alienated from reality, and elitist." Trying to make Buddha in a Traffic Jam only makes it worse. But Vivek succeeds in breaking the Bollywood's dominant code.

How does he do that? He discovers that "Within each of us, there is a seeker who is hungry for knowledge and wisdom. After working in the film industry for over six years, this is the first time I can feel this seeker."

Right in the midst of the near-impossible ordeal of trying to make an off-beat, politically incorrect feature film on a ridiculously low budget of 2 crores in an industry where a single star for a single movie may demand and get upwards of 50 crores, Vivek has an epiphany. "Can I, as a filmmaker," he asks himself, "tell the truth?" Then he answers the question with utter and unequivocal conviction: "My answer is clear. Yes."

It is a tremendous realisation; Vivek has found his purpose. As he strives to articulate it, he understands:

People seek the truth. In media. In art. In cinema. Since nobody tells the truth, and it is acceptable, we succumb to the apparent emotional needs of an audience like feeling happy or feeling sad; the truth remains the least priority for the artists of Bollywood.

It is this truth of a filmmaker and human being that this book chronicles for the world. A truth that we Indians must pay special heed to. For what is India, what is Sanatana Dharma, itself if not for truth? Satyameva Jayate Naanritam. This Rg Vedic injunction and prophecy could well be the theme of the book.

But in addition to the record of making a film, which is also the tale of his own reawakening, this book also tells the story of India. The story of India which, in a sense, is our own story – the story of each one of us. This is the story we all live through.

As Vivek puts it, "Everyone in India has a story for their failures, stagnation or decay." We know, as Vivek reminds us, that our country is so "full of problems." Imagine what would happen "If we solve even a fraction of our problems." We would, he says, "become a solution-rich country." A book like this inspires us to be "problem solvers, instead of being buck-passers."

* * *

Urban Naxal is packed with analyses, reflections, and solutions. It is a thinking woman's and man's book. It is also brimming with compassion, consideration, and passionate concern for our poor, "suffering, conflicted, mediocre India." How to turn our society from its addiction to mediocrity to a land of hope and possibilities? This is also one of the themes of the book.

As Vivek puts it, "After poverty, inefficiency is the second biggest curse of Indian society." In addition, there is corruption. Unrelenting. Endemic. As Suresh, one of his producers puts it pensively, "Forget Naxal areas, even in cities it's not easy. It's very difficult to do business in India. We have become an extortionist country." From being broke, "Financially. Emotionally. Mentally," from the point "where most people give up," Vivek overcomes impossible odds to make his film.

In doing so, he learns about the real India. Not the India that we see from the safe mode of our comfortable, bourgeois city-bred security, but the gut-wrenching reality of our complicated, poverty-stricken, but still so uplifting India:

I thought I knew India but last night I realized I had been window-shopping. Last night I felt I was back to where I belonged. An India where success doesn't lie in money. It lies in surviving. The complex India. The difficult India. The corrupt India. The honest India. The oppressed India. The feudal India. A regressive India. A progressive India. It's poor. It's filthy. It's hard working. It smells of struggle, of co-existence, of sweat. Its diversity, its disparity, the chaos, the conflict. The aspirational India, the ignored India, the defeated India... The real India.

It is this defeated and real India that actually saves Vivek. He realises that when we recover the simplicity, beauty, and sincerity of our inner beings, the whole universe conspires, as it were, to help, support, and guide us: "My faith in goodness is reinforced. I learn that if the intent is right, the universe creates a new logic. A new reality."

Again and again, the common people from urban taxi operators to adivasis in distant Dantewada come to his rescue. So do a variety of film industry workers and professionals. His wife, the exceptionally talented Pallavi also does a major role in the film as does his niece. The former also sings the defining theme song, Faiz's revolutionary anthem, "Chand roz aur mirī jaan faqat chand hī roz." Students and faculty of the Indian Business School produce and inspire the movie.

A big boost comes when Anupam Kher agrees to act in one of the lead roles, that of the B-school Professor and Dean, who recruits and brainwashes students, playing on their guilt, plying their idealism, to turn them into urban naxals. Vivek not only didn't have the money to pay Kher's regular fees, he couldn't even afford the actor's normal 5-star accommodation or meals.

But Kher, graciously rises to the occasion. He tells Vivek after listening to the script, "I think you have found the purpose. You have found your song. Mark my words, this film will change your life. Thanks for casting me and all the best." What is more, he lives in the ISB hostel like all the others, even eating the normal mess food. When it comes to the on-location shoot from a professor's campus residence, Kher is completely in his element, taking over and owning both the role and space.

Then, right in the middle of the making of the movie, Kher says to Vivek, "In every director's life comes a point when he finds his sur, his song. This film is your song. I can feel it." As readers and viewers we cannot but agree with Kher. Vivek has rediscovered his metier, his true calling.

The book is the story of such a miracle. That is what makes it inspiring.

* * *

But the book and film analyse a special, specific subject, as indicated in the title, Urban Naxal. What is this? Simply put it is the nexus between India's "Red Corridor," our "poorest and ironically the most militarized zone ... the nerve centre of the Naxal movement" and its urban cultural and intellectual support base. Who are the Urban Naxals?

They are, in Vivek's own words, intellectuals who "present this beastly and gruesome reality in a sanitized, romantic, and palatable packaging for which the media and its urban audiences have a weakness." They offer the legitimating and camouflaging ecosystem for what is an open, if internal, insurgency against the democratically elected government of the Republic of India.

Spread across several states and districts of India, this war has claimed many thousand lives, both of Indian security personnel as of Maoist insurgents. Vivek's book is full of facts, figures, questions, and ideas about this menace to India's sovereignty and integrity.

But we must never forget that both the book and the film are not expert reports or documentaries. They are original, creative works, literary and cinematic. India-haters, of whatever political or ideological stripe, have one dream. It is to capture power and install their own government in India. They hope to harness the disgruntled, some would say disenfranchised, members of our society, "the Adivasi, Dalits, Muslims, and other 'forgotten people', united under one common red flag," to "demolish the State," instead of including them in democratic process.

Vivek warns us against this real and present danger. According to him, Naxals are waging a conflict in which "the lines between war and politics, combatants, and civilians" gets blurred. Right in our midst, in our social circles and living rooms are people who support such dangerous and armed terrorists. Vivek believes that he has a story that "needs to be told." It is the story of "the invisible enemy" in our midst, perhaps more dangerous than a known and identified terrorist.

It is this invisible enemy who is the Urban Naxal.

Whether we agree with him or not, Vivek's story is not only worth telling, but worth attending to. What is more, he tells it unusually. In a film which reads like a book, with ten chapters. This, as Vivek and his whole team know only too well, is quite unlike a regular film: "It's born in a B-school, with the initiative of students. A movie in a book form is an 'out-of-the-box' idea and very appropriate for a student's film."

But why is it called Buddha in a Traffic Jam? That is because right in the middle of its making, Vivek is once more in a deep pit: "Again, I had no money. No work. No hope." When he discovers the way to get out of the crisis and actually finish the week he feels like "a Buddha, in a traffic jam."

A traffic jam is the worst possible situation to be if you want to get to some place on time. But if you discover your Buddhahood right in the middle of the impasse, it's a miraculous way of beating all the odds of life.

That is Vivek's story, the story of India, of Urban Naxals. It is the story of how his film was made, how his book got written.

That is why I decided to support this "Bloody Fascist Brahmin."

That is why I decided to break my rule to write this Foreword.

—Makarand R. Paranjape

Professor and Poet
Jawaharlal Nehru University, New Delhi

Contents

Book Four : The Struggle of Buddha

Book One

Buddha is Born

"If anything, if you can get somebody interested in something and get them excited, that's great. You should be praised for having opened the debate and having asked the right questions.
- Oliver Stone

1. Bloody Fascist Brahmin, go back!

6th March 2016

Black.

I am inside a mass of black. No earth. No sky. Just black.

And thousands of screams.

'*Bloody, Fascist Brahmin*... Go back.'

Hundreds of young students are baying for my blood. Angry. Vengeful. Armed with wooden sticks and hot blood.

They want me beaten up. Humiliated. And killed.

They are trying to break the car open to pull me out and parade me as a symbol of an upper-caste oppressor and punish me for exposing their nexus.

My guilt is that I am here to show my film. One of the smallest films of the decade. A film with no money, no studios, and no backers.

They do not agree with the film which has found resonance amongst students. They want the film banned. They want my voice killed.

I feel like a fetus about to be ripped out from the womb. Abortion by mob.

And none of them have even seen the film.

An Hour Earlier...

'Oh My God! We are screwed.' There were cars all around us, waiting for the green light, on a day when it had rained a bit and clogged the roads.

'Sir, this is Kolkata, a giant, blocked drain. A gutter without an outlet. Can I take you through the inner roads?' My chauffeur Prabhu asks me.

'As long as we reach Jadavpur University by 5.30 PM,' I say, looking at my watch. It's 4.30 PM. Before leaving the hotel an hour ago, I had looked up the Google Map. On a normal day, it takes 58 minutes to reach Jadavpur University from Park Street. But this isn't just any other day.

Prabhu is a big built, bald man in his 50s, maybe 60s. It's difficult to guess a hardworking person's age as they jump straight from childhood to middle age. And in most of the cases, even the person himself doesn't know his correct age. I think people in India age prematurely. A man who starts worrying about feeding his family pre-puberty will naturally age faster than others. Prabhu hails from a state which can put even West Bengal to shame - Bihar. His village is 100 miles away from Patna. He came to Calcutta to earn a living and feed his family back home. He did odd jobs, like any other migrant, and lived in a tiny room with 20 other Biharis. His life changed when a truck driver took him on as a cleaner, coincidently on the same day *Calcutta* became Kolkata. He has a better idea of India than those who have become millionaires just talking about the 'Idea of India'. He decided at an early age that the safest way to make money in this city of sins is through honesty and customer satisfaction. It's strange, how we find more honest and righteous people as we climb down the economic strata. More low-income people have surprised me with their honesty than the moneyed ones.

The entrepreneur in Prabhu never liked highways. He wanted to start his own business. He started off by buying a small Xerox and PCO shop with some of his own hard-earned money and some borrowed. Within few years, he was running a chain of three Xerox/PCO shops in the same lane. Next, he tried investing in a call centre. Just a few days after he finalized the deal, the local retailers went on a strike against FDI in the retail sector. His shops had to stay shut for weeks. As a result, he couldn't pay his EMIs and had to sell the shops. In West Bengal, you just can't be not affected by politics: the 'politics of the poor', as Prabhu describes it. 'This, perhaps, is the only place in the world where people hate development,' he tells me. *'Yeh bhadralok ki rajneeti kabhi Hindustan ko amir nahi banne degi'* He was talking about 'Leftist politics' as intellectuals describe it, and how the politics of the elite would never let India become rich. So, after this setback, Prabhu borrowed money again and bought a second hand Innova. He drives it as a private car, illegally, as he doesn't have enough money to bribe the officials and get an All India Tourist Permit.

Even so, everyone wants to feel confident and proud of something in life. Satisfied customers were Prabhu's 'confidence crutch'. His Innova looked brand new. Polished and scented. He had newspapers in all three languages, Hindi, English, and Bengali. Plus, *The Economic Times.* He had the latest issues of *India Today* and *Business Today*. There were small Bisleri bottles, a tissue box and a map of Kolkata. Management gurus define it as 'value addition'. He constantly smiled and doubled up as my local guide, providing me with historical insights on every lane. Intermittently, he brought in local politics and how due to it he is not being able to materialize his objective of owning a fleet of taxis and get his family to Kolkata. Ola and Uber have made it tough. But he isn't willing to succumb to competitors' games. He is convinced that he has to give quality to see a smile on his customer's face, only then can he succeed—. '*Seth khush hona chahiye... seth log khush hoga to hee paisa banega na, kyon seth*?' He was talking beyond customer satisfaction. He was talking about customer delight.

One needs delighted customers to build a loyal customer core and this base eventually gives profits. Slowly, but steadily. India is full of enterprising individuals but has failed to exploit their collective strength. We have never recognized the value of individual merit. Prabhu, if given equal opportunities, could be the owner of an Ola-like taxi service. Ideologically, there wasn't any difference between him and a multi-billion-dollar conglomerate, Tata, that recently bought a stake in Ola. Both believe in quality and consumer delight.

Prabhu turns the car to the left. And makes another quick left. It seems he has taken it upon himself to prove that Kolkata is indeed a city of the Left. We enter a narrow, serpentine lane which will take us to a small crossing from where another left turn, and we will be on the main road. This lane is so narrow that Prabhu has to pull back the side mirrors of the car. 'What if another car comes from the other side? Forget car, what if a scooty comes?' I ask him. 'No. It won't.' Drivers, like women, are driven by a sixth sense.

The lane is surrounded by derelict, shamelessly renovated, over-populated, encroaching buildings, falling from the top like an old tree, with some traces of colonial architecture still left in them: the only proof that this city was an Indian capital for 138 years during the British Raj. These tiny lanes don't have much traffic but there are more speed breakers than buildings. Why do we love making speed breakers? Maybe it's a subliminal reflection of our system's psyche that thrives on creating as many hurdles as possible on our way to success. More hurdles mean more corruption, more money for the law enforcers.

We reach the crossing only to realize we may have to turn back. A municipality water pipe has broken. There are people bathing from the leaking water pipe. Some are washing clothes and some filling huge plastic cans for household work. Kids are playing with water. Not realizing that as soon as they grow a moustache they will have to play with fire. Their mothers are shouting at them. The kids shamelessly disobey their commands until they get beaten up. There are cows, pigs, dogs, cats, and rodents – all quenching their thirst from a thin stream of water. A huge bandicoot is staring at a dog. After some snorting and whooshing, the dog backs out. Size matters.

Women are chatting, filling utensils, taking a bath in the open. One of them is singing while a young man is prompting her with lyrics. It's rare to see such condensed happiness, bonding, and rivalry in a space of 20 square feet. A rickshaw-puller joins in and starts washing his rickshaw. A few women who are semi-naked, covered with just a wet, sheer sari request him to wait until they are done with their chores. Nodding, he takes out his mobile phone and starts playing a game. Soon in India, more people will have access to 4G telephones than water.

'What if there wasn't a leakage, where would they get water from?' I ask Prabhu.

'They will create leakages,' he replies, honking hard. 'Don't think it's free!' He moves his hand over his bald pate out of habit that hasn't left him even after his hair left his head, and continues, 'They pay the municipality guys to keep it open.'

In 70 years of independence, we haven't been able to provide water to our citizens. I fear soon the waterless Indians will turn into bloodthirsty savages who would kill their own kin for water. Not out of any ideology or politics. Not out of hatred or revenge. Only out of their thirst. And this is where the Indian State has failed. Miserably. I wonder what is stopping Shekhar Kapur from making his film on the subject – *Paani.* I wish he makes it before that watershed day.

'Which gate?' Prabhu asks. 'Seth, we are about to reach Jadavpur.' Prabhu rings me back to here and now. It's 5.20 PM. I am ten minutes early. I look at Prabhu who gives me a I-told-you-not-to-worry smile. He promised. He delivered.

I ring up one of the students from Think India, a cultural student organization. Because they are against the Leftist ideology of armed struggle, they are considered right wing.

'Have you already reached Jadavpur?' He sounds hassled and starts talking to a fellow student in Bengali.

'Any problem?' I ask.

'No, no sir, please come to gate no 8. And please come slowly.'

Why is he asking me to do that? Perhaps they are not prepared. 5.30 PM is the official time. Maybe, they were expecting me to reach by six. How are they supposed to know that I am a time fanatic? How are they supposed to believe that a film celebrity could reach before time?

'Let's go in from gate no. 8. Do you know where it is? Or should we ask someone?'

'No sir. No point asking. I'll take you there.'

By now I had started trusting Prabhu's judgment.

'Are you meeting a relative?' Prabhu makes a simple query.

'No.'

He looks at me from the corner of his eyes. In sneakers, jeans, tee and an open shirt, I most certainly don't look like a politician. If my relative doesn't study here and I am not a politician, then what the hell am I doing here at JU – the nursery of radical politics? The story goes that when a pregnant lady crosses the JU gates, the baby in her womb starts talking politics. Prabhu makes a left turn. I look at the gate and realize it's not gate no. 8. It's gate no. 3. He explains that as there is a lot of slow moving traffic on the main road, to save time, he has decided to enter through gate no. 3 and take me to no. 8 from the inner roads of the university.

The old, yellowing walls of the buildings are densely plastered with posters which are covering up all the cracks on these derelict structures. If you want to kill someone with *poster-phobia*, JU will work as gallows for him.

'What brings you here?' Prabhu can't control his curiosity.

'I am screening my film here.'

'Do you make films? Where? Bollywood?'

'Yes.'

'What do you do?'

'I write and direct.'

'Which films have you made?'

I tell him the names of my films. He hasn't heard of any. The last film he watched was *Munnabhai MBBS*. Despite loving the film, he doesn't agree with Sanjay Dutt lying to his father in the movie.

'Whatever may be the situation, a good son must not lie to his father.' He shows me his moral compass. For him, there is no difference between me and Raju Hirani. He, like most of the audience, believes that a film represents everyone in Bollywood. He has no idea that for the last 45 days, the only thing I have been fighting against is *not* being part of *that* Bollywood. I have suffered because my film speaks a political truth that nobody wants to be told. I have been struggling that my film be seen as an alternate narrative. I am fighting a new battle everyday just to show my film to interested students. I have flown the entire night from Pune to Kolkata, changing planes, waiting at airports to reach just in time to screen my film at Jadavpur University.

Only after I arrived early morning in Kolkata, I was told by the students that the university had cancelled their permission last night to screen the film in the auditorium. But they have decided to screen it anyway. I have no idea where and how I will show it.

Prabhu takes a turn. Only to stop. The road is laid with posters. Some students are sitting on the road and making placards. The road looks like a horizontal graffiti wall. The energy and excitement remind me of my college drama competition days. The backstage was always the battleground for last minute preparations. Prabhu honks and the students pick up their posters from the road and spread them on their shoulders. Two girls are walking in the middle of the road, smoking and giggling. Prabhu honks again.

'What's the name of your film?' Prabhu asks me.

'*Buddha In A Traffic Jam.*'

Now the girls turn and one of them says something to Prabhu rudely in Bengali. The other girl looks hard at me. She whispers something to the first girl. And both of them start screaming. Some students leave their work and start staring at me. Some start moving. Some pick up placards. Some are yelling their lungs out. Some run towards us.

Prabhu instinctively races the engine, honks hard and maneuvers the car in the onslaught of students. 'What are you doing? Stop. Stop now.' I yell at him. He stops the car after a few hundred metres. Not because he has obeyed my order, but because it is a dead end, with staff quarters on all sides.

'If students have any issues, I'll talk to them. Why run away? Reverse the car,' I tell him. Prabhu gives me an amused look. He glances at the rearview mirror and whispers in Bengali which translates to 'Oh My God. We are screwed.'

In the flash of a second, the car is surrounded by hundreds of students. They are banging on the car. They want me to come out. They are screaming in Bengali. It's a scene where I know for sure that if I get out they will cut me into pieces. They start hitting the car with the rear end of the placards. One student jumps over the car. One falls on the bonnet. Then one student starts hitting the side mirror until it breaks and falls down.

All of us imagine ourselves in various dreadful situations. We see ourselves being robbed, being a cancer patient, being killed, but this is one situation I could have never imagined, even in my worst nightmares. I feel like a character from *Game of Thrones* being hounded by savages eager to drink my blood. But not before shredding me up. It's bright daylight, yet the car is dark from inside as all its sources of light are covered by the students' sweating bodies. It's almost indescribable. I feel numb. I am worried about Prabhu's car. If I don't get out now, they will destroy his car. His livelihood. His ambition.

'Don't make the mistake of getting down,' Prabhu reads my mind. 'Life is more valuable than a car.'

'I'll have to talk to them. Let me at least hear what they want.' I roll down the window a little bit to be able to talk to them. Before

I can say anything, they push their hands inside. Some hands start forcing the window down. Prabhu is in a dilemma. If he shuts the window, it hurts them and if he doesn't, they will break the window.

'Why are you damaging a poor man's car?' I try to talk to them.

'If you care for him, come out.'

'I will if all of you move back five feet.'

This makes them think.

Suddenly, from nowhere, a girl pushes herself in and bangs her placard on my window. I have never read such big letters from such a close distance. It was so close that I couldn't even read the entire sentence in one go. The girl starts shouting what I gathered was written on the placard 'Bloody fascist Brahmin. Go back Agnihotri'.

I try to maintain my calm. 'I am willing to talk and answer all your questions. What is it that you want?'

'We want you to go back. And never ever return,' the girl screams.

'But I am just showing my film... if you don't see it, it's fine.'

'There is no way you can ever show it here!'

'But why?'

'Because there is no place for alternative narrative at JU.'

She takes her hand out. Everyone takes out their hands.

Prabhu quickly rolls up the window.

The girl bends down. Looks deep into my eyes.

And then she spits on the glass.

I am not reacting anymore. I am not numb or nervous anymore. I am just observing. In movies, we use slow motion tricks to suspend time to emphasize the importance of that moment. I could see the spit moving towards me. Slowly, like in the movies. Every particle crystal clear, splitting from its mass and breaking into many drops. Each drop turning into a big bold letter. They splash on the window. All the particles scatter and make a random design on the glass. Through this abstract hazy foreground, I can see the distorted face of the girl still screaming.

'There is no place for alternate narrative!'

I can hear it in surround sound. I can read it on my window. In her spit. The venom.

2. A Film is Born

December 2010

I open the window and freeze. It's touching 5° centigrade. In winters like these, I like to be hit by the chilly breeze, first thing in the morning. I slowly open my eyes. I am mesmerized by what I see.

Dawn is breaking. The first light of the sun has just kissed the arched dome of the Taj Mahal. It looks like the first waxing crescent of the moon. But in warm amber. I wait for the sun to envelope the entire dome in its warmth, like how Shahjahan must've held Mumtaz Mahal in his arms on a chilly December morning. I am so dumbstruck that I forget to take any photos on my new iPhone.

Some moments get imprinted in our mind's photo album. Some in the Nature folder, some in Family, some in Travel, some in Food. But some photos don't fit in any category. This is one of them. It belongs neither to the Monuments' folder, nor Sunrise. At the moment, I am not a filmmaker or a teacher. Not a husband or a father. I see this magic like no one else can see. This is my view. My angle. My perspective. I don't believe in God but I do believe in Godly moments. I find myself shivering only to realize that my iPhone is vibrating. Why would Ravi Agnihotri call so early in the morning when he knows pretty well that I am on Christmas holiday with my family?

'Hello, Ravi.'

'Vivek sir, we have got the funds,' Ravi informs me jubilantly. 'I wanted to inform you before I go to sleep.'

'Wow! Great. Who is the funder?'

'*Woh sab chodiye* ... you just come to Hyderabad.'

'Yeah, but who is the funder?' I am curious, as if I am watching a murder mystery where the director has shown the murder in the very first scene and I don't want to wait for the climax. All I want to know is 'Who is the murderer?'

'I will tell you everything when you are here. Just tell me when can you come?'

'You know I am in Agra with my family. My cousin with his daughter from America is also with us. We had made this plan in advance. There is no way I can come now. I'll be back in Mumbai on 2nd, -January, 3rd I can be in Hyderabad.'

'Why delay when the investor is excited and ready? What if they change their minds?'

'If they are going to change their mind within 10 days then it's better not to work with them. Tell them I will be there on 3rd Jan.'

'OK.' Ravi takes a long pause as if waiting for me to change my mind.

'See you. Got to leave for Jaipur in an hour.'

'But how will you go? The entire highway is blocked.'

'Why?'

'Gujjars are agitating for 5 percent reservation. They have blocked all highways and railway tracks to Jaipur. It's everywhere in the news.'

'It's impossible for them to block the Golden Triangle. Christmas-New Year is the peak tourist season. There is no way government can let them block the main transport arteries. India will stop. It's 2010 not 80's.'

'Sir, don't believe me but please don't take the risk.'

I ask the reception about our pre-booked taxi. The manager tells me that the driver is a Gujjar and he won't come.

'How can he back out just like that?' I am losing my cool.

'Sir, these Gujjars don't listen to reasoning. We are sorry. And we advise you not to take the risk.'

The manager tries lots of taxi services. Everyone refuses to go.

I remember our local taxi driver who took us around in Agra. I call him. He tells me it's not possible to take the highway to Jaipur. Agitators are pelting stones at the cars and breaking window panes with *latths*. I plead with him and impress upon him how important it is for us to reach Jaipur. We can't cancel bookings as we won't get any other place due to the season's rush. I insist there must be some way. He tells me one can go from small village roads but he doesn't know the way and it's not safe unless *'you want to take a chance'*.

Chance is just another word for risk. All of us talk about risk but what is risk? Is it knowing that there is danger out there and still going through with it? Is it a price-payoff analysis? Is it ignorance? Stupidity or instinct? The human mind feeds on information. We feel comfortable and secure when we have all the information. Lack of information is like going into a dark alley. You are vulnerable to loss. It was chance vs choice. I made my choice.

Driving on dusty, bumpy, part-tar-part-clay roads, looking at yellow mustard fields covered with thick fog, moving in the direction of the unknown, I was thinking of another risk which I was going to take on 3rd January. Ravi has found a funder but I still don't have a story I'd die to make. For free.

Early 2010

Sometime ago, a young IT professional from Bangalore had contacted me on Facebook. He ran an NGO –Green Commandos–, and wanted me to become its brand ambassador. He spoke to me about environmental issues from a very socialist point of view. He also asked me to help him contact some celebrities. It was obvious that he was more interested in film celebs and I did introduce him to some big celebs. It was a good cause after all. After a few months, he informed me that he has got admission in the Indian School of Business (ISB), Hyderabad, and he was quitting his job. ISB at that time was listed as the 12th best business school in the world.

'What... you too, from socialist to capitalist?' I teased him.

He was a capitalist at heart who also wanted social justice. Most of the Indian students grow up with this dichotomy. Including me. He spoke to me about his ambitions, his future, the country's future and how he loved a movie that he had watched the night before. The movie was titled *Yamla Pagla Deewana*. It was obvious that both of us loved movies. But of different kinds. The only thing common between us was our last name 'Agnihotri'. His name was Ravi Agnihotri. A hardcore Punjabi from Ropar.

During one of his Sunday calls, he asked me if I was interested in mentoring a short film on the Naxal issue. These were the times when I had just come out of a professional dilemma, after an overstretched phase of self-denial and deep introspection. I had made two back-to-back big, multi-starrer films, without much struggle. Anil Ambani's Reliance, under the BIG umbrella brand, was setting up their film studio in a very big way. Reliance had signed me, along with five other reputed directors including Shyam Benegal, Vidhu Vinod Chopra, Sudhir Mishra and Madhur Bhandarkar, for multiple films, each at a vulgar price. I had arrived! But then, after spending two years on two scripts, the films never got made. I was out of work. Out of money. More than that, I was disillusioned with the film industry. What can an unemployed filmmaker do? Luckily, I knew how to teach. It was in my blood. I taught at Whistling Woods and some other media institutes. Mentally, I had resigned from Bollywood. I think all filmmakers go through this phase.

Ravi sent me a mail which had a short idea for a 60-minute film on Naxalism. He wanted to make it before his upcoming graduation in six-seven months.

He then called to ask if I would like to come to ISB to deliver a lecture and discuss the film project as well.

'Yes. Why not? I would love to teach at ISB. In fact, I have created a module called "I Am Buddha". It's about 'creative thinking for leadership'.' I soft sold Professor Vivek Agnihotri to Ravi.

'OK. Let me speak to the concerned people. Will come back on this soon.'

He called sooner than I had expected. He gave me a formal invitation for the lecture and asked for a convenient date.

This was my most hi-tech lecture. I had prepared a multimedia presentation. It worked well. I felt wonderful teaching at ISB, with its world-class beautiful campus. And started wondering if this was my new career. If this was where I should be.

Afterwards, sitting on sprawling lawns and sipping beer, Ravi introduced me to three other students. Pritika Idnani and Sandeep Goel from Delhi and Abhishek Mohanta from Chandigarh.

They had formed a team to produce this short film on the Naxal issue.

'Who will sponsor it?' I asked, like a commercial director.

'None. We have already created the seed fund. Each of us has contributed a few thousand and will put in more.'

One of them took out a file full of research on the Naxal issue. They also had a story prepared. Written by Navneet Skeria, DIG, Lucknow. He was on paid leave to do his MBA. It was about a Meera Sanyal kind of lady MD, whose chopper develops a snag and has to land in a tribal area. Stuck with the tribals, she lives with them, understands their problems and comes out with a business solution.

The film was to be called 'Break Even'. But what the students thought was a story, was in fact just a sketchy idea. It sounded more like a feasibility report full of complex jargon and data. Great presentations don't make great stories. I didn't want to dissuade them. I figured I had nothing to lose. If I mentored this film, I'd spend some good time with students at ISB. It won't be typical Bollywood.

'Who is your audience?' I asked

'We will sell it to the studios.'

I realized they had no idea about how the film business works. It was important for me to tell them the truth.

'Why do you want to make a 60-minute film?' I said. 'You will spend your hard-earned money and nobody will see or even care about it. You will see it a few times and then someday even you won't remember where you had kept the DVD.'

'But we have decided now. We have formed a production house and applied for private limited registration. It's called Friday Night Productions. Even if the money is wasted, we will assume it a part of our CSR (Corporate Social Responsibility).' Ravi was determined.

'You guys are the future CEOs of the world, why don't you think big?' I challenged them.

'Big? How?' Sandeep asked. He was the wisest amongst them with a sharp business sense.

'Make it for a larger audience. Make a full-length feature film. It will be seen even after hundreds of years.'

'But we don't have that kind of money. Maximum we can contribute is couple of lacs.'

'Don't contribute. Raise the money. Show your enterprise. This will be your real MBA. Even if nothing happens, you will have a first-hand experience of raising funds and learning from it. And if nothing else, you can always make this short film.'

There was silence.

'Write to your alumni association. ISB alumni are rich and powerful people. What if someone believes in the idea? What if you find a sponsor?' I urged.

Sandeep sensed the potential. He asked a few questions but agreed. Pritika liked Bollywood entertainers, so her choice was simple. Abhishek was convinced but waited for Ravi's reaction. Ravi was more concerned about the research he had done. Slowly, the discussion turned into a massive argument amongst them. Ravi got irritated and lost his temper. He sat in a corner, sulking.

More beer cans opened.

'But what about the script?' Ravi asked me after a long awkward pause.

'Why do you insist on making a film on the Naxal issue? Who cares? Nobody cares about the Naxal issue. Who wants to see some people in jungles? The new, aspirational India wants to see entertainers in the cozy sofa of a multiplex. Not some preachy film on issues with no solution.'

'But our CEO finds a business solution,' Ravi jumped in.

'What solution?' I asked.

'That we will think of,' Ravi spoke like a typical Bollywood producer.

'If you couldn't think of one for the last six months, what's the guarantee you will find one before the release of the film? Even if you find a solution what will be its credibility? So many governments, agencies, corporates, economists, political scientists haven't found a solution. Why should we look like fools? Giving a solution just because we have to make a film?'

Sandeep asserted that it was not a good idea to make a social issue film. Soon, everyone was convinced but for Ravi.

'Ravi, it also doesn't make business sense. Shooting in jungles is complex, expensive and very time-consuming.'

This made sense to Ravi.

'Why don't we shoot the film here at ISB? Set the story in a B-school,' I argued. 'What if there is a professor who uses a student for murder? It's simple but with lot of potential. A crime thriller coming out of a B-school.'

In my interaction with students, which I did a lot on my second trip with my co-writer Rohit Malhotra, later in November, I realized that most of them wanted to take a job outside India with top MNCs. Nobody was interested in India unless out of family compulsions. It wasn't like they were pissed off with India; they were just not interested. These students played poker, drank beer, smoked pot, attended standup comedy shows and dreamt of having an IT professional for a wife and driving a BMW in an American suburb. In their minds, they were not part of a suffering, conflicted, mediocre India. They wanted to be rich and successful. It's sad that we teach enterprise, but not vision. This was a new, shining India. An India, outside of Bharat.

They were trying to own the crime thriller idea. Everyone wanted to make a Cannes-worthy idea. Filmfare awards wasn't their scene. The dorm was full of smoke. And ideas. In times like these, everyone turns a storywriter. Soon, we had hundreds of brilliant ideas. The only problem was they didn't connect with each other. Pritika had suggested that everyone should do only what they specialize in. Ravi and Sandeep were given business and finance whereas production and logistics were given to Pritika and Abhishek. I was supposed to crack the script while they used their networks to raise funds. Assumption was that ISB would come at a substantial discount as location. But Abhishek warned us that the administration had refused to give the location to the *3 Idiots* unit.

Ravi picked up his laptop and started making spreadsheets of revenue models. Sandeep started figuring out their *connections,* who could sponsor. The blueprint was getting drafted. Revenue share was getting structured. Logistics and production milestones were being identified. The release and promotional plans were falling into place. A list of film festivals was being downloaded. We had a movie and a perfect business plan. The only things we didn't have were the funds, and a *story.*

'Do you think we can do it? We will do it only if you say yes.' They threw this vital responsibility on me.

There is a famous fable about a man called Sheikh Chilli. He built castles in the air and in his vivid imagination established big businesses and became a tycoon. Conquered lands, became emperor, married a princess, had great children but in the end the castle in the air vaporized and Sheikh Chilli found people ridiculing him and laughing at him. He became the joke of the town.

'Are we being Sheikh Chillis?' I asked myself. I had had bad experiences with my last three films. It had taken me some time to rebuild and reinvent myself. I was ready for a new career in teaching and writing. I didn't want to fall back into the same trap of making a small budget film and getting stuck with it until it squeezes you out, sucks out all your emotional energy and demoralizes you until you are dead creatively.

Sheikh Chilli's dreams soared because he didn't care about the laws of nature. In his world, there was no gravity. Hence, he climbed new heights of fantasy. But this is the real world. A world of gravity. Everything can come down like a pack of cards. But ambition, conviction, and confidence make a lethal gravity. Together they create such a pull that like-minded forces create an ecosystem that leads to the idea's success.

'Let's do it.' For me to commit without a script was the biggest risk I have taken as a filmmaker.

More beer. There was camaraderie in the dorm. Nothing unites people like having a common dream. It was only later that we learnt that everyone was seeing a different dream.

When my aircraft took off from Rajiv Gandhi International Airport, Hyderabad, I had no idea that a few months later, on a Christmas vacation, lost in the wilderness due to the Gujjar agitation, struggling to find the tar road that leads to Jaipur, with no food and no water, I would find the idea that would change my life.

3. Being Reborn

December 2010

The Agra-Jaipur highway is blocked. Gujjars are lying on railway tracks blocking Delhi-Mumbai route – the bloodline of the Indian Railways. There's police everywhere and they do not let us anywhere close to the highway. Distantly I can see thousands of Gujjars agitating with all kinds of gaudy political banners. On the shoulders of the highway, food is being cooked. A lot of vendors are selling bananas, cucumbers, *bidi*, cigarette, cheap water. Agitations, *dharnas* and strikes are good business for some. Lots of children from close by villages are amused at the sight of ugly OB vans and wondering why these reporters are in such a panic when the agitators are relaxed.

Gujjar agitators have damaged some Rajasthan State Roadway buses which sit there like disowned aluminium boxes. I'm sure they will remain there long after the agitation is over. After a lot of paperwork, reports will be made. Months will go by and they will rot in police stations. We are a slow country. There are multiple agencies and multiple procedures overlapping one another. Since no one wants to be answerable, the buck stops nowhere. By the time the government recovers from one strike, another springs up.

I fail to understand what kind of democracy allows damaging of State property and revenue losses. It reminds me of my student days in Bhopal, where at the smallest pretext we students used to stone buses and, in some cases, burn them. Nothing has changed except that now it has become more dramatic, thanks to TV. The losses to the government will run into thousands of crores. We now know that the recent Jat reservation agitation costs the states Rs. 34,000 crores, as confirmed by the president of the PHD Chamber of Commerce. It would be interesting to see a comparative study between the State's investment in infrastructure and the loss to the

State exchequer on account of agitations and protests. It's quantifiable. If we add loss of productive time, inconvenience to citizens, loss of education time and other intangible factors, the losses will out-value investments.

Political parties, when in opposition, provoke communities, engage them in identity politics to put pressure on the ruling party. Our political parties are always in election mode and therefore they make promises to potential vote-bank communities without bothering to analyze their legal and financial implications. This forces the ruling party to shift focus from governance to political management. Interest groups get involved and the issue overshadows everything else. To score back, the ruling party starts appeasing other communities and identity groups. It's a vicious cycle. The practice of wooing and appeasement of minority communities was started by Prime Minister Indira Gandhi. Prime Minister VP Singh's politics of Mandal converted it into a competitive political mafia. Identity politics today has become India's biggest socio-political malaise.

Gujjars are a pastoral community. The name Gujjar is derived from the term *gaucharana*, meaning 'to graze cows'. They are spread across India, Pakistan and Afghanistan. Rajasthan alone has around 70 lac Gujjars constituting around 7-8 percent of the population – more than enough to swing an election.

The immediate provocation for the agitation is that both the ruling Congress and the Bharatiya Janata Party promised them a five percent quota in government jobs and educational institutions but the problem lies in implementing it. Since this agitation is near Delhi, media has covered it extensively. Otherwise we would have never known about it.

It's Christmas time and the Golden Triangle is full of tourist cars. I see some cars taking a diversion through mustard fields, towards the villages. Cops advise us not to take the risk and go back to Agra but I decide to follow the cars. If so many people are taking the risk, all of them can't be fools. My adventurous family agrees. My wife and children are Mumbaikars. They have no idea how ugly political agitations can get.

We have been driving for hours on dusty roads going nowhere; we are passing dull, dark villages, turning back from blocked roads, getting misdirected by locals, waiting in the fog for local vehicles to pass in the hope that following them might lead us somewhere. We follow a milk van for an hour only to realize later that we have driven some 30 kilometres backwards. The problem with small roads is that they have no signs. Local people remember them. If you don't know the roads, then it's your problem. Sometimes these roads will take you to a smaller road and then another smaller one and then stop at a farm. We have lost the other car with my NRI cousin and his daughter. My wife is feeling sick. The kids are hungry and thirsty but there is no food and no water. And no mobile network. My daughter is crying. I am trying to tell them what a memorable adventure this is. I am finding different creative ways of lying to them instead of telling them that we are lost.

The sun is setting. It's getting chillier. And darker. The sky is painted in indigo. We have been driving for nine hours now. On a normal day, it takes four hours to reach Jaipur from Agra.

A part of me is struggling with the script which will take me out of the mediocrity I have been getting sucked into lately. Another part is extremely worried about the turmoil that I have invited upon my family. I try to ease the tension.

'Where are you from?' I ask the driver, who is looking more lost than the dusty roads.

'Haryana-Rajasthan border,' he tells me with pride.

'Doesn't this affect your business specially when tourists are pouring in?'

'Yeah. But then what can a poor man like me do? This is not the first time I am seeing this. Last time the army came. There was a lot of firing. Hundreds of people died. What's the point when nothing is going to happen?'

'Why do you say that nothing will happen?'

'*Sarkar* will never listen to them.'

'Why?'

'Because they don't deserve it.' He passes the judgment without blinking.

'What are you?' I ask him to understand his mindset.

'I am a Jat.'

'But Jats themselves have got reservation.'

'Because we are entitled. They are not.' He says it with total clarity.

The car bumps into something. 'Be careful' I scream.

It's pitch dark. The car's headlights can't penetrate the thick fog enveloping us. We don't know what hit the car. We don't know where we are. It's getting bumpier.

I have always been interested in political news but never the politics *per se*. Similarly, I know caste dynamics but never understood caste politics. How does caste entitle someone for State benefits? How do we quantify 'backwardness'? Isn't empowerment in our times directly connected with money? Shouldn't it be then financial entitlement? Money buys you opportunities, not the caste. Not anymore. I don't think I had heard of so many castes, sub castes, sub-sub castes until the Mandal agitation. Diversity *per se* is certainly a beautiful thing. But politics around diversity and desperate and unethical attempt to keeping everyone happy is an ugly game. Diversity, in a competitive, electoral politics is the reason why we are in constant conflict, and therefore, poor and stagnated.

Something strikes the car's bottom. By now we are used to it.

'Is this the first time you have driven like this?' I try to kill time.

'I drive all over India. But only on highways. Strikes are everywhere. Wherever you look—*jahan dekho wahan chakka-jam*.'

'What do you do in that case? Wait there?' These are practical questions.

'I keep extra money to give whenever we are stopped either by a cop, octroi person, taxi association, local goons or agitators. Agitators let you go after some time. *Kuch le de ke, chupke se,* on extorting money. Others have a fixed rate. Agitators can demand any amount. I have accepted it as cost of running the taxi. Now you should have money for mobile phone and bribe, then only you can drive a taxi. But we don't give from our pocket. We recover it from the tourist.'

'How?' I am alarmed.

'Don't worry, not your type of customers. We cover it up from pilgrimage tourists. People who visit *dhams* before dying, those people are generally easy with money.'

'Why not my kind of tourists?'

'Because you will go from Agra to Jaipur and go to your hotel.

The pilgrim tourists travel with us for 10-15 days. In every *dham,* there are many agents for everything. We have a *setting* with them. Hotels, restaurants, *chaiwala*, sadhus, pundits, everyone is a part of it. That's where we really earn money as commission.'

'Really?' I had an idea about how *pandas* and *pundits* fleece poor people who come to these *dhams* but I didn't know that they pay commission to taxi drivers.

'Sab yoonhee chalta hai sahib. Yahan paise ki kadr hai insaan aur uske hunar ki nahin. Kabhi chaliye. Maza aayega. Bahut bada jaal hai yeh sab It goes on like this only. Here money is valued, not man or his talent. Come with me sometime. You will enjoy it. It's a big nexus out there.' he tells me.

Suddenly the car stops with a thud. He is the first to get down.

By and by, everyone gets down. We can't believe what we see.

'Vivek, he has been driving on the fields,' Pallavi, my wife, says with controlled anger and frustration.

Forget the bumpy road, we have driven about 200 metres in a dry field. Now the wheels are stuck. I can't even get angry at him. What's the point?

My children are scared. For Mumbai kids, this kind of darkness is possible only in Harry Potter movies. My cousin's daughter had heard all kinds of horrible stories about India. Now she had her own story to tell.

We see a bike. In situations like this, one only thinks of the worst. *'What if they are some drunk Gujjars, returning from the protest... what if they rob us?'* All kinds of horrible thoughts occupy my mind. I am sure everyone is imagining some kind of trouble. The bike stops. Three men start speaking to our driver in Haryanvi. I can't fathom a word. Haryanvi doesn't sound very friendly. Especially when the bike riders' faces are covered with *gamchas*. They get down from the bike and move towards the car.

'What's the matter?' I ask the driver.

'They are coming to help.'

We wait for the car to come out of the field. It's extremely cold. In open fields like these, the wind bites you. The fog is getting thicker. We have mobile phones but they don't work. We are literally disconnected from the world. I am not struggling any more. I am not stressed. In fact, I am at peace and enjoying this 'straight out of the movies' scenario. One good act has the potential to change everyone's energies.

I stand alone. Freezing but loving it. When you stand nowhere, you are closest to yourself. Slowly the world fades out. All I see is our driver pumping the accelerator and trying to come out of the pit his car is stuck in. I imagine him taking commission from sadhus, bribing umpteen number of middlemen, driving for hours and finally reaching his home once in a blue moon with some saved money that can pull the family through until his next visit. He will never know which part of his income belongs to him and which part to middlemen. It will depend not on his hard work, not on his merit, not on his honesty; it will depend on how many hurdles, middlemen, he finds on his journey. He will spend all his life calculating, scheming, manipulating just to survive in this vicious economic cycle. One day he will die, without even realizing his true worth.

What has caste got to do with this? Social disparity in modern India is a function of economic disparity. We have been trying to find socio-political solutions for fundamentally economic problems. An economic problem needs an economic solution. How does one eliminate middlemen when everyone is a middleman in one way or the other? Middlemen never let talent shine. But how do they survive? Who protects them? Bigger middlemen? The driver's words echo in my mind: *Sab yoonhee chalta hai sahib. Yahan paise ki kadr hai insaan aur uske hunar ki nahin. Kabhi chaliye. Maza aayega. Bahut bada jaal hai yeh sab.* His statement was more than skin deep. I try to go deeper. What he is trying to say is exactly what most of the Indians say, irrespective of their economic strata. It's a hopeless situation. Nobody is interested in change. We celebrate mediocrity. We do not value merit or talent. Money is the real merit. It's a monstrous nexus.

The three men push the car while our driver accelerates. One of them goes and gives him some instructions. This time the driver doesn't pump the accelerator and the car comes out. The driver indeed knows his car but they know the earth. There is an India that runs on manuals and systems. And here's this, the other India that runs on common sense.

I am sure if everything stops, these three men will survive; it might be difficult but they will find their way out. I bet my family will give in, in no time. My family is Systems India. These men are Common Sense India. And in between, there are middlemen. The middleman is the real connect between the two Indias. We had looked at these men from a Manuals & Systems point of view. The manuals of urban life picture such men as goons. Rapists. Murderers. They turned out to be our saviours. My children are still scared. What if they get the car out and then run away with the car? And all our belongings. And...What if something like this actually happens? Nobody will know until morning. We will be lost in the fog. Our screams won't reach anywhere. We will believe and hold on to anybody who offers help. We will be at his mercy. At his command. We will be slaves to his agenda. How vulnerable will we be? How hapless will we be?

And, suddenly, I think of the Adivasi in the jungles of Bastar. A voiceless, faceless native that no one cares about. He is surrounded by middlemen who are working for a sinister design created by people who are hiding their greed behind the masks of a certain ideology. He is miserable. Suffocating in his own emptiness. He is struggling to come out of this vacuum. He holds every hand which offers help. He is at their mercy. He is the pawn in the game played by this nexus. This is the *jaal* the driver was talking about. He did not offer any logical argument; he was just telling me the way it is. The nexus siphons off all the natural resources and money that should rightfully belong to the Adivasi.

The Naxals who claim to work for the tribal's cause, know that there can be no revolution. So, what's their motivation? They are the messiahs of the Adivasis; this is the only narrative I had heard so far. They are fighting with the State for tribal upliftment, empowerment and justice– fundamental rights of any Indian citizen. Is it possible then that they are also part of a nexus? Where do they get the money from? And arms? Why do all our films justify Naxals? Where is the Adivasi in our films? Why is it that in a digital age he is not on the path of development? Why are we not told about the truth? And what is the truth? Is there another side to the truth? I want to explore it. Can I, as a filmmaker, tell the truth? There are moments when questions are raised only to reinforce the answer. My answer is clear. Yes.

My mind is churning with questions, overlapping one another. For the first time, I feel I want to research a subject. I suddenly connect with the India I grew up in. And I am embarrassed of my mediocrity. Suddenly I am not hurrying up. I have slowed down. Hurrying is an internet and mobile age syndrome. We hurry when we are not interested. We hurry when we don't care. This time I am interested and I do care. I remember telling my students at ISB that nobody cares for such stories. It's true we don't care when something isn't important. We tend to take it for granted. But when more than fifty percent of India is Naxal-infested, this becomes a very important issue. What is the reason for calling someone, fighting with a gun in Kashmir, a terrorist and another man with a gun in Bastar, a revolutionary?

After fighting mediocrity for a long time, I have found something which I truly want to do. This is the film I want to make. The crime thriller idea was only to sustain my mediocrity. This is a real idea to discover the truth. Explore Naxal politics and try to find out how the nexus works and present an alternate narrative.

The temperature has dipped sharply. Also, when you stand out in open for a long time, the chill permeates right to the bones. My hands are numb. But I feel the fire in my belly.

The headlights of the car flash in my eyes as it climbs the functional wall of the farm. The villagers offer to ride ahead of us to show us the way to the highway. Stress has a strange quality. It blocks all our positive thoughts. We saw the bikers as a danger. It never occurred to us that in such a dark and difficult time they were actually a helping hand. It is a paradigm shift moment for me. I was so distanced from my roots. Somewhere in the race to survive in Bollywood, I started telling stories that I believed people wanted to hear, and not the ones I wanted to tell. The ones which ought to be told.

I suddenly notice that the land is flattening. Bumps are receding. Rough patches are less now. We will soon be on the highway.

The car is running at 100 kms/hr. Its 10 PM. There isn't much traffic. In the backseat, Pallavi and my kids are sleeping. I am fully awake. I am thinking: what if our getting stuck in the field was part of a design to help me find my voice? Does the universe really conspire?

Standing alone in the middle of nowhere, on a foggy, freezing night, isolated in time and space from rest of the world, I had found my song.

My Buddha.

4. An Encounter with the Real India

The climb to Amer Fort is very steep. The cobbled path is made of huge blocks of stone. With extraordinary foot traffic, the stones have become very smooth and slippery. A lot of people prefer to ride elephants. Some to feel like a Maharaja and some because they can't walk up. A small group of people is protesting against the inhuman practice of people riding elephants up to the fort.

'Nothing *janaab*, do you really think they care about elephants?' our guide tells me.

He is sure that the protesting group will finally be called for negotiations and that's when they extort the authorities.

'Elephants will never stop. Where will all these *mahouts* go?' he poses the real question.

On one hand, there is a group of poor humans, elephant–keepers, whose survival depends on elephants. On the other hand, there are human interest groups whose survival also depends on elephants. Soon it's going to become an elephantine problem for the government of the day.

I try to race up with my son, holding my brand-new Canon 5D EOS camera in a way that even if I slip, nothing will happen to the camera. It's a very common human trait that if we are holding something expensive and are about to slip, we try to save the expensive thing first. Is it because we think our body is repairable?

We reach the main courtyard and wait for the others. My son is running around. He is living in the moment. He is also amused. In India, he hasn't seen such big structures other than the five-star hotels. If these palaces are monuments of monarchies, five-star hotels are modern monuments of capitalism.

Our guide offers my son an Eclair. Indian guides are wonderful people and it's no strange coincidence that his name is also 'Raju Guide' as a lot of guides name themselves after one of the most extraordinary characters of Indian cinema, made memorable by Dev

Anand in *Guide*. It's sad that now this profession is taken over by uneducated and unemployed youth with no real knowledge or interest. They learn very basic stuff about the place and blabber it in their local accent which is impossible to comprehend. Most of the time their real interest is in taking you to stores and restaurants which give them commissions. He tells me it costs a hefty bribe to get a license for the job.

'*Kya karein, karna padta hai janaab*— we are helpless. Indians rarely hire guides as they are not interested in history; all they want is photo, photo, photo. And foreigners have become very smart, they know that guides fleece them, so they haggle a lot and prefer guides with *gora* accent and the government doesn't do anything for us.'

Everyone in India has a story for their failures, stagnation or decay. This man is blaming the tourists, the government, but not once will he look at his own growth, his own competence and the quality of his service. Like any other industry, the Indian tourism industry is also full of mediocrity. Inferior quality of service and lack of professionalism. And to top it, our attractions are mostly chaotic and dirty.

While we wait for the others to climb up, I look at the gigantic building and wonder how they made it happen with just camels, horses and elephants. It's an architectural marvel. An excellent example of defense, design, engineering, material science, structural design, water and waste management, cooling techniques, rich aesthetics, symbolism, lifestyle and comfort, and above all stability and durability. There is so much inbuilt art everywhere. On the gates, windows, floors, roofs, walls and the furniture. We rarely get to see such optimum use of science, technology, and aesthetics in modern buildings. Our modern buildings are structural and design blunders; they are aesthetically challenged and weak. It's a sad commentary that in independent India we have not built even one building which is an architectural marvel and which can stand the test of time. If these old buildings are a celebration of excellence and precision, our modern buildings are a celebration of mediocrity and corruption.

'What are you thinking, sir?' Raju guide asks me.

'Just admiring the excellence of the man.'

'We built this city, *janaab*,' he tells me with pride.

'We?'

'*Janaab*, though it's known for Rajputs, in reality, Amer was built by Meenas. I am also Meena.'

I look at him, suspecting that he is trying to manipulate history, but I am curious.

'Just now you were telling me that Amer is the centre of Rajputana history.'

'*Janaab*, don't go by what is told. Isn't all history wrong? We are taught a wrong history. We are told a wrong history. *Jiski laathi uski bhains*– strength triumphs. After a thousand years, some other Raju Guide will call it somebody else's history. Whoever rules, writes his own history. There is history and there is truth, and the truth is that we Meenas ruled it before the Rajputs. It's our land.'

History in independent India has been treated like the ancient tale about five blind men and an elephant. An elephant is brought before the blind men and they are requested to identify, recognize and give their own interpretations of it. Each blind man catches hold of one part of the elephant's body – trunk, ear, leg, tail and stomach, and describes the elephant according to the part they are holding.

Nehru judged history and filtered it to what should be told to an independent India and what should be hidden. He made sure that the history reinforced his ideology and made him look like a hero. His daughter Indira Gandhi and later her daughter-in-law Sonia Gandhi tuned our history to further their political agendas. In independent India, only a certain kind of narrative is allowed; the one that suits the ruler's agenda.

The city of Amer is spread over 4 square kilometers and the fort is at top of a hill. This city was first built by Meenas and later it was ruled by Raja Man Singh. Meenas are an Indo-Aryan tribe with origins in the Matsya dynasty of Vedic India, ruled by king Virata. It is believed that after spending twelve years in *vanvasa* in forests, the Pandavas spent their thirteenth year of *agyatavas,* living incognito, here. In modern history, the Meenas ruled many parts of Rajasthan until taken over by Rajputs. Meenas are classified as a Scheduled Tribe in Rajasthan. They oppose the Gujjars' demand for Scheduled Tribe classification, fearing that their share of reservations will decrease.

The Meena tribe is divided into several clans and sub-clans like Ariat, Ahari, Katara, Kalsua, Kharadi, Damore, Ghoghra, Dali, Doma, Nanama, Dadore, Manaut, Charpota, Mahinda, Rana, Damia, Dadia, Parmar, Phargi, Bamna, Khat, Hurat, Hela, Bhagora, and Wagat. Bhil Meena is another sub-division among the Meenas. A sub-group known as Ujwal Meena seeks higher status and claims to be Rajputs, thus distinguishing themselves from the Bhil Meenas. Other prevalent social groupings are Zamindar Meena and the Chaukidar Meena. The Zamindar Meenas, comparatively well-off, are those who surrendered to the Rajput invaders and got settled on the lands believed to be granted by the Rajputs. Those who did not surrender to Rajput rule and kept on waging guerrilla warfare are called Chaukidar Meenas.

If a community of fifty lac people can have such a complex and competitive caste dynamics, how complex would it be to fathom the caste dynamics of India, with over three thousand castes and over twenty-five thousand sub-castes between one hundred and twenty-five crore people? Infused with politics, all these groups and sub-groups end up becoming interest groups and vote banks, fighting with one another endlessly without realizing that all of them have a common need – money.

Finally, everyone is here. I take some pictures, experimenting with the exposure, learning elementary photography. The quickest way to learn technology is to just do it. If we are afraid of technology, it seems very complicated and scary but when we are not afraid and ready to explore, it becomes a very playful gadget. I am very happy with the results. In fact, I am happy after a long time. Not the kind of happiness we feel on vacation. But the kind that we feel after cleaning our wardrobe. Relieved and light. Revived and fresh.

I haven't made a film for the last three years. Not because I didn't try. I tried to mount four brilliant film projects but each time they were shelved just a few weeks before principal photography was supposed to begin. It's impossible for people who don't work in showbiz to understand the pain and agony of a film getting shelved. You give a film your blood and sweat. It takes so much from the maker. It sucks all your imagination, experience, physical and emotional energy. And leaves you empty. When a film is shelved, you start feeling demoralized and defeated. You become desperate. You start succumbing to mediocrity. And mediocrity is very addictive. Anything which makes us escape from the challenges of life is addictive. The awareness that you are living a mediocre life is worse than being mediocre.

I had failed four times. If a couple of films don't take off, the industry starts looking at you like a failed director. But four? That makes you a jinxed director. Like a *manglik* girl who is jinxed for marriage until she finds another *manglik* boy. I didn't understand then that I wasn't jinxed. I had become part of a jinxed game. Like the common man of India whose life is jinxed because he is a very small, inconsequential part of a big, jinxed *jaal*. This feeble common man is in the business of improving his life but the people who control his life are not in the business of improving his life.

The people who controlled my films weren't in the business of film-making. They were in the business of the stock market.

In a romantic way, last night the chilly breeze in the fields took away all my baggage. Till now, I was playing to the gallery. Last night I felt like playing for myself. What I like, enjoy and understand. This thought alone gave me a sense of freedom. I feel lighter. And energetic. After living in Mumbai for fifteen years and working in Bollywood for five years, my worldview had become very simple. Or dumb, as I understand it now. Like in our messy movies, the barometer of my life got shrunk to 'If you are rich, you are successful'. If you have a box office hit, you are a great director. If you have a star, you are a greater director. Like everyone in a metropolis, I was struggling to survive. Like everyone in Bollywood, I have been struggling to succeed. Like everyone, I have been seeking a safe, economical and convenient route to success – tried and tested. Following a design. A formula. I have been living a second-hand life. I had become a dehydrated filmmaker. Not a storyteller but a me-too, mediocre narrator.

I thought I knew India but last night I realized I had been window-shopping. Last night I felt I was back to where I belonged. An India where success doesn't lie in money. It lies in surviving. The complex India. The difficult India. The corrupt India. The honest

India. The oppressed India. The feudal India. A regressive India. A progressive India. It's poor. It's filthy. It's hard working. It smells of struggle, of co-existence, of sweat. Its diversity, its disparity, the chaos, the conflict. The aspirational India, the ignored India, the defeated India... The real India.

5. The BIG Factor— A Twenty-thousand-rupee Marvel

2008 - 2009

I have made two big multi-starrer films: *Chocolate* and *Goal.* They were never planned. They just happened.

I had made a telefilm for Zee TV called *Chocolate.* Kumar Gaurav, Pallavi Joshi, Nikki Aneja and Kay Kay Menon acted in it. I shot it in the Alps, Switzerland – a rare for Indian TV. The Zee programming team didn't want to be held accountable for their creative judgment, so they welcomed tried and tested 'foreign film ideas'. Plagiarism was in fashion. *Chocolate* was based on *Usual Suspects*, a DVD that was hot at the time.

Later, I was shooting another telefilm with Rajesh Khera and Rajeshwari Sachdeva when Khera asked to leave for an hour. He had to go to collect his cheque from a producer. While writing his cheque, his producer expressed her desire to meet me as she wanted to make a film with me. When Khera told me this, I couldn't believe it. Those days I was seeking funds for a film on Bofors called *Aarambh.* Rajit Kapur and Naseerudin Shah had agreed to act in it. I had done a few readings with them. Rajit Kapur, who was producing the film, backed out at the last moment. I waited for long but the money wasn't coming in. Nobody wanted to invest in a politically charged film. I thought this was my chance.

My producer Raagini Sona had seen *Chocolate* and loved it, so she asked me to make it a full-length feature film. When I told her, I was interested in making the Bofors film, she said unexcitedly 'If you insist', but also laid out a condition that the film had to be shot in the UK, as they were getting a subsidy of forty percent from the UK government. Obviously, you can't set a Bofors film in the UK. In the next fifteen minutes, she convinced me to start my film career with *Chocolate* and make it into a multi-starrer film. And make it *big.*

In those days, stars used to do films only after seeing the DVD of a Hollywood film. If it wasn't seen, tried and tested in Hollywood, they wouldn't do the film. I never had to give the script to any of my stars. All of them had seen *Usual Suspects* except Anil Kapoor whose son had seen it and spoke highly of the film. Since plagiarism was commonplace and to an extent a professional compulsion, I became a part of it. Moralities change with changing times. At that time, it wasn't an immoral thing like copying a south Indian film isn't immoral now. All the respected and legendary writers, directors, music directors, action masters, choreographers, poster designers, trailer makers and even critics were copying from Hollywood films. In fact, a leading critic and trade expert Taran Adarsh lifted paragraphs from an American *Usual Suspects* review for the review of *Chocolate*.

This was the copycat era. Costume designers were copying from other designers. Heroines were copying makeup and hair styling from foreign magazines. Music companies were stealing from other companies. Readsure DVD library was the most famous in Mumbai's own Beverly Hills area – Juhu-Versova-Lokhandwala. The manager at the library used to recommend films this way: *'Ramu has kept it for a week… this one is Gupta's favourite… Maheshji has asked for this… Anurag has seen this one ten times... and this one has a long queue as every filmmaker is asking for it…'* That's how we knew who was copying which film. One of the superstars whom I worked with told me 'If it's an original script, I won't do it. Bring me a Hollywood DVD', and before I could react, he justified it by saying 'They have already done their R&D. It's tried and tested. Why do we have to think again?' I am sure today he will refuse to do a film if it even smells of a Hollywood film. Those were the times of underworld, extortions, and murders. Everyone wanted to play safe. In life. In business. In creativity.

A few days after the release of *Chocolate,* I received a call from Ronnie Screwvala's office. Ronnie was the founder and chairman of UTV. He had seen success with *Rang De Basanti* and now wanted to start his own in-house production. He had seen *Chocolate* and wanted me to make a cutting-edge film for him. I narrated the Bofors film but there was zero excitement.

'Can we make something brighter... entertaining... cutting edge... big?' He asked me. He wasn't interested in a small film.

I was just back from London after spending a good time in Southall – the world's largest Asian ghetto. I had heard the story of Southall Football Club which was on the verge of shutting down because no one was willing to pay the county charges. It was a meagre amount but everyone's ego had come in the way. I threw this as an idea at him.

'OK. Let's make this.' Ronnie is a very quick decision maker. He is a man of few words but when he says something, he means it. A rare breed in Bollywood.

This is how my second film *Dhan Dhana Dhan Goal* began. I never got a breather between these two films to reflect upon or to understand the business of films. UTV insisted on bringing in Anurag Kashyap to write the script. Nobody at UTV knew that he was primarily a dialogue writer and not a screenplay writer. So, he brought in a fresher, Vikramaditya Motwane. Vikram was struggling to make his own film and in the interim period, he was helping Anurag with sundry stuff. Together they wrote a script which everyone at UTV felt was too small in vision. Ronnie asked me to go to Mahabaleshwar and rewrite the film. And make it *big*.

'Big' is a very attractive word. I started chasing the 'big' dream of UTV. I wrote a big script. For the big stars. Saif Ali Khan and Priyanka Chopra were doing the film but Saif backed out at the last minute due to some complications. I got a feeler from John Abraham and in no time, he was cast. Priyanka backed out because she felt John was a lesser star than her. Knowing this, Bipasha called me and insisted that I cast her in place of Priyanka. John and Bipasha were in a relationship, so the producers thought they could save on coordination and date issues. Arshad was a friend who came on board easily. Boman met me once briefly and agreed to do the film as this was his real big film after *Munnabhai*. This is how casting is done in Bollywood – with relationships, equations, and money. If a star says he read the script before signing the film, and shot exactly to the script, my assumption is that he is either lying or he is Aamir Khan.

We shot it *big*. India's first football film, shot entirely in British football clubs, including Old Trafford, the home ground of

Manchester United. It was a very difficult film to make. There were a lot of nuanced ego problems between John and Arshad Warsi. John and Bipasha. John and me. John and other actors. It worked for the film as John and Arshad were anyways conflicting in the film, but it cost the production house a lot of money. In Bollywood, people concentrate more on lifestyle, vanity and interpersonal equations than their craft. Though we made a *big* film, a Bollywood film remains only as big as its star. I was in Bollywood's 'big' club.

It was no coincidence that just a few weeks before the release of the film, a gentleman called Mahesh Ramanathan called me from BIG Films, a film business unit of Reliance. He wanted to meet me urgently. To make some Big Films.

In 2005, Reliance Industries split. Mukesh Ambani got Reliance Industries, while Anil Ambani got telecom, power, entertainment and financial services. His new company Reliance Big Entertainment forayed into the untapped market of video rentals with BIGFlix. It simply didn't work. They launched their film business in a big way, by signing six directors, including me. I signed a three-film deal. The money was big.

I had spent years working on a superhero subject. It was a simple story, rooted in Indian mythology. And that was its biggest problem. There is a mindset in Bollywood that doesn't let Indic ideas flourish.

After months of work, when we were about to put the cast and crew together, I was asked to hold everything, for BIG had hired Prasoon Joshi as their creative consultant and he was supposed to evaluate every film. Prasoon was coming from his success with the lyrics of *Rang De Basanti* and he was the advertising industry's poster boy, Bollywood's 'intellectual import' and a writer of exceptional calibre. I was asked to narrate the script to Prasoon. I wasn't comfortable with the idea. *'How can a lyricist judge a script?'* I asked. Mahesh Ramanathan, the COO, convinced me that it was just a handshake meeting and one would narrate just the theme as a formality.

We met in a boardroom of Reliance with their chairman Amit Khanna and Prasoon Joshi – both lyricists. The entire atmosphere was like a government job interview. Amit welcomed us warmly. Prasoon kept quiet. We sat across a *big* boardroom table. As soon as

I started narrating the background and relevance of the story, Prasoon took a deep breath and said, 'Can you just tell us in two lines.... the gist?'

'It's a full-fledged feature film. A mythological. How can I narrate it in two lines?'

'It's an interesting subject.' Amit Khanna, who had approved the subject, tried to bypass him.

'Yeah, I think we must make films like this.' Prasoon swallowed some more tobacco juice. 'But why don't you change it to a Superheroine?'

I thought he was kidding. I smiled.

'No, seriously. Why do we always have to have superheroes? Why not superheroine?'

My hero was based on the character of Karna, one of the greatest warriors and the only one who defeated Arjuna. Karna, it is believed, conquered the world. My film was based on the 'conquerer of the world' who derives his power from the sun.

'But the protagonist is Karan. Not Kaali. At least, metaphorically.'

'Why can't the protagonist be Kaali?' Without waiting for my reaction, he turned towards Amit and asked him, 'Why don't we invert the pyramid?'

There was pin drop silence for a moment.

Prasoon turned towards me and said with a victorious smile, 'Let's invert the pyramid, Vivek.'

'Yeah, great idea. Let's invert the pyramid,' Amit seconded it.

'First, let's make a pyramid and then think about inverting it,' I tried my hand at humour.

'It's time we have superheroines. Why such bias? Today's woman is empowered. She is no less than a man,' Prasoon raised a fundamental question.

This wasn't the first time some one had thought of this. I have been hearing this since my advertising days. A lot of Hollywood studios even made superheroine films. They didn't work because the largest consumption of such films is amongst men and young boys and they like to see a superman and not a superwoman. I chose to keep quiet. I had learnt in my advertising days not to question a client's bad idea as the idea would soon die its natural death and though he would forget about the idea, he would remember the questioning of that idea.

'What are you thinking? I think it's a superb idea... also, heroines are easy to cast... invert the pyramid,' Prasoon tried to persuade me.

'I have no issues with that but it will be a completely different story. I'll have to go back to the drawing board and start from scratch. New research. New writing. But that won't be the story I want to tell. What I want to tell is here, in front of you.'

Prasoon immediately understood my discomfort.

'OK. Let us come back to you on this.'

That day I learnt that in the *big* fat world of Bollywood, the problem isn't whether the pyramid should be inverted or not. The problem is there isn't any pyramid.

Prasoon is a poet at heart. But poetry must die at the Box Office. A typical dilemma all creative souls fight in this business. I wondered how does he survive in a world which believes in throttling the truth.

As I walked out of the *big* boardroom, I knew this project was going to be shelved. They were not interested in the film. They were interested in something else.

After a couple of months of no action, Mahesh asked me if I would like to wait on this or start another movie.

'So, it's not happening?' I asked Mahesh.

Instinctively, I wanted to quit but Mahesh gave me all sorts of logic. Instinct is like a loving wife, who whispers her concerns in your ears but gives in to your logical arguments.

'Finally, he told me that he wants the film to happen but Prasoon is not letting it happen.

'So, this time no Prasoon Joshi.' I laid down my condition.

'Definitely. We will just send him the script for reference.'

I started working on a new script. It was called *True Story*. It was set between the Emergency and Y2K. It was a story of a *Madrasi* boy, whose father is a clerk in the Customs & Excise department and maintains a journal of all corrupt officers, thinking that some day he would expose them and eradicate corruption. His innovative and meritorious son tries to earn a living but faced with the corruption starts using his father's journal to raid the raiders and becomes a big shareholder of corrupt India. It was a conflict of a middle-class father and son in the times when choices were limited and we were like a Communist democracy ridden with the quota and license raj. It was about the changing aspirations of the youth post liberalization. The film was mainly about the relationship between a cowardly father and an ambitious son set in a changing India.

We were a month away from the shoot. As promised, Mahesh mailed the script to Prasoon, for his reference. Mahesh told me that Prasoon had read a few pages and liked it so he wanted to meet to hear the basic story and he might have some suggestions which I could accept. I like my scripts to be discussed, debated and criticized. You get various perspectives. It helps the judgment.

I asked him to print a script, just in case, but Mahesh didn't feel the need. 'He is a writer himself, I am sure he would want us to read the script,' he said. Mahesh was convinced that it would be a five-minute courtesy meeting. He was desperate to make the film. When you have a boss like Anil Ambani, you want to show him results and move up the corporate ladder. This film was Mahesh's ladder.

Reliance has a huge office in Andheri but the meeting was fixed in a very expensive business centre of Taj Lands End in Bandra. Along with my co-writer Rohit, I arrived on time only to be told that Prasoon would be delayed by half an hour. We kept ordering tea. '*Dekh lena, paanch hazaar se kam nahin aayega chai ka bill*,' Rohit repeated, worried about the bill.

Prasoon eventually arrived after three hours and asked that we read the script. Mahesh was always in a 'yes sir' mode. He ran and got four scripts printed. At that time laser printing was very expensive and if I remember correctly he paid around twenty thousand for four scripts. In Bollywood, people shamelessly waste money on stuff that will never get shown on the screen but they don't invest in writing.

'This is an anti-corruption film,' Prasoon said.

'No, this isn't exactly an anti-corruption film, it's a father-son relationship film, like *Shakti* wasn't a film on smuggling. Similarly, corruption here is just a subtext, that is to put the relationship in context....'Doesn't matter, let's make it a corruption film.' Prasoon didn't wait for me to finish and narrated an anecdote from his childhood his father resisted corruption when some corrupt contractor tried to bribe him with *boris* of potatoes and how he threw the potatoes down the hill and the man out of the gate. This resonated with me immediately as my father had once asked me, when he found out that I had stolen a book from a bookshop, to go back to the book shop, return the book and give an apology in writing.

"If we are making a film on corruption, we must ensure that there is no corruption at the thought level", Prasoon advised.

This made an impression on me and I remembered it almost at every stage of making this film.

Mahesh kept looking at twenty thousand rupees bill for the printing of the scripts.

When films go into creative ping-pong, the first thing that gets affected is your payments. BIG wanted us to sign the star first but we needed money to develop the script. Mahesh neither had the courage nor the skill to handle the situation. Who would bell the cat?

I was desperate but not enough to agree with a wrong idea. Most of the movies are made this way. They start with an honest, sincere and powerful idea, but on its way to the screen get screwed by so many middlemen that by the time they reach the audience they have no soul left. Sadly, my film on middlemen had to fight the middlemen. Tragedy of India.

Nothing worked for BIG. Barring one small film of Shyam Benegal, no film ever got made. They started acquiring big films and lost big monies in all of them. BIG almost shut down. But by this time, a lot of middlemen had made lots of money.

'Why are there so many middlemen? Why are there four people to do one job? If Prasoon is taking all the decisions, why do they have Amit Khanna? Why does Prasoon want to invert a pyramid which doesn't exist? What if they have actually inverted the pyramid of filmmaking?' Rohit kept asking me questions as if I knew the answers. All I knew was that whatever they were doing, they certainly weren't interested in making films. I felt I was in a wrong place. I felt Prasoon was in a wrong place. Also, BIG was in a wrong business.

I didn't give up. I tried to make two more films with independent producers. They almost went to floor but then the recession impacted the film industry and the producers backed out. By this time, I was broke. Financially. Emotionally. Mentally. This is where most people give up. I had also given up. Not on life, nor on my potential. I had given up on the Bollywood style of filmmaking. I had given up on mediocrity. I had resigned from Bollywood. As a demoralized, broken, confused, and defeated man.

The whole day of going around seeing Jaipur following the ten-hour journey the previous day, had taken its toll on everyone. By dinner time, everyone was exhausted. As they slipped inside their quilts. I took out my laptop and started with the research. I didn't get up from the corner of my study couch until I discovered a unique and dangerous nexus between the Naxal mafia and middlemen disguised as intellectuals. Like Prasoon would have desired, I had inverted the pyramid of intellectuals.

I had found the theme of the film: Intellectual Terrorists.

6. 'Jesus is coming'

January 2011

The sky is clear and Hyderabad is not as cold. My taxi is running on an empty highway outside the Rajiv Gandhi International Airport.

'Why is this airport called Rajiv Gandhi Airport?' I ask the driver.

'Rajiv is Indira Gandhi's son, sir' the driver answered in his Telugu accent.

I am forty-five minutes away from the meeting which may help me realize my passion. This film isn't important because I want to make it or some kids at a B-school want to make it but it's important because a truth like this hasn't been told before. If it has any chance of getting financed, it's going to be from someone outside of Bollywood. Bollywood can't finance this film for they have no clue about this dimension of India. It's going to be somebody who is bold enough to disrupt the *status quo* of an agenda-driven narrative.

I have good vibes. Something tells me that it will work out and I may not have to go back to the days of despair and agony. I feel confident. Since the debating days in my youth, I always close my eyes for a few minutes and measure how I feel before stepping out on the stage. There is something that tells me the end result. It's also backed by solid logic. Why would anyone call me to Hyderabad if it were not serious? The only problem is that I am carrying an absolutely different script idea with me. It's not what the students sent to the potential investor. Since we are meeting directly in the investor's office, how do I tell the students? From a film that justified the cause of Naxalites, it has become an anti-Naxal idea.

The pyramid has been inverted.

I get down at Phoenix India's multi-storied building on Jubilee hills. The ground floor is full of Audis. I am taken to the boardroom. Ravi and Sandeep are already there, busy setting up the PPT presentation.

'Look Vivek, we had mailed it to over a thousand people in our network and this investor responded immediately. I have already met their MD who has tentatively agreed on the budgets. It all depends on today's meeting. We have to make this happen.' Ravi is extremely excited and stressed.

'While I was in Rajasthan, I had time to relook at the idea. I have made some substantial changes.'

'See, you are an expert in scriptwriting. You decide whatever is best for the film. Just impress him. We have to make the film in February. Somehow make him agree to invest.' Come what may, Ravi wanted the movie to be over before April when they will graduate.

'Look at the presentation' Sandeep starts showing me the slides.

The presentation is full of data, graphs and jargon. Also, it has far too many slides. He stops at the budget slide. It had a budget of one crore with basic breakups.

'This is wrong. How can you make a film for one crore?' I had thought it was a partial budget.

'But we have already sent it to them,' Ravi says as if 'this is *it*'.

'But it's impossible.'

'But it's our only chance. We will make it happen. I promise you.'

Before that could go any further, the investors enter the boardroom.

Suresh Chukapalli, the potential investor, is a self-made man. Hailing from a village in Guntur, Andhra Pradesh, he started as an automobile entrepreneur and slowly got his feet firm into steel, power, cement, realty, and mining. He is the founder-director of the $1-billion Lanco group. He is a well-connected man. He is fond of movies and some top Telugu stars are his close friends.

He is also in the AIKYA family of ISB. Aikya means Unity. AIKYA, ISB's unique host family network programme was initiated for connecting students with the local business community. Since its inception, AIKYA has grown multi-fold.

Suresh is wearing a crisp white shirt and a pleated black trouser and shining black shoes. His upper pocket boasts a shining golden pen. He looks vanity-conscious. He is a man of few words and doesn't care much for frills. He maintains such a quiet on his face that it's difficult to gauge his mind. His son, Avinash, also joins us.

We are also joined by Gopikrishna Patibanda, managing director of the Phoenix group. Gopi is an engineer by education. There is a quickness about him. He doesn't seem like a guy who will ever say no. He is such a simple guy that you can't believe he runs an over twenty thousand crore company. If Suresh is the vision, he is the technique. He talks only business. With a smile. Everyone calls him Gopi *saar*. But he likes to address everyone as 'Boss'.

'Boss, call me Gopi,' he tells me with a gentle smile. While shaking hands with him, I had no idea that I found a friend for life.

'They sent me a mail. I couldn't believe that a film can be made for one crore. So, I asked them to make me meet you. If only you say it can be done, we would be interested.' Suresh tells me in a Telugu accent. He tells me that he googled me and then saw all my films on YouTube and loved *Chocolate*. He is very impressed by my cinematic style. I realize that this will be an advantage for me in the negotiations.

'First let's see the presentation, understand the project, let me tell you the story, then we will discuss monies.' I tried to create some room for myself. I had done some mental calculations and had figured out that it wasn't possible to make a film for one crore. The students had not cared to add professional fees of the crew and actors. They assumed that it will be a new cast and crew. The kind of film I want to make requires seasoned actors. There is no way it can be made for less than two crores. I don't know how to present this bad news to the investors. It is a tricky situation. There is always one magnetic element which drives any deal. In this deal, 'one crore' is that magnet.

'Start' Suresh orders Ravi.

Sandeep plays the PPT presentation, made over many nights of hard work. Adlibbing, he explains the CSR angle of the film. How they want to give back something to society. In the next few slides, Sandeep presents statistics on Naxals and related issues. I have made many presentations during my advertising days and narrated scripts innumerable times to different groups of decision makers that I have gained expertise in gauging the mood of the quorum. Also, I am a director. I can read people. Their body language. I know this is not working with Suresh and his team.

Under one roof, there are three sets of people with three different reasons to make a film. The students' payoff will be a laurel in their CV, the status of a producer and a remote possibility of making some money. Suresh's payoff is that for a throwaway price of one crore he gets to test the waters, become a film producer, that is every first-generation rich businessman's desire in India. For me, this is the last chance to resurrect myself. More than that, I want to make this film. From my gut. In my case, there is no choice.

'Please stop,' Suresh interrupts. He says something in Telugu to Gopi. Gopi just shakes his head. And smiles. Suresh continues, 'Let's listen to Vivek. All this data we know.' He turns to me, smiles and asks, 'You really think it's possible in one crore?'

These are the bottom line people. Sandeep and Ravi are the jargon people. I am a storyteller. So, like everyone else, I should also be doing what I can do best. Tell the story. Listening to a film script is also an art which comes only after many narration sessions. I know if I narrate the script, he will not be able to make out head or tail of it. He will get bored and lose interest. He is stuck on this magic figure of one crore and if I have to get him to spend more money, I have to engage him.

'Have you ever been extorted by Naxals?' I ask Suresh, knowing that they have business stakes in mining and infrastructure, the sectors most affected by Naxals.

'You sit with me someday and I will tell you,' Suresh looks at Gopi and smiles.

'Do you think it's easy for businessmen to do business in these areas?' I ask.

'Forget Naxal areas, even in cities it's not easy. It's very difficult to do business in India. We have become an extortionist country,' Suresh tells me pensively.

'Why is it that our films only glorify the cause of Naxals? Why is that the other side of the story is never told? This film is a story about the other side. A point of view never told.'

'Yeah, nobody cares. It goes on like this only. But do you think people will be interested in this story?' Suresh comes back to the brass tacks.

'Perhaps not. But if I say that maybe there is a Naxal in this room... right now... amongst us... what would you say?' I throw an intriguing question at him.

Suresh looks at Ravi and Sandeep, then me and then at his son. Before he can question my premise, I add:

'Do you think it's possible for these Naxals to run their operations without sympathizers in the government, police or media? Do you know that they are planning to take over cities...our industries? It's not me who's saying it...it's in their document. How can they plan this without installing their people in all key places? How do you know that the money these ISB boys are asking for is not going to be used to champion their cause, strengthen their position in cities? Imagine someone in your own company, working for the Naxals... against you...and you will never know about it... Where will we go then, what will businessmen like you do then?' I can see Suresh is shifting in his chair.

'Don't you think it's important to tell the other side of the story and expose them before they attack us?' I ask.

'It's a very big problem. The real problem is that politicians use them for votes. Nobody cares about businessmen in India. Some people in media talk as if they are reformers...saints... I'll make you meet my friend...he is an IPS officer. He'll tell you what all goes on.' Suresh looks at Gopi, speaks to him in Telugu and then continues talking to me.

'Yeah, we will arrange your meeting this evening if he is here, else next time when you are here. You must meet these people and then only you will know how cruel and barbaric these people are.'

I know he is engaged.

'Imagine a professor at ISB is a Naxal who uses young students to further his own sinister agenda?'

Before I can go past a few scenes, he tells me, 'We are doing this film. You have to make sure it's done in one crore.'

'But there is one issue.' I take him by surprise. Suresh looks at Gopi.

'When Sandeep and Ravi sent you the budgets, they were looking at a smaller film, but I got a bit ambitious and said why not add value to it so that it has a shelf value, something which is not just a quick business project but also makes us proud. I want to cast some known faces. This value addition will cost us more.'

Ravi almost faints in his chair. He tries to dissuade me, cover it up as a misunderstanding. He is too desperate to just take whatever money they give and put some scenes together and have a film ready on their graduation day on April 4th. He is a result-oriented manager.

'Let Vivek talk,' Suresh tells Ravi.

I get up and walk to the whiteboard and write down four basic heads of film budgeting. I had produced a lot of TV shows. If nothing else, television makes you a budgeting expert. I put figures and explain them. I want Suresh Chukapalli to not just finance the project but also take its ownership.

Suresh looks at the bottom line figure of two crores, speaks to Gopi in Telugu for some time and then he gives me a blank look.

'Who are the actors you are thinking of?' he asks.

'Some known and good actors as the key here.'

'What about the professor?'

I had started my TV career with Anupam Kher's media company and have good relations with him. Also, he is an actor par excellence and a natural choice for playing a professor. Bhaskar Shetty, his manager, is a kind person and a friend who I am sure will give me a cut on his fee.

'Anupam Kher' I announce.

'And the heroine?'

'Gul Panag' Ravi replies.

'Who is she?' Suresh asks.

I had understood by now that the only way to get a higher budget sanctioned is an attractive cast. Star-struckness is one of three major reasons for people to invest money in films. Launching their child and proximity to heroines being the other two.

'Though she doesn't have much to do, I am thinking of a Mahie Gill kind of a heroine… rustic…' I am trying to gauge what he thinks.

'Yeah that is fine. I like Anupam Kher but we will invest only one crore and fifty lacs.'

'But… these are expensive actors…'

'That is OK. We will do it. One and fifty then' Ravi replies desperately.

'Ravi, we will need more money.'

'Vivek, we will work it out... will find some sponsors. OK Gopi sir, we will do it.' Ravi is not willing to consider anything as he is too desperate and it's visible. Between quality, time and money, one can choose any two. Only two. Ravi is a kind of manager who will always chose time and money. That exactly is the problem, with most of the B-schools: No emphasis on quality.

'What about the marketing budgets?' Suresh asks.

'We will sell it to a studio,' Ravi says.

'Even I know some people.' Suresh mentions some big names of Bollywood studios.

'Boss, one of our partners, Ram Mohan, is a big distributor and president of the distributors association. We will take his help,' Gopi tells us.

'Viacom's CEO is an ISB alumnus.' Ravi can't be left behind.

'Even Ronnie Screwwala's executive assistant is an ISB alumnus,' Sandeep adds.

The problem with the Indian entrepreneurial mindset is that even before going to the drawing board it starts looking for *jugaad* and connections.

It is decided that Phoenix will be fifty percent stakeholder and Friday Night productions of ISB and my company, Vivek Agnihotri Creates, will be twenty five percent partners each. Suresh refuses to route the money through Friday Night. He insists that I produce the film. Ravi is not happy with this. Maybe Suresh can see what I can't. Years later I will thank him for his sound judgement.

'OK, you can discuss the nitty gritty with Gopi,' Suresh gets up and comes close to me, holds my hand and speaks softly, 'Vivek, please take my son also in your film. He is interested in acting. He won't let you down.'

'I am sure we can do something,' Ravi answers for me. He knew about this demand but hadn't told me. There is no place where I could fit his son in any major role. I have learnt through experience that in a tricky situation honesty helps the most, maybe not instantly, but most certainly in the long run.

'Yeah, please create a good role for him.' Suresh looks at Ravi for affirmation.

'Honestly, there are just four main roles and he can't do any of them. I'll see what is the best I can do. You will have to trust me and leave it to me. I'll do whatever is correct for the film,' I tell him honestly.

'OK. I trust you. Please meet my IPS friend before you leave for Mumbai.' Suresh shakes my hand and leaves.

The meeting is over in less than an hour.

Again, no one is interested in the script.

Sandeep, Ravi and I are waiting for the car outside Phoenix House. Jubilee Hills is a very posh area. Swanky cars are passing by and I look at the faces of people inside them. Some are smiling, some are stressed. Some excited. Some bored. Everyone is carrying a success story. A failed story. Some have got more than what they asked for. Some have got less than what they deserve. Exactly like us. Ravi and Sandeep have got fifty percent more than what they wanted as the budget. I got twenty five percent less. Suresh got his son to act in a Bollywood film with Anupam Kher at a throwaway price.

In films, one struggle ends only to start another. If this film has to happen, we must shoot in February as the course ends in April. That's less than a month. I have made big commercials, big TV shows and only big films. The post production budget of my earlier films was more than the budget of this film. I have no idea how I will make this happen. Like they say, God only knows.

As I drive towards the airport, I go past a long wall painted with advertisements of detergents, sexologists, marriage counsellors, local gyms, and private massage parlours. Somewhere in between this graffiti of various art forms is a bold graffiti that reads, *'Jesus is coming.'*

7. A Hundred Owners

January 2011

I don't know how I will make the film in a budget of one and a half crores. The overtime payments of *Goal* were more than four crores. The special effects bill must have been around two crores and here I have to make an entire film in less than the VFX budgets of my last film. It is possible only if everyone works for free, and locations and camera equipment are free.

It's time to invert the budgeting pyramid.

Amit, my production manager, has been negotiating for the last one week with people and his total is still nowhere in the range of one fifty. We are exactly thirty days away from the shoot. I am becoming restless. I try to escape behind Arnab Goswami's *News Hour*. Pallavi hasn't yet understood how Arnab's shouting and screaming can de-stress me. He actually does de-stress me. I pick up the TV remote and increase the volume.

Suresh Kalmadi is fired as the chairman of Commonwealth Games Organizing Committee in one of the biggest ever–a Rs 70,000 crores scam– under Sonia Gandhi's regime. Sonia Gandhi will go down as the most corrupt national leader in the Indian history.

Over hundred people have died in a stampede in the Sabarimala shrine. As a child, everyone is scared of some kind of an accidental death. Some are scared of car accidents, some of air accidents, some of fire, some of getting killed by a thief. I am scared of dying in a stampede. For as long as I can remember, stampedes at religious places have caused hundreds of deaths each year. Still, we put up with it as if it's a natural calamity beyond our control. What kind of mindset do our rulers have where it's OK for poor citizens to die in floods, droughts, heat, cold, riots? And stampedes?

Bhimsen Joshi has passed away. A young bride remembers her last three lifetimes. Villagers have christened her as a goddess. A weak looking man is rounding up weekly news on a Hindi news channel which is a video version of *Manohar Kahaniyan*. It's disgusting. I try to switch channels but I can't. I am stuck with him. I don't know if it's the remote or the TV's fault or something wrong with the Tata Sky set-top box. I want to switch over to *Times Now* to see what Arnab is up to on the CWG scam and Kalmadi's sacking, but I just can't. This is why I like mechanical devices rather than electronic.

The call centre of Tata Sky is a little better version of MTNL's call centre. After pressing a few options, I find a customer service executive. After he finishes his mandatory welcome and disclaimers in Hindi and English, I tell him about my problem. Initially he refuses to accept that it's their problem.

'*Sir, problem aapki taraf se hi hoga. Yahan to sab theek dikha raha hai.* It seems fine at my end,' he tells me. He is talking too much and trying to be over-familiar. He is irritating me.

'How the fuck does it matter where the problem is? The transmission is going via your box and if I am not receiving the transmission from the rest 199 channels out of 200, then whose job is it to solve the problem?' I am losing my patience with his *sarkari* approach, monotonous voice and accentuated rubbish English. These are the times when I curse myself for giving up my application for the green card while studying in the USA. After poverty, inefficiency is the second biggest curse of Indian society.

'Please turn everything off for two minutes and then restart,' he advises.

I do this, while he holds on.

'No, it is still not working.'

'Ok. I am lodging your complaint. Somebody will come to attend within twenty-four hours.'

'Twenty-four hours?' I am shocked. In the fleeting world of news, twenty-four hours is a very long time. Especially in a world of Twitter, where the politics of the narrative can bend either side within twenty-four minutes.

'No. I want somebody to come now, else I will write on Twitter about your pathetic service. It's been over half an hour that I am struggling with the problem.' I am angry. Furious, maybe. In India, when everything fails, anger works.

'*Sir, ek problem hi to hua hai. Kyon apna khoon jalate hain, koi aafat to nahi aayee hai. Subah subah hi bhejta hoon kisi ko.* I'll send someone tomorrow early morning,' he tells me very sweetly.

Sir, ek problem hi to hua hai. Solve ho jaayega ... koi aafat to nahi aayee hai.

Very often we misread problems as crises. A crisis denotes a dangerous situation. A situation in which the probability of success and failure or survival and death is almost equal. More in favour of death and failure. A crisis happens when we can't solve problems. Problems seem scary. We are trained to be scared of problems. 'Don't go there in the dark... a ghost lives there,' parents tell their kids. We create ghosts in our children's minds and all our lives these ghosts do not let us see problems as just any other phenomenon of life.

When a child gets lost, we don't tell him that in his experiment with space, he got lost as he is not adept with the directions. With this result, it can be deduced that he needs to learn directions before venturing out onto unknown roads. Instead of this, we yell at him and scare him from solving a basic spatial problem. When the child gets lost again, he sees it as a crisis, and panics. He takes all the wrong decisions. In the process, he gets more lost and scared. He doesn't see it as a problem and doesn't attempt to find a solution. I am not saying we should leave our children to get lost. I am asking what if we teach them to look at 'getting lost' as a problem? They may find solutions and reach home safely.

We, as human beings, have conquered the world and now, a bit of the universe, because we explored. Without exploring, one can't find a new ground. Every exploration begins with a problem. Every new ground is a solution. We stop our children from exploring. The child grows up thinking, what if I explore and fail? A possibility of failure or loss in a situation is considered a crisis that stops us from taking chances. To actually go behind the mountains and see if there is really a ghost or not. Hence, we run away from crises. This fear becomes a ghost in our minds, scaring us off new possibilities.

Problems are meant to be solved. In our education system, problems and solutions are related to the Science curriculum. In History, Sociology, Literature and other humanities subjects, there are explanations and interpretations, but not problems. Problems are related to complex symbols, terminologies, and equations. This is why most people are so scared of technology. When our TV set conks off, we do not look at it as an opportunity to understand the engineering of a TV set, understand its circuitry and explore a new science.

Problems bring challenges. Challenges mean new experiments. Experiments bring learnings. Learning means discovery. Discovery means evolution. Evolution is the only purpose of life. A problem is not a curse but a means to actualize life. Newton didn't look at the apple as a crisis. He looked at it as a problem. 'Why does it fall on the ground and not fly up in the sky?' Then with step-by-step experiments, he solved it. Finally, he discovered gravity, which became a milestone in human evolution. It's not that gravity did not exist before him. He just solved the problem.

India is a country full of problems. If we solve even a fraction of our problems, we will become a solution-rich country. It will enhance the quality of living. We will be problem solvers, instead of being buck-passers. Instead of being risk takers, we have become ticket takers. Solutions are what we call innovations. Innovation makes civilization grow. Similarly, self-growth is not possible without small innovations in day-to-day life. I learnt this, when confronted with my life's biggest problem.

I turn the TV off and focus on my problems at hand. I have to cast some seasoned and fantastic actors, get a crew of top-notch professionals, shoot outdoors (outdoor shooting is more expensive than a local shoot in Mumbai) for thirty-five days in Hyderabad, record music, finish editing, sound and final mixing and everything else in one crore fifty lacs. Plus, deliver it latest by April which is just three months away.

If I have to make it happen I need to think differently. The solution to this problem is not in negotiations or number crunching. It lies in the approach. My manager Amit has been doing it wrong. Despite his hard negotiations and pleas, the budget is not narrowing under three crores. We need to cut another crore and fifty lacs. Even if I use my goodwill, it won't go below two. To cut fifty lacs more, I need to stop every leakage, ensure everyone and everything work at cent percent efficiency. I have to understand the circuitry of filmmaking. Its design. Its engineering.

I have to find the pyramid and then invert it.

I stand in front of a complex circuitry. An overtly interdependent business yet extremely collaborative. Just take a look at only one department:

Camera.

A cameraman is nothing without a camera. The camera is supplied by a vendor. A camera needs attendants. The number of attendants depends on lenses and accessories, which depends on the cameraman's brief, which depends on the demands of the script. A lens means nothing without a focus puller. Then you need lighting. Lighting involves transportation and light boys who need electricity which is provided by an electrician who needs a generator which requires diesel, and if there happens to be a petrol pump strike, you are screwed.

Now, the camera needs to shoot a scene. It requires a stage for actors to perform. Actors need costumes, makeup, hair styling. A stage needs art direction which requires construction and props which need setting boys who need carpentry and painting tools which take them to production managers who control budgets. Budgets determine which camera is to be used. Which depends on the cameraman's brief. So, everyone is interlinked, interdependent and interlocked.

I must break it apart and re-engineer it with fewer steps, like an assembly line.

In modern history, if any one innovation has revolutionized manufacturing, it has to be the 'assembly line', launched about hundred years ago, at Highland Park, Detroit, Michigan, by Henry Ford and his precocious team. Ford broke his Model T's three thousand parts into eighty-four steps performed by workers on a chassis pulled down on a rope.

The official website of the $110-billion Ford Motor Company chronicles it under the heading 'Innovation':

'The new process (of assembly line) revolutionized production and dropped the assembly time for a single vehicle from 12 hours to about 90 minutes. By reducing the money, time and manpower needed to build cars as he refined the assembly line over the years, Ford was able to drop the price of the Model T from $850 to less than $300. For the first time in history, quality vehicles were affordable to the masses. Eventually, Ford built a Model T every 24 seconds and sold more than 15 million worldwide by 1927, accounting for half of all automobiles then sold.'

Bringing the product to the worker instead of moving various teams of workers to the product became the idea that overhauled the manufacturing industry as a whole. Ford solved a problem.

I break down filmmaking process:

Vision and R&D (The Drivers)
The Drivers, people with the roadmap – Director, Writer, Director of Photography, Editor – they require vision and conviction.
Technique (The Engineers)
The Engineers, who translate a vision – Sound Designer, Art Director, Costume Designers, Action Director, Music Director etc. They require skill and delivery.
Motor (The Mechanics)
The mechanics run the machine to specs – Light boys, Spot boys, Makeup & Hair Stylists, Setting boys, Fighters, etc. They require efficiency and productivity. These people require attention to detail and hard work.
Circuitry (The Programmers)
The Programmers work outside of the workshop and manage the circuitry of the film – Colorists, Data Managers, VFX Artists, Sound Recordist, Mixing Engineer etc. They convert raw elements into cinematic presentations. They require precision and energy.
Maintenance & Quality control (The Inspectors)
The Inspectors consolidate the film as per the specs – 1st Chief Assistant and other Subordinate Assistants, Focus Pullers, Script Supervisors, Continuity In-charge, Sound Mixer, Production Managers, Accountants. They require focus and discipline.
Optics and Packaging (The Imagers)

The Imagers create the perception of the film – Strategists, Communication managers, Public Relations, Designers. They require creativity and understanding of society.

Nobody came from Tata Sky.

It's been two days, and my TV is still stuck on the same *Manohar Kahaniyan* news channel.

I decide to tweet, tagging Tata Sky.

In some time, I receive a call from an engineer. He asks me if I am home, so that he can come personally to attend to the problem.

This is the first time that I realize the actual power of social media. Its usage for grievance addressal can open up so many horizons. Brands can't mess around with the customers. It can be so useful for public help, warnings, building public opinion, influencing policy, delivery of governance and above all as a check and balance for the narrative.

My hero has to be a social media influencer.

Finally, the Tata Sky guy comes. He turns on the TV and switches channels.

'It's working alright,' he tells me.

I take the remote. Yes, it's working perfectly.

Why does it happen that when you go to a mechanic, suddenly your car starts working? Why does the stomach ache disappear the moment we enter the clinic? Good old Murphy.

'But, when I tried... Maybe there is magic in your hands. Thanks.'

'It was nothing. Just moisture,' he tells me casually.

Why did it never occur to me? The solution of the remote lay outside of electronic technology. It lay in chemical science.

The solution to my problem of budgeting doesn't lie in money. It lies in the ownership of an idea. It doesn't lie in a financial equation. It depends on a creative equation.

On my notepad, I write down the motivating factors, the payoffs, for each set of workers.

The Drivers: Primary – Creativity and fame. Secondary – Money.

Find people who are hungry to show their craft for acclaim and are in between two films. Share profits.

The Engineers: Primary – Climbing up the ladder. Secondary – Money.

Find new talent, give them the ladder.

The Mechanics: Primary – Money. Secondary – Food.

Find old, experienced workers who deserve appreciation, guarantee a minimum package. Bonus on profits. Feed well.

The Programmers: Primary – Technology. Secondary – Recognition, credits.

Find good assistants to leaders, make them do out-of-the-box work, give opening titles.

The Inspectors: Primary – achievement. Secondary – Experience.

Find people who want to work with me to learn; challenge them.

The Imagers: Primary – Experiment. Secondary – Appreciation.

Find young disruptors, innovators who are looking for a break. Pay token amount.

I call Amit to fix my meetings with the crew.

In the next one week, I meet all the heads of departments, technicians, and vendors for a cup of tea where I explain the importance of the subject, the role they can play, not in just making of the movie but also in the ownership of the film. In short, I talk to them from my heart with absolute honesty and sincerity. I make them equal partners in the creative process. My lighting vendor and chief electrician Barmu can't believe that I narrated the entire script to him and shared costume and set designs with him. I tell them why it is important for them to participate in the film. How they can contribute in filmmaking irrespective of their position and department.

Nobody has ever involved them in the filmmaking process. These people who work at the bottom of a hierarchy, as spot boys, light boys, setting boys, even the walkie-talkie attendants and many others keep working on film after film without knowing anything about the subject. They go outdoors but don't know the names of the city where they shoot. They keep moving shoot after shoot, following dead instructions without ever knowing what they are doing, and why. Did the workers on *Sholay* have any idea what kind of history they were participating in?

I involved everyone. *Everyone.*

In the end, everyone works for money but sometimes it takes a backseat when a film fulfils one's larger need. I am pretty clear on those larger needs, the motivations of each set of people. This note becomes my successful prescription. It becomes the solution to the budget problem.

To the driver group, I offer back-end share of profits, if we ever make any, plus the money for a month's work and five free days. I promise them space to experiment. I assure them that this film will become their show reel. These people work on a film-to-film basis. Between two films, they are very often free for two to three months or more. In their minds, this is a 'no income' period. I offer them an opportunity to do something for their creative soul, experiment, stay in a great B-school, shoot easy, drink beer and also get paid some money. It sounds like a creative picnic. Everyone agrees to my terms.

To the engineer group, I offer head-of-the-department positions and independence. Normally in these departments, the budget is very difficult to control as the requirements keep changing. They deal with fabric, tailoring, construction, labour etc. So, in return of such a break, I ask them to work on a turnkey basis, on a package. Their fees, material, manufacturing, execution, transport etc. all in one fee. Another problem with these departments is that they always have to struggle for the payments and in the end, after the shoot is over, a certain percentage of their dues goes into bad debt. I offer them fifty percent advance and balance one week before the end of the shoot and in return I ask them to cut their package by twenty-five percent which they happily do.

I am relaxed as at least the most volatile departments are locked and they cannot increase my budget.

Motorists generally don't get consistent work. Especially, if they are a bit older. I get such people, recognize their efforts, guarantee them five days' extra money, stay in the campus with all of us, fifty percent advance and in return, they have to lock their fees and not charge me for extra shifts as I plan to work a little more than regular shifts. I get a big discount.

I give them what they want and I get what I want. It's a win-win deal. Everyone is hired on a fixed package and there is no scope for even a rupee to go up. But we are still fifty lacs over. Location, stay and food alone are costing sixty lacs. I resolve that if I have come thus far, it's in order to go further. I don't know how, but I have faith.

I personally sign contracts with them and offer them a packet of *motichoor laddoos* and took selfies with them. One thing common in all the selfies was the confidence on each face. The kind of confidence one has on owning something that's very precious to him. In this case, it's the film.

For the first time, a film is going to have a hundred owners.

Book Two

In Search of Buddha

"Marxists say God is a fraud. But God has lasted thousands of years, Marx could barely last a hundred years."
- Anonymous

8. The Red Corridor: A Day as Usual

April is one of the most pleasant months in the forests of Dantewada district in Chhattisgarh's Bastar region. The early morning breeze flowing from Indravati river and brushing along *champa* and *chandan* trees work as a perfect catalyst for meditation. In the evening, the same breeze brushing through *tendua* and *mahua* leaves works as an aphrodisiac. The Indravati river, which starts its journey from the Vindhyas, converts into a picturesque delight at the point where Chitrakoot Falls are located.

It is believed that due to its heavenly fragrances of *chandan* and *champa* forests, Lord Indra and Indrani came down from heaven to stay here for some time. One day during his regular walks, Indra got lost and reached a small village Sunabeda, where he saw a beautiful girl Udanti, fell in love with her and stayed back with her. After waiting for Indra for a long time, Indrani couldn't control her patience and sorrow and went around asking people about Indra. Everyone knew about the Indra and Udanti; they gave her solace and gently broke the news to her. When she broke down, they suggested that she stay with them as part of their family. Unable to hide her scorn, she cursed Indra and Udanti that they would never meet again. It is believed that she transformed into a river and stayed with the local tribals. Indra and Udanti rivers flow there separately, without meeting each other due to the curse of Indrani.

Spread all around Indravati is Dantewada. It gets its name from the goddess Danteshwari, an incarnation of Shakti. No wonder Dantewada's population has more females than males. Dantewada is surrounded by the dense forests of Dandakaranya, full of *aavla, bahera, harra, dhavala, kusum, mahua* and *tendu* and many other medicinal plants. Besides deep forests, Dandakaranya, from the ancient times, has been a habitat for different types of Adivasi communities.

Dandakaranya is spread over hundred thousand square kilometres, and it literally means 'the abode of the *Rakshasa* Dandaka'. Aranya is Sanskrit for forests. It was the kingdom a *Rakshasa* tribe called Danda, and it was also a colonial state of Lanka, ruled by Ravana.

It's in these forests of Dandakaranya, according to the *Ramayana*, that Lord Rama, Sita, and Lakshman spent thirteen of their designated fourteen years of exile. The forest is described in the *Ramayana* as 'a wilderness where many hermitages are scattered, while wild beasts and *Rakshasas* roam around.' Deadly creatures, demons, and exiles resided here and posed formidable risks for the sages who had to cross it in order to reach the Vindhya mountains for meditation. The plot for the divine objectives of the Hindu Trinity– Brahma, Vishnu, and Mahesh– to uproot *Rakshashas* from the path of the sages was formulated here. It's in these forests, one evening somewhere in the middle of *mahua* trees, that Surpanakha met Lakshman and fell in love with him. When Lakshman insulted her by turning her down, with a heart filled with rage, she demanded her *Rakshasa* brothers Khara and Dushan kill Rama and his brother. Rama won the battle.

The perennial river Sabari, which flows through forests, is said to be named after Shabri, a tribal woman who had offered berries to Lord Rama. Shabri could have been from one of the many tribes like Gond, Maria, Bhatra, Muriya, Halba, or Dhuruva living here since the time of Rama.

Tribes residing here have never travelled out of these jungles and have no exposure to the outer world. Till date, they do not have any reference to a civilized life and the modern world. They feed themselves on the abundance of forest produce and by hunting animals in the forest.

'The jungle is our life. We exist as long as jungles exist,' I was told by a young tribal man when I had visited Bastar in the late 1970s. In Bastar, traditions and rituals are closely linked to these forests and trees. The tribals believe that their gods and goddesses reside in this jungle and, therefore, every tree is sacred. The *saja,* the *mahua,* the *semal*, the mango, the *karanji*, the banyan, the *peepal*, the *salfi* trees are symbols of good fortune and prosperity. The number of *salfi* trees in a house is an indicator of the wealth and prosperity of the household. The drink that is made from its fruit is an integral part of their culture. If the drinks of *salfi, chind,* and *mahua* are not offered during ceremonies of birth, marriage, and death, the ceremonies are considered incomplete.

People revere trees just as they revere their parents and their deities. For they have never seen anything other than these forests. They don't know that outside these forests lies an India that has been to the Moon and Mars. An India that is the world's largest producer of films. An India that has over one billion mobile subscribers making it the second largest user of mobile telephony. An India which has the second largest English– speaking population, after the USA; whereas, the India that some of these tribals belong to, doesn't even have a language.

Dandakaranya has long been isolated from the outside world, and accessible only via forest pathways. Even when the British Raj tried to connect India through road and rail networks, this region remained geographically isolated and constitutionally excluded. India got independence, but nothing changed here. Feudalism prevailed and the only reason outsiders came here was to exploit its rich mineral wealth of iron ore, bauxite, tin, granite, marble, limestone, and corundum. These tribals are isolated from the rest of India– demographically, geographically, economically, socially, culturally, politically and psychologically. India has many Indias within. But they are not on the radar of the mainstream narrative. This is the lost India. This is an India that no one cares for. Hence, no one tries to find it.

On one of those April mornings, as the sun was rising above the mountains, the birds were singing songs and the breeze laden with the fragrance of *champa* was hitting the dew on the leaves, a young girl was collecting red ants in a make-do bag made of tender *mahua* leaves. It's another thing that for this little girl it was an adventure to catch red ants without realizing that she is, perhaps, the victim of such abject poverty that her family has to survive on red ant chutney despite India being the second largest producer of calorie content. She has no idea that the India she lives in is the fourth largest agriculture producer in the world, producing more food than all the countries of European Union combined. She has not even the faintest idea that while she starves, India wastes as much food as the whole of United Kingdom consumes, which is over forty percent of its total food production. In her India, food means a fresh and delicious chutney made of red ants and drinks made from *salfi, chind,* and *mahua.*

After filling her *mahua*-leaves bag with red ants, she starts to walk back on a familiar, yet bushy path back to the river where she would take a *dhongi* to cross the river to her village in Abujmarh. The sun is just warming up. She stops under a tree to listen to a bird singing songs as if she has seen the change of the weather.

BOOM. BOOM. BOOM.

She hears loud sounds. The entire forest fills with birds squeaking all over the sky. For the next half an hour or so there are lots of firing sounds. Then they become sporadic.

The date was 6th April 2010. It was a Tuesday, an auspicious day for Hindus. Tuesday, according to Hindu belief, is dedicated to Hanuman, son of the wind god Vayu and an ardent devotee of Rama. Hanuman fought Rama's war against Ravana. It's in these jungles that Shabri advised Rama to meet Sugriva – the *vaanar* king– who appointed Hanuman to find Sita.

On this day, sometime between six and seven in the morning, a bus full of eighty Central Reserve Police Force (CRPF) was returning after opening a road for the troops, to begin an operation called Green Hunt. In 2009, the central government of India deployed over hundred thousand paramilitary forces comprising CRPF, Indo-Tibetan Border Police (ITBP), Border Security Force (BSF), and one of India's most specialized, experienced and successful unit in fighting asymmetrical warfare, Commando Battalion for Resolute Action (CoBRA), supported with ten armed helicopters from the Indian Air Force, in Bastar, Odisha, and Jharkhand, in what is known as the Red Corridor, a Naxal theatre.

Apart from the paramilitary, there were two hundred thousand State Armed Police Force (SAPF). The Indian Army is also present here under the pretext of training the paramilitary forces. The Army chief along with his seven army commanders made an assessment to induce around sixty-five thousand troops to battle the Naxalites in this theatre. The Indian Air Force's Chief Marshall declared his 'full support to Green Hunt operations' with additional fleets of MI-17V5 helicopters, besides the already engaged MI-17 choppers. The government is also planning to send over a couple of thousand troops of Naga battalions of the Indian Reserve Battalions (IRB) into the Red Corridor.

These forces come with advanced satellite phones and Unmanned Aerial Vehicles (UAV) engineered and supported by the National Technical Research Organization (NTRO). To bring in sharpness and precision to this operation, the Defense Research and Development Organization (DRDO) has developed specialized UAVs with 'lower frequency radars' to track down the Naxals in these dense forests. The NTRO has imported about a dozen hi-tech drones from Israel for surveillance purposes. The central government is simultaneously working on cloning a new commando unit on the lines of Andhra Pradesh's deadly Greyhounds.

The Red Corridor, one of India's poorest and ironically the most militarized zone of India, is the 'nerve centre' of the Naxal movement. According to the South Asia Terrorism portal, between 2005 and 2011, over two thousand Naxals have lost their lives along with almost the same number of civilians and armed forces personnel. This indeed is the longest, deadliest war in independent India.

While the CRPF team was returning, Naxalites blew up the bus with improvised explosive devices (IEDs), commonly known as landmines. Though overwhelmed by the heavily armed ambush of Naxalites firing from the heights, the CRPF men fought back and the encounter lasted until all eighty men fell one by one and those who survived ran out of ammunition.

The Naxals then climbed down and shot the wounded men and looted their weapons. Seventy-six CRPF men were killed by over a thousand Naxals comprising of a supporting cast of local militia and *sangam* village associations. 'It was a total siege,' a police officer reported. 'The CRPF men were attacked not just from three sides, but even from the open area.'

Some defenceless surviving CRPF men pretended to be dead but Naxals searched bodies, shot the pretenders and looted all weapons and ammunition. Only three rifles were found at the site of encounter. It was a swift affair and perhaps the deadliest in the history of independent India. Even at the Line of Control (LOC) and in Kashmir, where our forces have been fighting an unending battle with Pakistani forces and terrorists, we never lost so many soldiers in a single attack.

This attack came two days after the Naxals triggered a land mine blast in Odisha's Koraput district, killing eleven security personnel of the elite Anti-Naxal Special Operations Group. And five days after India launched its new Biometric Census, the largest census in the world, with the ambition to cover the people of this area which has been isolated since Rama walked in these jungles.

The young tribal girl waits for some time and then heads back home. She stops at the river, takes a ride in a *dhongi* and crosses over. Her mother makes a delicious red ant chutney called *chapura* and feeds her family, thanking their gods for the food. The girl picks up a stick, pretends it's a gun and starts shooting imaginary enemies – Boom. Boom. Boom.

For her, it's just a usual day.

9. A History of Violence

I not only want to understand the geography, history and politics of the Naxal movement, but feel the pulse of it. I want to understand its design and figure out where it is heading to.

I juggle with data and research. My writing studio is filled with analyses, articles, timelines, and all available opinions and essays on the Naxal movement.

I know that data can't become a film. But, research helps find insights into an issue. Sadly, Bollywood doesn't invest in R&D. That's why most of our films have no insights to offer. As a result, small, independent films have become the R&D lab for the Indian film industry. These films have to do an extraordinary research, for their only strength is transporting the audience to another universe, where they can feel and relate with the characters, their concerns, and their behaviour. In the mainstream films, the world is unreal, devoid of any real human concern, and the characters are like caricatures. Hence, this kind of cinema ends up becoming 'Escapist Cinema'. Like a circus.

This is why we get to hear dialogues like 'The only purpose of cinema is entertainment, entertainment, and entertainment'. It's not true. If cinema is only entertainment, then what's the difference between cinema and a circus? It's because of this unshakable belief of the Bollywoodians in this maxim that our cinema has never been taken seriously as an art and has hardly been a catalyst for real impact in society. I am not denying the contribution of Raj Kapoor, Guru Dutt, Bimal Roy, Hrishikesh Mukherjee or Raju Hirani in the mainstream cinema, but nine out of ten films have diluted the impact made by such masters, whose cinema not just entertained but made us think, feel, and act.

I have all the possible material but not the perspective which can give a new insight into an issue which has been discussed, debated, and analyzed to such a level that now it's become boring for the audience. People have formed their opinions. Some find Naxals messiahs for the oppressed and some think they are the villains who stall India's growth story. And none is willing to listen to the other. I have to find the truth. But if the truth is not popular, it seems like a lie. That is another tragedy of mass communication. Which is why most of the filmmakers take a populist stance. In our films, so far, we have shown a terrorist or a Naxal as a product of injustice or oppression. But my research proves otherwise. It's an ideological act arrived at either by total brainwash or a lure for money or power… or both.

My assistant gives me seven hundred pages full of violent acts in Naxal-infested areas. She has marked some pages with red tags.

'What are these for?' I ask her.

'I found them unusual as these are rarely reported in mainstream media and I had to dig into blogs, tweets, FB posts etc. to collate facts. So, I am not sure how authentic they are… so if you want you can ignore them.' She tells me like a typical assistant who doesn't want to take blame for anything.

I have never understood why we train our assistant directors to think like clerks or logistics managers and never like a director.

I shift my focus to the violence angle. When we think of violence in the Red Corridor, we tend to assume that it's always between Naxals and the forces. Because that's what we get to read in the mainstream media. Media, as a prerequisite, has to be anti-establishment, which is good for a democracy. Therefore, media always pushes a narrative which is sympathetic towards Naxals unless a sensitive and inhuman Dantewada kind of incident takes place. This file is full of Naxal attacks on the establishment.

I flip through pictures of thirty-eight Greyhound commandos killed by the Naxals in a reservoir in June 2008 in Odisha. Sixteen policemen slain in the jungles of Gadchiroli. On 18 March 2007, the Naxals attacked a police camp at Ranibodli, killing fifty-five policemen, including Special Police Officers (SPOs). Naxals ambushed a joint paramilitary-police team in Bihar, killing ten, wounding ten more, taking four prisoners, and robbing more than thirty-five automatic rifles from the State forces. On September

2010, they killed three policemen and took four hostages in an ambush in Chhattisgarh and at gunpoint made them promise that they would never take up arms against the insurgency again.

This is a never-ending list of Naxal crimes. Looting. Rapes. Murders. There isn't anything new in these reports. People know their crimes and it doesn't matter whether we illustrate one example or hundreds. Our audiences have become numb to the oppressor-oppressed stories. These are the things of the 1970s and 80s. Very Amitabh era stuff. In Ranveer Singh and Ranbir Kapoor's times, we need something which people don't know. A well-hidden secret from the public eye.

I am restless.

Naxalism started as a social justice movement, 50 years ago, in a half village-half town in Darjeeling district of West Bengal where some poor peasants forcefully took away land from landlords. The police were called in on 24 May, 1967 and police officer Sonam Wangdi was killed by arrows shot by tribal peasant leader Jangal Santhal and others. The next day, a large armed police contingent arrived at Naxalbari and they fired at the peasants, killing nine women and two children. In a young independent India, where social disparity and feudal oppression was the order of the day, this tragedy enraged the youth who wanted to build a nation based on equality and justice. Many young people joined this movement led by Charu Majumdar, a hardline leader of the Communist Party of India (Marxist) or CPI(M).

Majumdar later quit CPI(M) to form the Communist Party of India (Marxist-Leninist) or CPI(ML), which believed in killing "class enemies" to establish the "dictatorship of the proletariat". The movement came to be known as Naxalism and the young men and women who led this movement came to be known as Naxals or Naxalites.

But slowly, the immediate economic and social problems of the masses took a back seat and the battle for the supremacy with the State became the central theme. There has been a range of acts of violence inconsequential to the rights of people, but invariably end up harming the masses.

Naxals in Jharkhand have set aside their ideals and emerged as a mining mafia. A report claims that a multi-crore mining scam is being staged by the Naxalites. The Maoist extortion business is estimated to be around a whopping Rs 2,000 crore. All contractors have to pay five to ten percent of the project cost to Naxalites as 'protection money'. Trucks that pass through the 'Red Corridor' pay Rs 1,000 each per month. There have been repeated incidents of Naxals blowing up schools, trains, and railway lines, apart from government buildings which harm the common masses more than the politburo of governance. There have been reports that Naxals physically torture police informers by gruesome acts like hacking off limbs and even gouging out eyes. In July 2007, a group of armed Naxalites extorted Rs65,000 from a poor farmer in Chikmagalur in Karnataka. Such atrocities demonstrate that the Naxals have lost the principles for which they once fought and are adversely affecting the lives of the people they once sought to help.

I dig into the pages with the red tags. I remember my assistant finding them interesting. These are certainly not from the mainstream media. The first story I read opens up my mind. Slowly, the simple design of a complex politics starts to form. I focus on two cases.

Latehar is a backward district located in the north-west corner of Jharkhand. Surrounded by natural beauty and forests, Lateher is rich in mineral deposits. Almost half of its population is tribal and the balance is Dalit. Enough to attract Naxals. Like in most backward and rural areas, the government runs its infamous MGNREGS (Mahatma Gandhi National Rural Employment Guarantee Scheme) which guarantees a minimum of hundred days of employment per household per year. Populist government schemes, for their mammoth size and lack of State interest, always encourage corruption. Despite the welfare at the heart of these schemes, they are always hijacked by a corrupt nexus and the benefits never filter down to the intended beneficiary. MGNREGS is no exception.

Niyamat Ansari, a local activist, along with his colleague Bhukan Singh, used to help villagers access the benefits of this scheme. Soon, he realized that the villagers were not getting their due amounts. Together with Bhukan, Niyamat raised his voice against the looting of government funds by corrupt contractors. He had no idea that this whistleblowing would have fatal repercussions. From an unexpected enemy.

In February 2009, the Naxals, who are active in this area, held a so-called 'people's court' and accused Ansari and Singh of acting under the influence of the police and being 'involved in counter-revolutionary activities'.

When it became evident to Niyamat that the Naxals and contractors are working in tandem, he raised his pitch to expose this nexus. Naxals, guided by a local contractor, attacked Niyamat and Bhukan's houses with a severe warning to the neighbours against informing the police or even providing any kind of help. Naxals also put up posters against them with 'fatal' warnings.

On March 1, a formal complaint was registered by the police against several individuals. Niyamat identified and reported Naxals and also Shankar Dubey, a local contractor, as perpetrators of the attacks.

On March 2, about twenty armed Naxals, led by their local commander Sudarshan, came back to the village and started beating Niyamat. According to Human Rights Watch, 'When Niyamat's sister tried to protect him, she was shown the gun and was asked to back off, with the warning that she would be shot. She sat nearby and cried. After brutally beating him with *lathis* and assuming that he was dead, a village woman was told to inform Niyamat's family, with the statement 'Take him wherever you want to take him.' Niyamat's father rushed to his son and realized that he was still breathing. He roamed through the village to collect people and ask for help, but no one came forward due to fear. 'This was a scene from Dilip Kumar's *Mashal,* where he screams for help for his dying wife but nobody helps,' a student told me.

By the time he was carried on a *charpoy* and brought to Latehar hospital, he was dead.

In no time Naxals released a pamphlet taking responsibility for Ansari's killing. The pamphlet read: 'You all know that our fight against imperialism, capitalism, and *samantvad,* that is against class enemies, is going on and Niyamat and Bhukan from both these viewpoints are class friends. That's why we are also sad that Niyamat had to be executed. Despite his being under the influence of the police administration, carrying out anti-people, counter-revolutionary activities, and challenging the party, we gave him several chances to mend his ways in writing as well as verbally. He didn't show any improvement, and as a result, we were forced to give him the punishment of death penalty.'

Bhukan, who went into hiding, was warned by the Naxals: 'We are still giving Bhukan a chance to improve himself, on the condition that he appears in people's court and realizes his mistakes, asks for forgiveness and promises that he will improve.' Later, a hapless government took him and his family to the state capital. They were housed at an undisclosed location. Bhukan's sons Mandeep and Sandeep who were in Classes VI and VIII missed their annual examinations, but that certainly is of little concern when death is chasing life. Government officials refuse to divulge details on other activists, fearing the Naxals.

In Latehar, all voices against corruption were silenced.

A friend of mine, Vijay Ganti, who works with the State Bank of India and travels in the interiors of Jharkhand and Bihar for financing tribals, tells me that the poor tribals who work on MGNREGS are always in trouble. On one side, there are corrupt contractors. On the other, there are the Naxals, who support contractors to get money. 'While both the Naxals and the MGNREGS contractors claim to be working for the welfare of the tribal communities, in reality, they are engaged in a nexus to benefit themselves. Which is why they don't want anyone to create awareness about people's rights,' says Ganti. To reinforce his argument, he sends me a story which was never investigated by the mainstream media and brought to its logical conclusion.

Amrapara is a community development block in Pakur district of Jharkhand. This hilly area is rich in coal. It has a population of roughly sixty-six thousand out of which around fifty-five thousand are tribals.

In 2006, PANEM Coal Mines Ltd started its mining operations in Amrapara. With the advent of mining came money, which empowered the population with purchasing power. And new ambition. The texture of this backward block started changing.

These people who had no context of prosperity, suddenly aspired to become richer and more powerful. Life in this remote area began changing at a rapid pace. In the meantime, Sister Valsa John, an ordained nun, who had worked among the Santhal tribals of Jharkhand for over fifteen years, first as a school teacher and then as a human rights activist, formed a *samiti*– Rajmahal Pahar Bachao Andolan (RPBA), the Rajmahal Hills Protection Movement.

Slowly the *samiti*, mediating between mines and locals, started becoming a power centre. The resistance movement that was based on a principle of 'anti-greed', started lusting for money and power. This is the moment the middlemen wait for. They soon started alluring *samiti* youth on behalf of company officials, government servants, and politicians. This was a perfect playground for the Naxals. Slowly, Amrapara descended into an abyss of criminalization. Sister Valsa kept trying to work against the criminal nexus led by the Naxals and she was seen as a stumbling block to their evil aspirations. On November 15, 2011, a mob of fifty armed men, out of which over thirty were Naxals, broke into her house and hacked her to death.

According to a report in *Mainstream Weekly*, 'the immediate spark for Sr. Valsa's murder was provided by the rape of a girl working with her. Some days earlier, Surajmuni had been picked from Alubera, a weekly market by a group of young men, and gang-raped that night. The next day, her parents had reported the rape at the local police station and tried to file an FIR, but the police refused and chased them away. Thereafter, the parents had approached Valsa for help. On her advice, the victim and her parents had gone to the police station again. They had been rudely told to settle the case out of court and accept monetary compensation. But the rape victim had refused to compromise and demanded justice. At this juncture, Valsa had intervened and managed to get an appointment for the rape victim with the District Collector on November 16, 2011.

'For the criminalized youth, this was probably the last straw. Their anger flared as they realized that Sr. Valsa had become a hindrance not only to their greedy designs, but also to their easy access to women. Her brutal murder was the culmination of a process of dehumanization that had been set into motion by the company and the violent atmosphere of the mining area.'

According to Dumka inspector-general Arun Oraon, 'The Naxals are trying to make inroads into Pakur to extort money from a mining company. The Naxals, however, did not use firearms to kill her. They let the villagers do that as message—even an influential person like Valsa could be killed if Naxals did not approve of that person.'

Naxals admitted to their role in Sister John's killing. In an interview with the BBC, Naxal spokesman Somnath said, without providing any basis, that Sister John was 'working for the interests' of mining companies. Because she had 'let down the tribals,' he said, the Naxals had to 'resort to the extreme step (of killing her)'.

It's 3 AM in the morning. I am getting restless. This is not the Naxal movement I knew of. In a story of oppressor versus oppressed, we tend to look for a Robin Hood, the hero. In independent India's story, media has tried to make Naxals look like Robin Hood. Which is why incidents like the Niyamat and Valsa murders are rarely reported in detail and if reported, they always put the blame on the State.

Niyamat and Valsa were from the minority who were fighting oppression, injustice, and corruption against the marginalized section of society. They were working for the same cause as Naxals. Then why were they killed? I can smell a design which is akin to the underworld's strategy for keeping their supremacy. I dig into similar stories. As I turn the pages, umpteen stories of barbaric, gruesome, and brutal killings start unfolding, leading me to dangerous motives and the sinister politics behind it. Every case I probe indicates that Naxals don't want any development in their area. They don't want the children to be educated, they don't want roads to be built. They want tribals to remain in the dark.

And to achieve this perverse end, they can go to any extent of violence, even if it means killing an infant. A four-month-old baby was killed in a *Jan Adalat* in front of her mother as her father was a suspected police informer. Naxals burn mark sheets and transfer certificates of 10th and 12th students, so that they cannot go for further education and migrate from their villages. Families do not keep their children in the area as they fear that Naxals will induct them forcibly in the movement. I met some students in Nagpur who do not go to their villages and their families come to Nagpur to meet them. Naxals burnt fifteen vehicles of contractors who were building roads as they believe that roads will eventually lead to development. Dalit Patru Durge was killed because he was taking government help to get lift irrigation in his village.

'Sir, why are they so anti-development?' my assistant asks me.

I believe everything in this world can be converted into a simple design. Once we understand the simple design, it becomes easy to tackle the complex engineering of the phenomenon. For the last few months, I have been struggling to convert Naxal politics into a simple story. There are so many agencies involved. Today's Naxal movement is not the same as in the times of Charu Majumdar or Sitarammaiah or Paddi Shankar. Their story was simple. A *Zamindar* oppresses villagers, rapes their women, and takes their land. Some righteous young men, influenced by Chinese leader Mao Zedong's theory of armed struggle for revolution, pick up arms and kill the landlord, give their land back to the villagers and thereby bring justice. A central theme of many films.

There are no *Zamindars* today, so who are they fighting in the tribal areas? Why is it that after four decades of struggle, neither have the rebels achieved their objective nor have the tribals been empowered? Why is the government not being able to stop this oppression? Where do they get money from? Are all those intellectuals who openly support the Naxal movement on national TV, righteous people? What is in it for them? This is a movement being fought in jungles inhabited by wild animals, snakes and, the tribals– is it possible for it to survive for so long? That too without financial, intelligence, strategic, and logistical support? It's impossible for a movement to survive for so long only on good intentions. So, who are the masterminds?

While seeking answers to all these pertinent questions, I stop at a photo. It's a photo of a semi-naked young tribal girl's corpse from

Bastar. Her body is being carried on bamboo sticks, like a hunted animal is carried for cooking. Her eyes are open, still carrying hope. Her breasts are bare and innocence is flowing from every pore of her dead body. Her beauty is unexploited. Uncorrupted. In her, I find the simple story I was looking for.

I think about that girl with red ants.

10. Heaven and Hell

Whenever the Naxal issue pops up, people start discussing the politics behind it. Some are on the side of the oppressors and some on the side of the oppressed. But discussions always remain at the circumference. Very rarely do we talk about the centre. The tribal, who everyone is fighting for.

I relook at the picture of the tribal girl. No clothes, no context. I name her Vanbala after a poem by my father, of the same title.

Vanbala has no context of the real world. She doesn't know if this world contains anything other than these trees and forests and streams and snakes and birds and red ants. Her family's land was stolen by the landlord and her father was made to work on his own farm as a labourer. He also has to give away all the farm produce. A forest officer takes most of whatever her mother and brothers bring from the forest. Then there is a police officer who rapes her at will. For her, this is her life. Her world. Her heaven.

She has no idea of the hell she lives in.

A few years ago, I visited a maestro conductor in New York – the epitome of capitalism – in their massive and opulent apartment, in one of the poshest neighborhoods of NY, overlooking the Hudson river. It was Christmas and New York was snowing in. While I waited for the hosts to come out, standing at a never-ending window, I was captivated by the beauty of the snow falling on the oak trees around Hudson river and I thought of '*Gar firdaus, zamin asto, ami asto, ami asto, ami asto*– if there is a heaven on earth, it's here, it's here, it's here.'

The Maestro is a world-renowned symphonic conductor and composer with over fifty Grammy nominations and ten Grammy trophies that are displayed on a mahogany chest, just above the shining Steinway & Sons piano made of the highest grade close-grained, quarter-sawn Sitka spruce – a very expensive wood selected for its superb acoustic properties. The living room was full of murals, paintings, artefacts, souvenirs, china and the kind of stuff which I don't even know how to describe. I must admit this was, perhaps, the second time in my life when I was enchanted by such opulent urban living and was reminded of the contrasting smallness of my small-town, middle-class, deprived background. The first time I felt so was in an industrialist's house in Delhi.

The maestro's wife served me Silver Tips Imperial Tea – the world's most expensive brand of Darjeeling tea, sold at four hundred dollars per kilogram, in an expensive china cup with the choicest of the cookies and cakes, hand-picked from Pasticceria Rocco of the historic West Village in NY, while the Maestro sipped an expensive Cerretalto wine from his prized cellar. Slowly the discussions shifted from music, Hollywood, Bollywood to the recession. Yes, at that time the American financial downturn had just begun, what later came to be known as the Great Meltdown. Suddenly, his wife, who was sitting quietly thus far, became angry and for the next few minutes, she spoke non-stop, taking short breaks only to light her Dunhill.

'America is not the America we came to… it's hell,' she declared.

'You don't mean it,' I said, looking at her sparkling diamond ring.

'Everyone has gone bust, there is no security… no safety… when I walk on the streets of New York, I feel like I am walking in a jungle with beasts all around… everyone is exploiting everyone… the powerful and mighty are exploiting us, the simple people… It's a big hell….'

'You haven't seen India or some African countries yet to know what it feels to be in real hell…' I interrupted, to give her some reality check.

'I have read on India and I know it's a beautiful place. People love each other, you have families, parents look after children and when they are old the children look after them, they have values, culture… unlike us… America is hell… it's a hell of some other planet.' She meant every word of it. I could feel it. Artists can lie but can't hide. She lit another slim Dunhill, blew out the smoke and continued in an introspective, husky and broken voice.

'What is hell after all? When we think of hell we think of suffering… everyone is suffering…. nobody cares… nobody respects.... nobody loves... nobody helps.... You can't trust anyone... If that's not hell, then what is it? There are beasts all around to devour you... America is a land of suffering. People may look beautiful outside but inside, they are suffering. The more they smile, the more they suffer inside. People don't know that they live in a hell because nobody has told them so. Welcome to the world's most successfully hidden hell, the United States of America.' She stubbed out her cigarette.

I wasn't prepared for such a speedy paradigm shift. Especially in a place which seemed like absolute heaven to me.

Ironically, Vanbala doesn't even know her hell. This vast, lush and unapproachable jungle is her kingdom, of which she is the princess. I keep looking at her photo. I realize hell and heaven are such subjective concepts. What appeared heaven to me was hell to the rich maestro's wife. What appeared heaven to her is hell to me. Hell is not a place. It's a state of mind. A *fakir* walks barefoot in scorching heat, sleeps on a pavement and yet sings a song admiring the beauty of the world. Whereas a film heroine, living in a castle of fame, opulence and glory, drinks herself to death, escaping from her hell.

Vanbala didn't know about her hell, until the Naxals came.

Mainstream media hasn't done justice to this grave issue. Almost all the reports are mere copy-paste jobs. Nobody wants to go into the jungles to do real reporting. Which is why, the reports are only about the killings between the forces and Naxals, circulated by syndicates. There is a thirty-three page essay by Arundhati Roy on the issue yet it doesn't smell of the jungles. It smells of her. It stinks of her agenda. Why, I wonder? Why is it that most of the op-eds and essays from the so-called intelligentsia comprising editors, professors, historians, political analysts, social workers, NGO entrepreneurs, humanitarians, and civil society leaders favour the false Naxal narrative?

I am interested in understanding the psyche of Vanbala. And the psyche and motivations of that Naxalite who takes a conscious decision to spend his life in this hell in order to protect Vanbala from this hell. I find it in independent blogs. Where the mainstream media fails, citizens shine.

As I read more and more independent material, a story starts emerging. In the corner of a filmmaker's mind, there is a special projector which transforms the most complex and elaborate essays into many simple and short films. I can see the history of Naxalism in the theatre of my mind. Vanbala is the protagonist through whom I see the story of Naxalism unfolding.

Vanbala was a young girl, growing up in Naxalbari in West Bengal, when India got its freedom.

'What is freedom?' She asked her poor peasant parents while devouring half of her *panta bhaat* in one bite.

'*Gore log* will leave us,' her landless peasant father replied while putting salt and turmeric on his heels, badly cracked due to tilling in the scorching sun.

'What will happen if they leave?'

'We will get our land back from the landlord. Your brother won't have to plough the fields like an ox just for a handful of the crop which is rightfully ours.' There was hope in his voice. Little did he know that it was easier to get freedom from colonial slavery than from the *Zamindar*.

Before independence, most of the country lived in villages, inhabited by poor, landless farmers who were ruled by the exploitative *Zamindars* or *Jagirdars*. The *Zamindars* gave these landless farmers ploughs and seeds, made them till the land like bulls, and in return gave them a pittance of the crop. This was also the time when there were famines, droughts and India was starving due to food shortage.

In this background, these *Zamindars* were central to the exploitative enterprise. The village was his universe. He would charge *lagaan* as per his whims and fancies. He raped women at will. His *kothi* represented the exploitation of the farmer. The mystery around him, his moustache, his *pagdi*, his servants and his *lathi* made him an icon of terror. He was evil. He loved to see a hungry farmer. His heart would fill with joy when a farmer put his *izzat – pagdi–* at his feet. He loved the sound of the whip slashing the skin off a starving farmer's back. He could do all this because he was the owner of the land. And that's the only commodity that God doesn't make anymore. He owned God's most in-demand and rare creation – land. Thus, he was God.

He also owned almost all the gold of these farmers in mortgage. If you understand this man, you will know why we Indians have such a fascination with land and gold. In no other country do people invest in land and gold as we do. We are willing to stop eating fruits, buying new clothes and often we even look for a cheaper doctor in order to save for '*do beegha zameen*' – a patch of land.

The *Zamindari* system was a payoff of the colonial policy of ruling the land by adopting two forms of 'indirect rule' i.e. the *zamindari* land tenure and the princely states. While the *zamindari* landlord tenure system created conditions of lower bureaucratic penetration as also land/caste inequality, the princely states tended to have lower levels of government institutions and also often had tribals who were ignored and neglected and untouched by modern bureaucratic institutions. This was a perfect set up for the organized restlessness and insurgency in India that would come in the future.

India got independence. Two things happened simultaneously. One, business fell into Indian hands. In West Bengal, the *Jotedars* – as the *Zamindars* are called there – tried to manipulate the land records and deceive the landless farmers and the government. A free India needed manufacturing more than farming. Rich with cash and gold, this *Zamindar* spread his business interests to urban businesses. He owned or bought stakes in factories, mills, and trade.

On the other hand, Nehru brought in a socialist vision. He brought in huge dams and public sector heavy industries. The intermediate beneficiaries were these new factory owners who were hand in glove with corrupt officers and maneuvered tenders in their favour. That's why lots of movies have a reference to some government officer's visit for inspection and how the factory owner would treat him with goodies, women, and wine.

The foundations of the unprecedented corruption that we see today were laid by Nehru's economics. While a majority of new, free India was struggling to survive the aftermath of Partition, the rest were now trying to become self-reliant by going for higher education and starting new businesses. The Indian middle class thought that after freedom, the rich-poor divide would be bridged, but to their shock, they realized that despite Nehru's idealistic socialist policies, they were now exploited by the rich Indians.

To balance this disparity, the government launched a very successful 'Green Revolution', but instead of bridging the disparity, it widened it even more because, once again, the beneficiaries of this revolution were only the *Zamindars* who had the wealth to buy fertilizers and modern agricultural equipment. The might and influence of these *Zamindars*, in independent India's socio-economic fabric, was unchallenged as they were infusing their illegal money into the coffers of politics. No wonder then that most of the cultivable land at that time was owned by just five percent of the people – the *Zamindars*.

Every young boy and girl detested the *Zamindar* for exploiting his father, uncles, and brothers. For molesting or raping his sister, mother or neighbour's daughter. This young boy grew up with angst. And it was this angst that became the fodder for the Naxal movement.

With politicians and police on his side, the only hurdle to this *Zamindar* was this bourgeois, idealistic youth, influenced by the doctrines of Mao Zedong who led a peasant army to bring about a successful revolution. The void created by the State was slowly getting occupied by the youth. This idealistic youth had to rise. He had to protest. He had to fight.

Then, one fine morning, in Naxalbari, a group of hungry and exploited peasants, armed with crude weapons rose to fight for what was rightfully theirs – the land and the crop. They attacked landlords, seized granaries and stole paddy, burnt all land records and forcibly took the land. And gave it back to the landless peasant.

An uprising had begun. Illegal. And unconstitutional.

An editorial in *People's Daily*, the Chinese Communist Party's mouthpiece, called it 'spring thunder' and declared it a successful rebellion '... a Red area of rural revolutionary armed struggle has been established in India.' Thus, began India's longest and most lethal social war.

Influenced by Mao Zedong's political sentiments contained in his *Little Red Book*, Naxalism bases its ideology on the 'Historic Eight Documents', a set of eight monographs written by Charu Majumdar, who was deeply influenced by Mao's ideas and believed that similar conditions existed in India wherein militant peasants and youth could be mobilized to overthrow the government through armed struggle.

Like his hero, Majumdar also believed that war was nothing but politics with bloodshed. He was often found quoting Mao's now famous statement: 'Revolution is not a dinner party, nor an essay, nor a painting, nor a piece of embroidery; it cannot be advanced softly, gradually, carefully, considerately, respectfully, politely, plainly, and modestly. A revolution is an insurrection, an act of violence by which one class overthrows another.'

I mark this statement with a yellow highlighter and then underline it with a red pen. Instinctively, I decide to use it at as the penultimate statement in the film, coming at the very end of the movie, more as a cinematic tool to remind the audience how miserably this movement, in its current form, has failed.

Charu Majumdar laid down four conditions for the aspiring Naxalite.

One: Acceptance of Mao Zedong as the leader of the world revolution and his thoughts as the highest form of Marxism-Leninism of that era.

Two: Belief in the view that a revolutionary situation existed in every corner of India.

Three: Area-wise seizure of power as the only path for taking forward the Indian revolution.

Four: Guerilla warfare as the only means of advancing the revolution.

Majumdar wanted to bring the Indian State to its knees by attacking it with a web of underground organizations and thus bring about the revolution. Soon he found to his surprise that a variety of intellectuals like writers, artists, professors, journalists and almost everyone from the *Bhadralok* of West Bengal joined in as also a large army of moralistic, energetic and risk-taking students. They wanted to bring light to a dark India. Some people in Central Bihar still believe that Naxalite is made of two words '*naksha*', which means map, and the English 'lite' – light, and therefore, put together, it means making a new map of India with our lights.

Naxalism as an underground movement has mushroomed across fourteen states, which are recognized as dreaded dens of 'Naxalite insurgency'. It is spread over Andhra Pradesh, Odisha, Chhattisgarh,

Jharkhand, Bihar and West Bengal. To a lesser extent, this trend is also visible in Tamil Nadu, Karnataka, Maharashtra and Uttar Pradesh. It is estimated that Naxalites are active in more than forty percent of India's geographical area, which is known as 'Red Corridor'. It is now spreading its tentacles in Punjab, Haryana, Rajasthan and Gujarat. Delhi is emerging as the centre of Urban Naxalism.

Today's Naxalism isn't limited to *Zamindars* or class struggle. In recent years, many other issues have added up which have aggravated the already worsening Naxalism. Issues like farmer suicide, informalization of the formal sector and contractualization of the industrial workforce, rising prices and soaring unemployment, development-induced displacements that include the creation of SEZs, EPZs, IT Parks and industrial hubs, environmental degradation etc., apart from gender and caste-based violence, have given Naxals more avenues to wage their war against the Indian State. This is new Naxalism. Not the one Charu Majumdar had founded.

In 1972, five years after the Naxalbari incident, a comrade was interrogated by the police and when subjected to third degree treatment, he vomited out Majumdar's whereabouts. He was arrested and died within a fortnight in police custody. With him ended a short story of an oppressed man's war against the oppressors, called Naxalism.

Nobody at that time knew that in some isolated parts of India like Bastar and Andhra Pradesh, a few youngsters were still carrying the fire of Naxalism in their hearts and that they would soon spark the jungles with the flames of guerrilla warfare. The government of India has been fighting this world's longest and biggest civilian war for the last fifty years without much success.

Little did Vanbala know that Naxalism is just a vehicle to take her from one hell to another hell.

11. Vanbala

One fine morning, some young Naxal guerrillas enter Vanbala's hell with the intention of converting it into heaven. Upon their arrival, the tribals run away, fearing that they would loot them like the officials. Now the Naxals have no food.

This is when Vanbala meets them and gives them some *panta bhaat* and red ant chutney.

Vanbala is fascinated with the gun.

The young men tell her of the famous teachings of Mao: 'Wherever there is struggle there is sacrifice, and death is a common occurrence.'

She picks up the gun.

After seven years of training, she becomes a Naxal commander.

Under her guerilla comrade guardianship, the villagers stop paying taxes, bribes, and commissions to the forest officials, contractors, and mill owners.

Vanbala goes back to her village and forcibly takes the land back from the *Zamindar*, makes him drink her pee, parades him naked in front of the oppressed villagers and reinstates the land to the rightful owners – the landless peasants of her community.

She realizes that this is a war and it can't be fought on foot and at a close range in this manner. She needs to attack from a distance. In Sri Lanka, Liberation Tigers of Tamil Eelam (LTTE) is active in guerilla warfare and as they need money, they train other guerilla groups. Vanbala's group, People's War Group (PWG), learns guerilla war from LTTE. So now Vanbala gets expertise in explosion and landmines. Now she can attack from a distance and at her will. The dynamics of the war changes. It becomes a war between Naxals and the Indian State.

The gun becomes a symbol for land redistribution and the end of an oppressive and corrupt system. A lot of young tribals are fascinated by this quick form of justice and they also pick up guns and join Vanbala.

They track down sexual exploiters, make the entire village spit on their faces, tie them to trees, and leave them to rot to their death.

Vanbala leads her men and attacks the policemen who always sided with the influential and powerful. They kill many policemen.

Newspapers report the incident: 'The ambush in which policemen were killed was led by a woman known not just for her commitment to the Naxalite cause but also her beauty.' Her division is headed by Indravati (name changed), a 52-year-old from Andhra Pradesh, said to be fluent in seven languages including English.

They use violence to demand better wages and rates for their produce. And they get it. Insurgency spreads and soon the area becomes the theatre of a new kind of warfare. A parallel government starts taking shape. Personal justice becomes the order of the day.

'Apni Satta, Apna Kanoon' Our governance, our laws, becomes the motto. Kangaroo courts get set up.

Vanbala becomes the new establishment.

Establishment has to survive. Survival requires funding and an ecosystem. Therefore, it becomes a compulsion to form a nexus with the politicians, police, and the middlemen. They also start looting contractors, trucks, and godowns.

Vanbala now has a big enterprise. People to be fed. Arms to be procured. Ammunition to be replenished. And above all, terror to be maintained, so that the government officials don't dare enter the area and therefore they block all kinds of developments. And kill all of them. In lots of cases, even women and children.

Terror has a quality – its virality can't be controlled. Soon, villagers start to put a red flag on any piece of land and no one dares come close to them to claim ownership.

Naxals become service providers for interpersonal rivalries and start facilitating revenge on the condition that the person will join them and become a Naxal. Kangaroo courts are used for this purpose. *'Adha foot kam kar do'* aka 'Behead him'.

The localized movement takes a pan-Indian shape, to accomplish its real goal – to wage a full-fledged war against the Indian State. Slowly, the Naxals become successful in establishing an alternate

State structure. Stretching from the border of Nepal to Central India and Karnataka in the south. It's christened 'Red Corridor'.

An India within India.

Vanbala travels from village to village with a promise of justice in *jal, jangal aur jameen,* water, forest, and land, and provides justice through committees like the *Sangam* and the *Jan Adalat.* She starts appeasing the Dalit youths by invoking the name and images of Dr. Babasaheb Ambedkar and Sardar Bhagat Singh in Maharashtra and Punjab respectively. When above ground tactics fail, they create terror. They kill. They kill those who don't subscribe to their ideology. They kill to create a power and governance vacuum and soon they fill up this space. They attack schools because education promotes awareness and empowers youth with skills for a livelihood other than farming and forest-related jobs. This is how they keep the population in their area of influence out of the mainstream milieu.

They form '*Bal Dastas*', enrolling children in their fold with the purpose of brainwashing and conditioning these young and innocent minds with violent Maoist ideology. Exactly like the Taliban or the ISIS.

They recruit lots of women in their cadre by coercion and threats. Poor Adivasis part with their girl children. This inhuman practice is the reason for a large number of women in their cadres. They also use children and women in the forefront of engagements with the security forces.

It's not easy to enthuse, manage, and maneuver such large, widespread cadres, where it takes weeks of walking on jungle trails infested with snakes and scorpions, only to communicate. One thing that keeps them motivated is the power to kill innocent people with a promise to change their hell into heaven.

All the stories I read outside of the mainstream media lead to the missing links. But one theme which is common in all the stories is that a sinister politics is developing at the behest of Naxals. Be it from a first-hand account in a blog, a social media post, or the police reports. Only time will tell whether this is a fact or just a hypothesis, but it's worth probing.

If police and other sources are to be believed, the Naxalites, with the help of Dalit youths and the Islamist terrorist group Indian Mujahedeen (IM), want to have their own government in the country by 2025. The revolution will emerge from the conflict of Hindus on one side and Dalits and Muslims on another. Two consolidated rebellious, energetic forces pumped with raw adrenaline, will go for each other's blood. And then it will be opportune to hijack and change the narrative to oppressed, proletariat, and marginalized vs bourgeoisie, elites, and Brahmins. This attracts poor and intellectuals both. In this case, the Adivasi, Dalits, Muslims, and other "forgotten people", united under one common red flag, will demolish the State. That's the ambition. And they also have a plan.

'How will they achieve it?' I wonder. 'How will they communicate with the students? Students don't go to the jungles.' I take a long breath. 'There has to be someone, something, some system that connects the Dalit and the Muslim youth, from all the campuses of India, with the comrades in the jungles. But… then… you need time, organization, management, training, and funding for such a huge project… It's a logistical nightmare… how can they undertake such a mammoth and complex operation without getting noticed?' asks the Byomkesh Bakshi inside me. I understand that jungles are their home turf, where it's easy to annihilate the enemy and exist; but how is it possible to go unnoticed in the government's home turf, where the government machinery is omnipresent?

Naxals have a history with students. It had started with fourteen students of Osmania University, Hyderabad, who vowed to never marry and dedicate their life to the cause of people's revolution.

In 1978, the Radical Youth League was formed in association with Jana Natya Mandali and Radical Students Union, with 'Go to the village' campaign. Through these shows, youngsters would make villagers aware of their political situation, like how oppressed they were and the importance of an armed revolution for their empowerment and justice. They were the first political force that invaded the minds of villagers. This was the first political narrative introduced and with that one more decision taken, that no alternate narrative was to be introduced. Their leader Seetharamaiah, a sharp political mind and master strategist, created a network of these tough and fearless rebel students, who would integrate with the tribals and poor farmers to push their party's agenda.

In his famous speech, he turned around the dynamics of the

existing strategy. 'Unlike Charu Majumdar's maxim, we will not go looking for the class enemy, destroy him, and then organize. We will organize and if the class enemy comes in our way, we will destroy him,' he announced. He also gave a clever analogy which is frequently used by Naxals till date: 'If a poisonous snake comes a farmer's way while he is preparing his field for the harvest, then he kills it.'

They organized themselves and started annihilating all government machinery including security forces. Their justification for such destruction and killings of government servants and security *jawans* is oversimplified: 'What work do they have in jungles? If they are in the jungles, it means they are here to obstruct our mission.'

This movement has been successful primarily due to the enthusiasm, commitment, and organization of the students. And of course, the killer instinct.

I want to understand how have they organized themselves. What if they have sleeper cells in campuses? I look up the organizational chart of the Naxals.

The apex body is the Politburo, under which there is a Central Committee and the Central Military Commission. Under Central Military Commission there is Central Technical Committee, Regional Commands, Special Action Teams, Military Intelligence, Publications, and Editorial Board of *Jung*, Central Military Instructors Team, Tactical Counter Offensive Campaign, People's Liberation Guerilla Army (PLGA), and a very complex intelligence set-up known as People's Security Service.

The PLGA consists of three forces: Main Force has Companies, Platoons, Special Action Teams, Intelligence Units. The Secondary Force operates with Special Guerilla Squads, Local Guerilla Squads, Platoons, and District Level Action Teams. The Base Force has People's Militia, Gram Raksha Dals, Area Raksha Dals, and Self-defense Squads.

Then they have State Military Commission, State Committees, District Committees, Zonal Committees, Area Committees.

There are also Revolutionary Writers Associations and Jan Natya Mandalis to promote propaganda and forward misinformation to the young.

I am utterly confused and tired. Everything is becoming clinical.

I remember in 1985, a Leftist friend of mine had tried explaining the Naxal organizational structure to me, and finally exasperated, he'd said, 'Trying to understand the Naxal movement is like peeling an onion. In the end, you will have only tears in your eyes and many disconnected and scattered layers of the onion.'

'This can be a dialogue straight out of a film,' I had thought. Many years later, I used these very lines in my first film *Chocolate* for Anil Kapoor's character.

It's difficult for a militarily trained cadre to easily connect and communicate with a student on a campus. It's impossible to mobilize students if one is not working with them day and night. It requires easy access.

'How are they connected?' I ask. 'There must be some underground channels. This connection can't be ad hoc. It has to be a regular connection, disguised amongst the "real regular" connections.'

I am confused. My mind is numb. But I am breathing hard.

When the mind stops, the heart starts thinking. Heavy breathing is a sign the heart is doing a different chore. I want to go by my instinct and not the standard logic that is tailor–made to fit a template.

I try to look. For a foreign hand. If not, then, God's hand.

I discover that the Communist Party of India (Maoist) has close fraternal ties with North-Eastern terror groups. Most of such outfits have linkages with external forces hostile to India. The CPI (Maoist) has openly expressed its solidarity with the J&K terrorist groups. These ties are part of their 'Strategic United Front' against the Indian State. The CPI (Maoist) also has close links with foreign Maoist organizations in the Philippines, Turkey, etc.

The outfit is also a member of the Coordination Committee of the Maoist Parties and Organizations in South Asia (CCOMPOSA), which includes ten Maoist groups from Bangladesh, India, Nepal and Sri Lanka, with the aim to create a 'new South Asia'.

Slowly, I start to connect the dots. A plethora of front organizations starts revealing itself around which an Urban Naxalism is being woven. These front organizations are the offshoots of the parent Maoist party, which maintains a separate existence to escape legal liabilities. These Front Organizations (FOs) carry out a two-pronged communication attack—propaganda and disinformation. They raise funds for the insurgency and assist cadres in legal matters. These FOs are also used to provide safe houses to underground cadres and shelter to fugitives. They bring intellectuals into their fold who provide an intellectual veneer to the illegal, unconstitutional, and inhuman violence in the Naxal movement. In effect, these intellectuals present this beastly and gruesome reality in a sanitized, romantic, and palatable packaging for which the media and its urban audiences have a weakness. Such FOs exist in twenty out of the twenty-nine states of India. They are seeping into the strategically sensitive north-eastern states of Assam and Arunachal Pradesh.

Lately, they have begun targeting India's seat of power – New Delhi – and many other cities by setting up urban bases of these front organizations with the aim to penetrate and influence policymakers, judiciary, media, civil liberty, human rights, cultural, Dalit, women, and youth organizations. So far, the urban units do not indulge in violence but it is definitely a serious problem, posing a threat to our ambition of becoming the next economic superpower.

Then, suddenly, something strikes me.

Why do they have to connect with the student if they can have their professors in the faculty? They can enter a student's mind through this professor. It's easier, faster, exact, less risky, and seems organic.

This is the first time I don't have to think even for a moment. Instinctively, in a flash, I am taken back to my campus days. I remember my professors, the cultural committee professors, my drama mentors, and my debating mentors. My mind is becoming a dark edit room, with jumbled up footage from old movies of my life.

Flash.

I have written a play on price rise.

Flash.

My drama mentor professor sees the rehearsal.

Flash.

I am at his house.

Flash.

He talks and talks.

Flash.

He gives me manuscripts of his old plays.

Flash.

I am elated. Inspired. Motivated.

Flash.

I want to demolish the system.

Flash.

I change the play from 'price rise' to 'caste issue'.

Then some keywords and key images flash up as in the background a Faiz Ahmad Faiz couplet plays: *Chand roz aur, meri jaan! Faqat chand hi roz*
A few more days, my love! Merely a handful of days more.

Corrupt system.

Helplessness.

Oppression of youth.

Intelligentsia.

Arms.

Swords.

Students.

Dalit.

Revolution.

Blood.

Professors.

India.

New freedom.

India.

Superpower.

Boom. Boom. Boom.

I think I have a story. It's all there. It's all around me.

I am at the centre. I am the nucleus.

I am the story.

12. Zorba the Greek

I am not alien to the Naxal issue. There was a time when I was at the threshold of joining the Naxal movement. Today, it reads like a film script.

Flashback: My college days - Bhopal

I am in college. Motilal Vigyan Mahavidyalaya, Bhopal.

I have written a play for the annual function. The winning play will travel to various drama festivals. Before I start directing it, I want to take feedback from my dramatics professor, a middle-aged man who is also active on Bhopal's theatre scene. He writes, directs, and sometimes acts in plays, performed at Bharat Bhavan and Tagore Hall.

'Why is the theme price rise?' he asks me, looking at the title, *Mehangi Mehangai.*

'Because this is a current issue and people will relate to it,' I reply.

'Why do you think they will relate to it?'

'Because my hero is a product of a hapless society which has no control over demand and supply; hence price rise. The free market economy found support because of the belief that it will benefit the middle class and poor, but both have become the victims of capitalism. They have been conditioned by the establishment to believe that they can't fight against this monster called 'capitalism'. My hero is one of them but he always sees the comical part. It's only later when he understands the tragedy of it, he challenges the system. And this is something that every common man wants to do.'

He opens a new cigarette pack by tearing apart the cellophane packaging with his badly stained teeth. He takes out a cigarette and starts tapping it on the table. I don't know why people tap their cigarette before lighting it. Is it in order to consolidate the tobacco? Or does it give a feeling of power while tapping it? Or is it just a style copied from a film hero? He dresses like a typical government college science professor but there is something very cowboyish about his style.

'Why satire?' he asks.

'Why not a hard-hitting satire that would slap and wake up the people from their slumber,' I say.

'You expect the audience to sleep?'

'Not in the theatre… in their lives… the collective consciousness of this country is sleeping,' I emphasize.

He lights a cigarette. I want to smoke so much but I can't as we just don't smoke in front of our parents, elders, uncles, aunts, neighbours, father's colleagues, family friends, seniors, and teachers. In effect, we can smoke only with our friends, hiding in some shady corner.

'This is not the freedom we wanted,' I continue, 'where a few people control the power while the rest are left to die. The system must change.'

'Why have you copied Sharad Joshi?' he asks me softly.

I wasn't prepared for this. Yes, I have tried to imitate famous satirist Sharad Joshi's style in many dialogues. As a matter of fact, I wrote this play after seeing the premiere of his latest play *Andhon ka Haathi*. Being a close friend of my father, his daughters are good friends of mine. One of them even pointed out to me that I have taken some dialogues from a very famous satirical piece of his, *Parampara*. I am already feeling guilty.

'Sir, I am inspired by him,' I reply.

'Inspired or influenced?' he asks.

'Inspired.'

'Then why have you copied his style? His sentences? You are definitely not inspired; you are influenced by him.'

'What difference does it make? Inspired or influenced? As long as it's not plagiarism.'

'It makes a difference. An inspired mind creates new things. Like Gandhi was influenced by the *Gita* but inspired by Gokhale and Tolstoy. He didn't copy them in his works but he copied *Gita* all the time.'

'But what's the difference? In the end, he interpreted all three doctrines in his own distinctive style. I am just inspired by Joshi's style of satire.'

'You are influenced. And an influenced mind is not a free mind. It's an intellectual slave. Do you realize you are doing intellectual slavery of Joshi? I am sure a bright young man like you doesn't want to be anyone's slave. You should have your own unique voice.'

He lights another cigarette, from the previous one. I like the way he takes the first puff of his cigarette. He closes his eyes, takes a deep drag and holds it for a few seconds and then exhales, softly and smoothly, blowing out smoke rings. I don't know what has impressed me more – the smoke rings or the satisfied expression on his face? I am going to try it the moment I leave from here. If I get the rings right, would it be an influence or an inspiration? Or would I be simply aping him? I try to decode his theory. If I make circles and make the same face like him, I would be copying him. If I make rings with my own expressions, I am influenced. But if instead of rings I exhale squares or triangles of smoke and have a sad expression, then I would be inspired. And if I just don't smoke at all and blow no smoke with no expressions, then I would be called a revolutionary. An original revolutionary.

'You have to be original,' he dictates.

A cigarette can be such a useful metaphor for understanding life's most complex ideas.

He takes a strong puff and goes inside, leaving the half-lit cigarette in the ashtray. I want to steal a drag while he is inside but what if he comes out and finds me holding his cigarette? The temptation to steal is the most common human trait, only next to lying. 'Am I stealing Sharad Joshi's style?' I introspect.

He comes out holding some very old, dusty files.

'Here are some of my old manuscripts… I wrote these essays in college. These are original. Neither influenced nor inspired,' he confesses while throwing the files in front of me, letting the dust from the files mix with the smoke particles. Together, the dust and the smoke fill the entire path of a lone sunbeam, filtering from a hole in the window and falling on the overflowing ashtray sitting alone on the wrought iron table. If there was no dust and smoke, I would not have noticed the existence of the sun and its filtering rays inside this dark room.

'I wanted to change the world but when one has to choose between ideals and survival, men like me end up choosing…' he takes a deep drag and speaks softly as the smoke comes out in sync with the rhythm of his speech. 'Well, you know the answer. You can take a look at them. Read them. Innocence and intensity are a lethal combination. You will know why,' he says with a smile.

I pick up the files. There are some letters, which I could make out as the abbreviations of his name, and serial numbers on the cover, indicating that there is a series of files and at the centre, there is a scribble:

'You can knock on a deaf man's door forever.' - Zorba's Musings.

'Do you know who Zorba was?' he asks me.

'Yes, the hero of Nikos Kazantzakis' *Zorba the Greek.*'

'What did you learn from him?'

'That life is here… that the answers - if they do exist - are not to be found in books, but in life itself, as long as it is lived passionately, free of hopes, and expectations…'

'I do not agree with Zorba here. Zorba says this because he is not Buddha as yet. We can't live without hope, without expectations… we must expect our society to be just and fair,' he opined.

'It's utopia. A society can never be fully just and fair, sir.'

'Do you remember the famous dialogue from *Zorba The Greek*?'

'Which one, sir?' I ask.

'Do you know the best wisdom in the novel doesn't come from Zorba, it comes from the intellectual, Basil.' He speaks while lighting another cigarette.

I wait for him to take a deep puff and exhale, slowly and smoothly, blowing a series of smoke rings. It's becoming difficult for me to hold my urge to smoke and blow out a chain of smoke rings. Softly and smoothly.

'You have seen what happens when you hold a magnifying glass out in the sun and concentrate all the rays on one spot. That spot soon catches fire, doesn't it? Why?' He continues, imitating the actor in the film, 'Because the sun's power has not been dispersed but concentrated on that one spot. It is the same with men's minds. You can do miracles if you concentrate your mind on one thing and one thing alone.'

'But why are you telling me all this?'

'Imagine you are the glass,' he continues, 'and all the social issues are those spots which need to burn. Now tell me where is the Sun?'

I am lost. I have no answer. No ideas. All I can hear is the sound of the matchstick on the striking side. I smell phosphorous. I see smoke rings. Appearing and disappearing in the sunbeam.

'You have no Sun. Your Sun is Sharad Joshi, who can't be your Sun because he has his own Sun. Do you know what his Sun is?'

I shake my head. I feel nauseous like a non-smoker feels, after sitting for some time in a room full of smoke. But smoke is not the reason why I feel sick. I feel sick because I know what is he going to arrive at and I also know that it will shatter my comfort zone.

'His Sun is his suffering. His Sun is about human suffering. His empathy with human pain. His agony. His suffering. That's what makes him attack these evils with his writing. There is only one Sharad Joshi. He is inspired and influenced by his feelings about human suffering.' He pauses to balance the long ash on his cigarette and realizing that it can't reach the ashtray, he taps it on his left palm and continues, 'You can't burn anything if you have no Sun. Joshi's Sun can't be your Sun.'

'How do I find my Sun?' I ask softly.

'When you feel the human suffering as your suffering… that feeling… that pain… that anger becomes your Sun. That moment you find your Sun, you find your purpose. You find yourself. Otherwise, you remain a dropout from meritocracy. Like me.'

'But why only sufferings. Can't one find his Sun in happiness?' I ask.

'There is no Sun in happiness. You find happiness only after you find your Sun and burn. Only after you burn, you can burn the evil. Then you find happiness.'

He gets up. I also get up.

'Take these files,' he instructs and adds, 'You are a creative young man. Real creativity lies in the creation of an equal society. You must not follow the mob mind. Collective psyche is always dangerous for a society. Read these files and wander in the jungles of human suffering, inequality, and injustice and see what you relate to.'

'I'll try,' I say, picking up the files.

'I wrote them but never got them published. If you want, you can use them. Not to get influenced but to see the spectrum of human suffering. When you lie down at night, ask yourself what is that one issue that truly disturbs you and that you would want to change–, if you could.'

'You are expecting too much from me. I had come here just to take your feedback on my play.'

'Your play is not bad but it's not what you are truly capable of doing. Read this material and maybe after some reading, you will find your Sun and may want to relook at your play,' he says, opening the door. 'Who knows, your voice may become a mini revolution.'

'Me? How can I start a revolution? At the most I can create awareness.'

'You can start a revolution by becoming one,' he concludes.

I distinctly remember as I was leaving his house, a few students from different colleges were collecting outside in the lawns of his government quarter for *chaupal* - a forum for an exchange of ideas. Many years later, I learnt that some of them were arrested in the tribal villages of Chhattisgarh, on the charge of spreading Naxal ideology. I could have been one of them.

I want to arrest those moments in cinematic language. I start writing the one-liners of my film in longhand, on my old, crumbling idea pad.

1. *A bright student seeks intellectual help from his professor. Professor notices the curious yet aware nature of the student and gives him his personal, secret files.*

And, thus, he enters his mind.

13. Comrade Vivek Agnihotri

Flashback: My college days - Bhopal

It's late at night. 2 AM. It's too quiet. More than any other day. Am I going deaf? Zorba, are you here? No sound. Am I asleep?

My mind is going hyper. All kinds of bizarre thoughts travel in my mind like lost vehicles in a city, going everywhere but not towards the intended destination. There is no chain of thoughts, no links, no connects. They are scattered, fleeting, incomplete, and restless. If only my mind had hands, I would have punched some hard and strangled some. They are buzzing like bumble bees, in some deep corner of my mind. A prisoner had died once because of the sound of non-stop buzzing. He went crazy as he could only hear but not see. I can hear thousands of them in the closed and dark cell of my mind in which I am imprisoned. I am struggling to break the shackles but I can't. Sleep betrayed me at this moment of grave need.

I get up and take out the file that the professor gave me - 'Zorba's Musings'. I light a cigarette. A street dog starts barking. I take a deep drag and blow out small rings of smoke. Softly and smoothly.

I open the file. And get stuck on the first page which has only a dialogue from *Zorba the Greek*. I read the lines exchanged between Basil and Zorba several times and then just sit there staring at those lines. Slowly, the lines blur and I start hearing bumblebees again. But just then the sound fades. It's as good as silence. My thoughts are forming a logical sequence that is leading me somewhere bright but unknown. I read the dialogue once again, for the final time, before I flip the page.

Alexis Zorba: Damn it, boss, I like you too much not to say it. You've got everything except one thing: madness! A man needs a little madness, or else...

Basil: Or else?

Alexis Zorba: ...he never dares cut the rope and be free.

I see myself in the shackles of many borrowed ideas. Ironically there is no *'me'* in these ideas. No pain, no suffering which is mine. I want to write a play on price rise because it's in the news. I make a satire on it because it's a smart way of presentation. I have a few smart scenes because I want to look like Sharad Joshi. I have not suffered because of price rise. I have not suffered discrimination. I haven't experienced inequality or injustice. I haven't been oppressed or molested. I know the stuff only intellectually. Not actually.

I start flipping pages and try to read quickly. This file is an assortment of the professor's essays, plays, poems, and ideas. Ideas for the revolution. He is deeply affected by the caste system. His writings reek of hatred for the Brahmins. This makes me angry. 'Why did he give me his work despite knowing that I am a Brahmin?' I wonder. 'Maybe he has risen above the caste hierarchy and sees me just as a student,' I justify in my mind. For the next seven days, I stay locked in my room reading about caste discrimination, Maoism, and Naxal ideology.

My mother thinks I am overworked and offers me an extra glass of milk. My father thinks I am in love. My sister thinks I am smoking weed. My friends think I have become arrogant. Only my drama mentor understands me.

Present Day

I take out an old photo from my college days. It was taken by my sister on my first day at the college. They say that the first love, first kiss, first job and more such firsts are the most memorable moments of life. Likewise, my first day at the college is the most memorable moment, but for a different reason. As I entered the campus along with my friends, a group of boys called us. They were seniors and ready to rag us. Like savages they were staring at us, as we walked towards them. In the jungles, the hunter runs after the prey, here the prey was walking towards a gang of hunters.

I don't know much about the current ragging scenario but anyone who has survived the ragging of the 70s and 80s can survive any hardship. For the next six months, we were ragged every single time we came across the seniors. Our movements were restricted. We couldn't go out to the open ground, the lakeside, the main hall, the two-wheeler stands or the canteen, as all these spots were crowded with the seniors. Bus stand, canteen, and two-wheeler stands were their favourite spots. The reason was that there were few girls in our college, at the most ten or fifteen, who would invent new ways to avoid this bunch of ogling seniors. But using the canteen in free periods, pulling out their two-wheeler from the stand or to take a bus from the bus stand, was something they just couldn't escape. The moment the girls would go to the canteen, it would get filled with the seniors. Hundreds of eyes would stare at them. Penetrate them. Analyze their anatomy, making their own short, mental blue films. The worst part was that the girls knew they were being filmed by these staring eyes but they were not in a position to stop their visual rape.

Yes, a visual gang rape. Some boys would even pretend to be lost in thought while walking and collide with the girl or brush their hand lightly on their breasts. Sometimes, while girls were returning home, after their evening tuition classes, seniors would find them in dark patches of the streets and grope them.

A few years ago, in my Delhi *barsati*, on a cold night, I was narrating the situation of these girls to my female friends from Delhi. I asked them to imagine themselves surrounded by savages and monsters, saliva drooling from their mouths and they start closing in on you until you feel their hot breath all over your neck. Their eyes are penetrating and mouths lascivious in the anticipation of not just devouring you but to shred you apart, piece by piece. Hundreds of savages waiting for their turn, jerking off to get their stinky semen all over you.

One girl puked on my hand. Seeing her puke, another one puked, on my ZZ plant. Some moved to washrooms and some to the balcony to smoke. One short girl, short like really short, four feet something or maybe less, got so angry that she took a long puff and exhaled the smoke like she was a dragon, fuming fire on these boys. She started stabbing her cigarette in the ashtray as if she was hammering their skulls.

'You know pal, worst are these fuckers, who fuck you with their fucking eyes in their fucking mind. Bloody assholes, their dicks should be cut and thrown to the vultures,' she yelled at the top of her voice and went to make a stiff drink. A noisy scenario died with the longest silence.

One girl kept looking at me for some time and then held my hand and asked, 'Who gave you so much pain?'

My pain? This was the pain of an Indian girl. These girls were mostly from Delhi and a few from Bangalore and Mumbai. Normally, the story of an Indian girl's pain comes from the victims, survivors, or the feminists. A regular girl's suffering in her day-to-day life doesn't ever feature in the national feminist narrative. They have been conditioned to accept it as part of living, as an everyday struggle. A part of the culture that wants to crush their dreams. Their aspirations. Their confidence.

It shall remain a paradox that despite such suffocating, dark surroundings, these girls shine in their lives. As engineers, doctors, teachers, entrepreneurs, managers, scientists, cops or as efficient housewives. Whereas, such boys end up doing nothing with their lives. Outside the college and employment market, they are left with no option but to join politics and earn by either extorting or mediating for commissions. This is a standard template.

Flashback

College elections are on. Being a leader in cultural activities, I work with a large, cohesive group of creative, aware, and liberal students. These students are the most influential in such elections but they don't go to vote. Both the leaders of the National Student's Union of India (NSUI) and Akhil Bhartiya Vidyarthi Parishad (ABVP) are putting a lot of pressure on me to bring this group to vote for them. In a college of thousands of sex-starved young boys, these fifteen-twenty girls are the focal point of this election. They aren't just votes anymore. They are a status symbol. Both the parties want one of the girls to contest as their candidate. They want me to persuade them. Slowly, this pressure turns to threats. I want to change my college but my drama mentor convinces me that it's my purpose, my duty to fight such political hooliganism.

'Politics is bad if you want to use it for power but it's a remedy if you want to save the weak from exploitation,' he advises. He prepares me to become a politician. With his mentoring, I start my own political party with a satirical name - 'Jokers Party'. With a promise to empower and protect girls.

Present Day

I open my old college photo album and find a picture of all Jokers Party members. In checked bellbottoms and long-collared printed shirts, we look like a funny version of the Beatles. Or a derivative of the Klu Klux Klan.

As soon as we announced our party, one of the most attractive girls met me and expressed her desire to contest from our party. She wanted to democratically wrest political power from the seniors and assert her right to stop the visual gang rapes.

She was a senior army officer's daughter, and however clichéd it may sound, the girls from an army background are smarter and more modern than their civilian counterparts in cities like Bhopal. Similarly, this girl was very modern and beautiful. She had short hair, played table tennis and wore short skirts. For a city like Bhopal, in the early 80s, this was a fantastical reality. I liked her. In fact, loved her. She lived close to my house and every evening she would walk past my house. Twice. On her way to and then on her way back. I would make sure I was in my balcony and pretend as if I was there just by chance. In small towns, girls don't look at boys. Looking would be a sign of inviting him. Or accepting his invitation. She never looked at me, but instinctively, I knew she was aware of my presence. I knew because her walk changed when she crossed me. An awkwardness would come in her body language, a concentrated self-consciousness would capture her persona, which any boy in that high-testosterone age can sense from any distance.

One day, during summer holidays, when the days are long and evenings amber, she stopped in front of my gate and waved at me. I wasn't prepared for such an encounter. She signaled me to come down. I ran to the nearest mirror, splashed some water in my hand and brushed my hair with wet fingers, styling them like Amitabh Bachchan in Trishul. I sprayed some Charlie perfume and ran down anticipating various scenarios. By the time I came down and started walking towards where she was standing, I was convinced that she wanted to know some directions. Genuinely or as a pretense to know me.

'You keep looking at me and I know that you do and that is not a right thing to do. Is there anything you want to know or ask?' she asked me as soon as I reached the gate.

'No… nothing like that.' I couldn't even cook up a smart answer.

'Stop staring or I tell your parents and my parents.' She left without waiting for me to respond. I was so much in love with her that I couldn't call her 'bloody bitch' even in my imagination.

Her house was opposite the railway *fatak* on the Itarsi-Delhi railway line. There were a few *dhabas* and a *paan* shop there. We would sit at the *dhaba*, take cigarettes from the *paan* shop on credit, and wait for her to come out and as soon as she came out onto her veranda, we would kick our bikes and zoom past her house.

One day, I was studying in my ground floor study at the back of our bungalow when my mother called me from the first floor. There was a call for me from a girl. As I was climbing the stairs, my mother looked at me as if I had lost my virginity. First, I looked at the receiver of our shiny red dial phone, prepared myself for any kind of surprise, gained some confidence and picked up the receiver.

'Listen, I asked you to stop but you are still doing it… why are you doing it?' She asked me point blank even before I could say 'hello'. It was her.

'Doing what?'

'Why do you roam around my house? You also honk. My father will get to know sooner than later.'

'That's the way to my friend's house.' I cook up and then realize the blunder I had made.

'That road goes nowhere. It's a dead end and that is why you also take a U-turn and come back.'

I was ashamed of myself. I wanted to die. Then something took me over.

'I want to be friends with you.' Something made me say this. I was possessed.

She took a pause and spoke to some other girls, her sisters perhaps, and then came back on the line.

'Come and meet us at the club at 5.45. Don't be late because my dad will be there by 6. See you then.' She didn't wait for my confirmation.

I found her 'army-like' behaviour very cute.

We became good friends. I genuinely cared for her. She was impressed with my debating and dramatic skills. Unfortunately, till date, I don't know what the status of our relationship was. If there was a Facebook then, I would have called it 'in progress'. Most love stories in small towns die while 'in progress' and are eventually found at the end of a notebook or a diary as a poem. We met every evening and played table tennis, gossiped about college and killed time.

One evening in a game, she started to hit the ball very hard. We had only one ball and I was scared that it would tear. That was also the day when I understood the subtle difference between an energetic woman and an angry woman.

'What's wrong with you? Why do you have to hit every ball so hard?' I lost it.

'Because I am a whore. I am a slut. I am a bitch.' Even she lost it.

For the next half an hour I watched her tears falling on the TT table as she told me how a few boys from the opposing parties literally molested her, groped her, and humiliated her in a crowded bus. It's strange that in India most girls are raped, molested and groped in crowded places. She wasn't angry because she was groped. She was furious because she couldn't even react.

'They were touching me, feeling me, rubbing their elbows on my boobs, laughing and blowing smoke on my face and I couldn't even react. I kept looking down as if nothing was happening. Why?' She broke down, 'Why am I being denied to even react to my molestation?'

I tried to console her but she shrugged and asked me, looking deep into my eyes, 'Imagine yourself in my situation… what would you do?'

Next day, she withdrew her nomination.

At that very moment, I found my Zorba. My Buddha.

Flashback: My college days - Bhopal

Haplessness.

I see myself in a city of the blind and the deaf. I am screaming for help but nobody can see or hear me. I feel helpless; I stop screaming. There is no point.

Is this how we tame our citizens?

Is this how we make everything look quiet and peaceful? "Yes" is the only answer. No one screams anymore as there's no point screaming in a city of blind and deaf people.

I am choking. I feel her pain. I understand the struggle and helplessness of women in a chauvinistic society. I find my Buddha.

Rehearsals are not the same anymore. Each time I brief an actor, I feel as if I am faking it. I feel suffocated by my own creation. Joshi's writings, the conflict, and pain that they present, have become my standard of excellence. I feel embarrassed of my own creation, not because of its artistic or intellectual calibre but because it does not reflect my conviction. My core feeling. My actors are rehearsing but I am lost in my thoughts, trying to figure out how I can still change or improve the play, so that it becomes *my* play. I am a Brahmin. A vice-chancellor's son. Good in studies. Popular amongst girls. Well behaved. I have a Chetak scooter bought in US dollars. I am the only student who wears Levi's jeans and has a Sony Walkman with original Abba cassettes purchased in the USA.

My chain of thoughts is broken by a tap on my back. I turn around and find my drama mentor smiling at me.

'How is it going?' he asks me.

'Rehearsals are going fine but after reading your stuff, I am not happy with my writing. I think I must write something else.'

'Do you want to see a play?' he asks.

Ghasiram Kotwal is the most acclaimed among Vijay Tendulkar's many controversial plays. Ghasiram bartered his own daughter to Nana Phadnavis, a Brahmin and one of the most prominent ministers in the court of the Peshwa of Pune, to get the post of the police *Kotwal*. As a *Kotwal*, Ghasiram enforced strict and cruel rules in the city and threw innocent people in jail for the smallest offences. He had under him a large body of unscrupulous spies, everyone possessing ample means of harassing people. He used to procure women for Nana's lustful cravings. The word Ghasiram became a permanent synonym for oppression and tyranny. Later, when Nana's purpose was over, he ordered Ghasiram to be killed in the most inhuman way possible. The theme, how men in power use people to give rise to ideologies to serve their purposes and later destroy the same men when they become useless, stays with me.

On the one hand, I am enchanted by Baba Karanth's magnum production and on the other, I am disgusted with the system that hasn't changed since Ghasiram's times. In fact, it has become worse. I understand the impact that art can have on the mass psyche. Art, in times of revolution, can be the most effective weapon in the armoury.

For the last few weeks, my blood has boiled. I am angry and guilty. My anger is about the haplessness of a common citizen who is oppressed by the privileged section of society. I am guilty of belonging to that privileged section. I decide to drop my surname. From Vivek Ranjan Agnihotri, I become Vivek Ranjan. My friends from college still call me Ranjan, assuming it was my last name. This is my penance for being a Brahmin. For being a privileged one.

I stay awake the entire night and keep writing until dawn, with my Hero fountain pen, on the back side of the extra invitation cards of my sister's wedding. By morning, I have a new play. It's about discrimination against a Dalit woman. It's not a satire. It's dark. Hard hitting. Penetrating. Suffocating. And revolutionary.

The play proves to be a success. I am the new hero on the campus. My fellow students believe that I will topple the establishment. I am invited to debates from remote corners of the country. All my dramatic, literary, and debating work for the next few years remains revolutionary and inspired by the Naxal ideology of armed struggle.

I am affected by social evils. I want to topple the system. Plus, I have no future plans. The three main requisites for a student to be brainwashed and lured to turn a rebel.

In no time, I am burning buses and throwing stones at the Vidhan Sabha. And I am introduced to *desi katta* and rusted swords.

'*Badhai ho.* You are not a Zorba anymore. You have found your Buddha,' my drama mentor congratulates me.

'Thank you, sir.'

'*Cigarette peete ho?*' he asks while tearing the cellophane of a new pack of Wills Navy Cut.

'Sometimes.'

He lights two cigarettes and offers me one.

'Do you know that I was playing a game with you? A secret game. I wanted to check if you really have the mettle to be a comrade or not.' He takes a deep drag.

'And?' I take a deep drag.

He blows out smoke circles. Slowly and smoothly. I blow out smoke circles. Slowly and smoothly.

'And I am happy that you have won the game,' he concludes.

I have no idea that some day, in a distant future, his reply will become a dialogue in my feature film.

He looks at me with pride and opens the door.

'Good night, Comrade Vivek Ranjan.'

Present Day

I didn't even realize then that I had become his new recruit. I had become an Urban Naxal.

I write the next one-liner.

1. *The professor brainwashes the student and converts him into a Naxal activist and uses him for his ulterior motives.*

14. The New Big Idea: Urban Naxalism

I think I am heading somewhere. I have a student, who is me, and a professor who will mentor the hero and convert him into a Naxal. Sounds like a good plot for a film but it's just a basic idea. In film parlance, it is known as the Logline. It's not enough. The story is about the professor. I am just the medium to reveal his sinister political ambition. I need to find the professor's ulterior motives, the *modus operandi* and the dynamics of a possible nexus between academia and Naxals. But I don't know where to go from here.

Flashback: My college days - Bhopal

I am doing rebellious plays on class disparity.

I am participating in debates and always raising questions that align with Naxal ideology.

I am active in campus politics.

I am influencing, motivating, persuading, challenging, brainwashing, and coercing the oppressed and, therefore, socially aware students to come into our fold.

I am leading protests. I am throwing stones at the Vidhan Sabha. I am burning buses. I am part of rusted sword fights. Yes, in Bhopal, students would be delivered old swords which they would keep in water until it rusts. When you hit someone with a rusted sword, the rust infects the wound and causes tetanus.

In my mind, I am waging a war against the State. Not out of knowledge or enlightenment but out of haplessness.

Present Day

Why was I doing all that? My parents never taught me to damage public property. My school didn't teach me to break the law. What changed then?

I start questioning my drama mentor and subsequent professors in my post-graduation course in economics at the School of Social Sciences, Bhopal. Jana Natya Mandali, Radical Students Union, and

Radical Youth Movement were recruiting students and thousands of them were joining. In the garb of a touring cultural group, they would amplify the injustice and glorify revolution. There is no one who hasn't faced injustice. A friend who was fascinated with Naxalism had told me once, 'Revolution is the only purpose of life.' A Naxal army was getting built on the ground. A revolution had begun. A new India was taking birth in the minds of students. An education system rooted in the principles of utopian socialism, courtesy Nehru's fascination for the same, and the professors, enamoured of the Nehruvian dream, were feeding the young minds to wage a war against India.

Did they really care about me or was I just a pawn in a bigger game? What if I had not gone to Delhi and USA for further studies, would I have become a professional Naxal? Were those professors Naxals? Is this how they make inroads into urban India? Like a venomous, silent snake under your bed, getting set to attack and kill you? Was I helping that snake? Was I that snake?

My head spins.

I am standing at the window, looking at the empty parking lot. I see two boys hiding behind a broken car, smoking weed. Why don't they make weed legal? It used to be legal when I was a student. Government *thekas* used to sell them. Rajiv Gandhi spoilt the party.

My assistant walks in with more material and asks me if I am alright.

'Yeah, I am fine,' I lie to her.

'Is something bothering you?' She insists on finding out the truth.

'I feel like I am failing,' I whisper.

'And may I ask why you would feel like that?' she asks.

'I am feeling depressed, I can't seem to work; as though I am in the middle of an ocean, looking for drinking water. I feel creatively paralyzed, unable to write anything more. How will we shoot next month?'

'Sir, is this a writer's block?'

'No. Not at all. I think I have overcommitted myself. How the fuck will it matter if a professor mentors a student? There is no emotional connect. It's a very thin line. We should call up Suresh in Hyderabad and tell him that we are changing the subject and let's do a campus comedy like Ravi wants.' I speak like a defeated person.

'Sir, can I tell you something?'

I nod.

'Sir, I think this is precisely the time you must write, not when you are at your creative best but in such times of confusion. Especially when you are lost and have nowhere to go,' she speaks confidently.

As she talks I feel surrounded by the ghosts of all those filmmakers and creative artists who worked out of nothing. No offices, no assistants, no money, no experience and yet they spoke the truth that took our civilization forward. Some were ridiculed. Some were punished. And some were executed.

'It's not that I don't know where to arrive at. I know where I want to reach but I don't know if anyone would want to hear it.'

'Sir, why do we always think about what the audience wants to hear? Why don't we say what we want to say?'

Sometimes life-changing advice comes from the least expected quarters.

'Sir, our job isn't to help the world go around,' she continues, 'but forward, which is something altogether different from the ordinary. It is, simply, something else. And I am sure when you will write for yourself, you will write that "simply, something else" stuff.'

She waits for a moment and then gets up, leaving a few pages in front of me.

'I think I should leave you alone. I'd advise you to forget about all the material and just go through these four pages.'

I watch her leave.

Within each of us, there is a seeker who is hungry for knowledge and wisdom. After working in the film industry for over six years, this is the first time I can feel this seeker. I had been convinced that the only purpose of cinema is to emotionally stimulate the audience. Now I understand that seeking is also an emotion. People seek the truth. In media. In art. In cinema. Since nobody tells the truth, and it is acceptable, we succumb to the apparent emotional needs of an audience like feeling happy or feeling sad; the truth remains the least priority for the artists of Bollywood.

We have become a driver, surgeon, math teacher or a carpenter who is expected to do the same job each time, with the same skills and same precision. Only technology keeps improving, making it easier for the artists and in return making us dull enough to tell a duller audience that our world is bruised and bleeding. This dullness, this being regular, is the surety of the world. This ordinariness makes the world go around.

Like failure, chaos contains information that can lead to truth. I start to love my chaos. I realize I don't need a story, I need the truth. My truth. In truth, the work itself is an adventure. Only when the purpose of a creative endeavour is to discover the truth and explore human behavior is the journey of its audience extraordinary. That 'extraordinary' is what art is about.

I jot down three questions: Why did I become a snake? How did I become a snake? How can I prevent other young students from becoming snakes?

I start making concept maps, trying to be able to *see* the entire methodology of Urban Naxalism. And what it leads me to and what it reveals, stuns me. If this is true, I think, then a grave danger is looming over the internal security and the social fabric of this country. Somebody has to warn the masses.

The Naxal movement is engaged in Fourth Generation Warfare (4GW). This war is waged by a blurring of the lines between war and politics, combatants, and civilians. If they have reached this stage, we have no one but our political leaders to blame, who have used Naxals for their political gains and shunned them when not required. Like Ghasiram Kotwal.

The modern-day guru of Fourth Generation Warfare, William Lind, has aptly observed, 'If nation-states are going to survive, people in power must earn and keep the trust of the governed.' Addressing the American Council of Foreign Relations, he said, that 'the heart of Fourth Generation Warfare is a crisis of legitimacy of the State'. How true to the Indian model when he added that 'the establishment is no longer made up of "policy types" - most of its important functionaries are placemen.' Their expertise is in becoming and then remaining members of the establishment. Their reality is covert politics and not competence or expertise. When the 4GW will visit them, their response would be to 'close the shutters on the windows of Versailles'.

This fourth-generation war is complex and long term. It's decentralized, small in size, and lacks hierarchy. The strategy is to make a direct attack on the enemy's (in this case, the Indian State) culture, including genocidal acts against civilians and wage a highly sophisticated psychological and cultural warfare, especially through media manipulation. All available pressures are used – political, economic, social, and military. For this purpose, legal professionals are required, media professionals are required, creative people, varied intellectuals and academicians are required, and civil society leaders are required, especially those who are connected with NGOs. It begins with low-intensity conflicts where all the actors attack from different platforms.

I pick up the papers given by my assistant. It's the summary of the documented vision of the Naxalites – vision and strategy documents under an urban perspective plan – a blueprint for their urban movement/activities.

Out of these, the 'Strategy and Tactics' document and 'Urban Perspective' document catch my attention. These documents take a long-term approach as they believe direct confrontation for quick results won't help. The document admits that the enemy is very strong in urban areas and, therefore, he should not be engaged with until the conditions are favourable. And to make them favourable, it suggests, exploring and opening of opportunities, organize people through front organizations. Target the 'vulnerable group' of minorities, women, Dalits, labourers, and students through influencers who work undercover for a long time and accumulate strength. The document stresses on uniting industrial proletariats, the weak and students, and use them as vanguards who can play a direct role in the revolution.

The city becomes the money source, shelter for cadre as transit points, source of weaponry and legal protection, medical aid, media attention, and intelligentsia network.

So, an invisible Naxal-intelligentsia-media-academia nexus works as strategic fortification with the ultimate aim of taking over the Indian State to achieve Maoist rule. They have identified Pune-

Mumbai-Ahmedabad as the Golden Corridor. Delhi-Kanpur-Patna-Kolkata as the Ganga Corridor. And KKTs (Kerala, Karnataka, and Tamil Nadu) Chennai-Coimbatore-Bengaluru as the Tri-junction.

'Mass organizations are operating under the garb of human rights NGOs. These are manned by ideologues, including academicians and activists,' the Ministry of Home Affairs (MHA) has said in an affidavit filed in the Supreme Court, detailing the new strategy of the Maoist movement.

The affidavit cites the 'Strategy and Tactics of the Indian Revolution' document as a blueprint of the Maoist plan to seize political power. The affidavit states that one of the strategies adopted by Naxals is to mobilize certain targeted sections of the urban population through its mass organizations which are otherwise known as 'front organizations'. The MHA filed the affidavit in response to a notice issued by the Supreme Court on a PIL filed by former Madhya Pradesh MLA, Kishore Samrite, that the Maoist problem was spreading rapidly.

'The mass organizations mostly operating under the garb of human rights NGOs are organically linked to the CPI (Maoist) structure but maintain separate identities in an attempt to avoid legality,' the MHA affidavit says.

The affidavit further says that such organizations pursue human rights related issues and are also adept at using the legal processes to their benefit. According to the Home Ministry, ideologues and supporters of Naxals in cities and towns have undertaken a concerted and systematic propaganda war against the State. 'In fact, it is these ideologues who have kept the Maoist movement alive and are in many ways more dangerous than the cadres of the People's Liberation Guerilla Army,' the affidavit says.

The tactics employed are extremely effective and media attention grabbing. These range from using aggressive agitations and propaganda provoking Dalits to take up arms to programmes on anti-capitalist policies to target controversies in history (e.g. Is this what Dr. Ambedkar wanted in the Constitution?). They work with feminist groups, atheist groups, anti-superstition movements, intellectuals, students, labourers, slum groups, farmers, journalists, competitive exam centres etc. They take up genuine issues with the aim not to solve it but to create unrest and anger against the system and make people believe in armed struggle. This is how the 'vulnerable group' unknowingly becomes their vanguard. Like I became, under the mentorship of my professors.

Maoist documents stress on building a strong base in cities and mention three kinds of urban mass organizations: secret, open and semi-open, and legal; the last including cover organizations and affiliated activists. The forest-based rebellion survives mostly on what Maoist ideologue Varavara Rao calls the 'movement in urban areas'. From the urban network come logistics, moral and intellectual support, and the ideological argument for violence. The network is in several cities and sympathizers occupy prominent positions.

So far, the urban movement has served the Naxals in a number of ways. Take logistics support for example. In 2006, police seized empty rocket shells and rocket launchers in Mahabubnagar district, Andhra Pradesh. The kingpin, 'Tech Madhu', later surrendered to the police which led to the detection of an elaborate network the Naxals had built to manufacture rocket parts and transport them to different parts of the country. The network originated in the industrial centre of Ambattur, a suburb of Chennai where these were fabricated in separate foundries and stealthily transported in private commercial carriers to different parts of the country. The network spread across five states: Tamil Nadu, Andhra Pradesh, Madhya Pradesh, Chhattisgarh, and Odisha.

On many occasions, important top-level leaders of the CPI (Maoist) have been arrested from cities and towns indicating that front organizations in cities are used as shelters.

The detection of Maoist activities in towns such as Surat in Gujarat, clearly indicates that the Naxals are attempting to penetrate the urban working-class movements. Besides, there have been reports of the detection of Maoist activities in Haryana – in Jind, Kurukshetra, Panipat, Sonepat, etc. A closer look at these areas reveals that these are industrial hubs. In Delhi, the Naxals have reportedly infiltrated the Delhi Safai Karmachari Sanghatan (DSKS), a union of sanitary workers. In fact, according to a media report quoting unnamed intelligence officials, 'the rebels, the sources add, have plans to strike in the industrial belts of Bhilai-Ranchi-

Dhanbad-Calcutta and Mumbai-Pune-Surat-Ahmedabad to take their battle into the heart of India.'

Some instances of Naxal violence adversely affecting the trade and economy are damaging road construction machinery, shutting down and destroying bank branches, damage to railway lines, highways and telecom towers, thereby inhibiting communication and transport and destruction of the pipeline for transporting iron ore slurry in Chhattisgarh. According to reports, 'power and steel industry projects in Chhattisgarh with investments of the order of rupees one hundred and thirty billion were stagnated due to Naxalite disturbances'. All in all, it's a very grim economic condition which affects all sectors of industry and all classes of people. Micro-economic effects include lower tourist inflows, lower regional tourism market share, reduced usage of public transport, reduced long-term investments in agriculture and other potential sectors, reduced enrolment in schools, lower job availability and lack of substantial opportunities.

The Urban Movement has attracted students towards the Maoist fold in various parts of the country. In the 1980s, hordes of students from Kakatiya University and Regional Engineering College (now National Institute of Technology), Warangal, and Osmania University, Hyderabad, joined the then Progressive War cadres. Besides, according to one media report, '...security agencies believe that the front organizations have started a vigorous movement in the education sector, to rope in students from several reputed colleges for their cause... (they) warned the (Nagpur) city police about these student-oriented revolutionary organizations. People working under banners with hints of revolution, like "*sangharsh*" and "*kranti*" are under the scanner'.

Following the arrest of Himadri Sen Roy, a very senior Maoist leader, and Somen alias Sumanand, West Bengal State Committee Secretary, near Kolkata, police claimed that 'the CPI (Maoist) has initiated a drive to spread its network in the city (Kolkata) and its outskirts and the outfit has brought some youths and students from premier educational institutions like Presidency College under its fold in the last two years'.

In Bengaluru too, Maoist activities in colleges have been noticed. According to a media report, the police suspected that a group, known as the Karnataka Communal Harmony Group (KCHG), a congregation of intellectuals and activists, is a Maoist front. Apparently, top police officials visited the famous Jesuit college – St Joseph's – to investigate the involvement of students with the KCHG and the Naxals. In fact, in Karnataka, it was the urban movement that was stronger than the rural movement. Jawaharlal Nehru University, Hyderabad Central University, Tata Institute of Social Sciences, Allahabad University, IIT Madras, Jadavpur University are the citadels of urban Naxalism.

Moreover, if and when the Urban Movement catches on, the State will then have to deal with industrial unrest and urban terrorism. Urbanization has some obvious faults and the Naxals could well exploit these to their advantage. Also, the stronger the movement becomes in the urban areas, the more it is likely to contribute to the agrarian revolution – in terms of providing leaders and men and material to the 'people's war'.

The majority of the people in Maoist-affected areas and even their supporters and cadres have little to do with Maoism at an ideological level. They are only alienated and angered people with no real idea of the perceived sense of injustice, oppression, and loss of dignity. Naxals are cleverly exploiting this sentiment to their advantage – caste conflicts in Bihar, resentment against landlords in Andhra, discontent against forest laws in tribal areas, unemployment amongst youth and radicalism among Muslims are all given the prescription of capture of power through the gun as the ultimate solution of all their problems. While the local grievances need to be effectively addressed through improved governance and ruthless accountability, there is also a need for creating mass awareness of the ultimate designs and consequences of what the extremists stand for.

I make tea for myself. I stand and wait for the water to boil like we are waiting for Naxalism to boil in our cities. Nobody is talking about it. Why? Why is our media, our artists, our storytellers silent on this issue? Why isn't our intelligentsia talking about it? What if they are part of this nexus? Are they the urban terrorists? Urban Naxals?

Instinctively, I know the answer.

One liner:

3. The student finds out about the nexus between the professor, an NGO worker and Naxals who want to attack the State and the student decides to expose them.

It's not a film any more. It's a mission.

15. A New Angle

Mao Zedong had said, 'The final objective of the revolution is the capture of cities, the enemy's main bases, and this objective cannot be achieved without adequate work in the cities.' The charismatic Che Guevara too opined: 'The importance of the urban struggle is extraordinary.'

The Naxalites sure did bring about some equity and relief for the marginalized category of rural India from the rampant feudal ill-activities, but that has come at a huge cost to the entire nation in terms of both economic development and safety of citizens. Moreover, this movement no longer holds its people-centric approach. It has more or less become a terrorist group with only one principle—to seize power. Development of these areas is a steep challenge; not only are they economically and socially stunted but these areas have people suffering from a much more unfortunate condition of not being able to exercise their fundamental rights. The policy for rehabilitating the affected areas should be to start development from the grassroots level.

Masses have suffered from both ends, i.e. at the hands of the security forces as well as the Naxalites. Salwa Judum, which was a militia set up with the approval of the government to counter the Naxals, caused the displacement of more than fifty thousand families in Chhattisgarh alone. Security forces have also been accused of recruiting minors as SPOs (Special Police Officers) in the Salwa Judum. Salwa Judum has been alleged for practicing vigilante justice and their activists have been held responsible for heinous crimes like torture, rape, and non-judicial executions. In many Naxal-infested areas, there has been a visible nexus between Naxals, Salwa Judum, the police, and contractors.

The Home Ministry affidavit filed in the Supreme Court states that as part of their strategy, the Naxals are forming a 'rainbow coalition of various insurgent groups in India, so as to launch a united front attack against the existing State machinery'. Although the affidavit doesn't name any particular outfit, sources say there is an understanding with all insurgent groups from the North-East to Jammu and Kashmir.

'We have established a link between the Naxals and Manipur-based People's Liberation Army and the United Liberation Front of Asom (ULFA),' a Home Ministry official said on record.

Security and intelligence agencies suspect that Naxals have a new chain of supply of weapons and are not dependent only on the snatching of arms from security forces. Intelligence reports have also indicated a collaboration between the Reds and the Indian Mujahedeen. The recent seizure of bombs and explosives from IM men in Jharkhand, a Red bastion, point to a nexus between the two groups. It is suspected that the Naxals are providing explosives to the IM in return of arms and ammunition.

Recent studies say that the Naxals have well-established linkages with other insurgent groups and a few Muslim Fundamentalist Organizations (MFOs), which are actively involved in India. These links provide the movement not only with psychological support but also material support in the form of money and weapons.

J&K Terrorist Groups

Naxalite spokespersons, on many occasions, have openly supported the actions and cause of the J&K terrorist groups. The Lashkar-e-Tayyeba (LeT) terrorists who carried out the attack on the American Centre at Kolkata in 2001 had escaped to Jharkhand and taken refuge in a Naxalite sympathizer's house in Ranchi. In return for this and similar other favours the J&K terrorists who are well trained in handling sophisticated arms, impart training to the Naxalite groups.

The North-East

Intelligence agencies have also reported linkages between Maoist elements and the insurgent groups of the North-East i.e. the United Liberation Front of Asom, Nationalist Council of Nagaland, and People's Liberation Army (ULFA, NSCN, PLA). North-East insurgent groups like the PLA and NSCN follow the Maoist ideology and were even trained and supported by China in the 1960s and 1970s.

SIMI

It has emerged that the Naxals have openly supported the activities of Students Islamic Movement of India (SIMI) and both have been lately collaborating with each other.

Nepal

Naxalite groups in India have tried to sustain their fraternal and logistic links with Nepal's Naxals. The outfits of India, along with Communist Party of Nepal (Maoist), have decided to work towards carving out a 'Compact Revolutionary Zone'. The Indian groups have been extending moral, material, and training support to CPN (Maoist) cadres in guerrilla warfare, which has resulted in significant growth of Naxal violence since 2001. Cooperation between Naxals active in Nepal through Bihar, Jharkhand, Chhattisgarh, up to Andhra Pradesh, has provided the left extremists contiguous areas to operate, move, hide, and train.

South Asia

The Maoist groups of four South Asian countries, India, Nepal, Bangladesh and Sri Lanka, have joined hands to form the Coordination Committee of the Maoist Parties of South Asia (CCOMPOSA) to advance 'People's War' in South Asia. The objective of the Committee is to unify and coordinate the activities of the Naxal parties and organizations in South Asia and spread protracted People's War in the region.

ISI Links

The Inter-Services Intelligence (ISI) has been very active in Nepal and Bangladesh for long, especially along the borders, in their desire to encircle India and is giving support to numerous Indian militant groups based in Bangladesh. The ISI does not hesitate in providing moral and material support to these groups. This bond has been mutually beneficial to both the parties, as the left-wing extremists receive weapons from the ISI to be used against the Indian State.

LTTE Links

The Naxalite linkage with the Liberation Tigers of Tamil Eelam (LTTE) dates back to the 1990s when it was estimated by the intelligence agencies that the PWG used to acquire weapons, especially AK-47 assault rifles, from this organization. In the present context, the Naxalites are actively involved in Tamil Nadu with the discovery of a training camp organized by former PWG Naxals in the Periyakulum forests in Tamil Nadu. It has led security agencies to suspect a renewed nexus between the Naxals and the LTTE.

Revolutionary International Movement

The PWG maintains constant touch with the Maoist groups of 27 countries through the Revolutionary International Movement. A Turkish Maoist organization is known to have undertaken the task of publishing PWG activities through an Internet website.

Linkage with Left-Wing Philippines Groups

A few media and intelligence reports from Southeast Asia state that the Naxalites in India have also developed links with the left-wing extremists of the Philippines, and through them, with other groups of Southeast Asia. The increasing expansion of Naxalism got further strengthened with covert support from other groups with a similar ideology in the Indian subcontinent. India's 'all weather adversary' Pakistan has grasped the opportunity provided by Naxalism to further increase unrest in India and re-emphasize its dictum of 'bleeding India by thousand cuts'.

The US State Department's National Consortium for the Study of Terrorism and Responses to Terrorism has found that going by the number of terror attacks and the number of killings of innocent citizens every year from 2012 until now, the big-five terror group consists of the IS, Taliban, Boko Haram, al Qaeda, and the Communist Party of India (Maoist).

I wonder why Naxals are called rebels or insurgents and not terrorists. I look for the most acceptable definition of terrorism:

'Use of violence to terrorize people for achieving political objectives'.

My film must prove that Naxals are terrorists and Urban Naxals are intellectual terrorists, a point the mainstream media and intelligentsia always love to ignore.

The entire history of Naxalism is based on armed struggle. Their Strategy document clearly talks about an 'armed war' against the State and finally establishing their government in 2025 by toppling a democratically elected government through the barrel of the gun.

For Naxals, socio-economic justice is just an instrument to cover up their terrorism against the State. They support everything that negates Indian nationhood, be it secessionists in J&K, insurgents in the North-East, radical Islamic groups or armed ethnic groups.

In an interview in 2007, Ganapathy, the Secretary-General of CPI-Naxals asserted, 'We see the Islamic upsurge as a progressive anti-imperialist force in the contemporary world. It is wrong to describe the struggle that is going on in Iraq, Afghanistan, Palestine, Kashmir, Chechnya as Islamic fundamentalism. Our party supports the Islamic upsurge.' Commenting on the 26/11 massacre of Mumbai, Bimal, Politburo member, was quoted in *Hindustan Times,* saying: 'We do not support the way they attacked the Victoria station, where most of the victims were Muslims. At the same time, we feel the Islamic upsurge should not be opposed as it is basically anti-US and anti-imperialist in nature. We, therefore, want it to grow.'

Varavara Rao, referring to North-East insurgencies, stated on May 13, 2007: 'This is a time for all revolutionary, democratic, and nationality movements, like the ones in Kashmir and the North-East, to unite and something will come out of this unity'.

The Naxals stand against India's sovereignty, unity, democratic polity, and civilizational values and hence, will have to be fought and defeated at all planes – ideological, political, and physical.

Ajit Doval, the current National Security Advisor, has written that the Naxals have targeted democratically and legally elected politicians to prove their vulnerability and to erode the legitimacy and credibility of the system. He writes, 'Their attacks on police and para-military forces are aimed at demonstrating that the coercive power of the government is a myth as it is not even able to protect itself. Their holding *Jan Adalats*, imposing fines, and dictating terms for talks are calculated to undermine the government's ability to enforce its writ and authority and give credibility to their propaganda that government is only a "paper tiger". On the contrary, the State has been able to do little to demolish the contrived self-image of the Left Extremists as saviours of the people. The discordant voices within the government and display of confusion and indecisiveness immensely boost their morale. While the far-flung, tribal areas are in the news because of incidents of violence, what is lesser known is their fast-spreading influence in urban suburbs, among the trade unions, unemployed youth, students etc. much beyond the tribal areas.'

I have no doubt in my mind that Naxalism is the biggest threat to India, bigger than Pakistan and China. Such links are not possible to maintain from the jungles of Dantewada. Where is their strategic hub?

All the research points to Delhi and the National Capital Region (NCR) as the most active urban Naxal centre. Some of the organizations in Delhi that are under the scanner are the Revolutionary Democratic Front (RDF), Committee for Release of Political Prisoners, Democratic Students Union, Nari Mukti Sangh, People Democratic Front of India, and Mehantkash Mazdoor Morcha. Many of their members are said to be active in towns adjoining Delhi like Gurgaon and Ghaziabad.

Intelligence agencies stumbled upon the Naxals' strategy of setting up urban bases in cities like Delhi in 2009, with the arrest of Kobad Ghandy from Delhi, allegedly responsible for recruiting people from urban centres. More recently, Hem Mishra, a student of Jawaharlal Nehru University in Delhi, was arrested by Maharashtra Police for allegedly helping Naxals. His arrest followed a search at the residence of G.N. Saibaba, a professor at Delhi University.

Delhi being the media centre of India attracts all kinds of intelligentsia. Another reason for such high concentration of intelligentsia is that all central research and policy agencies are here and these agencies were used by the Congress government to employ intellectuals and use them to give an ideological endorsement to their political narrative. Since Sonia Gandhi's politics align with the left, it is but natural that most of these people are Naxal sympathizers. The 'ecosystem' that Sonia Gandhi has nurtured consists of such intellectuals, eminent journalists, historians, and above all NGO heads.

The next big question spinning in my head is about the bloodline of this movement – money. Money is one of the most important factors helping extremists to acquire weapons and explosives, raise their cadre strength by recruiting youth on regular salaries and carrying out mass mobilization programmes. They are reportedly collecting sixteen hundred crore rupees a year, which is big money for carrying out armed insurrection in an impoverished area. Where do they get it from? Is it possible that the money is routed through NGOs since no one questions them?

To further the military objective of the revolution, the Naxals surely would strengthen their cyber-warfare strategy. This is where students are most effective. They are cleverly using universities and colleges, which attract students from weaker sections, as easy sanctuaries for insurgents to thrive in the cities. Panic buttons need to be pressed right now, else the spread of the invisible Naxals in the sprawling towns and cities of India could shape up as a major destabilizing factor in future.

Invisible Enemy

At a tactical level, the most important advantage of 4GW warriors is the advantage of invisibility. Only quality operational intelligence can make them visible for counter-tactical operations aimed at pre-empting, preventing, and punishing the depredators. It is also the only instrumentality through which they can be tactically surprised and their advantage of speed and surprise neutralized.

An invisible enemy is the most dangerous of all. Like a snake under your bed. I shiver imagining that someone in my ecosystem – a writer, a lawyer, a journalist, a social worker, an officer, a professor, a historian, a painter, a filmmaker, anyone just anyone can be an Urban Naxal. What if?

I have found the angle I was looking for. If someone tells you there is a ghost next to you, you will most certainly laugh it off. What if I *show* you the ghost next to you? Will you still laugh it off? Or scream and run for your life? I have to show this ghost called the Urban Naxal to my audience. Someone you work with, someone you live with, someone you sleep with, someone you love, someone you respect, someone you trust turns out to be a Naxal, facilitating a war on your country.

One-liner:

The hero finds himself stuck in a web of half-truths and mirror images. He discovers that he has been trusting people who work for the

Naxal cause, overtly and covertly. Will he run away? Will he expose them?

It is 6 AM and I am working. I am absentminded, reckless, heedless of social obligations. It is as it must be. I have reached a point where the film can beat about the bush or become explosive by exposing the skeletons that have been meticulously hidden from the public eye by the 'ecosystem'.

I have to be a risk-taker and just tell the truth the way it is. Everything that bothers me. Everything that must be told. Fearlessly. My loyalty is to the inner vision. There is no other way work of artistic worth can be done.

16. Deep-Diving into Naxalism

I can see the story, its characters, and their destination. When a filmmaker reaches this stage, the first thing that overcomes him is insecurity. What if I am wrong?

My father used to say often, 'In crisis, walk.' His *mantra* has always worked for me. Whenever in confusion or self-doubt, I travel to unknown places. Unfamiliarity doesn't let you judge. You see the reality. First, you just look at it from a distance, fully detached from it. This gap, between the observed and the observer, is inversely proportional to bias. Bias develops with familiarity. Bias becomes a point of view which becomes our mindset and the dictating factor of all our actions. Before you can get familiar enough to interpret it, move. This way one can collect a lot of objective data which helps us reach near the truth.

Rohit and I fly to Hyderabad. We explore ISB from a new perspective, we explore Hyderabad, we meet Greyhound officers, we walk in tribal jungles, we talk to ex-Salwa Judum men, we listen to tribals. We learn about kangaroo courts. About beheadings, about rapes.

Two Indias stand in front of us. At one end, in a modern monument of one of the world's finest B-schools, are poker-playing, potential CEOs of the world who will shape our tastes, our choices, our purchases, our investments, and our careers. Our lives. And at the other end, there is a hungry, unaware, stagnant, defeated, hopeless India which will never know the pleasure of choice.

We see Naxalism in a new light. Thus far we had known about the clash between these two Indias intellectually. Now we have seen it actually. The poker-playing India will always choose Naxals over tribals as tribals have nothing to give. We are disturbed. And angry.

The days of the narrative that people pick up guns because of oppression and haplessness are over. Guns today are an organized business. With profits.

A new narrative has to be introduced. The nexus has to be exposed. The youth has to be cautioned to a possible threat of being adopted in India's bloodiest war without them ever knowing it. It's time to recap all the insights in the context of the Naxal-Urban Nexus and Urban Youth.

The Times of India of April 11, 2010, reported: 'The Jawaharlal Nehru University campus became a battleground on Friday night when members of disparate student organizations clashed over what was seen as an attempt to support the Naxalites and "celebrate" the massacre of 76 CRPF men. Members of Democratic Students Union (DSU) and All India Students Association (AISA) organized a meeting to celebrate the killing of 76 CRPF personnel in Chhattisgarh. They were even shouting slogans like "India *murdabad*, Maovaad *zindabad*".'

How can this be allowed inside a central university without the protection of the faculty and the administration?

Inspector General of police, Bastar range, SRP Kalluri has gone on record, as reported by *India Today*, as saying, 'I felt disappointed when I came to know that celebrations were held at JNU (by some students) after the killing of seventy-six jawans in the forest of Tadmetla in 2010.'

Under the headline 'Naxals have a new address: Jadavpur University', *The Indian Express* of Dec 10, 2010, reports that 'Kanchan, the arrested CPI (Maoist) state secretary, has reportedly told the security agencies that a recruitment process is on for the outfit's military wing and Jadavpur University has emerged as a major centre for the cadres. Also, the Naxals are believed to have a backup module among the university students. Kanchan has reportedly also said that 12 students from (Kolkata's) Presidency College are working actively as CPI (Maoist) cadres in Lalgarh.'

Hindustan Times of March 28, 2010, carried a column with the headline '1970s revisited? Kolkata youth back in Naxal fold'. The report interviews an IB officer, involved with tracking Maoist activities, who says, 'This trend is alarming. Many student and youth activists in the city campaigning for Lalgarh have visited the jungles and undergone arms training.'

Former Presidency College student, Ramen (name changed), is now a regular in Lalgarh. 'Initially, I got involved looking at the plight of people in Nandigram and Lalgarh on TV. Although I'm not exactly a Maoist, I believe in their cause and as a concerned citizen I'm working with them to help the downtrodden,' he told *HT*.

Maoist ideologue Varavara Rao said at a news conference in JU on February 26, 'Our support is growing among students of Kolkata. Though these students don't come from tribal areas, they understand the situation.'

I can feel in my guts that the next biggest threat to India's internal security is going to come from our campuses.

The last few months have kept India occupied with shocking and repeated revelations from campuses of renowned educational institutes like Hyderabad Central University (HCU), IIT Madras, JNU, Osmania University, Jadavpur University, Delhi University, Bhagalpur University to name only a few. The common thread in all these institutes-turned-battlefields is a protest against the ruling government in India in the name of Constitutional principles and democratic values. A closer look at all these cases reveals that there is no suppression of 'democratic principles' by the government. However, a picture has been painted so. Some faculty members too tried to escalate these protests through their active participation or supportive roles. All this left the common man of this country wondering 'How did students turn anti-India?' 'What is suddenly wrong with all these universities and institutes?'

While roasting chicken legs on a tandoor, a senior IPS officer from the Andhra cadre explained to us how urban Naxalism is seeping into our cities faster than we can imagine. 'In the cities, the frontal "mass organizations" are generally manned by ideologues, who include academicians and activists, fully committed to the party line. Such organizations ostensibly pursue human rights related issues and are also adept at using the legal processes of the Indian State to undermine and emasculate enforcement action by the security forces. They also attempt to malign the State institutions through propaganda and disinformation to further the cause of their "revolution". Whenever an incident like this happens, a sympathetic media protects them by blaming the forces. What they don't know is that the forces are extremely professional now and do not indulge in civilian contact.'

He details the mechanics of 'Mass Mobilization', 'as it will consequently lead to "Party Building" for them which will be proletarian vanguard in the revolution and through which they can build a "United Front" and perform military tasks for the guerilla warfare in the areas surrounding cities where they have established their base or which are also known as "Liberated Zones". Naxals form own organizations. Underground secret organizations which may not fit within the ambit of democracy, and open revolutionary organizations and legal democratic mass organizations, which can work within the ambit of democracy and law. They also infiltrate existing mass organizations and try to get into leadership roles to support their anti-State "revolutionary" agenda. They build several types of mass organizations simultaneously. From these mass organizations, individuals are selected, brainwashed into supporting and becoming members of the Maoist party. Mass organizations are the fodder for their party building in urban areas.'

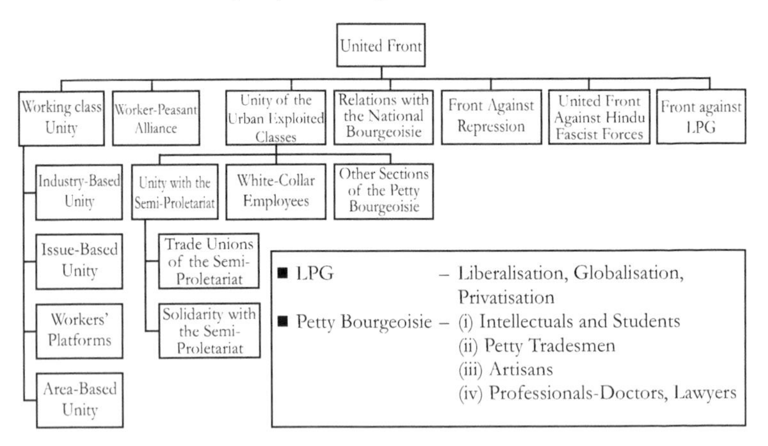

The Maoist documents have illustrated the hierarchy of mass mobilization in a compact flowchart.

The IPS officer has spent a good time in the Greyhound force and has nabbed more than a dozen Naxalites. 'I can smell them, irrespective of where they are hiding: in a forest or in a university,' he says with a smile while relishing the smell of charcoal on the southern spices of the marinade.

I must have a character like him in the film, I decide while chewing on the succulent chicken leg.

'If you want to understand the smartness of their strategy, just see how seamlessly an individual converts from being a participant in a mass protest to a loyal party member. The most interesting part is that most participants don't even know that they are part of the activist groups or party factions. The participants usually think that they are working for the betterment of democracy.'

His insights were real and extremely useful for the film. We learn that the aggressive, enthusiastic and active candidates are selected for activist groups. They are indoctrinated and made party members. 'Activist Groups' is the first level of selection and a transitory phase, post which, selected activists enter the party cell and start working as Party Member.

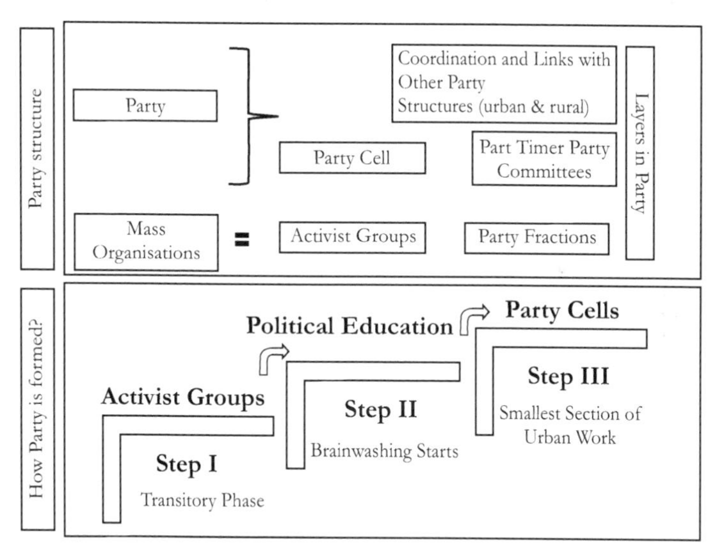

The details of internal links within mass organizations in urban areas were found in documents seized from Delhi University English Language Prof GN Saibaba. In the year 1991, he was allegedly sent from Andhra Pradesh to Delhi to spread the network of Naxals in urban areas. In mass organizations operating in urban areas, there are two wings i.e. Strategic Front and Tactical United Front. Strategic Front does not directly deal with the mass population. It encompasses Central Committee and the Maoist Politburo. Tactical United Front deals with mass organizations directly. These mass organizations are internally categorized from A1 to A7 basis the role they play and target population they mobilize.

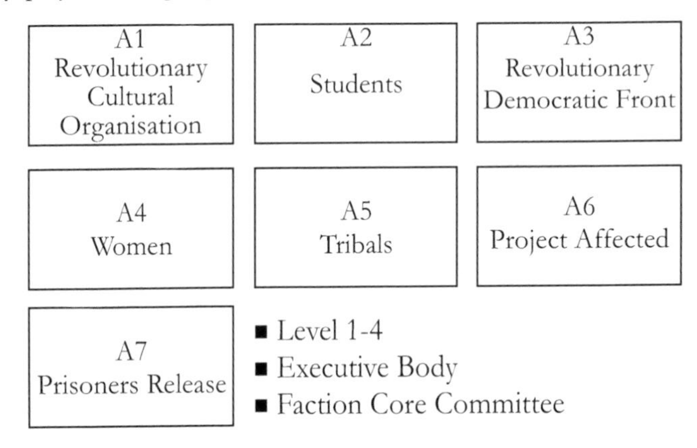

Out of this, Kabir Kala Manch is part of the A1 type of organizations which sing revolutionary songs and organize cultural programmes to mobilize people. A3 is Revolutionary Democratic Front (RDF) which has 222 organizations empathizing with Naxals and their ideology across India. RDF was banned in Andhra Pradesh and Odisha. A4 to A7 comprise organizations targeting and working on women, tribals, project-affected people and for the release of prisoners respectively. Executive Body controls and coordinates these seven types of organizations. One representative from each type out of A1 to A7 is part of Executive Body. It decides types of programmes or protests to be organized and their locations.

Faction Core Committee is only of five people and they control the Executive Body and all mass organizations through the Executive Body. The Faction Core Committee directly deals with Politburo members and the five people in the Faction Core Committee operate with different names and most of these organizations are not registered. In each organization, there are levels from Level 1 to Level 4 for participants. Based on aggressiveness, revolutionary traits, commitment, and reliability for Maoist work, Faction Core Committee decides the levels of participants in the organizations. The ratio of Level 1 to Level 4 is 10:1, which means if there are 100 individuals in Level 1, level 4 may have 10 or even less number of individuals. Once the individual is confirmed for Level 4, those interested in weapons and armed struggle are sent to jungles and others from level 4 who have grudges against the system are engaged in rest of the activities supporting the Maoist party and armed struggle such as courier, propaganda etc. The individuals do not come to know that they are being assessed or which level they are in.

Urban areas are important for Naxals to get cadre which has the skill set to perform military tasks, plus they become critical in order to develop international network, local intelligence, medical aid to rural guerrilla force, transit facility and cyber warfare.

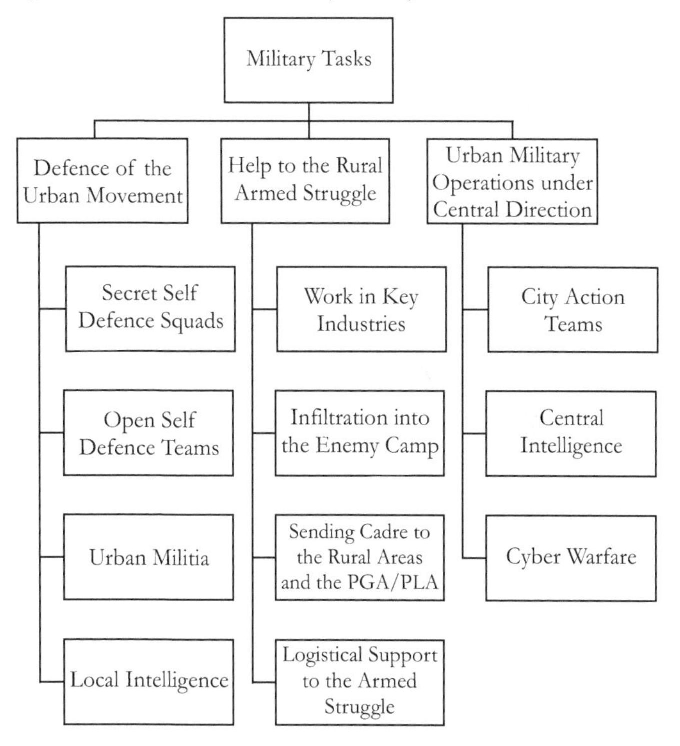

One more important dimension for the Naxals' focus on urban areas in the last few years is the recruitment ebb they are facing in tribal areas as tribals understood the hollowness of Maoist ideology due to the violence and harassment they experienced over last forty years. Naxals are not getting recruits for their *dalams,* the units in their Armed Guerilla Force. The number of surrenders has gone up manifold. Migration is highest in Gadchiroli district in Maharashtra as the youth there do not want to join the Naxal movement and they cannot go back to their villages due to fear of Naxals.

The history of students' and teachers' association with Maoism is as old as the movement itself. Youth and labour are the backbone of the Maoist movement. The Strategy and Tactics of Indian Revolution mentions the following about students' role in the Maoist movement.

'Among the urban petty bourgeoisie, students and youth constitute an important category. They react to the events and historically from the anti-British movement they played a significant role. In the wake of Naxalbari, their role is exemplary. Our party has good experience in organizing them. While working in urban areas, we must pay necessary attention to organize them... There is a need to emphasize the necessity of uniting with intellectuals. We need to allot sufficient cadre to work among them and some special effort be put to unite and organize them.'

'Our forces are capable of defeating any enemy provided we can see him. How does one fight an invisible enemy who can be even your brother or your son?' the IPS officer took a pause, emptied the last few drops from the bottle of Old Monk in his glass and said with a smile, 'or even your wife?'

I didn't tell him that I have seen such invisible enemies and that I have been a part-time recruit.

While doing my internship at Ogilvy & Mather, Bombay, Mani Iyer, the dad of Indian advertising and the then chief of O&M, had told me once that creative leadership lies in recognizing when to stop research and start writing the ad.

'When?' I had asked.

'When you have found what needs to be told.'

I know what needs to be told. I need to tell the story of the invisible enemy, the most dangerous terrorist.

The Urban Naxal.

Book Three

The Making of Buddha

"You have your brush, you have your colours, you paint the paradise, then in you go."
- Nikos Kazantzakis, Zorba the Greek

17. The First Draft

I call Rohit and tell him that it's time to write the first draft.

We set a few parameters.

One, we will stay absolutely honest and committed to the facts.

Two, we will neither overplay nor underplay any situation, dialogue, character or any visual.

Three, we won't be afraid to tell the facts as they are, in the language of the characters, even if it's profane in nature.

Four, we won't think about the censor board or the box office.

Last, but not the least, if any scene, dialogue or shot looks like we have seen it before, we will throw it out of the window.

I wipe the whiteboard, take a blue marker, and on its shining white surface, I write our scripting mantra, in big bold letters:

REAL. HONEST. FEARLESS. EYE-OPENER.

After setting these new rules, we now want to break some age–old rules of scriptwriting. I don't want the cliché style of narration. I want to change the format. After some discussions we realize that our biggest problem is that we have too many stories. Also, all our research is condensed in a book form in chapters, with no linear, seamless flow.

'What if we narrate it like a book… in chapters?' I ask Rohit.

'Sir, who will see it?' Rohit asks me.

'The same people who always cry that Bollywood doesn't experiment with new ideas and formats,' I quip.

This is not a regular film. It's born in a B-school, with the initiative of students. A movie in a book form is an 'out-of-the-box' idea and very appropriate for a student's film. Their top-of-the-mind reference for any narration is always a book. Also, 'but nobody does it' becomes my motivation to 'do it this way'.

We decide to write the script like a book. In chapters. A first for any Indian film. To my knowledge.

The cover

Despite the independence, democracy, judiciary, development, NGOs, social workers, a vibrant civil society, and above all, the longest and the most violent movement for social justice – the Naxal Movement, nothing has changed for the tribals in the forests of Bastar.

This is the saddest commentary on our post-independence growth story.

My challenge is to get it right at the beginning of the film, like the cover of a book, so that the new generation gets the point right away. Bastar – an area which has not changed in thousands of years.

Rohit suggests that we do a voice-over on some old paintings and photos, so that the audience gets to know the geography and some history of Bastar and its tribals. I think it's a cliché and nine out of ten writers will come up with the same idea. Bollywood works on a few given templates and this is one of them. The audience knows them too well and that's why our audience is always ahead of the story; they have seen it several times and make no effort to guess the proceedings. Predictability is what kills a film. I can't just let the audience predict what is up in the next scene.

I get up and add another parameter on the whiteboard.

REAL. HONEST. FEARLESS. EYE-OPENER. UNIQUE.

'Sir, don't make so many rules, else our script will read like a rulebook.' Rohit loves to pull my leg.

I believe in the power of visuals. Words should be used only when visuals fail to communicate. I decide to tell this tragic truth of Bastar in just two visuals. My co-writer comes up with an idea that I like. He suggests that in the first visual we show '*... a semi-naked tribal is cutting wood in front of a hut*'. In the second visual we show '*... a tribal cleaning a gun*'. This will show that nothing has changed except for that the gun has replaced the axe.

I open my Mac and write on a blank page of Movie Magic Screenwriter:

Fade in:

Bastar: circa 2000 BC

A semi-naked tribal is cutting wood in front of a naked hut.

Cut to:

Bastar: circa 2012:

A semi-naked tribal is cutting wood in front of a naked hut.

I am so lost in my thoughts that I end up typing the same description in both the shots. My co-writer starts laughing and points out the mistake and asks me to change the second line to '... *cleaning a gun.*'

I am about to change it but then, stop. What if we shoot it exactly like this, using the mistake as an opportunity? Suddenly, it makes more sense to me. With the tribal '*cleaning the gun*', he becomes part of a violent system and therefore an aggressor. Whereas if he keeps cutting the wood, he would come across as an innocent tribal, who has no context of the world around him. The gun makes him a participant in a scheme, whereas the axe makes him a victim of the scheme.

I let the description stay with its mistake.

For me, it simply meant that *for the tribal,* nothing has changed.

Sometimes, mistakes lead us to a truth hidden in the shadows of words. In the complex world of cinema, with each film, each scene, each shot, a filmmaker learns about so many dimensions of the human mind, that without the clarity of vision and strength of conviction, it's easy for anyone to get confused. Since in Bollywood stars are the focal point, they substitute for vision and conviction. Makers are convinced that a star will fill in for the lack of vision and story. Thank God, we don't have any such pressure. Like that poor tribal we also have something that money can't buy – a burning desire to find the truth and an axe of conviction to cut through the jungle of lies.

I am convinced that the universe is conspiring for us to reveal the truth. This is our '*a-ha*' moment. We have found our muse. The truth. This is why I love my job.

18. Prologue

There is a nexus between Naxals, Salwa Judum, contractors, and the police, who all claim to be working for the welfare of the tribal but instead the tribal has become a victim of this nexus.

Like any other war, this one has also propelled politics, ethos, and economics around it. On one hand, there are Naxals who want this tribal to succumb to their absolute authority. On the other hand, there is Salwa Judum, who wants this tribal to surrender to their strategy to counter the Naxals. Then, there is the police which wants him to blindly follow their diktats. On the circumference of this nexus, there is a contractor who wants the tribal to stay mute to his exploitation. Together, they behave like an army. A force that is out to silence everyone. To take them to their camps and save them from an enemy that wants to take them to their camps. This nexus has become a killing machine. The forests of Dantewada have become the killing fields.

We have many anecdotes recorded on my iPhone which narrate how Salwa Judum forced the tribal to go to their camps. We also have stories of how Naxals took away their young kids, trained them with guns when they had no idea why they were killing people. One uses violence to take them to the camps. The other uses violence to stop them from going to the camps. Thus 'Camp' is the dreaded word.

'A Tribal is ordered by Salwa Judum to go to their camp and on the other side, he is threatened by Naxals from going to the camp. When Naxals take away his son, he decides to stay back. As a punishment, Salwa Judum beats him up and rapes his woman.'

Since this is the first real scene of the film, I am tempted to open it with a bang. What lingers in my memory from the tribal village visit during my recce were the goats. There were too many goats everywhere. Tribals drank goat milk. I remember I almost threw up after smelling it. I decide to use goats in this scene. When the Salwa

Judum leader comes to the tribal's house, the first thing he tells the tribal is: *'I have heard a lot about your goats, heard that they give a lot of milk, won't you offer me some?'*

In dialogues, we decide to use the local dialect, as spoken by the tribals. I am very tempted to use a line from Buddhe, a tribal I spent a lot of time with: *'In naxaliyon ne bhatratmaa ki maa chod di hai–* these Naxals have fucked my motherland'. I make the Salwa Judum leader speak this line *'Yeh Bharatmaa tumhari maa hai madarchod aur yeh naxali tumhari maa ki maar rahe hain–* India is your mother, motherfucker, and these Naxals are fucking your mother'. This, perhaps, is the most profane dialogue ever spoken in the history of Indian cinema and we have no idea how this will go through the Censors. And the moral police. When you are driven, you can't see the dangers ahead.

In another scene, the Naxals have foisted their red flag on the tribal's house. Rohit suggests that the Salwa Judum guy take it out and beat the tribal with it. It's too obvious. We reject it. There are other ideas. For instance, after raping the tribal's wife, he covers her bare body with the flag. I am looking for a powerful image. A dry, stark, haunting imagery. What is the first thing he is going to do after beating the shit out of him and raping his woman?

'He will light his bidi,' Rohit says.

I close my eyes and I see him burning the flag with the same matchstick.

'Let the bloody flag burn,' I say.

In my mind, I have already burnt the Naxal mafia.

'The Salwa Judum leader burns the Naxal flag with his bidi.'

19. I am a Bitch

I am looking for an issue that can trigger off the spirit of activism in my protagonist. The humiliation of my table tennis friend at the two-wheeler stand in my college in Bhopal is fresh in my mind. To add to this, recently, in a Mangalore pub, a right-wing extremist group, Sri Ram Sene, led by Pramod Muthalik had beaten up some girls and pulled them out by their hair, for drinking and dancing and therefore violating Indian culture.

Subsequently, a consortium of 'Pub-Going, Loose, and Forward Women' started a 'Pink *Chaddi*' campaign on social media. The novel form of protest was initiated by four women: Nisha Susan, Mihira Sood, Jasmeen Patheja, and Isha Manchanda· As the protest grew, pink underwear started pouring in from locations all over India in solidarity and thousands of pink *chaddis* were sent to Mutahilik's house, on Valentine's Day.

This campaign made an impression on me and helped me understand the power of social media. I want to use this real-life example to show how urban, modern, and educated girls are treated in our society. The hero will fight for the cause. This will be my way of venting my anger against the exploitation of women and it will also be a tribute to my TT friend from Bhopal who I never met after college.

We get in touch with Nisha Susan and request her to let us use 'Pink *Chaddi*'. We promise her due credit. She isn't happy with the fact that a man would fight for the cause. And 'why not a heroine' is what she argued with Ravi, my co-producer, who was coordinating with her, and due to her feminist ego, she refused to let us use the name. For some feminists, the entire movement rests on hating men. I can't change their mindset. I change the campaign to 'Pink Bra Campaign'.

The second challenge is how to introduce these students. They aren't ordinary students. They are future CEOs of blue-chip corps.

In my mind these young boys and girls are urban tribals – the lost and vulnerable youth, going nowhere. Like the tribal, this youth has no context of India's real issues and all they are pursuing is a *flashy* job and a merry lifestyle with teenager-like freedom in some rich country.

If I have to pick up the most powerful images from my stay at the ISB hostel, it would be weed, beer, smoke, and cuss words. I chose to use these for the atmospherics, where these super smart students come up with bizarre theories. A girl comes up with a crazy 'drunk theory' and dances on top of the bar counter.

Rohit comes up with various 'drunk' theories. None of them are working. The problem is that the story should be unique, not heard before and yet should connect with the audiences instantly. They should be forced to think. I remember that I used to pose a paradoxical question to my grandfather who spent most of his time reading the *Gita*. According to the *Gita*, the soul is immortal. It can't be born and it can't die. It only changes the body. If souls are constant then how is the world population ever increasing? Where are these new souls coming from? Animals. Because animals are becoming extinct. That's why so many people these days behave like animals.

Rohit converts this idea into a fantastic scene where each friend describes which animal he behaves like. The buck stops at this girl. How is a pub-going, smoking, drinking, and dancing girl perceived by the sex-starved men? Slut. Whore. Bitch.

'In a B-School party, when a girl gets drunk and dances atop a bar counter in small clothes, a right-wing extremist group blackens her face and shames her.'

When I formed the Joker's Party in my college, the only avenues available to us to raise our voice were plays, articles, and speeches. We had to depend on donations and logistical support from the establishment and the authorities (government, college, political parties, police permissions etc.). Also, it was a logistical nightmare to reach the desired audience. I decide that, like the 'Pink *Chaddi*' campaign, my hero will use social media. He won't depend on the establishment. He won't need any permission from the authorities. He alone can wage a war against injustice. And reach his audience directly. Also, in Bollywood, new trends, and technology are always shown in a very narrow context. For example, if they have to show youth using social media, they show a boy and girl chatting or using Facebook. But this film is not set in la– la land. For the first time, a hero of an Indian film would be blogging, vlogging on YouTube and various platforms to connect with his audience.

We don't have a name for our hero as yet. Naming the hero is as complex a process as naming your child.

The Great Depression hadn't settled as yet. Banks have been at the centre of the meltdown. In the wake of the big subprime losses, Citibank's CEO Vikram Pundit had been in the news a lot. For our country, he is the reference for an Indian success on the corporate ladder. Vikram Pundit is what most of the ISB students want to become. I can't predict their future, but my hero has now got a name. 'Vikram Pundit'.

'The hero, Vikram Pundit takes it upon himself to raise his voice against moral policing. He runs a campaign on social media called 'Pink Bra', which goes viral and he becomes an overnight sensation as a student activist.'

We are satisfied with the chapter. But we don't have a title for it. Rohit says that it's mostly women who are victims of moral policing. He suggests that this chapter should be our tribute to the harassed women.

I remember the face of my TT friend from Bhopal. I see her screaming *'I am a slut, I am a whore, I am a bitch... I am a bitch... I am a bitch.'*

We title this chapter, *'I am a bitch'*.

20. The Secret Game

'You won the game,' my drama mentor's words echo in my mind.

This is the time for us to enter the classroom and introduce the professor. Introduction of the principal characters is one of the most critical jobs in filmmaking. For you don't get a second chance to create the first impression.

While doing my research at ISB, I made friends with a lot of professors. One of them played poker almost every night with the students. He was a sweet guy with radical ideas that he discussed with me at length. Two of his theories stayed with me. One, all CSR activities must result in profits. Second, that corruption in a developing economy, like ours, is good and works like a tonic.

Since the time I started watching movies, it has been professed that corruption is bad. What if the professor says that the 'corruption is good' and convinces the audience? This is a disruptive idea. Introducing an economics professor in a top B-school speaking in favour of corruption is a real, honest, fearless eye-opener, and a unique idea. It fits our mantra.

When the professor says, 'corruption is like tonic', the hero questions him, *'Isn't it time to change this tonic?'*

'In a classroom discussion, Vikram Pundit questions the professor's theory on corruption. Professor sees sparks of socialism in Vikram and invites him to his chamber.'

The next part was easy. All I had to do was write down my own experiences. Like my drama mentor the professor gives him a file titled 'Buddha In A Traffic Jam'. Zorba becomes Buddha but he is still stuck in a jam.

My hero Vikram Pundit doesn't sleep that night and keeps reading the professor's writings, doing his own research. What he discovers changes him. He discovers two different Indias within one. One drinking Coca-Cola and the other dying of thirst. One India is covered with gold jewellery and the other stripped off clothes and dignity. One is an India that's the beneficiary of reforms and the other India is full of socio-economic orphans, rejected by all the mainstream political parties.

He starts writing blogs, speaking about a repressive State apparatus that helps keep this exploitative system going.

'Vikram Pundit, with his revolutionary ideas, becomes a strong influencer and a strong anti-establishment voice on social media.'

In typical campus politics, like in any politics, when a new entrant creates disruption by questioning the *status quo*, the members of the establishment try to subvert the new voice and eventually threaten and demolish his argument.

I still remember that an NSUI leader Saingar Bhai had caught me by my collar, in front of the entire college and threatened to cut me to pieces if I didn't stop my anti-establishment speeches in the garb of Jokers' Party. I remember all the girls looking at me, standing around an old banyan tree and holding its branches as if those branches were their shields. I could see fear in their eyes.

Fear has always provoked me. *'You can cut me to pieces but can't stop what has been started by us.'* Saingar Bhai left my collar, combed his hair with an Ajanta comb, and spoke with a grin, *'You talk too much. Let me start with stopping that first.'* Then he slapped me. Really hard. For the next few, weeks all I could hear was an annoying whistle in my ears. It wasn't a slap. It was fear injected into me. It wasn't a whistle. It was a siren against the freedom of expression.

Vikram Pundit must also face resistance. While flirting with a lady in a bar, he is confronted by a man who threatens him with consequences. He orders Vikram to stop writing, speaking, and misguiding others.

'Saale, ISI ke agent, padhe likhe behenchod intellectual terrorists,' he screams in the bar. For a B-school student who has done his IIT, worked in a blue-chip Wall Street company, and has a price tag of seventy lacs per annum in the job market, such street-level goondaism can be nerve-wracking.

Rohit wants him to react. He wants him to pick up a fight. It's natural and obvious for a writer to think that way. But I have been in that situation. I am Vikram Pundit. I know how broken, how shattered, how demoralized, how scared and alone one feels.

Vikram goes back to his dorm and tears down all his research. He returns the file to the professor and tells him that the game is over. He had come here to learn business and not to become an activist.

The professor smiles. 'You have won the game, Vikram,' he says.

21. The Potters' Club

As a CSR activity, the professor mentors a pottery club run by his wife,Sheetal. The pottery enthusiasts make pots which are purchased by the government and the monies raised are donated to an NGO working in Bastar for tribal welfare. The NGO is run by Charu, the professor's protégé.

This idea of the Potters' Club came from my growing up days. I grew up in a colony of IAS and IPS officers. My father was the only educationist amongst them. I remember, many IAS officers' wives used to run pottery or handloom workshops, where they would get poor potters or weavers to create products to be sold in exhibitions as a formality and the remaining produce, the bulk of the total production they would sell to their husband's department. No other country can match us in inventing novel ways of corruption. Sheetal Batki is a similar middle-aged, bored housewife, who uses her husband's office for profit and to look empowered and busy. Ironically, her need to create a social space separate from her husband's, depends on her husband's official position. Sheetal Batki is an arts graduate who worked as a curator in Delhi's Modern Art Gallery and then married a much older professor, Ranjan Batki. To kill her time, she started pottery with the tribal artisans and using her husband's influence she sells it to the government's department of social welfare. The money raised is then donated to an NGO, Green Commando.

On the occasion of the inauguration of the yearly edition of the Potters' Club, the professor introduces Vikram to Sheetal who turns out to be the same lady that Vikram was flirting with. They will establish an undefined, unexplained intellectually charged relationship.

Here, Vikram also meets an Inspector General of Police, based after a real-life hero, KS Vyas, IPS, the man behind the Greyhound forces. In 1993, Naxals killed Vyas. The hitman, Nayeemuddin, turned approver and helped the force to kill and nab many Naxals.

In an informal chat with the IGP, Vikram learns that the casualties due to the Naxal insurgency are at least ten times higher than the casualties in the Kargil war.

'Now you tell me, where is the real war going on and who is our real enemy?' the IGP asks Vikram.

As soon as the exhibition is inaugurated, a senior government official informs the professor that the government has stopped all its grants. The NGO Green Commando works in the Red Corridor in Bastar and has been banned. Thus, his department will no longer be able to buy their pottery as the beneficiary of the profits is the NGO. Also, the existence of this NGO depends on the money generated by selling the pots to the government. The professor has already committed this money. He is in a dilemma.

He puts this academic challenge in front of his students, to work out a business plan to raise the amount committed to the NGO.

Vikram Pundit takes up the challenge.

22. Finding Buddha

Vikram goes deep into finding ways to help the tribals. Helping him in this endeavour is Charu, the NGO entrepreneur. Charu shows him another dimension of the Naxal issue. There is a chemistry between them. She impresses upon him that since nobody feels answerable for the Naxal issue, the issue has become an orphan.

'Out of one rupee, not even ten paisa reach the tribals. You know why? Because it's nobody's fucking job'.

Where should Vikram Pundit go from here? He has been challenged by his love interest. If he gives up, he will become weak and shallow. If he takes up the challenge, he will have to shed all his fears and insecurities and find a solution. He will have to give up being an elite B-school scholar. He will have to jump from the echelons of his pedigree and dive into the dark, filthy, and creepy underbelly of India. He will have to drop his perfumed Louis Phillippe shirt and wear the sticky and stinky sweat of a tribal. Like life, in every story, there comes a time when the writer has to make a choice.

A writer's job is most painful. And if he happens to be a director also, then to write a scenario, a dialogue, he has to become the character in that scenario. And it can become nerve-wracking. Sometimes, while writing, he is transported to the unknown corners of the character's mind and he starts perceiving situations and relationships from the character's point of view. This new perspective, new understanding, new learning becomes cathartic. Like crying is a cathartic exercise. A heartbreak can be cathartic too. Even the death of a loved one. New revelations and paradigm shifts start taking place when his own perspective dies. All his life he defends his conditioning, his perception, his opinion and his worldview, which are his crutches to hide in a comfort zone. When he starts writing, he makes a choice to either flow with the characters and let a new world reveal itself, however ugly or scary it may be, or to make his characters behave according to his own conditioning and therefore defend his position in the world. And when he chooses the latter, the audience rejects it as they are too familiar with this world and it is no different from their own world. They pay money to be transported to a new world. They want to meet new characters. They want to travel in new orbits.

I wanted Vikram Pundit to be like me but now Vikram Pundit has taken on his own life. His own mind; his own motivations. I let my story go. When you let your perspective die and start seeing things from someone else's perspective, a vacuum occurs. A hollowness. Exactly like when our first love leaves us. What do we feel in our guts? Emptiness. We can't breathe. We want to throw up. But there is nothing in the guts. There is only vacuum.

Rohit and I go out of the office. There is a metro line coming up. Whenever we stand outside, we keep guessing the amount of time that will be taken to complete this job. We have never seen any project getting completed on time. It's easy to add five or ten years and win a bet. I tell him I am bored of the same discussion. He tells me that there is a video clipping which is going viral.

A Pakistani TV reporter called Chand Nawab is covering the Eid traffic at a railway station in Karachi and every time he begins to speak, a passenger crosses the camera. Chand's rendering is very unusual and funny. It cracks me up. And then suddenly something strikes me.

Strikes *me*? Or Vikram Pundit?

What if Vikram gets the idea while watching this video? It will be a great transition from the previous scene which is too verbose and serious.

Standing in the shade of a peepal tree, we keep spinning the idea until the mosquitoes make it impossible for us to stay further. The sun has set. It's dark. In this darkness, we have found the brightest idea so far. We had never imagined that Chand Nawab will become our medium to find Buddha.

'Vikram is in the shower, confused, while his friends are watching Chand Nawab's video and rolling on the floor laughing. Amongst the laughter all around him, Vikram finds his Buddha.'

Vikram rushes to the professor's house and tries to understand the business part of pottery, where Sheetal tells him that these pots are unique as this art is unadulterated, uninfluenced by any other culture. In most of the world's art, there are influences of other cultures as people travelled and picked up motifs, styles, and images from different cultures and incorporated them in their pottery. But the art of this pottery, which is believed to be from Buddha's time, is untouched by outside influence. Not because the tribal protected it from any influence. Because no one ever went where these tribals live. No one. Ever.

'It's very difficult to sell these pots as in a world of adulteration, purity looks impure.' Sheetal believes it's not possible to sell these pots as no one is interested in these pots.

But Vikram Pundit believes otherwise.

23. Freakonomics

Vikram works day and night connecting the dots to solve the Naxal issue and finally identifies that the middlemen are the biggest roadblock. He makes a presentation to the Executive Council where he proposes that the fastest and surest way to kill Naxalism in the tribal areas is to have a business solution which can be achieved by wiping out the middlemen who siphon off more than ninety percent of a tribal's income. He recommends that the Pottery Club should connect the tribal directly with his consumers, by hosting his products on an e-commerce portal.

Rohit and I end up writing a ten-page monologue. I read the monologue and Rohit edits it. Then we do a role reversal. Finally, we have a short, crisp, and comprehensive presentation ready for Vikram Pundit. Interestingly, this didn't come from the ISB professors or the scholars. This solution came to two film writers while eating *golgappas* from a street vendor, next to my office, on a dull afternoon. We sit till 3 AM to fine-tune the presentation.

I feel content. For letting out the frustration against a failed system of corrupt and exploitative power mongrels and their middlemen.

VIKRAM

(He picks up an earthen pot and shows it to the committee)
This is just an earthen pot. Yes, you can say that. If I tell you this is not just a pot but 5,000 years of history – an example of a rare Indian art, I am not lying. Thanks to Professor Batki, who gave me this chance. A challenge to sell 20,000 pieces. Sir, while I was working out a marketing strategy, a thought came to my mind. We are the students of the tenth best business school in the world. As a student, we have a responsibility as well. I figured out why in spite of a booming economy and an industrial growth amongst the best in the world we are still a poor country. Our villages, our villagers, the poor,

the backward, the deprived, and the Adivasi have no share in this growth. All of you know this. But Sir... This one earthen pot can solve this problem.
Sir, I say that there are only 10 people left in the world who can create such an art. Not a single pattern, not a single design will be repeated. And it will all be patented. It will become a unique collector's item with the stamp of originality. They may have been made yesterday but they are worth almost the same as the ones made 5,000 years ago. Because the people making them are the same as they were 5,000 years ago. Uncorrupted! We sell it as a lifetime opportunity of possessing a piece of the great Indian history. This pot in front of you, sir, has one of the noble eightfold path of Buddhism. Imagine what a set of eight such pots will cost. Sir, sky is the limit!

People will buy it because it's for a cause. Helping the poor Adivasi! Now, look at the figures. Sir, this one pot costs less than a bottle of Pepsi. Because we – me and you – have never valued it. Just imagine sir, if we price it at say a 100 dollars, today the person who has made it does not get even a dollar for it. What can be a more screwed up system than this? Where does the rest of the 99 dollars go? To the wholesalers, retailers, agents, banks, government officers, octroi, transporters, warehouses, NGOs, and the unending list of middlemen. What if I wipe them out? Wipe the middlemen out and sell it online.

Sir, we do the entire marketing, selling, and transporting from IIB. By creating a perception value of 100 dollars, all we need is 10 dollars to execute it. We have everything here to make it happen. And the tribal will get the remaining 90 if we remove the middlemen from his life. Don't you think we can bring about an economic revolution? Yes, we can eliminate Naxalism by bringing this economic revolution!

(Vikram turns his laptop towards the dean)

Sir, I have created an entire application. I have tied up with eBay. They are ready to host us. It is just a click away. You click this tab and we go online. It's a bidding process. I am sure the figure Professor Batki said can be achieved and even more.

Vikram's solution will become the professor's problem. He isn't ready for this. His interest lies in the NGO, whereas Vikram is proposing to eliminate the middlemen. The NGO is the middle agency. If the council approves his recommendations and the institute decides to transfer the money directly to the potter's account, the NGO becomes redundant. How would this affect the professor, and eventually his wife, is what we need to develop.

We are more than halfway through the film. It's a big relief to be out of the web of research and being able to concise it in 60-odd pages. It feels like I was drowning and struggling to somehow come above the water and breathe. Just once. Breathe. But the real challenge begins now. One has to now swim across the ocean and there is no horizon in sight, forget a seashore.

'Professor rejects Vikram's ideas.'

We decide to take a two-day break. For creative detox.

24. Left Out

In India, people fight with all their might to kill an idea. The privileged people. The biggest problem with our establishment is that it has no space for a new idea. Art, cinema, and media haven't developed enough to present new ideas for adoption. They are engaged in the politics of survival and therefore the outcome is mediocre and very often regressive. Most of the ideas are perceived as dissent. As disruption. As treason. Sometimes ideas like Naxalism, become violent and seditious. Despite being a democracy, in our country there is very little room for an alternate narrative. Whenever a child comes up with an innovative idea, parents, neighbours, teachers, and society crush the idea by telling him *'Kyon apna waqt barbad karte ho, yahan kuch nahin hone wala–* don't waste your time.' It can't be that all of them are idiots. They speak from their experience. *'Aise hi chalta hai… don't be stupid '…. Nothing is going to change… you don't know their power.'*

Everyone is surviving because of illegalities and corruption. Everyone is, directly or indirectly, a part of the nexus. A new idea challenges and threatens this *status quo*. In such a hopeless and defeated society, the only way one can nurture his idea is either with muscle or by leaving the country. Majority of the population can't do either. Which is why the huge volume of these 'left out people' find their ideas crushed by a monstrous system which feeds on the blood and bones of innocent dreams.

Vikram Pundit has also become one of them. He questions Charu's silence on the professor's rejection of his brilliant idea. Especially when she claims to work for the Adivasis' cause.

'Wasn't it your fucking job to help Adivasis?'

Charu shows her helplessness.

Sheetal questions Batki's real motive.

'After a showdown with the professor, she shuts down The Potters' Club.'

This shuts Vikram's hope.

The professor questions Vikram and doubts his integrity. He tells Vikram that he was asked to make a marketing presentation but this had political undertones.

'I won't let you actualize your political ambitions.'

Vikram is left cornered. Alone. Helpless. Like any disruptive idea.

Rohit and I don't know how he should react. In a normal film, the hero will take law into his own hands. We decide that Vikram will go ahead with the eBay auctions and take on the system directly.

Rohit is so frustrated that he doesn't even write the proper description. He writes:

'Vikram fucks the system.'

On this note, we shut shop for the day.

I am fast asleep when Rohit calls me. It's past midnight. Our relationship is beyond time and space. So, I pick up the phone.

'Sir, what if Vikram actually fucks the system.'

'Of course. That's what we decided.'

'No sir, I mean he actually does it. What does any young boy do when he is angry and frustrated? When he thinks injustice has been done to him? He drinks and he has sex.'

'This is a long discussion, let's talk tomorrow.'

'Sir, I'll just take two minutes. What if instead of him launching the web auction, he goes to a whore and while in the act he figures out the politics of the professor and the establishment?'

I sit up and take a deep breath.

'Wait.'

I try to visualize. It's crude. Subliminally violent. Shocking. And disturbing.

'Let's put cheap posters of gods all over the room,' I tell Rohit.

'Vikram fucks a whore called the system.'

25. Lal Salaam

The Naxals do not tolerate critics. People who criticize them for killings, extortion or other abuses suffer threats and warnings. According to one local activist, 'The Maoists kill people, saying that they are police informers. They killed one man, who was doing good work on health and education, because he had a cell phone, and was, therefore, a police informer. Everyone has a cell phone these days. Will they kill everyone?'

So great is the fear of Naxals that most of the activists did not wish to be identified when they described threats and abuses. Said one tribal activist from Chhattisgarh:

'This is a fight over tribal land. All of them, the Maoists, security forces, companies, and government are there for their own benefit. Why are the Naxals in our area? For us? No! Not for us. They want our jungles for hideouts. The government–Salwa Judum– too never cared for us, they just don't want the Naxals. All they care about is what lies beneath our soil, the minerals. When we speak for the tribal rights, they get angry. They don't care about the people who live on the land. They only care about money.'

In the script, we have reached a point what in Hollywood parlance is called plot point number three. It's time to open the cards.

'In a kangaroo court, the Naxal leader orders to kill a government official for he hasn't given permission for a pipeline. The contractor, local police officer, and Salwa Judum officers are all part of it.'

A jeep arrives as the officer is shot. From the jeep steps out our professor and Charu. The professor, the Naxal leader, and Charu's NGO work in tandem to further their war on the State. The leader says that commissions have been committed and money has to be organized.

We detail out the mechanics and dynamics of this complex nexus. All my research on urban Naxalism and its *modus operandi* become the basis for this chapter.

The Naxal leader warns the professor that Vikram's idea of web auction will empower the tribal and that is against their strategy. He tells the professor about the Politburo's decision.

'Ask Vikram to stop it or kill Vikram.'

Charu is assigned the job of kidnapping Vikram with his laptop and bring him to the jungles where the leadership will take a call. Obviously, kill him.

This was the most challenging chapter so far. I am happy that we cracked it. I am proud that every single line in this chapter is authentic. It's so honest that after reading it, my assistant says that she can't trust anyone anymore. We know we have cracked it.

'Professor gives his cap to a young tribal kid and says "Lal Salaam". The naked kid salutes him back and screams "Lal Salaam".'

26. Blink

We now know that the professor is an Urban Naxal who uses Charu's NGO to route funds to arm Naxals in Bastar where they use it to run their mafia in tandem with the businessmen, contractors, police, Salwa Judum, and NGOs. The professor has used his wife and Vikram for this seditious act. Vikram's idea to empower the tribal has jeopardized their work of thirty years.

The plan is to kidnap Vikram and eliminate him.

Sheetal is the moral fulcrum of the film. She gets to know about the plan. She reveals it to Vikram.

'They are everywhere. Anyone can be a Naxal. If my husband can be a Naxal then your father can also be a Naxal. So, run. Run away.'

We are tempted to use action. But action costs money. We are still fifty lacs over the budget. I think of innovative ideas to make these moments experiential for the audience. I want them to feel exactly how Vikram would feel. I want the audience to become Vikram. Because in reality, we are Vikram Pundits. Escaping from terror, protecting ourselves from their ruthless attacks.

Kabir Kala Manch is the Naxals' urban cultural arm. It's time to pay a tribute to it. I decide to use it metaphorically. We set this chapter in the background of a cultural evening where a revolutionary play is staged by the students who are all protégés of the professor.

When Sheetal asks Vikram to run away he is faced with the biggest of human tragedies. He can't trust anyone. Should he run away from this deceitful, ugly, bloody world which wants to suck him up or confront them? If he confronts them what would be his weapon? A weapon or his courage? What if instead of running away, Vikram surrenders to Charu and thus, tests both his and her character to discover the truth at both ends? Humanity can't be fully dead. There must be some conscience. Some feelings. Some hope.

We test it out.

27. The Tao of Revolution

'Revolution is not a dinner party,' Mao had said. Yes, it indeed is not. What matters is how one looks at the revolution. To Naxals, revolution is about hoisting their red flag atop Red Fort. Mao had believed that if in the process innocents have to bleed it's justified for a larger purpose of revolution.

What is the purpose of this film? Is it just to expose the nexus?

I am not a textbook filmmaker. I didn't come here because there was a vacancy. There was no 'wanted' ad. I came here out of my own free will. Because I wanted to learn. Learn about the difficulties of human life and its solutions. I am not sure if I'll ever be close to understanding it all in this lifetime, but this profession of filmmaking has often taken me on a path of self-discovery. At this stage in life, I have learnt through experience that there is no higher human need than hope. Hope makes us believe in people. In ideas. In life.

Vikram surrenders himself to Charu. With no hope.

I have experienced that when confronted with honesty and courage, even the worst of the people tend to show their goodness. Charu believes in Naxalism because that's what she has learnt from the professor who represents India's biggest challenge – intellectual terrorism.

It's her moment of realization.

We use this moment as cinematic poetry. We make Vikram and Charu merge. The future CEO and the social worker. The victim and the murderer. The threatened and the threat. It's expressed through a poetic lovemaking scene. They become one.

But, in the end, one has to die for the other to survive.

In a clever move, Charu dons the bomb-laden vest and blows herself up over the kangaroo court – the establishment – and leaves behind goodness. Humanity. Hope.

'Charu sacrifices her life to save an idea called Vikram.'

28. Epilogue

'The only point in creating something is to watch it die. Like a story that must come to a climax, what I have done will not be fulfilled until the end has arrived.'

- Brandon Sanderson, The Hero of Ages

The climax is the most challenging part of any film. After two hours of viewing, all that the audience takes back is the climax of a film. This is where a lot of films fail. I am nervous like hell.

So many ideas are floating in my mind. I am thinking about all the great climaxes. I want to be inspired and make the climax scene kickass. I am conflicted inside. I am frustrated and my ego is not letting me surrender to any idea. It's like I am on ninety-nine in a game of cricket and want to score my century by hitting the ball out of the stadium.

We know that Vikram has to kill the professor. Kill the revolution. But every idea we think of has been used in some film or the other. That's all we have done in the climax of Bollywood films, either made the boy win the girl or made the hero kill the villain.

In the meantime, Mr. Anupam Kher's manager Bhaskar Shetty calls me and fixes up a meeting with Mr. Kher and I have no climax. I can't narrate the film without a climax.

Almost a week is gone and we are running absolutely out of time. Tomorrow is my meeting with Mr. Kher. We give up. I call Bhaskar Shetty to cancel the meeting. He doesn't pick up. I leave a message.

With heavy hearts, Rohit and I leave for the day.

I am driving back home. My house is less than a kilometre away from my office. When I shifted here in Versova on the eve of the millennium, it used to take me less than five minutes to reach home. Now it takes anywhere between twenty to twenty-five minutes. Somebody must calculate the value of time wasted in traffic and deduct it from the GDP. Everything is irritating me. The metro construction, the traffic, the roads, the honking, and the heat. As I wait, I notice a blind beggar singing a Mukesh song *'Sajan re jhoot mat bolo, khuda ke paas jaana hai, wahan na hathi na ghora hai, wahan paidal hi jana hai' —we all go to God on foot*. I am from the Kishore Kumar era. I never liked this song despite its wonderful lyrics. But this the beggar's song has touched me somewhere. Is it his voice? His expressions? His involvement? His oneness with the song? Or my frame of mind? Or all of the above? I open the window. Hot air brushes against my cheeks. My SUV fills with blaring sounds – honking, screaming vendors, the metro's construction, *azaan,* and his singing. Slowly, every other sound fades off and all that remains is his soulful singing. I find my song.

'Rohit, wherever you are, turn away and come home. I have understood our problem. So far, I was trying to impress and not express. All we need to do is express exactly how we feel, not what we think. '

People are honking badly. One auto driver is even abusing me in Marathi. I didn't even realize that the traffic in front of me had moved and I was standing there blocking everyone and causing a traffic jam.

Though his song made me cause a traffic jam, it has in fact cleared the traffic jam of my mind.

Pallavi brings chilled beer and *shami kebabs*. She makes really good *shami kebabs.*

'Garam garam hain, kha lo,' she tells me.

'Yeah, give me two minutes.'

Rohit has a young daughter and he wants to get her admission in the same school as my kids. Pallavi becomes the counsellor for the evening.

I open my laptop. I have no need to impress anyone anymore. I just want to express. Why should my hero kill the villain? Because everyone does that? What will a hero who wants to disrupt a corrupt system do? What would a man of ideas do?

Only an idea can kill an idea. I have got my climax.

He won't take out a gun. He would take out an iPad and with his app he will connect the tribal with the world market and bring in money to his doorstep. I had read that all value systems are functions of the economic system. Money in the tribal's hand will be an economic revolution which will destroy the Naxal armed revolution. An idea will kill an idea. A revolution will kill a revolution.

In the next twenty minutes, I type out a seven-page climax full of the professor's monologues on revolution and just one page of dialogues for Vikram who makes the professor surrender to his idea.

And, finally, I write: *The End.*

Beer is hot. Kebabs are cold and chewy. I still relish them. I had heard that a content man can sleep anywhere. Yes, and a content filmmaker can eat anything.

Before closing the laptop, I delete 'The End' and write:

'Revolution is not a dinner party' - Mao

29. Casting: The Art and the Science

They say writing a script is half the battle won. Once you start casting, you learn that the real battle has begun now.

Casting is an art. It's a science too. More of political science. Actors don't sign a film only on the merit of the film or their character. Films are signed for a variety of reasons. Someone needs money to buy a car, someone wants to send his child abroad for education. Some need to buy a bungalow. Some want to earn credibility and awards. Some want to prove themselves. Some want to do it because a competing actor is doing something similar. Some just want to have fun. As a director, one has to know the actor's current needs. In Bollywood, when nothing works, relationships do but it takes years to gain an actor's confidence and forge a relationship.

I am going to cast the professor first – Anupam Kher.

Back in the late 90s, when I wanted to diversify from ad filmmaking to directing television shows, Kher *saab* gave me a platform. It was a brief meeting at 7 AM in a five-star hotel's gym. He finished quickly and asked me to join him in his car. In a half an hour ride he agreed to produce my serial and also agreed to my financial expectations. My first serial was called *Yeh Kahan Aa Gaye Hum*. It was a musical thriller, for almost all episodes had songs and it boasted of being India's first digital TV show (in those times U-matic and Betacam were in fashion) and a stellar star cast consisting of Pallavi Joshi, Nikki Aneja, Girish Malik, Renuka Shahne, Makrand Deshpande, Rohini Hattangadi, Tinu Anand, Sulbha Deshpande and many young TV stars. There was a tall boy who I had seen struggling to work in Pallavi's earlier serial *Aarohan*. I had liked him a lot, so I cast him in a leading role. He later became a superstar in the South. He was R. Madhavan.

The pilot got approved by *Hindustan Times* group's Home TV. Home TV was headed by Karan Thapar, who had a concept of how a CEO of an entertainment channel should behave and dress up but he had no idea about the qualities a CEO must possess. He spoke only about two things: himself, and himself. With my management background, it was easy for me to predict the fate of the channel. In the several meetings that I had with Karan, I could sense that his reason for commissioning the serial had nothing to do with its content but with the fact that he wanted to use it as a bait for Kher *saab* to do a chat show for his channel.

In those days, film celebrities weren't keen on doing TV and Karan was going out of his way to persuade Kher *saab*. These were my first learnings in the film industry. I learnt that the content is secondary and personal benefits are supreme. I also learnt that the celeb media men actually are the middlemen who can go to any extent to get their work done. Once he got Kher *saab* committed to a chat show, Karan's behaviour changed. For one of the meetings, which could have been done on phone, he insisted that I meet him in his Delhi office. I had read Eric Berne's *Games People Play* several times and I knew that he was trying to change the equation by changing the territory. He made us wait for hours – the first sign of territorial assertion. Finally, we met him. He was dressed like a typical *bada saheb* from the colonial era with a twist in the colours. He wore a greyish suit and a bow with pink stars. His socks were fluorescent pink and yellow with parrot green polka dots. He spoke at length about how he wanted to revolutionize Indian TV. Every wannabe has a role model. In Karan's case, it was BBC. He told me that my serial was of BBC standard but it had a problem which he wanted to fix.

'Vivek, I like the serial but I have a problem with the casting,' Karan took me by surprise.

'But this is the best casting possible… it's like a casting coup.'

'Rest are fine, but I don't like Pallavi.'

'What? Really?'

'Yeah, change Pallavi.'

'Why? She is a TV star and national award winner. She is one of the best we have got.'

'But she is dark. I want someone fair,' Karan said without hesitation.

I couldn't believe that this discriminatory statement came from a leading journalist. I stared at his fluorescent yellow socks with parrot green polka dots for a few seconds and thought to myself that despite being the watchdogs of a dark, dirty, and discriminatory democracy, our top journalists like to remain in a Fair & Lovely world.

'Goodbye, Mr. Thapar'.

As expected, Karan shelved the serial. In times like these, producers choose to side with the channels. Kher *saab* stood by me. And it was his unconditional support that helped me get the serial commissioned by Zee TV within the next few days. *Yeh Kahaan* came to be known as one of the most stylish serials ever. During that period, I learnt a lot from Kher *saab*, especially his positive attitude and fearlessness, and made a bond for life.

I am driving to his office with two doubts: that the character is negative and that my total casting budget is less than what one major character actor took in my other films.

'Let me warn you it's a negative character,'

'I have no issues with negative characters. Some of my best roles are negative.'

'Yes, I know, but it's not that kind of negative.'

This catches his attention.

I narrate the script to him. He listens quietly. Narration is a very tricky task. In Bollywood, stars don't read scripts. They mostly listen to narrations. Narrating a film to a star is something almost every director hates. Stars are so bored, so uninvolved that every moment feels like death. I have never understood why stars are so uninterested in their core job. But actors like Kher *saab* are a delight to narrate the script to. Good actors always sit like a learner. They want to learn from the director, his vision, his motivation, his reason. They are involved. They react. They don't judge.

I finish the narration in precisely forty-five minutes. Experienced actors decide in the first ten minutes of the narration. As soon as I finish, he takes a deep breath and relaxes in his chair.

'*Kya aatma ki shanti ke liye bana rahe ho?*'

'Don't know about soul but I am making it because truth must be told... that's all I know at this moment.'

'*Marwaoge,*' he smiled in his typical style and added, '*Punditji*, I am doing your film.'

'Thank you, Kher saab.'

I have learnt that once someone buys your sales pitch, you should leave immediately. My problem is I want to request him to give me a discount on his price and I don't know how to approach the subject. Finally, I give in.

As I am about to leave, he stops me.

'Vivek, don't worry about money. I'll talk to Bhaskar. You must know why I want to do this film. I want to do this film because I can see the hunger in you. In every director's life comes a point when he finds his *sur*, his song. This film is your song. I can feel it.'

I am speechless. Not because of the praise. I have no words to describe the feeling when a creative person understands your inner voice.

Bhaskar calls me at night. Instead of negotiating any fees with me, he asks me to give whatever we could afford.

'In fact, Kher saab said that if there is anything we can do to help you make this film, please do not hesitate to ask.'

Anupam Kher is a good man and such moments are rare in this industry. I am going to cherish it and miss him, especially at times when I am going to miss good men.

It's time to crack other casting options. We don't have money for a casting director so we start casting ourselves. My assistants are extremely resourceful. We audition Rajkumar Rao, Deepak Dobrial and many other young and emerging actors for the role of Vikram Pundit but none fit the bill. We need someone who looks very urban, US-returned and a bit un-Indian in approach but very believable and dependable at the same time. When in the climax, he holds the professor's neck, people should believe that he is going to kill him instantly.

It's 8 PM and I am getting audition diarrhea. We have a problem. When I joined this industry, people used to say about stars, '*Kya acting hai*'. Now they say, '*Kya body hai*'. Most of these aspiring actors have the same body, same body language, same stance, and same mannerisms. They have the same routine: Get up, drink protein, go to a gym, drink protein, eat protein, run, swim, drink protein, eat protein. In the process, they have become proteins. A muscular mass of protein. They are muscular but weak. They are handsome with zero personality. They are trendy but style-less. They look dehydrated. They feel lifeless. If they have to be cast in a modern *Amar Akbar Anthony*, we won't be able to tell who is Amar and who is Anthony.

The ones who are great actors don't look like they belong to ISB. They fit more in a government college. Students in ISB have worked for a couple of years in big multinational corporations and their entire conduct is like that of a senior corporate executive.

I have decided not to compromise on the casting for this film. Why make this film at all? But time doesn't care about rules and we have no time. Just one week. It's almost midnight. I remember I have to go to a party. Bollywood parties begin after midnight.

In general, I don't like parties. Besides being too noisy and fake, they also screw up the next day. But in times like these, when I am failing to solve a problem, such parties help me de-stress and get a break from the problem.

WTF is one of the most popular open-air bars in Versova. Close to the beach, it also has an enclosed air-conditioned cabin with loud music on most days and karaoke on some days. It's frequented mostly by the film and advertising crowd. It's the kind of a place you get addicted to.

I give my keys to the valet. As I am about to enter the small Mediterranean door of WTF, someone yells my name. I turn around and find Shanoo Sharma. Shanoo tells me that she has started her own casting agency and she is casting for Sudhir Mishra, Dharma Productions, and Yash Raj Films. I had met her long back in a beach party of one of my assistants. She came across as a real Bohemian with tattoos, piercings and zero size hair. She struck me with her liveliness and laughter. She is Mukesh's granddaughter. She is the kind of personality you can't forget for life. I had liked her instantly and she always met me with warmth and affection. Her growth always made me happy as I love to work with energetic, happy and mad people. I tell her about my film and how I am still struggling to find my hero, heroine, and other main characters. She asks me if she could recommend a few names.

'Of course, That would be great.'

'Tell me something about your character.'

'I'll call you, let's party now.'

'Don't you worry sir; the party won't begin until I am in there. You tell me.'

'But I don't have money to pay you.'

'Let the money not stop you from great casting. You don't have to pay me anything. Just tell me.'

I briefly describe my characters to her. As soon as I finish she stubs her cigarette and her eyes light up.

'I will send two people you can't say no to. They are made for this film.'

'Really, do I know them?'

'Perhaps not. For the hero, you trust me with your eyes closed… there is this boy, he is just back from the USA… Indian boy, did college there… he is a politician's grandson… he has done a film *Yeh Saali Zindagi* with Sudhir sir… the movie is releasing soon. He will do justice to this role… he is just perfect.'

'But I don't have…'

'Sir, don't bother about money,' she interrupts. 'That's secondary… whatever you can afford you tell me… he isn't money-minded… also, he listens to me.'

His name is Arunoday Singh, she tells me.

'And the girl also I'll send… she hasn't done much besides a "blink and miss" role in Bhansali's *Guzaarish* but you trust me she is very good. She fits in this role to the T. Her name is Swara Bhaskar.'

I don't know either of them. But instantly my struggle is over. Struggle isn't a physical exercise. It's a mindset.

'Tell me what time and I'll send both of them for an audition. You meet them and be proud of me.'

'Thanks, Shanoo.'

'For the heroine, let me think and I'll get back to you.'

'I owe you. Let's go in and party.'

We move towards the door. She walks in but I stop at the door.

Suddenly, I don't want to party. I am feeling relaxed after a long time. I am hopeful. I know in my guts that this party can only disturb that. I call the valet and ask him to get my car. As I wait for the car I realize two things:

One, whatever quality this industry produces is because of people like Shanoo who want good films to be made. It's due to the indirect contribution of such people that we make some good films. When your intent to make a good film is firm, you start attracting such people in your ecosystem. The people we find in our lives are there to help us actualize an intent.

Two, I have met Shanoo only outside bars.

I get up late. After a long time, I have slept well. There is a message from Shanoo asking me for a time to meet these actors. I fix up post lunch meetings.

For Charu's character, I need a face which reflects both; her buoyancy as well as the pain. She should be compassionate. She should be ruthless. Both require intensity. Maturity.

I remember the face of a girl from Rakesh Omprakash Mehra's Dilli 6, who never speaks in the film but carries a lot of pain around her. She portrayed it with a kind of numbness which I had found very interesting. I ask one of my assistants to google her. He tells me her name is Aditi Rao Hyadri and he can reach her. Aditi is a vibrant girl and also a trained dancer. A background in dancing always helps as it brings in rhythm in the actor's movements. We do four-five auditions with her and with each audition, she appears better. I am keen to cast her but her managers have quoted a fee which is illogical, unrealistic and way beyond our budget. A lot of talented actors have not succeeded despite goodwill and critical acclaim because of wrong financial strategies. What they don't realize is that in the business of movies, your price is directly proportional to your ability to sell tickets.

I am told that Arunoday has reached. I look at my watch. He is bang on time. Punctuality is my weakness and I already like him. When Arunoday enters my room, I keep looking at his height. There are tall people and then there are some people who stand tall. My second connect is that he is also from Bhopal. He is the grandson of Congress veteran, the late Arjun Singh, and son of the leader of Madhya Pradesh's main opposition party, Congress. He is a very sophisticated man with a half-Americanized accent. He tells me that his only ambition is to do films with balls and meaning. This is my final connect. I ask him to listen to the script and send him to Rohit's room.

After a couple of hours, Rohit brings him to my room.

'So, what do you think?'

'I am doing the film.'

'There are some explicit scenes and I am looking for someone who does them naturally, unlike typical Indian films where both the actors look conscious, clinical, and apologetic.'

'Of course, I understand that. That's the only way.'

'I'll need time for readings and workshops.'

'Of course.'

'All of us will be staying in hostels at ISB.'

'That would be wonderful.'

'It will be hard work as we will be shooting overtime.'

'I understand.'

'I don't know if Shanoo told you we are working on a shoestring budget.'

'No issues. You pay me whatever you can afford.'

I lean back in my chair and take a deep breath. I realize I have put all my cards on the table.

'Is there anything you would want to ask?' I ask him.

'Yes, when do we start?'

In the last one week, Satya, my associate director and editor, has auditioned more than a hundred people for the small but very important roles of the Naxal leader and the Salwa Judum official. Both the characters have to speak in their native language and must look like they haven't been out of the jungles in ages. He shows me shortlisted tests but none are working. Most of them are too urban with big biceps. Those who are good actors look well-fed and successful. The film begins with both these characters and the actors will have to hold the scene for almost fifteen minutes. You can't just select anybody as the opening batsman.

'Is that all we have?' I ask Satya, despairingly.

'Yeah. In the given budget and the timeframe, that's all we have,' Satya replies.

I notice there are three folders on the desktop: 1. Shortlisted, 2. Rejected, and 3. De-stress.

'What is in 'de-stress'? I ask Satya.

'Means when you are totally fucked up in mind and depressed, just open this folder, play any audition, fall down on the floor laughing and that's how you get de-stressed.'

Assistants work very hard and under tremendous stress. That's why they invent their own clever ways to unwind. This is Satya's way of unwinding by looking at the auditions of really bad actors who fumble, get nervous and make funny faces and deliveries.

'Play the funniest one. I need to de-stress.'

Satya plays the tape of an actor called Indel Raja, a very short, misshaped man with curly hair and a certain madness around him. He auditions with Shah Rukh's flair, Rajkumar's arrogance and an accent which only his mother could understand. This fusion of styles is so funny that one can't just stop laughing. Other assistants also come in to participate in this laugh riot. I am feeling lighter after laughing for the five minutes of audition. Then, something strikes me. 'Why do we laugh when we meet real people?'

This man can easily be an RTO officer or a food inspector in a village in Chattisgarh. He is perfect for that role. Why can't he be a Salwa Judum official? A man who has always lived in the jungles and has no urban influence would look funny in an urban setting. I ask everyone to shut up and play the tape again. The 'De-stress' folder literally de-stressed me. I also find my Naxal leader in an actor called Gopal Singh. He is in the 'de-stress' folder too for he is very skinny and tall. Since the assistants see only well-built people for auditions, they found him very funny. The sad part of the film business is that we spend so much time with the unreal that when faced with the reality, we find it funny. His lanky figure is my asset. Normal thinking dictates a Naxal leader to be like a dacoit – well-built and strong. I know that these Naxals have to survive for weeks on red ant chutney. Gopal's skinny frame becomes his asset. Indel's ruralness becomes his asset. One never knows when his weaknesses can become his assets. I have found both my actors. They say God lies in details. I learn that sometimes God lies in the third folder.

My next meeting is with Swara.

When I meet Swara I remember that I know her. Sometime back when I had gone to Film & Television Institute of India's (FTII) Golden Jubilee function as a panellist speaker, Swara was assisting the organizers. She came across as a strong, energetic, and hard-working person. I remember, on the closing night, she sang revolutionary songs, which at that time I didn't know were propaganda songs of Naxals. In a night of unlimited drinks and music, everyone joined in chorus when Swara sang Faiz Ahmad Faiz's revolutionary song on freedom, now the anthem of Naxals, popularized by the Naxals' cultural front in urban India, Kabir Kala Manch, and its arms:

Bol, ke lab azaad hai tere,
Bol, zabaan ab tak teri hai,
Tera sutwan jism hai tera,
Bol, ke jaan ab tak teri hai.

Speak, for your lips are free,
Speak, for your tongue is still yours.
Your upright body is still yours,
Speak, for your life is still yours.

Swara is here to be auditioned for Pooja's character. Pooja represents the urban tribal – the marginalized, lost and forgotten urban population which is exploited by everyone. She represents the majority of our girls who are constantly being bullied, shunned and exploited by everyone, irrespective of their financial strata. Pooja is a moneyed kid, who hangs around with MBA students whereas she herself isn't chasing any career. She has no focus on her own life. She has no views, no opinions, and no direction. She is going nowhere. She is an urban tribal.

Swara is just the opposite of Pooja. Swara is strong, opinionated, focussed, aggressive and in control of her life. Though Shanoo has recommended her very strongly, I am not sure how she will portray the meek character of Pooja. Swara is very excited about the theme of Naxalism and believes that more films must be made on this subject. I ask her to listen to the script and send her to Rohit's cabin for a complete narration.

Rohit comes to my room after a while. Looking at his face I know something is bothering him.

'Sir, she has too many questions.'

'So, answer them.'

'Sir, more than the script she is questioning the system, the State, the society...how can I answer them?'

'That's her right. You don't have to convince her but you must explain your point of view.'

'I did all that but she doesn't look happy.'

I am keen to cast her as she is a good performer and is willing to work for the budgeted fees. I know it's impossible to get someone like her for that money. But Rohit is dead against her. I ignore Rohit's doubts as a writer's ego. Yes, writers don't like actors who ask too many questions.

Swara tells me that though she loved the subject, a few things are fundamentally wrong.

'For example?' I ask her.

'It's the State, the government which is responsible for the Naxal movement... that's what I feel.'

'Yeah, it's like saying parents are responsible for everything... isn't that obvious reasoning? Is there any onus on the children for the failure?'

We discuss politics for hours. She doesn't discuss the script with me but I can see that she is not very comfortable with our stance on Naxalism. It's rare to meet politically aware actors in Bollywood and I love to discuss politics. Rohit's stress is my delight. She asks me many questions about the production, marketing, and the music.

'I can introduce you to a very talented music director... his name is Rohit Sharma and he has already done music for an upcoming film called *Ship of Theseus*.'

'Sure, I am looking for offbeat music directors. Can you send him tomorrow?'

She calls and fixes up a meeting with Rohit Sharma.

'Rohit Sharma, a few more of our friends and I run a small band called Swang,' Swara informs me.

I figure out that this band mostly performs anti-establishment and pro-Naxal songs. Over extended meetings, I learn that Swara's mother heads the film department at JNU. She has grown up in JNU, listening to a certain narrative. Now it's easy for me to understand her stance.

In the last few days, we have had several meetings with Swara's manager. Each time he comes up with some new clause in the contract. I have been accommodating her considering that she wants to be secure but it rings a bell when her manager comes up with an unreasonable demand. There is a very cute scene in the film where Vikram and Pooja visit the professor's house for dinner. Pooja has given up drinking but eventually gets tempted and gets sloshed. At some point, she finds a statement by the professor so cute that she gets up and kisses him on his bald head. In the normal course, this would go unnoticed but Swara's manager wants us to commit in the contract that she would be kissing Kher saab only on his forehead and nowhere else. I argue with him that, but naturally she can't smooch him on the lips so it has to be an affectionate kiss to an elderly person. But he insists. I like to believe that I am chilled out and an accommodating director, but I am feeling uneasy with his illogical demand. I decide to call Swara. She is apologetic and blames the manager. Rohit keeps reminding me that her attitude is not in tune with our style of filmmaking. He doesn't want people with questions but wants people who have answers. I sign her up.

I have to yet cast for Charu and the professor's wife's character. Who can be my Charu? I start researching the castings of indie films. A lot of actors I like have a thick Maharashtrian accent. I want a thick Punjabi accent. I stop at Richa Chaddha. I meet her but she is not available on our dates. I call Huma Quereshi. Huma is family as she is distantly related to me. She had sent me her amateurish photo profile from Delhi. When she came to Mumbai I cast her for a film which eventually got shelved. She has grown up in Delhi and has a typical accent. She is a promising and talented actor and suits the character.

Sometimes we take things for granted. I had assumed that she would have all the time available but when I call her she informs me that she would be shooting for Anurag Kashyap's *Gangs of Wasseypur* in those months. Suddenly, there is a blank. I have run out of my options. I think about the myriad possibilities this industry offers. Anurag wrote *Goal* for me. I remember the fights we had. I remember, on the annual sports day of our children, who go to the same school and are in the same class, Anurag looked extremely happy as his first big film *Dev.D* was going to release. In that entire one hour that we spent watching our kids run and jump, he kept repeating that it's his first commercial film. It was bothering him that the industry doesn't perceive him as a commercially viable director. I remember how I sent a message to him during the interval. What had struck me was the heroine of the film, Mahie Gill.

Why not Mahie Gill?

Mahie enters with a smile, which keeps becoming bigger and more beautiful. Mahie's smile is innocent and her body language very sensuous. Her rawness is her sex appeal. She is a *desi* woman, simple and happy. Unlike most of the women stars who always look hassled and dissatisfied with life and irritated with people. Mahie tells me that she had been wanting to work with me and she had also auditioned for *Goal.* I feel guilty for not remembering such a talent. She likes the character; she is free on those dates and is willing to accept whatever money I offer her. For a moment I feel as if God is playing a prank on me. This perhaps is the easiest casting in a journey full of struggle, hardship, and hurdles. I know, in Mahie, I have found a friend for life.

We still have to cast for Sheetal, the professor's wife. For Sheetal, I had met a couple of reputed senior actresses but they were not willing to compromise on their fees. It is also true that they would cut their fees if the banner, director, and hero are big. In our case, all three are small players. In Bollywood, stars don't support small, meaningful cinema. They are more inclined to support a leave-your-brains-at-home kind of cinema, if only it can be called cinema. I wasn't surprised at all when this tall, sultry, award-winning actress who has done a lot of commercial films but is known for her arty roles, told me that all she cares about is money and if I could get her the desired money I don't even have to bother about narrating the story or the character to her.

It's a nuanced role that deserves an experienced actor who can subtly draw the line between her outgoing, flirtish behaviour and her deep empathy for a cause. I don't have many choices. In fact, none.

I have many guests at home. My house parties are famous for long discussions on films, politics and spirituality, and Bhopali meat. Very often, these discussions turn into arguments. Today's argument is about the CWG and 2G scams. Like always, it shifts from politics to films. I am always at the centre of any discussion but today I am just not interested. It's like noise. I am thinking about my immediate problems at hand. How do I adjust the fifty-lac gap in the budget and where do I find my Sheetal? I excuse myself and shift to my study and start juggling with the budget on my laptop. Knowing well that this exercise won't lead me anywhere. I am dejected, frustrated and stressed.

I call Ravi and tell him that there is no way I can cut down the budget.

'Should I stop casting? What's the point if we can't afford these actors?' I share my worries with Ravi.

'No, Vivek, we just can't do that.'

'How can you have the cake and eat it too? Either you can have these actors or the budget.'

'What do you think we should do?'

'There is no point making a film on this subject if the audience can't invest in the characters and therefore the actors become crucial for the film to communicate with the audience.'

My problem is what should be the problem of any filmmaker: how to communicate through casting? All the research, hard work, creativity, scripting and money go waste if the cast is not right. Good casting can sometimes save even a bad film but not the other way around.

Outside, in the family room, everyone has shifted from politics to singing. The entire house is filled with the sound of harmonium, *madal* and drunk chorus.

'Vivek, you go ahead with the casting, I'll write to all ISB alumni and more AIKYA families. I'll also try for sponsors but you go ahead, I'm sure something will work out,' Ravi tries to assure me.

'What if nothing works out?' I ask Ravi.

'We haven't come thus far to stop here. We have come thus far to go further,' Ravi tells me.

I realize it's true. Our ego makes us believe that we are designing and plotting things. Whereas we are just following a design. If we are following a design, then the design exists in totality. All we have to do is just follow. Flow. But we let our egos take over and believe that by doing extra stuff we can create a new design. Or we feel that we can't complete the design and hence we quit. This happens because we are conditioned about how much time we should give to an effort. A salesman stops calling after three calls because that's how he has been conditioned during his training. We are conditioned to assume that if a student doesn't pass an exam in one attempt, he is a failure. Who knows if the salesman's design requires more than three calls? Who knows that the student has to attempt an exam more than once to pass? Who knows that in the design of this film, perhaps Suresh Chukapalli is not the only man to fund this project?

Suddenly, there is silence outside. I go out to check if everyone has left. I come out to find everyone engrossed in Pallavi's singing. She is singing Faiz Ahmad Faiz's revolutionary poem: *'Hum Dekhenge... Lazim hai ke hum bhi dekhenge, wo din ke jis ka wada hai, jo lauh-e-asal mein likha hai... hum dekhenge' We shall witness, it is certain that we too, shall witness the day that has been promised, of which has been written on the slate of eternity.*

This is one of my favourite *nazms* and it also has a nostalgic connect as it was introduced to me by a Pakistani girl whom I almost married. Besides being a poet and a great singer, she was a Communist and during Zia Ul Haq's tyrannical dictatorship she went underground and spent a lot of time with me in Delhi. When I had visited Lahore, she gave me a cassette with the live recording of this *nazm* sung by Iqbal Bano. Pallavi learnt this song from that recording I had saved despite the invasion of CDs. Pallavi notices me and smiles at me. Such moments, when a singer looks at you in the audience and without speaking, just with the eyes, communicates the highest form of sharing, are rare and beyond description. Such sharing is not just romantic, it's reassuring and soulful.

I sit down and surrender myself to amazing lyrics of Faiz and Pallavi's soulful voice. Slowly, all my stress and frustration is disappearing. Long after the song is over and others have started singing, I keep looking at Pallavi and wonder why was I looking for the diamond all over the planet when it was in my own house.

Why did I not think about casting Pallavi in Sheetal's role? After we got married, Pallavi decided to focus on our children and from working round the year without any break she cut it down to just shooting a day or two in a month. From a national award-winning actor and a busy star, she had chosen to become a wife and a mother. That was her choice but why did I choose to forget how fabulous an actor she is? In marriage, the biggest blunder we make is that we forget the core values of a person for which we marry him/her. I stand guilty.

I call Rohit to share my eureka moment.

'Sir, you will have a long life… I was about to call you as I got an idea,' Rohit tells me as soon as he picks up the phone.

'Even I called you as I've also got an idea,' I tell him, 'but you tell me first.'

'Sir, I was wondering what if Pallavi*ji* plays Sheetal?'

I just can't believe it. Ideas float in the universe. People who are tuned on to a certain intent catch those ideas, often at the same time. Both Rohit and I were focused on a problem and, therefore, we could get the same idea at the same time. Coincidence? Or the unfolding of a design?

It's not easy to convince Pallavi. She asks lots of questions, not to judge you but in order to understand the subject and the character. I know Rohit hates it but we have no other option. She is also reluctant to leave the kids with the domestic help for a thirty-day-long outdoor schedule. It takes a lot of convincing before Pallavi agrees to make a comeback in films. After marriage, this is the first time I am going to direct Pallavi. A rare opportunity for a husband to direct his wife. And a great opportunity to work with such an accomplished actor.

Finally, I have a cast in hand. I call it a day.

'Sir, what about the Adivasi?' Satya runs behind my car to remind me.

'You don't bother about him. I have already found him.'

'Who is he?'

I remember Buddhe, the Adivasi who had been my guide during the research. Nobody can understand what he speaks. It's impossible to direct him as he doesn't understand what we speak. But there is one thing that only he has. His eyes speak. Like an uncorrupted Adivasi.

The real Adivasi.

30. Music: The Third Eye of Cinema

My daughter was eleven years old then. Girls at that age are full of dreams and questions. She dreams of becoming a singer and she has questions about every film. In my friend circle, she is called the young critic. Listening to her review after watching movies is our post-screening ritual. Today, when we came out after watching a film with our group and after everyone opined that the film was pretty good, all she said was 'If it's really so good why did they have to fill it with blaring background music?' 'Why, what's wrong with the background music?' I asked. 'I think you need background music only when you can't say something with dialogue or performance,' she said.

Children's worldview is more creative yet more logical than us. We as adults accept lots of illogic and flaws as part of an imperfect life. The role of art should be to get us out of this gutter by showing us new perspectives, giving new insights and taking us to new universes and characters but, unfortunately, Indian cinema, barring a few spurts here and there, hasn't helped us learn new aspects of human behaviour and life per se. In fact, Bollywood has singularly contributed to the collective dumbing down, in collusion with the music companies. These companies are more thieves than music promoters, who have killed our rich music and replaced it with machine-made melodies. Over a period of time, resigned to the marketing bombarding, we have learnt to put up with inferior quality of cinema, music, and literature.

The best barometer to test this hypothesis is the children's reaction. Today's children do not endorse such crappy work because they have choices on YouTube, iTunes, myriad TV channels, and various other social media platforms. Quality doesn't exist in isolation. We understand quality only in comparison. We compare it with our own world, our own reality. When the quality of our world becomes uncreative and shallow, we start accepting substandard work. The children's world is full of imagination, creativity, discovery, exploration, and adventure. Hence, when they compare our art, especially cinema, they find it very illogical and mediocre.

Modern Bollywood music doesn't do anything to our senses besides making us tap our feet. It's very rare to find memorable melodies which linger and unravel their layers, slowly, like matured wine. The lyrics are empty and the arrangement is desperate to make us dance. The so-called emotional songs are neither emotional nor musical.

I have no scope for songs. Even if I want, I don't have the money. The excess budget of fifty lacs is always haunting me. At this point, I want to believe that if Ravi raised this much, he will surely raise another fifty. This is my only consolation. My only hope. I have only four lacs for the background music.

I have always given a lot of importance to music in all my works and spent good money on recording songs. In my first serial, *Yeh Kahan Aa Gaye Hum*, I did over a dozen great songs with Pipi and the great poet Yogesh*ji*. Pipi is Salil Chaudhary's son and an extremely talented music director. He got his name because when he was born Salilda was composing in the hills and a PP (Person to Person) trunk call had to be booked to inform him. Pipi and I started our careers together. My first ad film as a producer/director was also his first as music director. When I made the serial, I brought him on board for the music. Together, we introduced a lot of talent. Shankar Mahadevan used to sing jingles mostly and hadn't got his big break in Bollywood. We did a lot of songs with him.

In *Chocolate*, I forced Pritam to do a hard rock song called *Khalish,* written beautifully by Mayur Puri who was an associate director in *Dhoom* and had come to meet Pritam during one of our recordings. With *Chocolate*, his talent was explored and I am proud that today he is a top lyricist. In *Goal*, though *'Billo rani'* was a chartbuster, some of the other songs by Pritam and Javed Akhtar were experimental and presented some awesome music. Both the films had exceptional background scores and *Chocolate*'s score was so good that the music company insisted on including it in the album. Both the albums made lots of money for the producers and music companies. In this industry, very rarely do the creators earn money out of profits from their work. It's always the middlemen.

Rohit Sharma is a very simple man and very non-filmy. Looking at his simplicity, I decide to lay all my cards in front of him.

'I have no scope for music. I also don't have money. The film is in chapters and I want to use music just to bridge the chapters. I need ten bridges and I have only four lacs for it,' I tell Rohit, honestly.

Rohit is a shy man. He looks down, then smiles. It's more than a smile. When we don't know how to react, we smile like this. He takes a few sips of the tea. Smiles again.

'If you can tell me more, it will help me understand how much work is required,' Rohit says.

I start telling him more in detail about the bridges but soon I find myself narrating the entire script. The reason could be that he looks trustworthy and non-judgmental. It is not just a narration but a discussion. He is socially and politically very aware and understands poetry very well. After listening to the long narration, Rohit takes out a headphone and jacks it in his phone.

'Please, listen to this.' He plays a song on his phone.

The song begins with beatbox, humming, whistling and abstract scanning until the vocals begin. The song which plays is a famous Faiz Ahmad Faiz *nazm*:

'Yeh galliyon ke awara, bekar kutte,
Kaale, peele, neele sab rangdar kutte,
Ki baksha gaya jinko jauke gadai,
Zamane ki fatkar sarmaya inka,
Jahan bhar ki dutkar inki kamai,
Bus truck, train aur tramon mein,
Beshumaar kutte!
Das, bees, challis nahin, bhai, sau karore kutte!

Oh, these vagabond, useless street dogs,
Colourful in all hues - black yellow blue…
The pleasure of beggary is their sole inheritance,
The abuses of all, their one sole possession,
The curses of the world their only earning.
Buses, trains, trams are stuffed these countless dogs.
Ten, twenty, forty… Nay! One billion street dogs!

The song is in A cappella style – group singing without musical instruments, where singers create all the sounds. I like its rawness and the emphasis on the lyrics. Unlike Bollywood songs, here every word finds meaning. I know I want this song in my body of work. This is the first time in my career I have heard such an unusual composition. It's so good, so 'cool' and so 'zingy'.

'Sir, this is from our stage shows...I played it because this reflects the mood of your film,' Rohit tells me.

'I have no space for songs but I need this song. I may use it in the future, give me the first right of refusal,' I request Rohit.

'If you want, I can try some other stuff.'

I need this song. I am wondering where to use it in the film. There is no space. No money. But I am greedy.

'No, I want this.'

'Sir, I will have to talk to my other band members as we have been singing it for a long time and it's our performance's most popular song.'

'OK. Talk to them but make sure they agree.'

'If they don't, I will make better songs for you.'

'But I don't have space for songs.'

'But you have bridges...what if I create songs for those bridges which also help take the story forward and set the mood for the next chapter?'

I had not thought about it. It's not a bad idea. But money? I can't afford to get tempted. This is how budgets go haywire.

'I told you my budget. I can't raise it even by a penny,' I warn Rohit.

'What if I do the songs in the same amount?' Rohit tempts me.

'I am not a novice. It's not possible in this amount. You need an arranger, lyricists, singers, studios... impossible.'

'Sir, did you ever think that you can make a movie on such a shoestring budget? Still, you are making it possible because you want to do it badly, no? Similarly, I want to do it badly, so I will make it possible... I have my own studio, I arrange myself and most of the lyrics we write ourselves and we are a band so we sing also ourselves.'

I think for some time. Not about what Rohit just offered, but about my luck. Everyone in the industry believes that things happen not because you are talented but because you are lucky. They say that if you are lucky, you would meet the right person at the right time. I never experienced it, never understood it and never believed in it. But I was always curious about it. *'Is this that lucky moment?'* I wonder.

Rohit meets me again but this time with a tall gentleman with a deep baritone. His name is Ravinder Randhawa. He is Swara's live-in partner. Their band Swang primarily creates leftist music, about the oppression of the tribals, jungle, and *zameen*, and other forms of class struggle. I have heard such songs in Kabir Kala Manch's functions. Swara was singing some of these songs at the FTII golden jubilee function. After talking to Ravinder for some time, I realize that his politics is very clear in his head. He strongly believes in his radical leftist ideology and doesn't care about another point of view. Strangely, the way Rohit and Ravinder have interpreted the film is not what I am making. My idea is to expose such people who support, overtly or covertly, the Naxal movement and here I am sitting with such persons asking them to do music for my film. I am stuck in a very delicate situation.

'Look, I am not sure if you would like to work in this film as it's opposite of the ideology you follow,' I warn them.

'This is our professional work and that is our personal belief and we won't mix those two,' Ravinder and Rohit both speak almost together.

This is how we legalize hypocrisy. We write against the exploitation of women and at the same time we accept it in our workplace. The irony of Leftist intellectuals lies in its supporters like Ravinder. Here I am making a film to expose and crush Ravinder's personal beliefs with a powerful medium like a film and he is willing to contribute to my cause on the pretext of professional ethics. Most of our Leftist leaders and intellectuals do the same. They fight for the weak and the poor and use this for their personal materialistic growth. It is this hypocrisy, disguised as professionalism, that makes them so rich.

After a long meeting and exchange of ideas, I have realized that Rohit is a powerhouse of talent. So is Ravinder but I am not very comfortable with him as he is very reserved and doesn't smile. I can't trust people who don't smile from their hearts. A smile is the most natural human trait. When someone doesn't smile, he is behaving in an unnatural manner and one should be cautious of that. Leftists don't smile much, as if it's an ideological code. There are various codes that we follow. Some people stay away from non-veg food, whereas some avoid women at any cost. Nazis wore a stiff uniform and a stiff face. They never smiled. Similarly, I have observed that Leftists don't smile. They have only one expression on their frowning faces – anger. Together, as a group, they give a sense of an army marching forward, in order to stop the 'motor of the world'. They give an illusion of a mass movement for the empowerment of the weak but in reality, it is a mass movement against development.

In the Naxal theatre, the antagonist isn't the oppressor, it's development. When they oppose development, the victim starts negotiating and that's when they extort the victim to keep their bank accounts growing. If the 'motor of the world' stops, the Naxal movement will be the first victim. Gangsters use guns for extortion, Naxals use 'anti-development' protests. Ravinder is reinforcing my findings with his ideas. He is making it sound as if the entire world is suffering. Yes, everyone is suffering, if you look at it from a pessimistic point of view. But if you look at the statistics of last fifty years, you will find clear indicators showing that poverty, hunger, famines, violence, discrimination have all gone down dramatically. Average lifespan has increased, man is more productive, people spend more on humanity. But these people paint a scenario where you feel helpless and in rage want to destroy the system. Exactly like media, which creates an illusion of mass outrage out of some stray individual, agenda-driven opinions.

I narrate the script and ideology to Ravinder, who very patiently listens but again without a smile. Whenever ideological scenes come, he shifts his body weight. In the end, both of us sit as if a Hindu and a Muslim are sitting together for dinner and someone raises the question of cow. Or a pig. Ideological beliefs are stronger than religious beliefs. There is silence in the room. Before Rohit can break the awkward silence, in that short moment of stillness, I think about using his fire to my advantage. I decide to use 'anti-thought'. I think whenever we transit to the chapters dealing with the Naxals, I can use his anti-State songs. But to ask him to write ten such songs for free will be absolutely unfair. What if I use Dushyant Kumar or Faiz poetry? Will I need to buy the rights? Aren't they in the public domain? As I try to articulate these queries in my mind, Rohit smiles and leans forward.

'Sir, what if we use a couple of Faiz songs, some folk songs, and rest Ravinder can write. In that way, I'll be able to give you a song for almost every bridge.'

I don't waste my time in solving the dilemma. Did he read my mind or the power of my need hypnotized him?

'What about rights?' I ask immediately.

'We had contacted Faiz Saab's daughter in Lahore, we can talk to her again.'

'Great. Go ahead. But remember, I can't increase the budget.' I reiterate my financial limitation so that he doesn't retain any hope of extra budgets.

We get the license from Faiz House for fifty thousand rupees. Instinctively, I want to go ahead even if there is no budget. In the worst-case scenario, I'll pay out of my pocket and use it in some other film.

'Make it fifty-one thousand,' I tell Rohit when he comes to sign the contract. I don't know whether to feel happy for getting such great literary work for so little or to feel sad that such heritage work of masters sells for such a tiny amount whereas trash sells for lacs.

Finally, we are talking about eight bridges with lyrics and two proper songs. Rohit suggests that we do a fresh song for the 'I am a bitch' chapter, and '*Bekar Kutte*' for the pre-climax. I am tempted to have one more song for the love-making scenario between Vikram and Charu. I want to use '*Chand Roz*' there but it would cost another couple of lacs, so I drop the idea. 'Don't be greedy', I tell myself. 'You should be proud that despite the shoestring budget you are getting songs written by Faiz Ahmed Faiz. Don't ask for more.'

This film is making me reinvent myself. Every day. Every moment. On one hand, I am happy with small victories over hurdles but, on the other hand, I am also tired and frustrated.

We are just a week away from the shoot and still up by fifty lacs. Ravi is assuring me every day that the money will be organized. I am really worried, so I decide to go to Hyderabad and meet him and if need be, meet Suresh and Gopi and tell them honestly that it's not possible to make the movie in this budget.

I fly to Hyderabad, one last time before the shoot, to resolve the suspense of fifty lacs.

31. Technology: The Second Pillar of Cinema

The road from Hyderabad airport to ISB is world class. It feels like my own private road. Intermittently, a few cars overtake us and disappear ahead in no time. In a crowded country like India, people love to speed up on such roads. But my chauffeur is not accelerating over seventy kilometres. I ask him why he can't speed up on an empty, four-lane highway.

'Saar, not allowed,' he replies in his Telugu accent.

'But who is going to notice?' I ask him, looking towards the barren land all around.

'Saar, it's a rule.'

'But everyone is going over hundred… I am sure even you can.'

'Saar, it's a company rule.'

Instinctively, I know I must not talk him into breaking the rule.

One big problem with India is that people do not care about the law. They don't follow rules because nobody gets caught. And in that rare chance, if they do get caught, everyone knows they can get off easily either by bribing or using a *jugaad.*

This driver is a man of integrity. Integrity isn't just honesty. Integrity is being honest even when nobody is watching. India needs such collective integrity for it to shine. We can be a developed nation but in order to become a civilized nation, we need citizens to follow rules. Because when you break rules, you make the system ineffective, inefficient, and unproductive.

'How long have you been working with your company?' I ask him.

'Twenty years.'

'In twenty years you haven't broken any rule?'

'I tried my best not to.'

Rest of the forty-five-minute journey I think about the hidden philosophy behind the driver's simple maxim: 'I try my best not to break rules'.

Normally, we are told from our childhood 'don't do this... don't do that,' so often, that we actually want to break rules. In independent India, instead of building our own indigenous communication tactics we follow the authoritarian ways of the British, which was based on the carrot and stick style of management. People follow rules not because they want to but because they fear the stick. That's why when we jump the red light, we check if there is a cop on the other side or not. Cops also hide behind trees or in a blind spot to get a sadistic pleasure in catching the offenders. A little shift from 'Do this else...' to 'try your best not to break rules' can motivate more people to follow rules and increase the effectiveness of the system.

When I get down at ISB, I want to tip the driver but he refuses.

'Against the rules, saar.'

'I insist... for your kids,' I try to persuade him, lure him.

He takes out a small piggy bank of CRY, an NGO working for homeless children, and asks me to put the tip in it. I put the money in his piggy bank and leave thinking that this world has been running because of some very good people.

Ravi tells me that he has tried all his avenues to raise the fifty lacs but in vain. Sandeep gives me some ideas on sponsorship.

'In the worst-case scenario, let's cast new people and save money from there...'

'Can we cut down the number of days and save some money...'

All kinds of suggestions are thrown by the students as the number of beer cans keeps diminishing.

'Vivek, we will have to meet the Dean also tomorrow and give him a list of the ideas and see if he has any observations,' Ravi tells me.

'I don't have to take your Dean's suggestions now.'

'It's just a formality. We have to keep him in the loop.'

We have a small argument on this issue and I take a moralistic, principled stand that I won't narrate the script at all.

'He is our Dean after all.'

'Yours, not mine.'

'How does it matter if you just tell him the concept in brief?'

'I know he will have problems with the way this film is scripted.

I know he can't visualize the impact and it will jeopardize the film.'

These students aren't ordinary students. They are the future CEOs of Fortune 500 companies. They are bloody good negotiators and I find myself walking to the Dean's office with Ravi and Sandeep. On our way, we have a quick lunch at the canteen. The food is mostly south Indian but delicious.

'How much does it cost you per meal?' I enquire.

'Dirt cheap…peanuts.'

I make a quick mental calculation and figure out that if we can get the food for the unit at the same rate we will end up saving about two hundred rupees per person per day for hundred and fifty people for thirty-five days which equals a little more than ten lacs.

Ravi calls the contractor and we decide to meet after meeting the Dean and in the meantime, he will also work out his logistics.

'Is it possible that we ask the Dean to not charge us for the location and the stay?' I ask Ravi.

'Impossible. Aamir Khan wanted to shoot *3 Idiots* here but they refused. That they are letting us shoot itself is a big exception. Let's not disturb that.' Ravi tells me.

'Something needs to be disturbed, if we have to make the film,' I sigh.

The Dean's room has glass on two sides and brings in a lot of sun. He is a short, energetic man and has a very warm relationship with the students.

'Ok. Tell me. I have been very curious to know what these young men and women are up to,' the Dean says with a smile.

I tell him the story, trying not to show the professor in a really bad light. He listens patiently with a child-like smile as if exploring a fantastical world of Disney characters. He asks some valid questions. His eyes light up when he hears me narrating how the hero wins the battle not with guns but his ideas.

'Ideas… that's what we need in this country. Nice, efficient, productive ideas.'

'Thanks.'

'Wonderful subject. I also believe that the Naxal issue has only a business solution.' He looks at Ravi and adds, 'Great job. Let me know if you need anything from me. All the best.'

'We only need your blessings,' Ravi tells him.

'That you always have.'

'Actually, we need your help,' I speak out of turn.

Everyone looks at me. I can sense Ravi isn't happy with my interjection. However confident or aggressive he may be, I have seen him be extremely shy of authority.

'These students wanted to make a documentary with their own saved monies. I challenged them to make a feature film and make a business out of it. It's a first of its kind in any B-school. They have proved their effectiveness by raising the money but we still run short of some money which is stopping us from realizing your students' dream.'

'No Vivek, that's OK… that's our problem.' Ravi pleads with the Dean, fearing that he may get upset and not allow us to shoot on the campus, 'Sir, you don't bother, we will handle it.'

'Wait,' the Dean addresses me. 'Please tell me how I can help.'

'If you can give us a discount on the location fee and a rebate on the hostels for the crew's stay, we can make the film without a glitch.'

'Absolutely no problem. I think this film must be made at any cost not because my students are involved in it, it must be made because it's important.'

He calls the administrative officer.

'They will be shooting a film here. Let them use our facilities with no charge at all and if possible, provide them accommodation for a token amount.' He looks at me, 'Anything else?'

'No. Thanks a lot. I'll remember this gesture all my life.'

'But I have one condition.'

The next few seconds of suspense almost kill us.

'I won't allow generators, cables and lights on the campus.' He looks at his watch. 'Mr. Agnihotri, meet me when you are here to shoot. All the best, gentlemen.'

The meeting has lasted only twenty-odd minutes but in these twenty minutes my faith in 'good people' has got reaffirmed.

I calculate a saving of twenty-five lacs. If the caterer gives us food on subsidized rates we will save another ten. But we will still run short by fifteen.

Ravi and others open beers to celebrate the financial assistance from the Dean but I am stressed as I don't know how to shoot a film without lights and cables and generators. To make matters worse, my sound designer Girish is insisting that we do sync sound. He is assuring me that the sound quality will be substantially high with the sync sound. The only problem is that it costs a minimum of four lacs extra. Though I agree with him fully, my priority right now isn't sound but the film itself. How to make it happen.

I call Saini, director of photography for all my films, and give him the bad news.

'Sir, even if I cut down some lights, how can we shoot without generator and cables?' Saini asks me a basic question.

'What if we avoid lights totally? What if we use some kinos for the face lighting which we can plug in their lines.'

'Sir, everything works on power.'

'I know Saini, but can we think out of the box and come up with something?'

'Sir, I don't think it can be possible.'

'Saini, this film is very important for me. Please help me.'

'Let me think.'

Saini has some great qualities. Simple, loyal, hardworking and non-confrontational. His only aim has been to match up with my vision and energy and add value to it. I know I am making an unreasonable demand. I tell him a Dushyant Kumar *sher*. Though it's written for a different context, right now it best describes our situation.

Kahan to tay tha chiranga har ek ghar ke liye
Kahan mayassar nahin chirag is sheher ke liye.

Where the light was promised for each home,
now not even a lamp is available for the entire city.

It rained last night. Dry leaves of winter, burdened with dust and smoke, look washed off like a car looks after being washed off all the sticky dirt mud after a long drive. Leaves are shining like a bride's skin just after her *haldi* ceremony. There is still some drizzle, so light that the wind is making it dance to its beats. The sprawling lawns look deep green under the cast of the dark clouds. Peacocks are singing.

There is a small gap in the clouds through which filters the divine light of the morning sun. I wish I also find such a 'ray of hope'.

I am impatiently drinking cup after cup of tea. I have always felt confident even under insurmountable pressure. My confidence is intact but I feel nervous about the fate of this film and, therefore, my fate that is now attached to this film. I am committed to it. My energies, my thoughts, my experience, my desire, my ambition, my vision are all in sync to make it happen exactly the way it's conceived. But this isn't enough to generate the extra amount of fifteen lacs required. Saini calls me.

'Sir, I thought about it and if only we shoot on 5D cameras can we avoid the lights and generators. But we will need ultra-prime lenses,' he tells me like nothing has changed between last night and now. Sometimes his simplicity is irritating.

'Are you serious? 5D?' These cameras are used for still photography and the video mode is used by music video or documentary makers. I have heard that in some action films in Hollywood it's been used as a safety camera fixed in a corner with wide lensing to capture a less-than-a-quarter-second shot.

'I think we can do it but it will require a certain discipline. The focus is very critical and artists have to cooperate to fix the focus which may take some time.'

'We can take care of that as we have very professional actors.'

I quickly do some mental math. If we cut out the generators and lights, it will also reduce light men, their wages, travel, lodging, and boarding. It will roughly save me twenty lacs. I jump with excitement. We have a surplus of five lacs. Of course, it's subject to the caterer giving us the subsidized food. I am already thinking about what I can do in five lacs. PR? An extra day of shooting? Songs which I want but can't have?

'Saini, let's rock it. If you are confident, so am I. I am back tomorrow, let's meet in the evening and crack it.'

'Sir, if you are ready to do this, we will have to make some investment in equipment, like we will need a monitor, lens focus grid, a slider, and a grip for handheld shots.'

My happiness hasn't lasted even a few seconds.

'How much?'

'I'll have to do some research but I have a rough idea.'

'How much?'

'Approximately, eight to nine lacs but someone is coming from the US and if I get it from there we can get it in seven lacs. But he is leaving tomorrow so will have to tell him now. '

I saved twenty, five more than required, and invest seven back in the tools required to save twenty and end up running two lacs short. Ironical indeed.

I have no idea how to react, 'I'll call you by evening. It won't be late as it will be early morning in US.'

In the last twelve waking hours, I have gone through a roller coaster of emotions. Relief, pressure, relief, pressure.

The caterer is waiting for us when we reach the mess.

'You look very tired, have a *kadak* masala chai,' the caterer tells me and waves at a waiter.

Am I looking so stressed?

'From a director I have become a *munim*,' I tell him.

'Don't worry, saar. God is great. He tests us.' He gets up, gets a box of *mithai* and adds in the same flow, 'Some *prasad* from Balaji, Tirupati.'

I am totally off sweets. He insists. I pick up a small piece.

'Saar, don't mind but why be a miser when accepting God's *prasad*?'

He is right. God's *prasad* is a metaphor for God sent opportunities. We don't accept them in totality. We try to mould the opportunities to our present reality without realizing that opportunities come to create new realities.

Ravi and Sandeep come from their class. Ravi informs me that they already had a long chat with the caterer and he needs some more details.

I give him details and he quickly does some calculations and puts a paper in front of me with some numerical values.

'See, if you are not fussy about dishes, I can give you the same food that we give in the mess.' He writes some figures and adds, 'That way I can extend some further discount as I cook the same food with extra quantities so I have a marginal cost. I don't want to make profits as Ravi told me it's for a noble cause.'

I am looking at his break-up. I am not interested in how much it costs me but how much the subsidy is going to save me.

'If you don't have a problem with eating simple food here in the mess,' he continues, 'I can save you one and half lacs,' he takes a long pause and smiles. 'Only if you have one full piece of *prasad*.'

I take the biggest piece from the sweets box.

He writes 13.5 and circles it.

'This is the best we can offer. That too because it's for a noble cause and on top of that you ate full *prasad*.'

From running over half a million short of the budget now I have an excess of one and a half lacs. These one and a half lacs sound more than a million.

I fly back to Mumbai. Looking out at various moods of the sky, my mind remains occupied in trying to understand the relevance of *prasad*. What is the opportunity here? What is it that I must open up to at my fullest and not restrict with present reality?

As my plane hovers over a well-lit Mumbai, I figure out that I am meeting some very good people. From the driver to the Dean to Saini to the caterer. The restrictions that the Dean imposed turned out to be an opportunity. Not just to save money but to experiment with a new format and to learn new technology. If we can pull this off with 5D cameras and make it look like a film, then we will be pioneering this art.

Maybe the universe is presenting such good men as an opportunity, which is why all the common logic is getting defied to make the film happen. My faith in goodness is reinforced. I learn that if the intent is right, the universe creates a new logic. A new reality.

32. Production: The Spine of Cinema

After writing the script, Alfred Hitchcock used to say, 'My film is ready, let's shoot the bloody film now.' In my case, we have the script as well as the budget in place. Plus, one and a half lacs surplus (I still don't know what to do with it). But I still can't utter those golden words.

The shoot is just a week away. I am leaving the day after tomorrow, two days ahead of the crew, for Hyderabad.

Swara has some questions. Just as the drama we had over the scene where Pooja kisses the professor's bald pate and Swara's manager having a problem with it was settling, he raised another issue. There is a scene where she is supposed to take off her shirt and throw it at the audience. He wants me to delete it from the scene or change it to suit Swara.

'She has got such a sexy tattoo on her chest, why would she have it if she has problems in showing it to the world?' I lose my cool and tell him that I will speak to Swara. I should be careful with what I say. Such statements can be interpreted by angry feminists as interfering in a woman's choice.

Before calling Swara, I remind myself several times that it's just one week to the shoot and since everything has fallen into place, I must not lose my cool under any circumstances. She understands the pressures and demands of a small budget film. It takes her some time to realize that I won't agree to the 'kissing' and 'shirt-throwing' clauses. She gives in. I take a deep breath. Even before I can breathe out slowly to complete the feeling of relief, she raises more doubts. As I try to answer her queries, she starts raising issues which I feel are beyond the scope of the script as they aren't script-related but ideological disputes. We have been discussing for more than an hour without going anywhere. Instinctively, I know that if I start reasoning any further, I'll lose my cool and it will end up in an argument. The timing is not right. I lean back and take a deep breath, again.

'I have noted down all your concerns. I'll discuss your script points with Rohit and get back to you by tomorrow and will also have the revised contract sent tomorrow.'

Rohit asks me why I am even listening to her questions. Strangely, with Swara, I was defending the script and now when she is gone, I am defending Swara's arguments.

'It's our film, our ideology, our voice. She cannot piggyback her ideologies on us. If she is so convinced about her beliefs, she can make her own film,' Rohit says and while getting up to leave, he adds, 'I am not changing a thing in the script even if I have to fight with you forever.' A convinced and driven co-writer is always an asset.

I am on my way to the airport. It's exceptionally crowded. Normally, I am very happy and relaxed before the start of the shoot but something is bothering me. I don't know what it is but you know when something is missing from an otherwise perfect arrangement. I call up Rohit. We love to open our chat with the politics of the day but today he is different.

'Sir, I couldn't sleep properly as one thought kept bothering me and if you don't mind I want to share it with you.'

No filmmaker likes to hear about doubts, confusions, queries and disturbing thoughts first thing in the morning.

'Rohit, you know now nothing can be changed in the script.'

'It's not about the script. It's about Swara.'

'It's OK. You don't have to think too much as I have decided to call her and tell her simply that no script-related changes can be considered at this stage. I am sure she will understand.'

'Sir, that exactly is the problem. She will understand for the time being as she can't argue with you but later, while shooting, she will again raise them and she will keep raising doubts as she can never be convinced about a political stand that destroys the very premise of her political ideology.'

This is the first time I have ever looked at an actor as an ideological entity. Aren't actors supposed to act? Acting means pretending to be someone else and making people believe that you are what you aren't.

'Sir, if she continues to have issues with every damn thing on the sets, from the vanity van to what the professor says, then we are in big trouble,' Rohit's voice has an urgency and serious concern.

Deep down, I know that Rohit is making sense. With experience, I have learnt that if any crew member or an actor has too many doubts even before the beginning of the film, he or she will eventually become an irritant and a liability for the production. Some people can never be satisfied with logic. A film is a filmmaker's point of view and interpretation of a story. Nobody has a right to question his interpretation before the film is exhibited. Questioning the premise of a film is neither intelligent nor professional. I can feel the conflict between my instinct and my rationality. The rationality is forcing me to tow the standard practice of managing irritants while my instinct is forcing me to replace the irritant. And make the film with absolutely no pressure from anywhere. Isn't that the fundamental reason for going through such stress and struggle to make this film?

I call up my office and ask the production manager to stop Swara's contract for some time. I have no idea who will replace her. I just can't think of anyone who will fill into Swara's shoes at such short notice, especially when I am not in Mumbai. I need to think of someone who will blindly follow me.

As I am checking in, my music director Rohit calls me. *Shit*, I was supposed to give him a final go ahead on the number of songs. Rohit tells me that he will send the songs to me before the beginning of the shoot. This is the worst by-product of digital technology – late deliveries. He tells me that if I want another song for the lovemaking situation, it will cost me around three lacs more.

'I just can't afford it,' I repeat myself.

'Sir, please try to take out money from somewhere for I can guarantee that a song at that moment will take the film to a different level,' Rohit pleads.

What should one do in a situation like this when you know how badly you need something but there is hardly any money in the pocket?

'Rohit, I have one and a half. Can we do it in that?'

'Sir, no. The arranger will take a lac and for any decent female singer we will need another fifty plus studio, mixing etc.'

'What if we don't do any arrangement in the song... what if we have suspended, unplugged kind of music, won't we save one lac?'

'Even for unplugged we need a few musicians... it will cost money.'

'What if go full realistic... just a harmonium to back up?'

'We can look at it but still, we will need a singer...'

I quickly scan through all the singers I can ask for a favour but I'll still have to pay them some money. Nobody works free in Bollywood unless someone is madly in love or needs something out of you. I am in no position to offer a favour to anyone nor do I know any female singer who is madly in love with me. Rohit suggests that he can sing for free if I want. But I am thinking of a female voice. A female singer who loves me unconditionally. Sometimes, we can't find our glasses because we are wearing them, exactly like I couldn't think of the only person who loves me unconditionally and is a great singer to top it.

'Have you heard Pallavi sing?' I ask Rohit.

'Yes, on TV. But not in person.'

'You go and meet her today and listen to her. If you like her voice, let's record it with her. If you have to pay someone for playing the harmonium, forget about him and request Pallavi as she can play the harmonium also.'

'OK. I'll call her,' Rohit says after a long pause. I am not sure if he said yes because he is happy with the idea or he is just giving in to a producer/director's demand. I don't care anymore. I feel good about it and I am going to do it exactly what is right for me and the film. It's not that the film will work better if Lata *didi* sings the song.

While I was speaking to Rohit, Vikram Khakkar was trying to call me. He has recently got married to my niece Aanchal Dwivedi. I assume he must be calling from his honeymoon and would ask me to recommend some good eating joints. Wait, why didn't I think of Aanchal? Aanchal is an established TV actress and that too of some calibre. She started her career with me. Should I ask Vicky as he is her husband now? But they have just got married and I don't know how Vikram would take it. I am not sure if I can ask her to take her shirt off as she also comes from a small-town, middle-class family like me. Even if they agree, how would I adjust the dates, for I need her in the first few days of the shoot and they are out on their honeymoon?

'Vicky, what's up? How is the honeymoon treating you?'

'*Kahan chacha*, we are still in Mumbai as some show came up and I got busy with it. Will go later.'

I see an opening.

'Would Aanchal want to work in a film?'

I explain the project and the demands of the role to him.

'Oh, so you want her for natural acting because your character is exactly what she is,' Vicky tells me jokingly.

Sometimes, we fail to see our youngers for their worth.

I call Aanchal and I just inform her that she will be smoking and drinking throughout the film and will be taking off her shirt.

'No issues, *chacha*. I'll do whatever you want.'

'You are my niece but I must tell you that I don't want any doubts or hesitations later.'

'*Chacha*, you have a blind follower in me. Tell me when do we start?'

'Day after tomorrow.'

I make the customary calls to sort out the logistical issues emerging due to casting changes. Now I have a competent actor who I am very comfortable with.

Later, on the flight when the stewardess offers me a welcome drink, I ask her to give me a chocolate instead. I want to eat something sweet. Not because it's customary to eat a sweet after a good act, I actually want to feel like those chocolate commercials, models who look ecstatic after eating chocolates. I want to feel like them. Happy. And ecstatic.

33. The Shoot

When in Rome, do as the Romans do.

This becomes our mantra during the entire shoot. We are staying on the campus. Everyone is staying in dorms with four independent rooms and a common hall and a kitchen. Saini, the actors and I are living in independent one-room apartments. We are following the lifestyle of the students and most of their timings. Breakfast. Work. Lunch. Work. Chill on the lawns. Beer. Poker. Midnight parties. Sleep for a few hours.

My crew tells me that this is the first time they are working without regular shift timings. When you break the working norms, people become relaxed and work for their inner satisfaction. I can see the results. We are knocking off shots at a good speed and with better nuances. It's more like a picnic. Some people have already started saying that this is the best shoot of their careers.

The first day of the shoot is one of the most difficult scenes in terms of logistics. We are shooting the 'I Am a Bitch' chapter. We have dressed up the institute's bar and for some reason, it's not working out. We have two 5D cameras and one set of lenses. We are stuck. Saini is trying to light it up with all correctness but it's not looking aesthetic. If it was the last day of the shoot, we would have accepted it but not on the first day of the shoot when your creative expectations are the highest. Also, we have called students to fill the bar and there are too many colours on their clothes.

'What if we turn the whole thing red? That way we will neutralize too many elements,' I tell Saini.

'But it will look tacky,' Saini tells me the truth.

He is right. An idea strikes me. What if I ask all the students to wear black? Then we will have only two elements: red and black. It's classy, quirky and apt for the title 'I Am a Bitch'. I am sure everyone has one black pair of clothes. Saini agrees immediately.

While the students are off to change, I sit down chatting with Pritika and her boyfriend. I learn that he sings rock and plays the guitar. He tells me that they have a band of five and their drummer is a girl. I like the idea. It's visually different. I ask him if he can get all of them and play a piece in the film. He immediately agrees and gets the other musicians from their classes.

Once ready, the shot looks wonderful. I am happy. Just for a moment. When Ravi and Sandeep called these students to be part of the crowd in the bar, he didn't tell them it can take forever. They assumed that it will be a maximum of a couple of hours. These students work by the clock. They have scheduled stuff to do and now they are getting impatient. Despite a lot of pleading and persuading they aren't ready to shoot. I use my 'student's mind' and make an announcement.

'Anyone who wants to have chilled beer and just have fun with us can stay and the rest can leave.'

Only ten or fifteen students leave out of a hundred. The rest agree to stay back for two hours on the ups.

This is Aanchal's first day of shoot. She doesn't even know her character well. She is nervous as it's her first film. But I have seen her grow. I know that she is a very spontaneous actor. Too much of briefing will make her think and then she will do calculated acting. I tell her that she should play an alcoholic. That's it.

If the students have to be let go in two hours we can't shoot too many angles. Also, they are not actors. We can't have too much movement of characters as the focus is very critical and complex in 5D cameras. I decide to shoot the entire scene in one go. This is the advantage of digital technology. I have shot all my films on 35mm film where every foot counts. The band plays real-time. The audience reacts real-time. Aanchal dances real-time. We knock off the entire scene in no time. We still have one hour and a song to shoot. I decide to continue this style of 'capturing the act' rather than constructing it.

It's a film of students and I have real students whose real behaviour cannot be matched by extras. One of the reasons this scene is working out is because of amazing chemistry between the students and Arunoday. He spent the last couple of days in classrooms and evenings with the students. Also, he looks and talks like one of them. Aanchal is like water. She merges with the environment. I give her dialogues and ask her to speak the way she would speak in real life. The students actually start pulling her leg and the scene turns out to be outstanding. It's time to shoot her dancing where she has to throw her shirt off. She asks me about the choreographer.

'Why do you need a choreographer?' I ask Aanchal.

'How will I do my steps?'

'When you dance in a party, do you have a choreographer?

'Yeah, but…'

'Just dance like you'd dance in a real bar, drunk.'

'But how will I know the continuity of steps after each cut?'

'There won't be any cuts. You just dance without bothering about the camera. We will adjust to your movements. And don't bother about the cuts as there will be only one take.'

Aanchal has no idea how to react to this unusual style of shooting. I say 'Action', she gets on the top of her act and dances so naturally that everyone forgets that it's a shoot. Students are already high with the free beer and no one is performing anymore for the camera. When the camera stops existing in a performer's mind is when he performs best.

A lot of technique is used in cinema to construct reality. We have reality all around us. All we need to do is put the camera in cinematic angles and shoot. The first day of shoot determines how the rest of the shoot will evolve. I know that this is going to be a very creative learning. Sometimes technological constraints become opportunities. For the first time in my career, I am not thinking of shot division and camera angles or lensing. All I am doing is creating a real situation and asking the actors to behave like the character. It is creating an organic beauty and innocence. Nothing is manipulated. Nothing is forced. The simplicity of the shots is bringing me closer to the truth. The absence of cinematic tricks is making it become more cinematically real.

Everything is running smoothly. There are no set timings. We fix the call time depending on what time we sleep. The youth energy is very intoxicating and addictive and all of us are sucked into it.

Also, there aren't any cables, logistics, and extra people. The atmosphere is that of a student's film. No set rules, no timings, no discipline. Our film shootings are so stressful and chaotic because everyone is in a panic mode. This happens because of the shift timings. There is a day plan and one has to achieve it within that time so everyone is racing against time. Here, there is no race. No panic. No chaos. Slower is faster. There is only fun and when work becomes fun and fun becomes work, everyone is smiling. That's exactly what Kher *saab* noticed when he arrived on the fifteenth day of the shoot.

'Why is everyone smiling?' Kher saab asks me.

'Because you are here,' I reply with a smile.

My production manager informs me that Kher *saab* wants to stay in a five-star hotel. I had spoken to Bhaskar and he had agreed to Kher *saab* staying on the campus. But he insists. We have no scope for any kind of budgetary improvisations as our last penny is counted. Booking a suite in a five star is impossible. I also know that it's suicidal to engage with actors in logistics on the first day. I don't want to start with him on such a note. Also, he is charging us much less than his market price. I try to persuade him.

'Kher *saab*, we always stay in five stars but this time we decided to stay here on the campus and believe you me it's been such a wise decision.'

'Yeah… but I am not used to all this.'

'Why don't you stay here just for one night? Experience the evening and tomorrow I'll shift you to a five star. I know it's not as comfortable but it is a once in a lifetime experience.'

After some thinking, Kher *saab* agrees. I have ensured that his apartment is in a location where peacocks hang out.

We have an exceptionally long dining table scene where all principal actors are conversing. We are shooting it in a real professor's house which looks like a modern art museum and is a director's delight and a cameraman's nightmare as we are not allowed to shift any artefact. This is the first time in the last fifteen days that I have seen Saini worried. This also happens to be Kher *saab*'s first day of shoot with us. In the last fifteen days Arunoday, Aanchal, Mahie Gill and Pallavi have become good friends and have lots of inside jokes to crack with the students. This is one major disadvantage of joining a shoot in the middle. By this time, the groups are formed and there are back stories to bond around. Kher *saab* is not very comfortable with small cameras hidden somewhere. He isn't used to shooting without lights, cables, people and the usual chaos and energy of the shoot. Normally, if something is required and it's not on the sets, there is panic of a kind which if an average person sees he may end up believing that a war is in the offing. But here we wait patiently and happily while the concerned person makes the arrangements.

The day and the shoot don't go the way I had visualized. Something is missing. I can see that Kher *saab* is getting isolated from the group of Arunoday, Aanchal, Mahie and Pallavi as the acting styles are very different. I try to tell Kher *saab* a few times but he is convinced about the way he wants to play the character of the professor.

We knock off the most complex scene with a lot of difficulties as something goes wrong in each take. This is how some scenes become jinxed when the fundamental bonding element goes missing.

I am not being able to enjoy every day's ritualistic beer drinking session after the pack-up. I can sense the same enthusiasm is also missing in the actors' group. Even Saini is not in his usual spirits.

'What is missing?' I ask Saini.

'It's the chemistry, I think,' Saini puts it simply.

'Yeah, but they are all great actors. It's the acting styles I think.'

'Sir, even I felt the same. I think you should talk to Kher *saab* as we can't shoot like we did today… broken and retakes.'

I agree with Saini. Cameramen can see what others can't.

I go to Kher saab's room.

'Why don't you join all of us outside on the lawns,' I ask him.

'I have been shooting non-stop for the last month, so a bit tired. Have you booked the hotel?'

'Yes,' I lie. 'Please join us, you will love it.'

I know I can't get out of this hotel issue and my heart is sinking. His hotel bill itself will be in the range of two to three lacs. This would mean cancelling the song and at least one day of shoot.

Kher saab joins us with his single malt, making beer-drinking students self-conscious. Almost everyone here has grown up admiring his acting. But he is an extremely sociable person and takes no time to make people comfortable. Also, he has a great sense of humour. Soon, everyone becomes comfortable with him. Before leaving after midnight, Kher saab again reminds me to book the hotel.

We are set to shoot a small scene in the same house but the professor has some work and we can get the location only after ten. I utilize this time to sort out Kher saab's hotel issue and realize it is actually making our schedule go haywire. This is when Dattu, Kher *saab*'s personal assistant, informs me that he wants to meet me.

'Vivek, there are two things I want to discuss with you.'

When an actor says 'I need to talk', the director feels exactly like when his wife tells him 'We need to talk'. I am sure some complication is waiting for me.

'One is a good news for you and another bad. Which one you want to hear first?'

'Kher *saab*, in the destiny of this film, I can't remain happy for a long time, for in the end, I know I have to struggle.'

'If you are feeling like this, it means you are becoming a true filmmaker.'

Only Kher *saab* can find positivity in the most hopeless situations.

'Well, first the good news, that I have decided to stay here,' Kher saab says with a very serious face, and then smiles. I feel so relieved that I don't wait for a moment before relaying the news to my production manager who sounds so happy that instead of saying 'wonderful' or 'congrats', he ends up saying 'have a nice day, sir'.

'I think there was something not quite right about yesterday's scene. What do you think?'

'Yeah, I think the chemistry could have been better.'

'The chemistry was bad because of me. I think I was acting like Anupam Kher and not the professor, which I understood later, because all the co-actors were reacting to the character of the professor the way they have interpreted it in relation to their characters. If I play it like the way I did yesterday, either I am going to look bad or they are going to look very bad. Therefore, I think I must surrender to the world that you have already created.'

'I couldn't have articulated it better. Let's do it this way from today.'

'No. Not from today. But from yesterday because I am going to ask you to reshoot the scene as I want to do it the way it must be done.'

I don't know how to react. On the one hand, it's the correct idea but on the other hand it's going to cost me one full day and the corresponding monies.

'I warned you that there is a bad news. This is it.' He looks at me for some time and realizes what I am thinking. Kher saab is one of the most perceptive persons you can find in Bollywood.

'Don't worry Vivek, I'll finish rest of your scenes very fast. I have never shot the way you are doing it here, so please help me find the *sur*.'

You are lucky to find good actors. You are luckier if they want to cross limitations. You are luckiest if they are ready to surrender to your vision. Here I have an actor, with *Saaransh* as his first film, where he played a seventy year plus character while still in his late twenties, who is willing to surrender to my vision, and I am worried about the budget. The invisible design of this film has a pattern. Each time a hurdle pops up, it opens up an opportunity for me. Each time I have surrendered to the problem, I have been moved ahead to a better idea. I haven't reached thus far to surrender to a hurdle.

'Ok. We shall reshoot the scene.'

The scene turns out to be one of the best so far. When a scene lacks drama, humour, action or thrills and if it is still engaging, the credit should go to the actors. Good actors can make any camera angle look great but not vice versa. When the scene was being reshot, it felt like it was the professor's house. Kher saab spent quite some time getting familiarized with every nook and corner of the house. He spent time with the owners and tried to understand how they behaved inside their house. Once I said action, he behaved as if he had been living here for decades and teaching these students for a long time. He owned the place.

This scene has Pallavi speaking long monologues about the history of pottery. Pallavi was getting stuck at a couple of places because she was trying to put weight in few words. I asked her to speak it like she is narrating an ordinary anecdote without emotionally investing in it. After her take, Arunoday tells me that this is the first time he actually understood the history of pottery. Pallavi is a revelation to me in this film. She has never done a role like this where she is smoking, drinking, flirting with a young man yet has a wonderful relationship with her husband. Where she blindly follows her husband, yet is empowered. Pallavi is playing such delicate nuances with such ease that I feel the industry, including me, has never known her true potential. There was only one exchange of dialogues between Pallavi and Mr. Kher but both of them improvised it into a banter so common in a mature marriage.

The only irritation has been that Mr. Kher keeps getting calls from his father almost every hour. A couple of times he called between the takes. There is some understanding between him and his father that whenever he calls, Mr. Kher has to pick up the phone. I have noticed this since my early days at Kher *saab*'s production company. Their discussion lasts for less than few seconds.

I have an idea. What if I use this trait as part of his characterization? The professor has no one to talk to. What if his father calls him exactly like his father and keeps giving him sundry news that he heard on BBC?

'Kher *saab*, if next time you get a call, I won't say cut. You continue shooting and instead of telling your dad you are in the shoot, you tell him that you are in the class.'

Everyone thinks I am kidding but I am serious. Kher *saab* instantly understands the dimension this can add to his character.

'You behave exactly like you behave with your dad,' I tell him.

'But I never lie to my dad,' Kher saab replies.

'I am sure this much sacrifice we can make for the character.'

'But who is the father?' Saini asks me later.

'I don't know. Maybe he is the Murtaza Arzai of this film.' Murtaza Arzai was the invisible devil in my first film *Chocolate* – everyone has heard of him, everyone is scared of him but nobody has ever seen him. The Arzai character was inspired by Kayzer Soze of *Usual Suspects*.

We are on the last day of the shoot. We have two major scenes to shoot and they happen to be the most important scenes of the film. One where the professor's real identity is revealed and the climax. We had done a mock rehearsal with camera angles and all possible logistical issues. As I am readying to start the shoot at 6 AM, I get a call from Bhaskar who informs me that Kher saab will have to leave early evening as there is no other flight connection for him to reach the location of his next shoot. It's impossible to shoot two most important scenes before nightfall. But Bhaskar leaves me with no option.

I am nervous, irritated, upset. I start to compromise in order to save time and finish the scenes somehow. I know if I leave it now to be shot later in Mumbai, I'll never be able to complete it.

The way the climax is written, everyone expects cinematic drama. I decide to shoot it extremely natural. I don't want the audience to feel the camera or editing or acting but I am not being able to explain to the people who have been part of its development. I lose it with Rohit and Saini. When you lose your cool, people just start following you blindly. I even lose it with Arunoday who wants to know why he won't kill the professor. 'We don't kill people even if we get to know they are terrorists, that's why,' I tell him, leaving no scope for further discussion. Kher saab senses it and realises that I am not focussed.

'*Punditji*, please chill and focus. I will leave only after finishing these scenes,' Kher saab calls me '*punditji*' sometimes, when he has to underline a point. 'We will finish them very fast,' he comforts me.

'Action.'

Vikram Pundit takes his hands off the professor's neck, tells him that he is going to fight his violent ideology with his idea, to build a '*nayi soch ka naya Bharat*– a new India of a new mindset– and challenges him, 'Do you still want to play a secret game?' Silence. More silence. The hero walks away leaving the professor standing alone in the middle of the classroom – his citadel.

'Cut.'

The last shot of the film is done. Before time. A rarity.

We have wrapped up the scenes before Kher saab's scheduled time to leave. We still have half an hour left. Everyone is busy outside with Kher saab for customary goodbyes and selfies. I haven't yet called for a pack-up. I am thinking if I have left anything. Is there anything else I can do in the next half an hour with Kher saab? I stand alone in an empty classroom looking at empty benches and the blank projection screen. That's how a filmmaker is left after the wrap-up. Empty. But this emptiness is like a mother would feel in her womb after delivering the baby. I don't know about others but I hate wrap-ups. I want the shoot to go on. It's like an affair which you don't want to end.

A phone rings somewhere. Kher saab has left his phone on the table. It's his dad. I run to give him his phone. When I give the phone to Kher saab, I think why not close the film on a shot where his father calls and the professor confesses his guilt to his father which he can't do with anyone in the world. His dad is the only factor which hasn't been resolved.

When everything is over for the professor and there is frightening silence in the empty hall, his phone rings. Professor tells his father 'Sorry, dad.'

The End.

One can't have a better ending than this. Last minute ideas are the finest extract of creative juices. Just two words, *'Sorry, dad'*, resolve everything. The film ends on hope and a desire for forgiveness. Kher saab instantly agrees and we shoot it with such ease.

The image of a tiny professor, with droopy shoulders, standing in a dark and empty hall, seeking forgiveness from his metaphorical father in a defeated and broken voice, *'Sorry, dad'*, and then wiping his glasses to clear all the dirt settled over a long time, gives me goose pimples. Let the audience decide who is the furtive 'daddy' of this devilish revolution.

I know it's a job well done and it's also time to wrap up.

'OK friends, since everything has turned out so well, if I leave now I won't feel good. So, I am not going today and I will leave tomorrow and all of you are invited for a party from my side,' Kher saab throws an open invitation for a wrap party which we had no money for. I owe it to him.

It's 3 AM and the party is still strong. Kher saab pulls me to a corner and puts his hand on my shoulder and smiles.

'*Punditji*, in my three decades of acting and after doing over 450 films, I have learnt one thing that when a director finds his true calling it starts showing in his work, in his body language and in his eyes. Throughout this shoot I have noticed that spark in you. I think you have found the purpose. You have found your song. Mark my words, this film will change your life. Thanks for casting me and all the best.'

I try very hard to control my tears. As soon as Kher saab leaves, I hide behind a tree and I cry. I don't know if the tears are flowing because someone finally understood my quest or because I am going to miss this shooting experience or because I have no idea what will happen in the future. I feel like a Buddha, in a traffic jam.

34. The First Screening

The Times of India group has a division called MediaNet. Under this, they sell editorial space in their newspapers. Yes, they sell the *editorial* space. One can pay and get whatever one likes printed. If you really want to know what is wrong with India, I'd advise you study the MediaNet model of the *Times of India* Group.

They have started a new vertical where they give free coverage to your film in most of their editions and in return they come on board as co-producers, taking fifty percent of the profits. This business is focussed only on small films. Their executives have been chasing me for my film. They are putting a lot of pressure to partner with us. It's a tempting offer for we won't have to spend money on the advertising of the film. It is exploitative but then beggars can't be choosers. Making a non-starrer film in India instantly makes you a beggar and open to exploitation. Like the father of a dusky daughter.

Right now, I feel like the parent of that dusky daughter and MediaNet appears like *that* exploitative groom who is only interested in the dowry and not the bride. They are trying every tactic possible to take my film. They are showing me dreams and pretending as if this film is the best thing that happened after the advent of *Times of India*. Why are they so desperate? Because they are getting fifty percent ownership of the film for doing nothing. Also, they want a 'last in, first out' deal which means they will recover their investment first and then share fifty paise with us from every rupee earned.

Ravi is after my life to tie up with them. I ask *TOI* to wait until the first cut is ready but they insist on signing the contract just after seeing a few scenes as a formality. If you are proud of your product, you want people to buy it only after understanding its features. I have been warning them that it's a different kind of film and I do not see any brand fit with *TOI*'s image. But they won't take no for an answer. Also, they smile too much, as if they are pleading.

Finally, under pressure, I agree to show them the rough cut. They come with a full force of executives with Blackberries and laptops. After fifteen minutes into the film, some executives come out and start making some calls. They keep going in and out of the editing room.

'Satya, I guess they are not liking the film.'

'Sir, why are you thinking negative?'

'In fact, I am thinking positive. I hope they don't like it and the deal falls through. That will be good for us.'

At halftime, they come out one by one and huddle outside in the smoking area. After a good half an hour of conferencing outside, their boss wants to meet me before watching the second part.

'It's a very interesting film... very hard hitting... very dark... very well shot... very well acted... amazing direction...' the Boss takes a long pause and then adds, '... but....' He starts looking for words.

'But you can't take it, am I right?'

'Yes, of course... right... I mean how do you know?'

'Will tell you someday.'

'Vivek, it's a fantastic film... one of the best I have seen in a long time... I still have goose pimples... especially the first chapter... Oh, my God... unbelievable.... But I don't think *TOI* will ever associate with this film as we are a marketing organization and we have families as our audience and this film isn't humorous or a family film.'

'But didn't you always know that this is a political drama?'

'Yeah, but we thought it would be like a Bollywood political film... entertaining...*masala*... still, let me talk to my seniors.'

'Sure.' I get up to show him the door.

He stops before leaving, 'But how did you know that we won't take the film?'

'Because this film has a pattern. Anything that I want from my heart happens.'

One of the executives who wants to write films calls me to say that they haven't taken the film because of its political message. It doesn't surprise me at all as it was obvious. This is how films are commissioned and acquired by the studios. These executives didn't even see the full film to know what it says. They didn't bother to ask themselves how this film will connect with the audience. They aren't concerned about the people who will eventually pay for the tickets and make them richer but instead, they are concerned about only one person's reaction who happens to be one of the owners of the Times Group: Vineet Jain. If there is corruption and incompetence in thought at such a preliminary stage, then how does one expect these studios to deliver great films? Vineet Jain can become the world's richest and most successful man, but in my eyes, he will always remain the destroyer of the fourth pillar of Indian democracy. He and his elder brother Sameer Jain single-mindedly corrupted and crippled Indian journalism.

When I was working with McCann Erricson in Delhi, we got to handle the *TOI*'s hundred and fifty-year celebration account. The celebration ran for over a year. Sameer and Nandita Jain were planning to modernize *TOI*. I was handling the account and got a chance to work closely with Nandita. Vineet Jain had joined the group and though he was in Switzerland, all the marketing material was sent to him for his comments. This was the time when Nandita launched *Saturday Times* in colour which later on became *Bombay Times*, *Delhi Times* and so on. I had then sensed a transition from the old school of journalistic practices to the modern approach which believed that even charity is done to make profits. The younger Jains wanted to assert themselves as the largest, biggest, oldest, first, best and so on. I remember that once my boss Mrs. Tara Sinha questioned the ethical stance of the campaign, to which one of the younger Jains had replied, 'Everything is fair in love and war.' I wanted to warn them at that time that yes, everything is fair in love and war but only *truth is fair* in journalism.

Bombay Times isn't a gossip tabloid. It's a symbol of everything corrupt in our system. If you have money, you can buy space every day and slowly people will start believing that you are a star. That's why people who appear in *Times* supplements fall flat when their stardom is tested at the box office. Vineet Jain's Medianet is an extortion business, aimed at desperate people who want to be in the news, hiding behind maxims like 'Profit, profit, profit', which is the media equivalence of Bollywood's 'entertainment, entertainment, entertainment'.

The first cut is ready. When I see the first cut, I feel satisfied. Because I have been able to live up to our mantra and the film has genuinely turned out to be: REAL. HONEST. FEARLESS. EYE-OPENER. UNIQUE.

I am also happy with myself because I am absent from my own work. The film, like a yacht, has its own sails. The sails and the wind danced together, while I was there only to ensure that the ship remained on course. In Zen, they say that a good teacup is the one that doesn't smell of its potter. The film feels Zen-like.

It's about two hours twenty minutes in length and I know that it should be well under two hours but I am going to cut twenty minutes only after getting everyone's feedback. For the first screening, I have invited Suresh, Gopi, their partners, all the students, actors, heads of departments and some very close friends whose feedback I trust. Everyone is very excited. I know deep within that it's going to surprise everyone. Unlike with my previous films, I am neither nervous nor tense. In fact, I am patient.

A salesman with a good product is eager to sell it. The film is over. Now I have to bother about final post-production and finances for releasing it. But I am not worried at all as I know that Suresh and Gopi will put in the money after seeing the film. After a long time, I feel so confident, so self-assured. So optimistic. I call up a nearby pub and reserve a table for twenty-five people. I want to treat everyone. I may be broke but I have a credit card.

Lights go down. *Buddha In A Traffic Jam* begins.

We run the film in one go. Slowly, the audience is getting segmented in their responses. Some people react to nuances and some don't react at all. There are very awkward silences at times. Normally, you get to hear a lot of rustling and coughing in theatres but here it feels like everyone is stuck to a posture. I like Arunoday a lot. Aanchal is fantastic. Mahie is awesome, Pallavi is outstanding and Kher saab has anchored the film brilliantly. I make mental notes of parts to be chopped. There is nothing we can touch in the last thirty minutes of the film.

I go out the moment Kher saab says sorry to his dad, to receive the guests outside where refreshments are served.

You know the impact of your film by the energy that people exude after the trial. The energy is very encouraging. A young couple is so moved by the film that they have too many things to discuss. Instead of the film, they want to discuss the politics of Naxalism. Like most of the youngsters in metros, they didn't have much idea about Naxalism before seeing the film. What else can be the purpose of a film? Nobody feels that it's long. The Indian audience is very patient with film lengths but international audiences don't appreciate films that are longer than a hundred and twenty minutes. There is a legend that this length was invented by Alfred Hitchcock as he believed that the length of a film should be directly related to the endurance of the human bladder. Ninety to hundred and twenty minutes was assumed to be the endurance time.

It's been more than ten minutes but Suresh, Gopi, and the students haven't come out. I go inside to check and find all of them in a serious discussion. As soon as I enter, I feel wrong energies. When they see me, their expressions change.

'Vivek, there are some very serious issues with the film,' Ravi tells me as if he is the judge and I am the judged.

'Obviously, it's a serious film so it must have serious issues,' I try to loosen up the atmosphere but nobody laughs at the joke. Their collective expressions are like someone has died and they don't know how to break the news to me.

'Vivek, we are sorry but we can't go ahead with this film. We won't be able to invest anymore.'

'But this is just the first cut. We still have to finish it and of course, the balance payment has to come from you for us to finish it.'

'Don't misunderstand but there are too many cuss words and politics,'

'But you knew about it, no?'

'It's also not entertaining. Too dark,' Ravi intervenes.

'What is entertaining?' I ask him.

'*Yamla Pagla Deewana*.'

This is when everyone laughed. They just couldn't control it.

'Vivek, we will think and get back to you but my first reaction is we can't be associated with this film. We are business people. We have to work with everyone. I hope you understand. Whatever is spent is spent, I have no problems and if you want to get funds from somewhere and finish and release the film, please go ahead. But we can't do it. Still, we will discuss and let you know.'

Before leaving, Gopi hugged me and said, 'I loved the film. You have made it brilliantly. I am there for any support.' I know he means it. He adds, 'I have some connections in a few studios, I'll connect you with them.' I am experienced enough to understand the real meaning of his last sentence.

Technically the film is shelved. It is shelved because it worked. It hit them hard. It made them realize that it's a very risky film for their business empire. Their faces had dropped because they knew that their decision was selfish. They were scared to associate themselves with the alternate thought that the film presents. They are mainstream businessmen working with the establishment. They can't upset any groups like politicians, Naxals, Leftists, intellectuals, and media. Plus right–wing fundamentalists. The film scared them. If I had made a cliché film, they would have invested more. Now I have nowhere to go. The shelving of the film would mean all the emotional and intellectual investment that I made goes waste, plus I have no money in the bank. I don't even know how I'll pay my bills. My heartbeat stops for a moment. I feel I am sinking. I rest on a chair and take deep breaths.

The lights go off as the booking time is over.

I stand alone in the preview theatre feeling exactly like one feels after everyone leaves the cremation ground for you to mourn alone.

Dark and empty.

Book Four

The Struggle of Buddha

"And the day came when the risk to remain tight in a bud was more painful than the risk it took to blossom."
- Anaïs Nin

35. Who is Gudsa Usendi ?

2014

The first week of January is never as chilly in Mumbai as it is this year. We have long windows on almost all sides of our fifteenth-floor apartment. One side faces the sea and the other, mangroves. Perfect for the chilly sea breeze to cross-ventilate with full gust. We love our windows open, but this year they have been mostly closed due to the unexpectedly chilly winter. Having just come back from the Kashmir Valley, after doing a recce for my next film, where temperatures were subzero, I am feeling a bit warm and suffocated, so I open the windows, letting the gush of air fly the newspaper off Pallavi's hands, who hates to be disturbed while reading her morning paper, and therefore, creating a small storm in Pallavi's morning teacup.

Before I become a victim of this storm, I run after the scattered pages of *Times of India*, *The Hindu,* and *Hindustan Times* which have flown all across our living room and study, and have become intermingled with each other. If we make the mastheads and typefaces of all the major papers the same, it will be difficult to tell which page is from which newspaper as all of them speak in the same voice. Negative, pessimistic, and manipulative. As I try to arrange them back in their original form, a particular news item, in the 'States' page, catches my attention.

'Noted Maoist leader Gudsa Usendi and his wife surrender to Andhra police.'

In another paper, the same news has a different headline:

'Who is Gudsa Usendi, the "invisible" Maoist?'

I know this name – Gudsa Usendi. I had first read about him when in May 2013, the Naxals killed twenty-seven Congress leaders in one of the most barbarous attacks in the modern history of humanity, in Darbha Valley of Sukma district in the Red Corridor. Some two hundred top Congress leaders including former minister,

Salwa Judam founder and an aggressive anti-Naxal activist, Mahendra Karma, Congress chief Nand Kumar Patel, veteran Congress leader Vidya Charan Shukla, and prominent lady tribal leader Phulo Devi Netam were travelling through the thick jungles of Darbha Valley in a convoy of twenty-five vehicles when they found the road blocked by trees, felled by Maoists. When the cars stopped, the Naxals triggered a thirty-kilogram IED, completely blasting one vehicle and leaving a five-metre crater in the ground. In a panic to escape, vehicles collided with each other.

As soon as the vehicles jammed, over two hundred and fifty Naxals opened fire from hilltops on all sides. With no way out, the Congress leaders surrendered. The Naxals made them identify themselves. When Mahendra Karma identified himself, they beat him up, stabbed him repeatedly and sprayed him with bullets. They beat in his head with gun butts. Seventy-eight stab wounds were found on his body. Then they started firing at random, killing most of the leaders. Nand Kumar Patel's son was also with him. They broke his son's head with an axe in front of his eyes, stabbed him mercilessly and then kept firing bullets on his corpse. Vidya Charan Shukla's personal security guard couldn't bear the beastly killings and shot himself. The survivors have recounted how after the killings, the Naxals, who had a large number of women cadre, danced around the mutilated bodies.

The Naxals used automatic weapons, a bomb and modern wireless communication throughout the operation.

A four-page statement was issued by the Naxals, taking full responsibility for the attack and justified it as the punishment for Salwa Judam founder Karma.

The statement was signed by Gudsa Usendi.

Gudsa Usendi was closely in touch with the media, sending audio clips, press notes, updating them about attacks. But no journalist ever met him. No wonder he was also known as the 'phantom spokesperson' for the Maoists.

What really interests me is a statement of Usendi to a reporter, Suvojit Bagchi, in 2010, 'We have to kill informers. If we don't kill them, we will not be able to survive.'

So, who is this man called Gudsa Usendi?

An article in the magazine *Governance Now* says, 'Gudsa Usendi is just a name: the person using that name changes from time to time. Usendi, those in the know of Naxal operations in the region say, is the title used by the spokesperson for the Dandakaranya special zonal committee.'

There is a legend that in June 2000, in Potenar village in Abujhmarh, Chhattisgarh, in the middle of the night, police surrounded a hut while hunting for Naxals. Five ultras were killed, of whom one was identified as seventeen-year-old Gudsa Usendi. As if to pay back the compliment, a year after his death, the Naxal spokesperson of Dandakaranya took on Usendi's name to keep his memory alive. The practice has continued ever since.

'Gudsa Usendi is always in the picture but never seen, only read and heard,' says a former Naxal. He is like the Murtaza Arzai from *Chocolate*.

Gudsa Usendi is the *invisible enemy.*

Three years ago, when I exposed the 'invisible enemy' in *Buddha In A Traffic Jam*, the people who initiated the project dissociated themselves from the film, killing an idea in the womb. They left me alone to struggle with the film. The idea of 'invisible enemy' was my interpretation of Urban Naxalism, which they didn't understand. Instead of encouraging it, they got scared. No wonder. All innovations first scare people. But they weren't just any people. They were the producers of the film. After two years, once again, I feel convinced about the film's theme of 'invisible enemy' and my belief in the film stands reinforced.

Suresh never spoke to me after that. The students graduated and took up jobs in multinational corporations. Everyone else I understood, but why did Ravi try to sabotage his own baby? This kept baffling me until I found out that after graduating from ISB, he had started working for Suresh's LANCO group.

Two years is a very short time in a filmmaker's life if he is in the making of his film. But the same two years can feel like a lifetime if he is waiting to release his film. When Suresh refused to fund the film any further, the first feeling that hit me was of denial. Then defeat. Then depression. On the one hand, I was so broke that I was planning to quit films, sell off everything and move to Bhopal. On the other hand, I had invested everything I had in the film – my time, my savings, my experience, my ambition, my thoughts, my feelings and above all my future and my conscience. I was totally spent. Emotionally. Morally. And financially.

In such moments of utter dejection and agony and darkness all around, a little ray of hope came from Vikram Bhatt who offered me *Hate Story*, an erotic revenge drama. I had mentally resigned from Bollywood and was already contemplating taking a teaching job somewhere and spending my life peacefully. Vikram was desperately seeking a stylish director for his story of revenge and sex. And I was desperately seeking money to explore my new career options. There was a strong compulsion for me to meet him.

Vikram narrated the story of a woman journalist whose lover, a tycoon's son, in a barbaric act, gets her uterus removed, to settle scores with her for exposing his company's malpractices. The girl pledges to destroy him, brick by brick. The twists and turns were interesting and the theme was modern. He wanted to shoot immediately. The money was less than what I deserved, but I was to get it immediately. It was enough to clear all my liabilities and loans and still be left with some. I was not very comfortable with the erotica genre because in Bollywood people label you. But erotica was an integral part of the film because when the girl realizes she can't conceive, she uses her sexuality to her advantage and destroys the hero's empire.

'Sir, every director in the world wants to make erotica. You can follow taboos or you can be the director who made India's first erotic thriller,' Rohit had advised me.

When you are defeated, your risk-taking ability also dies. I almost decided to say no, but then *Buddha In A Traffic Jam* kept flashing in my mind. With some of the balance money, I could finish the film and show it to studios.

I said yes.

Hate Story, with an absolutely unknown cast of Paoli Dam and Gulshan Devaiah, no songs, no publicity on TV (we didn't get censor approval for TV), turned out to be a sleeper hit.

I still remember the exact feeling, at the Director's Association (IFTDA) meeting, attended by the who's who of Bollywood, ranging from Ramesh Sippy to Ashutosh Gowariker, David Dhawan to Vipul Shah, Madhur Bhandarkar to Sudhir Mishra, when everyone stood and applauded the success of *Hate Story*, I smiled at the irony of life that a film that was a cakewalk for me was being celebrated but the film that took everything out of me was lying in the cans. A film that tells the truth that impacts our lives was struggling to survive whereas a story that has been told a million times was getting accolades.

Success brings forgotten friends. I got a call from Bhushan Kumar. He worships Vaishno Devi, the goddess of money and success. Bhushan wanted me to make something like *Hate Story* for T Series. In Bollywood, people just want to imitate a successful film.

I am here to learn the art of films. I came out of my own free will and my will dictates that I explore new themes. I didn't know if I could repeat the same genre again. Coincidentally, Bhushan's uncle Kishan Kumar, who is my neighbour, has properties and other business interests in Goa. The wife of the then Goa Inspector General of Police had written a script. My guess is that Kishan wanted some favours from the IG who wanted a favour from Kishan in return, and that is why he wanted to produce the IG's wife's script. Kishan asked her to attach a director. She was a friend of my close friend. That's how I met her. The script was clichéd and not well structured. When Kishan asked me to direct this film, I could see an opportunity to make some money to pay my debts and market *Buddha*. I signed the film with the condition that I would rewrite the entire script. He agreed, she agreed and Bhushan agreed to produce this love story with me, instead of a hate story. I started writing the film and it worked as a detox after an intense film like *Buddha*, and *Hate Story*.

While I was working on the script, Anubhav Sinha, the director of *Ra.One*, who used to visit his estranged wife, our neighbour and a very dear friend, asked me if I could help him by directing a film for his new production house. He told me that he had bought the rights of a German psychological thriller which was a very subtle and nuanced film about a homosexual man who gets attracted and then obsessed with his new neighbour. The film explored human emotions, new worlds and the mind of an obsessed person.

To suit the Indian market, Anubhav had already changed the protagonist to a girl. The premise was that a fat girl gets attracted to her neighbour and gradually gets obsessed with him. We decided to make a classy, slow, and creepy psychological thriller. We signed Priyanka Chopra's cousin Barbie Handa, who was pretty but big in size, which suited the character. Since Anubhav was in deep financial trouble after his first two films *Warning* and *Gulaab Gang* turned out to be box-office disasters, we never discussed money and I asked him to pay me a fair amount if the film made money. My motivation for doing the film was its complex characters and an opportunity to explore the human mind.

After I finished a short schedule in Goa and came back to Mumbai, I saw a huge poster of the film standing at the reception of Anubhav's office. I was flabbergasted to see Barbie standing almost naked in the poster.

'What is this, Anubhav? Aren't we making a psychological thriller?' I confronted Anubhav.

'Yes,' Anubhav replied calmly.

'What is this then? The nude girl and all?'

'I have decided to market it like an erotica as we don't have any stars besides you, and with *Hate Story*'s success, it is easier for me to sell it like an erotica.'

I was stunned. It's not that I had anything against erotica but I just didn't want to repeat the genre. Also, I had agreed to make a psychological thriller and not an erotic thriller. I couldn't believe that a director who never got tired of narrating incidents of how his work in *Ra.One* was sabotaged by the star-producer and his coterie was doing exactly the same thing.

'You are a friend. Our sons have grown up together and people think they are twins. On top of that, you are a director. A creative person. You have started a production company so that you can make good films. How can you even think about doing this?'

'As a producer, it's my prerogative.'

I believe that a creative person always sides with good quality. I tried to question Anubhav, the director.

'You have been telling me stories about how on the sets of *Ra.One*, you were forced to compromise. I hope you remember that agony. You still want to do this?'

Anubhav wasn't prepared for such brutal questioning. He took a long pause. In an awkward situation, a small pause also feels like a never-ending hollow tunnel.

'In retrospect, I think I should have compromised,' he replied without looking into my eyes.

Till date, I have no idea what happened to me. I just stood up, in a reflex action, with a genuine smile.

'In that case, I am quitting this film. I will have nothing to do with you ever.'

'But what about rest of the shooting?'

'You are a director yourself. I am sure you can do a better job since you know exactly what you want to sell.'

And I walked out of his room. I should have been hurt. Disturbed. And angry. But I wasn't. I was still. And numb. I had no reaction. This is how emotional paralysis feels.

I am told Anubhav shot the rest of the film. During its release, he sent a cheque of eleven lacs through the Film Director's Association's (IFTDA) secretary Ashwini Choudhary and president Ashoke Pundit. They gave me a single page gagging contract which basically asked me to shut up if someone asks me if I had directed the film or not. Though Ashoke tried a lot to persuade me to take the money, I refused. He said that people forget rifts but money always comes handy. I wasn't convinced but I promised to keep quiet as my fight was about a principle and not with the film. My fight was with the Gudsa Usendis, the invisible enemies, disguised as producers.

I am happy today that I never took any money or bullshit from him. It's better to die a pauper than surrender to unethical and uncreative producers.

I got busy with the love story for T Series. It was titled *Junooniyat*. I signed Pulkit Samrat and Yami Gautam. I shot the first schedule in the Kashmir Valley and Amritsar. When Bhushan and others saw the rushes, they were spellbound. Bhushan told me that he was very ambitious about the film and wanted to market it uniquely. Everyone was very happy. The word spread. Everyone at T Series started talking about the chemistry of the lead actors, the emotions, songs, and photography. I started to prepare for my next major schedule in Patiala and Shimla.

At the same time, Bhushan's wife Divya Kumar, fresh from the fluke success of her film *Yaariyan*, was mounting her next film and was struggling to cast some decent actors. Then came the news that she had signed Pulkit and Yami for the film and my dates were allocated to her film's schedule. Same actors, same genre, same production house, same music directors, same locations and same marketing people. How was this possible? When I confronted Bhushan, he told me without any guilt that it was his wife's birthday and she asked for her film to be released before mine on Valentine's Day and he couldn't say no as 'how can I say no to madam... it's my birthday gift to her!' Bhushan's birthday gift to his wife became my film's coffin.

I want to walk off this film but everyone advises me not to. I have one film stuck, another I have left and now leaving this also will seal my career forever as no one likes directors who take stands against a producer's corruption. The film got postponed indefinitely. Again, I had no money. No work. No hope.

I sit for a long time looking at the headline 'Who is Gudsa Usendi, the "invisible" Maoist?' When I had invested everything I could, to expose Gudsa Usendis, I had no idea that someday I would be surrounded by so many of them – the invisible enemies. They control the narrative here and just won't let me create an alternate narrative. I feel blank. But this blankness isn't of defeat. It's of determination. If I really have the burning desire to tell my story, if *Buddha In A Traffic Jam* is my purpose, then I'll have to fight the Gudsa Usendis. I'll have to tell the story and expose these invisible enemies of India, so the people of my country can finally see '*Who is Gudsa Usendi?*'

36. The Intellectual Mafia

For months nobody has come to meet me. I too don't feel any need to meet anyone. But I am getting extremely frustrated as neither is Bhushan confirming the shoot nor is he shelving the film. And *Buddha In a Traffic Jam* is ready but going nowhere.

When you don't have a regular job and feel low and confused with life, you tend to indulge yourself in something to escape. Some find comfort in alcohol, some in watching movies, some in overeating, some in excessive shopping, some in depression. I found myself diving into politics. I took to Twitter and Facebook for politics and social commentary. I belonged to a club which is the secular club of Bollywood. Like them, I also hated nationalists and loved Leftist activists. I also believed that in Kashmir, the Army is the real villain. Naxals are fighting for the oppressed lot. Media is a responsible fourth pillar. And the intellectuals are always right. Slowly, I learnt that they are a country of their own, with their own constitution. They are well connected and work with precision to manage a fake secular narrative. Their narrative is fake because their constitution is fake.

They mislead people by talking about secularism as an antidote to communalism. I could see through this fakeness. Slowly, I started seeing their hypocrisy and realized that a lot of these intellectuals were directly or indirectly connected with 'invisible enemies', working for the same purpose. I started speaking against their constitution. They started avoiding me.

I could see their hypocrisy because in these two years of desperation and despair, I had travelled a lot. I had decided to write a book and travelling in small towns in India is very cheap. I had got disconnected from my roots and felt secure in the intellectual bubble of Bollywood. I was proud of being creative but I had lost touch with the basic element required to be creative, the earth. Far away from the la–la land of Mumbai, I met a new India and her people, struggling to survive the scorching sun and mammoth corruption. This Indian doesn't want to leave India because his life is hell. He is in hell because the mainstream narrative is always talking about intangible issues like secularism and never about the education, health, jobs and security of this common man of India. The people I saw on TV and films were not the people I met in real India. The more I travelled, the more real Indians I met and with this new understanding, I reached where I belonged – outside the club.

Whenever I met people from Bollywood, I felt like a failure. Maybe it wasn't coincidental but after *Hate Story*, people's perception of me got divided. Commercial minded producers, directors, actors started loving me, whereas film-wallas who thought they were here to change the world started avoiding me. Commercial film makers have only one god – Audience; one temple – Box office; and one religion, one ideology – Money. Despite being in a majority, their voice doesn't find any credence because like other businessmen they don't want to disturb their equation with their God – the Audience. They believe in destiny and follow the maxim never to underestimate anyone – 'You never know when someone's fortune will start shining.' Till date, I don't know what caused the club members' boycott; was it because of the genre of the film or was it due to my rebellion against their fake political ideology?

The club members are different. Their religion is socialism and secularism. They claim to want equality and justice but their ideology is founded on intellectual discrimination. They start with hating and condemning commercial filmmakers. By increasing the scope of their condemnation for "social evils" and humanitarian issues, their voice finds resonance amongst other intellectuals. They praise, support, and promote one another. They have an impeccable networking system. This system finds its strength by condemning a common Indian's choices and confronting his beliefs. If he wants to feel proud of his *jawans* they will accuse the army of atrocities in Kashmir. If he wants to feel happy about his festivals, they will raise the issue of drought and farmer suicide. On Diwali, they raise the issue of pollution and on *Karva Chauth,* they paint the festival as regressive.

Through their control over the narrative, they hold common people responsible for disturbing the social fabric and thereby, keep them in perpetual guilt. They create and revel in moral one-upmanship. But life isn't all about ideological correctness. Ideology is always culture, civilization, evolution, economics, social structure, and geography-specific. They want to deny this fact. They want to be the custodians of a universal moral charter and profess a narrative that protects their elitism.

We have moved from nationalization to liberalization to globalization but our narrative remains stuck in the 1960s-70s. They hide their regressive ideology behind a fake humanitarian concern in the name of art or indie cinema. All film festivals are their properties. If you are not part of the club, you'll never be invited to these festivals. David Dhawan, Rohit Shetty, Feroz Nadiadwala and other commercial filmmakers, whose one film makes more money than the films of all the filmmakers of this club put together, are never seen in such festivals. The media loves this club because it helps the media's agenda. The media gets intellectual support and in return, they get good reviews. They have become the voice of Bollywood. When I started questioning this unfair equation, they started unfollowing me. Then they started blocking me on Twitter. And, slowly, from their lives.

Discrimination isn't always gender, race or colour-based. The most damaging discrimination is of the mind and ideology. I was discriminated against by almost all my Bollywood friends, whom I used to hang around with because, like them, I also believed in a certain ideology but found it fake and alienated from reality, and elitist.

Everyone needs a villain and Narendra Modi became the media's and the intellectual gangs' main villain as 2002 was tailor-made to suit their agenda of secularism. Secularism was nothing but a ploy to attract Muslim votes and keep a control on Hindus from asserting themselves. In order to give it sanctity, the Congress regime under Sonia Gandhi patronized every creative and intellectual voice that helped her further her agenda against a potential contender, Modi, by giving them alms.

Since I always believed that development is the only solution for India's economic and social evils *vis a vis* secularism and that's what *Buddha In A Traffic Jam* also professed, it was natural for me to be aligned with Modi's agenda of development than the Congress' agenda of secularism. Also, Congress was drenched in the politics of favouritism, sycophancy, and corruption.

I was the first filmmaker who openly started supporting Modi and this hurt many. Modi was looking very strong and a lot of indicators were predicting his victory. This is when I found a letter signed by some Bollywood personalities, led by screenwriter Anjum Rajabali, that warned Indian citizens of a fascist invasion if they elected Modi. I could not fathom how a democratically elected leader could be called a fascist. Fascism exists when there is no other side of the story. In Modi's case, only his opponents' side of the story was in circulation. I could see through their divisive strategy. They were trying to reduce the debate to secularism vs communalism instead of the real issue of development vs corruption. When I raised questions about the intent of the petition signed by the liberal and Leftist filmmakers of Bollywood, out of whom most were non-practicing filmmakers cum activists like Anand Patwardhan, they started labeling me as communal, *bhakt* and Sanghi. This was that *critical point* when I should have withdrawn. But I decided to fight and take them on. I called up some journalist friends to write an article against the petition, only to realize they weren't friends anymore. In these changing times, where mainstream media ends, social media begins.

With no avenue left, I published a blog titled '15 Communal Questions to The Secular Bollywood', which went viral. The response came from unexpected quarters – the real India. People who couldn't articulate their thoughts but felt strongly against the intellectual discrimination and fakeness of secularism started connecting with me. Mine was the lone Bollywood voice of dissent against a very powerful cabal of Leftists who wanted Modi's head. They say that big fires start with small sparks and that you climb Mt. Everest by taking a small step. Here is the blog which started the fire and paved the way to change my social life forever:

15 Communal Questions to The Secular Bollywood

April 17, 2014

Yesterday, certain Bollywood personalities led by my very dear friend and renowned scriptwriter Anjum Rajabali, issued an appeal to the public at large.

In their appeal, simply put, they have warned us that India is in grave danger from divisive and communal forces led by a 'man-they-won't-name' (read Modi). These A-lister personalities have reaffirmed their faith in secular nature of 'their' India. They have appealed to all Indians to stop these communal forces by voting for only secular parties. In order to save India's cultural diversity, its pluralism and above all 'secularism'.

Suddenly, it reminded me of Indira Gandhi's era where she always cautioned us about looming dangers from CIA conspiracies. Then Rajiv Gandhi started warning us against foreign elements trying to destabilize India. Sonia Gandhi led UPA has brought us to this. Where Indians are pitted against Indians.

Armed forces and Bollywood are India's two most secular institutions. Mr. Anjum Rajabali and his ilk, in their obsession with Modi-hate, have betrayed the film industry. I am sorry your appeal has obfuscated us more than enlightening.

I have few questions and I am sure you would like to answer to help me help India.

1. I am going to vote for Modi. Am I secular? Or communal?

2. I have decided to vote for the only man who says repeatedly that India is his religion and her Constitution is his holy book. If I vote for 'that man', how will I threaten the secular fibre of India? Pl. enlighten.

3. Millions of Indians (read Hindus) love Modi. They respect him. Adore him. And some also worship him. Like many worship Shahi Imam of Congress. By hating their leader, calling him a grave danger to India, aren't you playing a communal card? Aren't you questioning the judgment of millions? Aren't you hurting the sentiments of millions? How is your appeal secular?

4. Secular, as I understand, means that religion should not play any role in governance. If it's true, then why were you quiet for last 10 years when the ruling party was continuously giving alms to Muslims? Did you and your fellow signatories utter a word when PM M.M. Singh said that minorities have first right over natural resources?

5. You say India is vulnerable. Yes, I agree. India is vulnerable to poverty, unemployment, corruption, crumbling institutions, terrorism and Naxalism (Coincidentally, I see a lot of your signatories have certified Naxal leanings). What's your hidden logic that you find 'secularism' as the only threat to India and not the above evils? Pl. enlighten.

6. Do you want me to believe that India will collapse if 'the-man-you-won't-name', Modi, comes to power? You write –' The need of the hour is to protect our country's secular foundation'. Some of you are learned men. Where does this 'secular foundation' come from? India was always a Hindu nation. Until it was invaded and looted by Moguls, British, and Congress. India has survived that. India is secular because of its Hindu culture. With its millions of gods and goddesses and millions of reincarnations, no one understands secularism better than the natives of this country. If Hinduism wasn't secular in its DNA, it wouldn't have survived for thousands of years. It's the very secular nature of Hindus that it never ever invaded or attacked any other country or civilization. Hinduism encompasses all other faiths and religions and not the other way round. Hindus have let Muslims and British rule us. It's the Hindu sensibility that has let an Italian run this country for 10 years. There is a Shahi Imam who also appeals to vote against communal forces. Who are these communal forces? Hindus? Or a party which believes in Hindu secularism and is led by 'the-man-you-hate' who says 10 times a day that his only mantra is 'Justice for all. Appeasement for none.' So whom are you pointing your fingers at? Who is threatening India?

7. Your representatives, in a Times Now debate, said that they are not pimping for any party. But you are asking us to choose. If it's not Modi-led BJP, then who do you want us to vote for? There are only two national parties. BJP and Congress. Who is secular, according to you? Unless you meant SP, BSP, AIADMK, LJD, TMC, NCP etc. What is compelling you to talk in cryptic language and not naming 'the-man'?

8. Mr. Robin Bhatt, your spokesperson, at Times Now admitted that Modi is secular. Mr. Hansal Mehta, on the other hand, in the same programme, confessed that he hates Modi. How is it that even before the ink dried on the letter, your signatories are distancing themselves with 'personal' and 'official' positions? Are you a political party? Like AAP? Or is it that AAP is speaking through you? How can there be two opinions if some passionate 'saviours' of 'art & culture' have come together for a cause they believe in, so passionately? Is it possible that some people like Robin Bhatt and many others have signed it blindly because of your deep association with them in the Writer's Association?

9. Why is it that most of the signatories also happen to be part of the same association that you have very constructively nurtured? I happen to know some of them closely. Are you sure they feel neither obliged nor compelled? Is this their absolute free and conscious voice? If they felt so strongly about India's vulnerability, how come they have never ever uttered a word about politics of any kind? How come they never spoke on social issues at least?

10. If your fellow 'secular' filmwallas feel so strongly about the 'secular foundations' and its preservation thereof, how come they never uttered a word against the Muzzafarnagar riots? Or against Shri Mulayam Singh Yadav? Or Azam Khan? Or Abu Azmi?

11. I have an observation to make. Why is it that the Leftist crusader of truth, Shri Anand Patwardhan, while speaking only looks down, never looking in the eyes? You are a genius scriptwriter who studies characters. Is this how men with convictions address the most sensitive issue which can shatter the secular foundations of Hindustan?

12. You know Bollywood is the biggest brand India has. People follow Bollywood more than cricketers and politicians. Your appeal has created an impression that entire Bollywood endorses your views. Have you written a disclaimer in your letter that these are your personal views and have nothing to do with Bollywood? Maybe not. But when media called it Bollywood's stance, did you try to call the same editors to deny it with the same enthusiasm? Or are you taking advantage of a position that was never to be misused for political or personal gains?

13. Do you seriously want us to believe that secularism is the sole issue in these elections? And not development? Are you telling me that hungry, jobless people will ensure more communal harmony then well fed, employed people? Do you seriously mean that a corrupt India, lawless India, uneducated India and a weak India has better chances of preserving 'secularity, inclusiveness & pluralism' than a modern, educated and strong India? Or is it that like many Maoists/Naxals/Leftists, you also see development as the biggest threat to your own existence and political agenda?

14. Shrimati Sonia Gandhi also issued an appeal a few days ago. Is it a coincidence that your appeal is reinforcing exactly the same? Can you vouch it for yourself and the other signatories that none has ever been a beneficiary of Congress's alms? And that none of you have any vested interest, no political agenda? And no one is firing from your shoulders? If not, where was the need to get organized and send an appeal in such a hurry? Did you send this mail to all listed film professionals or just to those who you knew will sign blindly?

15. Last but not the least, I have two young kids at a very impressionable age. Next time if we happen to meet what should I tell them... 'This is your secular uncle? Because he did not vote for Modi.' Is that the only thing you have reduced yourself to be called a 'Secularist'?

In conclusion, my fellow filmmakers, I'd like to make a small correction in the mission statement of your appeal where you write:

'However, one thing is clear: India's secular character is not negotiable!

Not now, not ever.'

I find it narrow and rhetoric. Hence, I'd like to make a small correction to suit the aspirations of millions of Indians:

'However, one thing is clear: India's United character is not negotiable!

Not now, not ever.'

And also add: 'Jai Hind.'

The blog became so viral that I was invited to my first political panel discussion on TV by Barkha Dutt for her iconic show *The Buck Stops Here*.

When I reached the venue, Anand Patwardhan was already there. I said hello with a smile to which he gave a very cold response. He asked me why I had opposed the petition. I gave him my reasons but he wasn't willing to listen and instead kept telling me how bad the Gujarat model was. He was confident that Modi could never win. Every pore of his body was oozing hatred for Modi and his supporters.

'Don't they have a right to choose the leader they like?' I asked Patwardhan.

'They don't know anything about Modi,' he replied.

'How can you say that?'

'Because I know.'

In his tone, manner, and content, there was so much authoritarianism, entitlement, arrogance, hatred and contempt for these common supporters of Modi that he did not realize that he was professing exactly what he condemned – fascism.

'If Modi is so bad why are people connecting with him?'

'Who connects with Modi? I don't know of any.'

'The poor man who sells mangoes on the streets connects with Modi.'

'I don't care about the man who sells mangoes,' Patwardhan got angry and almost screamed, 'Modi must be stopped. He must lose.'

I kept looking at him and wondered how his frail body could contain so much hatred and anger. His aura was dark and negative.

The other panelists were Nandita Das, Alyque Padamsee, Sam Balsara. All urban, sophisticated, English-speaking elites and Barkha was making it sound as if entire Bollywood was against Modi. I told her that this letter wasn't the voice of Bollywood but of an 'intellectual mafia'. I could sense that Barkha was rattled. Nandita gave me a dirty look and Patwardhan got furious. I could see what they felt about me. The way an orthodox caste-conscious Brahmin feels when touched by a sweeper. Barkha got a bit upset at my remark and though she asked me 'What do you mean by intellectual mafia?' she didn't let me answer. A patent trait of liberals. This is when, for the first time, the liberal gang started hating me and trolling me.

I knew at that very moment that I would never be invited by Barkha on *NDTV* again and that is exactly what happened, but 'Intellectual Mafia' became legitimate jargon in social media.

In the meantime, I was in advanced stages of discussing an independent release for *Buddha* with established distributors and both promised to release my film only after the elections.

But after this show with Barkha, they stopped taking my calls and till date, I don't know what made an advanced negotiation stop without any further discussion. I found it strange and I had no idea then that suddenly I had created lots of Gudsa Usendis who didn't want me to succeed with this film. They were using all their tactics to destroy me. I had only two choices: speak up or shut up. I spoke up.

I wrote another blog which again went immensely viral. With this blog on 'Intellectual Mafia', I went for a frontal attack and discovered an audience for my voice.

Intellectual Mafia

To cover up his illicit romances, rising corruption, the undercurrent of a revolt and massive defeat and humiliation by the Chinese, Nehru nurtured an 'intelligentsia' which justified his impractical economics and failed politics to the masses. The coterie of intellectuals he created was immoral. Historians know that whenever a king has surrounded himself with immoral thinkers, debauchery has begun. These short-sighted and opportunistic intellectuals justified 'socialism'. Socialism has corruption in its very DNA. Nehru chose Big State over Big Market. More State-sponsored programmes meant inefficient system, red-tapism, favouritism, weaker economy, and corruption. It meant bigger disparity between masses and policy makers. More subsidies, doles, freebies meant more arrogance of rulers for they were the ones distributing alms. They became the givers. And us, the obliged masses, the takers.

Thus, India arrived at State vs Masses. Corrupt vs Masses. Intellectuals vs Masses. Givers vs Takers.

Emergency was declared. Sanjay Gandhi took over. He created an army of morally corrupt, foreign-educated intellectuals with no track record. Their biggest strength was their unconditional loyalty to the Gandhi family. This tradition has continued. Loyalty over merit. Scheming over competence. Loot over contribution. Corruption grew. Guilt grew. Fear grew. With every scam, the family started making the intellectual wall bigger and bigger. Today this wall is full of scammers, crooks, agents, brokers, pimps, lobbyists, character assassins, land sharks etc. disguised as lawyers, journalists, NGOs, feminists, advisors, professors, socialists etc. Simply put, beneficiaries of Congress's largesse.

Their strategy was simple. Moral domination. Nehru was a thinker. But Rajiv, Sonia, and Rahul are no intellectuals. They took a different route. They redefined morality. Secularism included. Anti-Congress was new immoral. Pro-Hindu became anti-Muslim. India was morally polarized. Morality is subjective. No one can say with guarantee what is pure morality. Masses were forced to choose between moral standards (Secularism, unity in diversity, inclusive etc.) and quality of life (development). People who wanted quality of life were made to feel guilty. Hindus who wanted to celebrate their religious freedom were made to feel guilty. Muslims who wanted to be part of mainstream India were made to feel guilty. They filled India's psyche with fear, hate and guilt. They hated all indigenous, grassroot thinkers. They hated Sardar Patel, Lal Bahadur Shastri, Morarji Desai, Charan Singh, Chandrashekhar, P.V. Narsimha Rao, Atal Bihari Vajpayee, and now Modi. They are the land grabbers of Sainik Farms and Adarsh Societies of India. They run NGOs. They run media. They coin useless and irrelevant jargon to confuse the masses. They have designations but no real jobs. They are irrelevant NRIs who want us to see a reality which doesn't exist. They want a plebiscite in Kashmir. They defend stone-pelters. They want Maoists to participate in mainstream politics. They want Tejpal to be freed. Yaqub to be pardoned. But they want Modi to be hanged. They are the hijackers of national morality. Secularism included. They are the robbers of Indian treasury. They are the brokers of power. They are the pimps of secularism. They are the Intellectual Mafia.

And the hell broke loose.

37. A Fight Begins

In 2014, after my blog on 'Intellectual Mafia', I started losing friends in the film industry but started gaining lots of fans and followers outside the industry. These people started putting pressure on me to write more. They also started showing interest in *Buddha*. When Bhushan Kumar abruptly junked the T Series film, I sat and reflected on my life.

I picked up some old canvas, cleared the dust and started painting. I made many paintings and instead of selling, I gifted them to friends, I wrote more articles. I started teaching. I travelled. I started meeting all my old friends who had nothing to do with films. A new ecosystem started building up and slowly, I started connecting with people. I found my voice. And my lost confidence.

This is when I received an email from the Mumbai Academy of Moving Images (MAMI), India's number one film festival, then chaired by Shyam Benegal, that *Buddha In A Traffic Jam* was officially selected in the India Gold category which features five or six best films of the year. I couldn't believe it at first. And I didn't know if we would be able to send it for the screening as we didn't have the censor certificate which was mandatory, and I was sure of not getting it without major changes. Thirdly, the cut required background music, post-production, and some publicity material. I neither had the time nor the resources to send the film to MAMI. Life has never given me anything easily. If it was easy, it didn't last. It's never been an easy walk by the river, but a risky trek in rough terrain and extreme weather.

I decided to at least show the rough cut to as many studios as I could. I met Siddharth Roy Kapur, MD of UTV, who instantly agreed to do a screening. Very strangely, he didn't come for the screening and instead sent a creative director who had just joined, and a young girl who had no idea of Indian politics. They loved the film and told me that this was one of the finest films they had seen in a long time and it should get a well-planned release. I wasted a lot of time with them and in the end, was told that 'as a policy, we can't be associated with a film of this kind'.

I went to Viacom but almost the same story was repeated there. Viacom has also done many films which were 'different and bold' like *Gangs of Wasseypur*. Another thing that bothered me was that these studios can afford to lose hundreds of crores on mindless films which help neither the audience nor the producers, have no archival value, nor do they help society at large but when it comes to standing up for *Buddha* kind of films, they have a policy. I showed it to all the big studios, small studios, studios which were not studios, producers who wanted to become studios but after showing extraordinary appreciation, all of them backed off. How can you love something so much and still not invest in it? It happens only in Bollywood.

It's really strange but true that the films which win national awards or are selected by MAMI and other international film festivals, which deserve to be celebrated by the country and the studios, go through spine-breaking struggle, agony, humiliation, and hopelessness. Studios, producers, actors, and the entire film fraternity should invest in them and showcase them to a large audience to promote good cinema and develop audience taste for them to be able to make better films. We have invested large sums, time, and emotions in dumb cinema and by and by the audience has stopped appreciating any movie which has logic or reality. The industry makes you feel as if you have committed a cardinal crime by making such a film. This is the reason that in a social function you can identify the makers of such films with droopy shoulders, under confident body language, standing alone in a corner, and getting drunk, whereas the maker of a mindless comedy loaded with *double entendres* would be surrounded by top stars, producers, and media. We are a defective film industry.

We had only seven days left when I sent the film to the Central Board of Film Certification (CBFC) on a Friday. In the meantime, I got to know that CBFC needs clearance from the Animal Welfare Board which is based in Chennai. On Monday morning, the agent threw a bomb at me. He asked for two lacs to get the clearance within the deadline. I failed to understand why a certificate would cost two lacs to which he said that officers would have to be bribed. This was blackmailing and a film that is anti-corruption can't be made by bribing people. I was so angry that I immediately called up the Chairman of the board and asked him on what basis his people could take such huge bribes. He told me very cordially that they charged only five hundred rupees, and in order to protect filmmakers from such touts, they had gone digital. He said the board meets every Wednesday and any application that is received by Tuesday evening is reviewed at the Wednesday meeting and the decision is immediately uploaded on their site. So, in effect, clearance is given in less than twenty-four hours and that too for just five hundred rupees and a simple e-application. I was in shock. Not because of the transparency and efficiency of the authority but because of my own ignorance. Somewhere, some good work is taking place which will eventually transform India, but the media never lets the goodness be part of the main narrative.

'Please file your e-application today and on Wednesday by noon we will list you.'

On Tuesday morning, I drove to the CBFC office.

The small CBFC office in the Malabar Hill area of Mumbai doesn't look like it has anything to do with films except that its name has 'film' in it. I was expecting red tapism and someone to ask me to come only after taking an appointment, but I was treated with a lot of dignity and I got to meet the main officer immediately. I explained to him why it was crucial to certify the film within the deadline.

'Why didn't you inform us about the film's selection in MAMI? You would have got the certificate on a priority basis.'

'I had no idea that you guys consider such things.'

'It's really unfortunate that our filmmakers go to any length for their films, but nobody ever comes to meet us with their problems. They just criticize us without even meeting us once. In modern times of negative media, government servants are always the suckers as nobody listens to their point of view. Everyone needs villains and filmmakers have found it in us. May God bless them all.' He then looked at me as if he was about to ask me to leave. 'I'll organize your screening tomorrow early morning and if you get the animal clearance by noon and make the desired changes by the evening I can issue the certificate by Wednesday evening.'

'Thank you very much. I really mean it.'

'Thanks for what, sir? It's our duty. We also like it when our films are selected for prestigious awards. All the best.'

When the film ended, I was called by the screening committee in the semi-dark hall of Liberty cinema. There were four men and a lady, all from different strata. One gentleman who looked like their leader because he had some forms in his hand, smiled and spoke softly.

'Congratulations for making such a daring film. All of us just loved it. This film requires at least a thousand cuts…'

I exhaled all the air from my lungs and waited for the bad news.

'But we discussed and have come to the conclusion that we will certify it with no cuts because we believe this is a very important film of our times and it must be released in its true form, else it will lose its meaning and impact.'

'You have made a very good film. I learnt a lot,' said another member.

'There is a small correction you will have to make because it's a constitutional obligation, else we would have passed that too as there is an abusive word used with 26th January, which you will have to change… as it's a constitutional requirement.'

I immediately calculated that this would take a lot of time and I would miss the deadline. But if you really care about something a lot, you also find quick solutions. Luckily for me, the character who had said the lines was a Telugu actor and the way he had said it sounded more like *'chhaaabbeees januaree'* than *'chhabbis january'*. I saw an opening and agreed instantly.

Instead of reworking the scene, I just punched 'chaaaubbeees january' and changed that bit which matched his lips perfectly. By noon, we got the animal clearance and by 5 PM we submitted the corrections and by seven in the evening I got the adults category 'A' certificate. A few minutes before midnight, we submitted the film to MAMI. Just a few minutes before the deadline.

With this exercise, I learnt two major lessons. First, never go by hearsay and always check out the facts yourself before accusing anyone of corruption or dishonesty; and second, corruption takes place mostly when you are ignorant, desperate, and seek shortcuts.

The first screening of the film at MAMI was attended mostly by film industry colleagues. A lot of them came to check it out as they just couldn't believe that my film was in MAMI. In the film industry, they want you to fail both commercially and critically. For some, it was indigestible that I could be present in both the spectrums. The screening was so formal and the reactions so controlled that it made me nervous. People weren't laughing at the right places. There was no rustle of clothes on the seats. No coughs, no uncivilized mobile phones ringing. It's a torture for film people to see a colleague's good film. When the professor's true identity is revealed, they started getting a bit itchy. Sitting behind them, watching their response, it seemed as if their true identities were getting revealed. By the time the film ended they were confused about how to react. Some of my very good friends left without meeting me. Overall, the response wasn't very encouraging; as a matter of fact, it was depressing. Pallavi always understands my confusion so she came and stood next to me, to comfort me. For a wife to see her husband's creative pain in waiting for four years for his movie to release can be very heartbreaking.

'Mark my words, this film, hundred kilometres outside of Mumbai, will find its real audience,' I told Pallavi, holding her hand tight.

We didn't have to wait that long. The next two screenings, on following days, were more informal and full of young students and non-filmy people. The response was encouraging. In the third screening, the Q&A went on for a very long time and it wasn't restricted to only the film but national politics. Fenil Seta wrote a very good review on his blog. On social media, genuine appreciation started pouring in. The common thing amongst them was that all of them called it an 'eye-opener', which later became a cue for my marketing plan.

Reliance's Big cinema had backed out as sponsors of MAMI as it was going through a massive financial crunch and there were rumours that it might shut down. That is when elder brother Mukesh Ambani came in as the sponsor and the festival was taken over by Aamir Khan's wife Kiran Rao and Vidhu Vinod Chopra's wife Anupama Chopra. From down-to-earth, genuine filmmakers like Shyam Benegal, the festival now was in the hands of corporates, critics, powerful people's wives and their admirers. This was the year when MAMI officially transformed from a cinema lovers' festival to a corporate club festival. I learnt this when I reached Chandan cinema with Pallavi for the closing award ceremony. We were official nominees, yet we were asked to sit in a corner seat in the tenth or twelfth row whereas the front rows were all occupied by commercial stars, star wives, their friends and people who are inconsequential to indie cinema. I was officially nominated; my wife Pallavi, besides being a senior actor is a national award winner and has been on the jury of the national awards, but nobody was ready to recognize those who did not make great press.

I met Anurag Kashyap, the self-proclaimed messiah of indie films, and asked him to see the film once and help me with its marketing but he pretended to listen to me while looking for someone more powerful and left the moment he saw Anushka Sharma. This was the time when he was also cozying up with the same stars and star directors whom he had condemned all his life. It's understandable why indie filmmakers give up and become sycophants of stars to survive in this industry. I found it very funny and tragic at the same time that the festival was organized to promote the best cinema of our country, but their makers had no place of dignity in either the auditorium or their hearts. That day I saw the change with my own eyes. The MAMI organizers' agenda wasn't to promote these films anymore but to promote themselves. MAMI is just another club of the elites.

A dead film had been resurrected. With the honour and dignity it deserved. There was a tweet from a very close director friend whose films I had promoted blindly, without even seeing them, where all he wrote was about Pallavi's song. It was a very diplomatic tweet. He was monkey balancing between our friendship by doing lip service without saying anything about the film, good or bad, and also managing his high ratings with the people who wanted to kill the film without even seeing it. In this moment of happiness, his tweet hurt me.

MAMI did two things for me: it gave the film the respectability it deserved, and it made me realize that my journey from here on was going to be lonely as Bollywood would only pull this film down. I had to find my audience. My market. My space. And my voice. All alone.

The film started getting invitations from film festivals. We won the Best Original Screenplay award at the Madrid Film Festival. The response was overwhelming. I had heard about 'standing ovations' but never received one. The response was way beyond 'standing ovation'. It was the connection. Instead of clapping and taking selfies, people engaged in discussions about Naxalism and other related politics. Almost every time, the discussions became intense with the audience getting into arguments with each other. The film was evoking a definite response. It was stimulating and engaging the audience.

'How did you know that the film will work outside Mumbai?' Pallavi asked me after a tremendous response at Delhi.

'Because I know that the India Bollywood sees is not the India we live in. And this film is about the real India, real Indians and real Indian issues that impact their lives.'

It's true. The adulation, the connection, the support was coming from non-English speaking, small-town youth; the most ignored people in the national narrative. Bollywood filmmakers and other intellectuals have a fantastical idea about Naxalism. They are so isolated from the reality that when they saw the film, they perceived truth as a lie.

A senior film journalist who works with India's largest Hindi media group and is also involved with the group's film festival, which primarily encourages the spirit of indie cinema, came to my office to request me to send the film to their festival. He told me about his Leftist background and how he hates Modi's regime. I connect with Leftists very easily as I have been in their shoes. He kept pushing me until I sent the film. Then he saw the film at a screening at MAMI.

'I don't agree with the film but that is your freedom of expression,' he told me after the screening.

The film was never shown at his festival. It hurt me a lot.

That day I decided to fight. I decided to not rest until the release of *Buddha In A Traffic Jam*.

38. Kanhaiya, Azadi, and Buddha

'Afzal hum sharminda hein
Tere qatil zinda hain'
'Tum kitne Afzal maaroge?
Har ghar se Afzal niklega'
'Bharat tere tukde honge
Inshaallah, Inshallah'
'Hum leke rahenge azadi…'

'Afzal, we are ashamed
Your murderers are still alive'
'How many Afzals will you kill?
An Afzal will appear from every home'
'India, you 'll break up into parts
Inshallah, Inshallah'
'We won't stop till we get azadi…'

I am watching a viral WhatsApp video where a group of students is screaming these slogans. I think it's some students in Pakistan displaying their extreme hatred for India. But they don't look like Pakistanis. Their accent is also different. Is it Kashmir? As the video progresses, I realize it's neither Pakistan nor Kashmir. In my wildest dreams, I couldn't have ever imagined that these are the students of Jawaharlal Nehru University (JNU), shouting anti-national slogans, inside the campus, right in the heart of India's capital. Fifteen kilometers from the Parliament, the temple of democracy.

I stand up. My breathing is getting heavier. I am trembling with disgust. I have never felt such rage ever before. I love India and I am very proud of India. I love students and I am very proud of our students. It was beyond my understanding that the students whom I hold in such high esteem are passionately seeking the breakup of my motherland, my *karmbhoomi*, my love – India. How can they celebrate a dreaded terrorist who attacked our Parliament?

Is this the beginning of an end? Has the Naxal movement finally revealed itself in urban India? What I see in the video is exactly what we depicted in *Buddha*. Is the theme of my film taking on a life? I fill a glass with ice and water and gulp it down like a traveler in a desert drinks water. But I am still thirsty.

A couple of days ago, on the cold night of February 9, 2016, an official cultural event had turned into a political rally. The event was against the hanging of Afzal Guru, a Kashmiri terrorist convicted for the attack on Parliament on 13 December 2001 and hanged on 13 February 2013. The event was led by the president of Jawaharlal Nehru University Student's Union (JNUSU), Kanhaiya Kumar, Kashmiri students Umar Khalid and Shehla Rashid and other student leaders of Leftist parties that are sympathetic to the Naxal movement. Kanhaiya Kumar and his fellow students shouted anti-India slogans including the prayers for India's break-up and eventual devastation.

Kanhaiya Kumar and his gang get arrested on February 11th on charges of sedition. A 'war of narratives' begins in India. Rohith Vemula, a PhD student at the University of Hyderabad, had committed suicide a few weeks ago, leading to widespread Leftist protests around the country, because he was supposedly Dalit – the insinuation was that he had been driven to his death by caste oppression. Anybody who saw these protests in isolation is politically naive because it was just a scene in a screenplay.

It connects now with the Kanhaiya episode. The screenplay started with the Film and Television Institute (FTII), where a section of the students went on strike over the appointment of a new Director; then the IIT Madras row over the Ambedkar Periyar Study Circle (IIT Madras had de-recognised the students' association after a complaint that it was creating hatred against Hindus. The ban was later lifted.); then Vemula; and now it looks like it is culminating at the citadel of Urban Naxalism – JNU.

Looking at the *modus operandi*, I can very easily see that Kanhaiya Kumar and the gang is just the front organization for the Naxals. Kanhaiya is being used by the faculty as an 'intellectual terrorist' to wage war against the State. They assume that the Modi government is new and not settled as yet, and therefore it's the right time to strike. In no time, the usual suspects like Barkha Dutt, Arundhati Roy, and all other Naxal sympathizers come out openly in support of Kanhaiya. A civil war-like situation is being created, the government is attacked for suppression of dissent, curbing freedom of expression and for being anti-Dalit. It's a full-fledged war between the Leftist forces and the State. All front organizations and supporters have come out of the closet. JNU is the battlefield and Kanhaiya their puppet.

In the chaos of the Kanhaiya episode, the media keeps a vital development in the Red Corridor hidden from us. In the last quarter, security forces have achieved greater success than ever in tackling left-wing extremism and there was over a thirty per cent decline in violence perpetrated by Naxals this year.

Seventy-six Naxal cadres were killed in the first few months of this year in comparison to fifteen in the same period last year. According to the Home Ministry, as many as six hundred and sixty-five Naxals were arrested and almost the same number surrendered as compared to just above hundred last year in the same period.

Almost at the same time, the Home Ministry cracked down on a number of NGOs which got foreign funding in the past couple of years. In the second half of 2015, the Indian government cancelled registrations of more than ten thousand NGOs across the country, including Greenpeace. With the increasing fatalities, arrests, and surrenders of the cadre, the tightening grip of the security forces, decrease in funding through NGOs, the Naxals have been feeling the heat, hence FTII, Vemula, and Kanhaiya seem obvious and logical tactics.

I heard Kanhaiya's speech and it took me back to my college days when student politics wasn't as sophisticated and well-oiled. When media professionals had not become brokers. It wasn't limited to ideological confrontations but also involved *desi katta*, swords, *guptis*, hockey sticks, crude bombs and Rampuriya *chakoos*. In the midst of all this there were speeches and sloganeering by the student leaders and their mentors from either Congress, Akhil Bharatiya Vidyarthi Parishad (ABVP) or Leftist parties.

Those speeches were mostly about how to make the university a better place for students. Only leaders from Leftist parties used to gives speeches which were about a utopian social engineering, and freedom from the State. Listening to Kanhaiya, I felt as if I was listening to a pop version of speeches I heard decades ago. Barring Kanhaiya's personal mannerisms and dialect, his speech was straight out of a Communist template. A narrative which hasn't changed a bit with the changing times.

It appears that Communists have a 'speech template' and all their leaders are given training in speaking the same way. The strategy is simple: take an unattainable, high moral ground, raise concerns over all evils of society, divide people but never present a plan to eradicate these evils. They have mastered the art of creating a fake narrative. In any society, there are always some people who are perpetually dissatisfied with everything. To an extent that even if you give them *azadi*, they will find problems in that too. From my student days until Kanhaiya, they have been fooling people without suggesting any solutions. Ask Kanhaiya how he will get us *azadi* from poverty and *Manuvaad* and Brahmanism and I am sure he will shift the goalpost. This is why I do not trust Leftists. They only raise questions. Never give answers.

I won't go into the details of Kanhaiya's speech as it's a function of his political agenda, but I'd request him not to mention *Manu Smriti* without studying and understanding it. *Manu Smriti* doesn't speak of the "caste system." It talks of *Varnas*. Varna is not caste. Nor was "Manu Smriti" a "law book" enforced by the State. Hardly anyone reads the *Manu Smriti* in popular Hinduism. It's time Communists stop using *Manu Smriti* as a polemic to exploit uneducated, poor people. Their strategy is to use innocent people to further their agenda, which is why I do not agree with Communists.

I'd also advise Kanhaiya and his supporters not to talk of freedom of speech as JNU is the last place where dissent and freedom of expression (FoE) is practiced. People with 'If you aren't anti-State, you are an enemy' kind of attitude must not give us sermons on FoE. FoE is part of an Indian's native intelligence. By native, I mean Hindus like Kanhaiya and me. It's native Hindu civilization's strength and openness that Muslims and Christians are accepted in mainstream culture. Dear Kanhaiya, if you chose to blame one hardworking *chaiwala* for all the evils, just because he represents Hindu aspirations, it shows your lack of understanding. It shows you have thoughts but your mind is not *azad*. To understand what I am saying, you may have to consult *Manu Smriti*.

Another reason I do not subscribe to the Communism of Kanhaiya is that Communists practice violence. Tens of thousands of innocent people have been killed in Naxal-infested areas and millions remain poor and oppressed. Your comrades do not allow TV in tribal areas as it can instill greed in the Adivasis. They would want to make money and the only antidote to your poison is money. Communism is not an ideology, it's an economic system, but the mentors of Kanhaiya fool people by projecting it as an ideology. Liberalism and even Fascism are ideologies but Communism is not. That's why I don't subscribe to this erroneous politics.

Communism is really good only as textbook material. In practice, it destroys societies and their spirit. Look around the world and you will find that wherever Communism reached, people lost their freedom. Their voice. Their lives. First, it makes you angry, then hapless and then a victim. It does not allow dissent or debate. Communism's only contribution is that it has encouraged poverty, mediocrity and violence. I shun such hypocrisy.

The Dalai Lama is a living example of how much *azadi* Communism allows. He has been living in free India as a refugee, away from his motherland, because of Communism. West Bengal is another living example of how Communist ideology destroyed the entire region. Today, Kolkata is a monument of poverty and failure. I can bet you will never meet anyone who has been benefited by Communism or terrorism. In modern India, Communists have acted as intellectual terrorists.

So, people who are excited and want to portray Kanhaiya as a hero or a youth icon aren't in love with Communist ideology. They have nothing to do with JNU. They don't want any *azadi*. They are supporting him because they don't want Modi to grow. Because Modi means *azadi* from corruption, sycophancy, and middlemen. Public relations czarina Niira Radia's phone conversations with senior journalists became public knowledge in 2010 and showed how compromised our media persons are. But even she will vouch that most of our media men and women don't want this *azadi*.

Hence, Arvind Kejriwal.

Kejriwal fails.

Hence, Kanhaiya.

It's as simple as that.

Kanhaiya represents aspirations of just a few thousand students of JNU. Even they will flip once they have to earn their bread and butter. India is too big and has millions of real students who actually want *Azadi* from such negativity, pseudo-intellectualism, and broker–ship. Students who want to be proud of their nationality, their Constitution, their government, their people, and their culture– Kanhaiya does not represent their aspirations. He is not a genuine–youth icon. He is a trained, well-funded student leader on hire. By calling him a youth icon, you are insulting millions of Indian youth/students who at this very moment are studying hard and getting prepared to create wealth and repay their motherland by getting her *Azadi* from poverty and 'traders of poverty'.

I feel as if someone has taken the script of *Buddha* and is playing it in real life. The only difference is that in the end, unlike Kanhaiya Kumar, my hero Vikram Pundit, instead of destruction of India, professes the idea of reconstruction of India.

As I hear Kanhaiya Kumar and his gang chant slogans like '*Bharat se azadi.... Le kar rahenge azadi.... Brahmanvad se azadi... bhookmari se azadi*' (Freedom from India... from Brahminism... from hunger) in this viral video, I want to ask him how he envisages such *azadi* will be brought about. I am sure he has no ideas and that's where *Buddha* comes in, which shows an alternate way to find *azadi* from poverty and oppression. My resolve to release the film has become stronger and absolutely unconditional. Because I know that *Buddha*'s time has come.

Buddha must win.

39. *Vande Mataram* at JNU

March 11, 2016

The road from Ahmedabad to Bhuj is straight, long and empty.

I am travelling to shoot an experimental short film, a first for me. I have never travelled with such a small crew of just seven people. I love to drive around India. For the recce of *Junnoniyat,* I travelled more than sixty thousand kilometers in an Innova and wrote the entire script while on Indian highways. I love this isolation from the world. But this drive isn't so peaceful, as my DA (Director's Assistant) Naireeta (pronounced Noeereeta), a young Bengali girl with utopian dreams and unrelenting energy, is constantly on the phone, but I can't stop her as she is doing something which I have been waiting for, for long. She is talking to the head of cinema studies at JNU, Ira Bhaskar, and at this moment in my life, nothing can be more crucial than this.

Since distributors and studios were backing out regularly, and the Bollywood club was trying to sabotage the film, I realized that the only thing which comes between the film and its audience is an old, corrupt system of distribution. What if I completely avoid it and reach my audience directly? Of course, the digital route is there but that opens up only if the film gets a technical release in theatres. What if I completely avoid the traditional route of distribution? It wasn't the time to think out of the box; it was time to demolish the box. Completely. I quickly made a marketing plan with just three slides and zero budget.

Slide 1:

Where are we?

- No money
- No infrastructure
- No marketing/ PR/ media support
- Strong-muscle, organized opposition

Slide 2:

Where do we want to go?

- Reach the audience directly, no middlemen
- Out-of-the-template only
- Become the New 'New'
- Establish an 'Alternate Narrative'

Slide 3:

How do we reach there?

- Disruptive marketing
- Target universities/ institutes with cinema/media department
- Institutes with political image as the drivers
- Promote the event on social media, create word of mouth
- Use students as brand ambassadors
- Make teasers with ordinary people
- Do technical release in 10-25 screens
- Release digitally

The first institute we wrote to was JNU. Kanhaiya and his gang's anti-India sloganeering and his subsequent arrest on sedition charges triggered an intense nationwide debate on the suppression of dissent and therefore curbing of freedom of expression. JNU became the symbol of freedom of expression. What could have been a better place to screen *Buddha* than this projected 'Mecca of dissent'? What could be better timing than this when the entire nation was discussing the role of Urban Naxalism?

So, I wrote to Ira Bhaskar, dean, cinema studies, JNU. Once. Twice. Thrice... Naireeta called her several times. Messaged her many times. She returned the call only once, to tell Naireeta that– '*Abhi mahaul theek nahi hai.*' The atmosphere isn't conducive now? We explained to her why it is so important and relevant to show the movie now, and she promised to get back, 'I will speak to the faculty and get back.'

I thought of asking my music director Rohit to seek Swara's help (who is part of his band Swang) in convincing her mother as Swara and Swaang strongly advocate freedom of speech. Rohit met me with Swara's partner Ravinder Randhawa, who offered to talk to Ira as he was anyway going to Delhi.

Ravinder came back after a couple of days and told me that they tried to reason with Ira, but she said '*mahaul* is not good, hence *no* film can be shown'.

'*Akela chalo re*...when feeling low, walk alone,' I tell Naireeta who is feeling bit depressed.

'How can you not flutter an eyelid, sir? It was such a good opportunity for our film to make some noise,' Naireeta counter-questions me.

'Because Ira hasn't said no. There is still some hope. Let me talk to her directly.'

Ira promises to get back, but she doesn't get back. At all. She doesn't answer calls. She doesn't acknowledge us.

I need to think up a Plan B. An alternative strategy.

I am going through tweets and news. Everywhere, the intellectual ecosystem is trying to make Kanhaiya a youth icon. Kanhaiya has been exploiting his newfound fame and has been giving anti-State speeches, flying business class, attending seminars and raising questions about the government's tactics to curb freedom of speech.

I come across a tweet from a friend, a sensible director and a wonderful human being, Hansal Mehta, where he informs that his film *Aligarh*, based on the life of a homosexual professor, will be shown at JNU the day after.

'Nooooooooo. How can they?' I ask myself. There must be something not correct. But then I read tweets from the writer of the film, the movie's supporters and many JNU students confirming the screening.

This means that the '*mahaul*' for some films is '*theek*'.

It's time to act. It's time to jump into a fight.

I take out my phone and write two tweets addressed to the leader of the FoE movement, Kanhaiya Kumar, who is also the elected president of JNUSU.

Dear Kanhaiya,v want to show #BuddhaInaATrafficJam @JNU but they aren't allowing.Film shows how India can get real 'Azadi'.Pl Help

RETWEETS 500 LIKES 272

9:40 AM - 11 Mar 2016

Why isn't #BuddhaInATrafficJam allowed to screen at #JNU coz it exposes sinister politics? Or coz it features @AnupamPkher or selective FoE?

172 93

Around 11 AM, I start getting several calls from unknown phone numbers. At about 11.45 AM, Anupam Kher calls me to find out why the media is calling him. He wants to know if we have any documentary evidence to substantiate that JNU indeed discriminated against our film. I brief him and mail him all the documentary evidence. By 12.30, Rahul Shivshankar of NewsX breaks the news and soon, almost all TV news channels start beaming the news on how *Buddha In A Traffic Jam* is stuck in the JNU jam. Calls start pouring in. News channels insist on talking to me live.

Almost every channel and newspaper cover it in their headlines. Social media is abuzz with the controversy, deciding the balance of power between the left and the right. Only two channels, who have been extra vocal about JNU and the FoE issue, never mention it – Barkha Dutt's *NDTV* and Rajdeep Sardesai's *India Today.* Also, as expected, nobody from the film industry, not even the champions of FoE, stand up in my support.

I have finished the day's shoot and am standing alone looking at the never-ending salt pans of Bhuj which have turned golden under a gigantic sun setting behind Pakistan's horizon. Beyond the border Barren land all around me. The only things one can see are the sky, the earth, the sun, the horizon. And a mass of silence. Nothing in between. I am part of the same air, same temperature. I am not outside this landscape. I am the landscape. I am sure our *rishis* wrote the eternal truth in the *Rigveda*, *'Tatvam asi,'*– Thou art that– while meditating on such uninterrupted landscapes. I am feeling like that. Uninterrupted.

As the evening breeze of March brushes my face, I feel that Buddha is not any different from me. I am him. I am Buddha. And like the hero of the film, I am also stuck in a traffic jam created for me by the invisible enemies. I have figured out that I can't play this game of politics as a filmmaker alone. I have to become a player of the game. I decide to make my voice heard and give life to *Buddha In A Traffic Jam*. I take out my phone and open a poster-making app which I have never used, I click a picture of the sunset and I make a poster. Knowing well that there is no turning back from here, I type a hashtag #IAmBuddha and publish it.

March 15, 2016

I am back in Mumbai. My inbox is full of people extending their support, requests for interviews, and abuses. In this chaos, I get a call from a student of JNU. He asks me if I would be interested in screening the film at JNU. Without any hesitation, I say yes. He says he will figure it out and get back. Oops, I have forgotten to ask his name.

March 16, 2016

I get a call from him again. He says that he has got the permission for 18th March between 5.30-8.30 PM from the student's body, JNUSU.

'How many students are you expecting?' I ask him.

'Sir, approximately hundred. We will also get a few friends from outside so say, hundred and fifty,' he tells me.

'What's the capacity of the auditorium?'

'About two hundred to two fifty.'

'Won't it look empty?'

'Sir, more students want to come but they are scared of the faculty. But we will try to convince them. Please don't say no now. It's a matter of our prestige.'

'Let me think.'

'Sir, since you said yes we got the permission.'

Oops, I again forget to ask his name. I don't want to call back to know his name and sound desperate.

But his proposal has also put me in a real dilemma. JNU is at the centre of national news. Our film is in the news. All political groups are watching the controversy keenly. If we go, it may appear that we are trying to milk the situation. If we don't go, the film doesn't get the platform I have been fighting for, for so long. What if we go, and there aren't enough students? What if it becomes political? What if they try to sabotage it? What if they write bad things about the film? What if it's a ploy by those whom the film exposes? I have been wanting to show the film at JNU and now when the opportunity comes knocking on my door, I am worried about how many people will come to see the film. In testing moments, it's always the sceptic mind that takes over.

I call Kher saab. He takes a long pause after I inform him about my fears that there may be a chance of not many people coming to see the film, and media and opponents of the film, who suddenly popped up from nowhere, will try to show pictures of an empty hall to suggest that no one is interested in the film and therefore justify Ira's discriminatory action. Anupam Kher listens to me patiently and then he says something I needed to hear most.

'Vivek, our real job is to make movies and show them to our audience. Even if ten students come, we must show the film to them. Just because ninety people don't want to see the film doesn't mean we can take away the right of those ten people who want to see it. A film is successful even if it changes just one heart. I think your film has that power. In the end, you will get what you deserve.'

'Will you come?'

'Yes.'

In the film industry, no star worth his salt will ever do something like this. He is the only person, besides my wife Pallavi and my DA Naireeta, who wants me to screen the film, whereas everyone else is telling me why I shouldn't be showing it anywhere before the formal release.

In the evening, I again get a call from the JNU boy. This time I ask his name. He is Saurabh Sharma, joint secretary of JNUSU.

'Sir, now everything is fixed, we students have contributed ourselves and raised money for the projector and a screen. There are over hundred confirmations. Sir, everybody thinks JNU means only Kanhaiya and anti-national students, so no one cares about students who love India. We may be small in numbers but we do exist. For their sentiments please don't say no.'

'But who is saying no? We will come.'

'Is it a yes?'

'Yes.'

March 18, 2016

I reach Delhi, guarding the hard drive which has the film's digital print. I have no idea what is in store.

The organizing boys come to meet me and try to understand from Naireeta the various technical requirements.

'Sir, we will start the screening at 6 pm sharp as we have permission only till 8.30 pm. After that, the students start leaving for dinner.'

'That's OK. We can start even at five or five thirty.'

'Sir, five may be too early as there will be a lot of sun.'

'What has sun got to do with us?'

'Sir, the screening has been shifted outdoor at the admin bloc.'

I am blank.

'What? But, why?'

'Sir, they refused to give us the auditorium saying there will be too few people. So, we decided to screen it outdoors but admin gave permission only from 5.30-8.30 PM.'

No filmmaker worth his salt would allow his film to be shown outdoors before the theatrical release. That too with bad projection, bad sound. That's not what we work so hard for.

'But how can we screen it outdoors? You can't begin until it's dark and it doesn't get dark before seven. Why can't you make another request to the admin to give you the auditorium? If you want I can come or I can request Mr. Kher to speak. That may make the difference.'

'Sir, firstly that will never happen. Secondly, after the auditorium's cancellation, there has been an amazing response from the students who were silent so far and now they are coming out in open and committing to attend the screening and I have a feeling that the auditorium won't be able to take five-six hundred students.'

'What? How many students did you say?

'Sir, five to six hundred.'

For a filmmaker like me, who has shown the film to a maximum of hundred and fifty people in one screening, this feels like heavy showers in the desert of Jaisalmer.

Never in the life of this film had I imagined these kinds of numbers at JNU. But this is also true that never in my life had I imagined that someday I would be forced to show my film outdoors, prior to its official release. For everyone, it has become an event. For me, it is the future of the film. Inside me, there is a conflict between a filmmaker who wants a perfect screening and a man desperate to tell the truth. Naireeta can quickly make out whenever I am confused.

'Sir, you always say that in the moments of confusion never follow your fears but follow the design of things.'

Five hundred students won't even wait for the film to get over and will start posting comments on the film on social media. One bad word and that would be the end. These aren't just five hundred students but they are five hundred live cameras ready to broadcast to thousands of people in an instant. If life is about taking chances, this is that chance. I am taking this chance.

I quickly write to Ira Bhaskar, inviting her for the screening. Kher saab is insisting that he wants to go half an hour early just to walk around and interact with the students. So, we leave at 5 PM to be there at 5.30.

When we reach JNU, we feel like we are in a different world. Definitely not the world we were promised. The entire arena outside the admin bloc is jam–packed with electrified students. The car can't move further so we are forced to stop about four hundred metres before the venue.

'You still want to walk?' I ask Kher saab.

'Only if I can get out.'

Kher saab's desire to walk gets crushed instantly by thousands of students shouting '*Vande Mataram*'. This is not the JNU I had known. The cop-in-charge whispers in my ears '*Kam se kam paanch chhe hazaar ladka hai.*' Five to six thousand students?

We try to walk towards the stage but it's impossible to move even an inch. It's not that we have never been amongst charged up fans but this seems like an unregulated crowd of uncontrollable students. That too in JNU. This is when more than two dozen girls come from somewhere and form a human chain around us and help us walk to the screen.

When the organizing students want to start the film, the other students won't let the film begin until we speak to them. I look for Saurabh but I am informed he has gone to an NDTV debate with

Kanhaiya. This is when someone announces my name to speak to students. I go up on this makeshift dais and I choke looking at the sea of students, charged and exhilarated like sea waves on a heavy monsoon day. I am a little overwhelmed. I didn't come here to give a speech. I look for Naireeta but can't find her.

I have been a debater but never ever gave an impromptu speech and that too in front of so many politically motivated students and a battery of media cameras looking for a political controversy in a politically volatile institute. I know students want me to speak on the current political controversy. What do I say? Do I talk about the film? Or just say a few good words and hand over the mike to Anupam Kher? I am holding the mike but my mind is blank. I look around. There are students on the ground, on the stairs, on the terraces, on trees and on top of cars. The sun is setting behind the redbrick admin bloc, and entire JNU is filled with the chants of '*Vande Mataram*'. It seems like a historic moment. Then I see some twenty-odd students raising back flags and screaming '*Agnihotri wapas jaao… Sanghi wapas jao…*'. Why are they protesting against me? They haven't even seen the film.

Rejection has an amazing quality. It gives you strength. I don't know if it was the chanting of *Vande Mataram* or the sloganeering against me. Or both. I am taken over by some force. And I speak. From the heart. Like I have never done before.

'Friends, I visit a lot of universities and colleges but this is the first time that I have witnessed such energy. Also, let me tell you one more thing. Right behind this campus is the IIMC, the Indian Institute of Mass Communication. I am an IIMC alumnus. It has been a few decades now. These walls, these sketches, this atmosphere, these trees, nothing has changed. Only one thing has changed… for the first time, I am hearing chants of *Vande Mataram* and *Bharat Mata Ki Jai* here. If this is not a revolution, then what is a revolution? If this is not freedom, then what is freedom?

'When I was a student like you, in those days, we had only two choices, to either wear Bata shoes or Corona shoes. The problem today is that you are faced with too many choices and that leads to confusion. That deprived society where young boys were being told that there is a design out there where you have to fit in as either an engineer or a doctor, I have studied in those times.

'In independent India's history of 70 years, one narrative which never got a chance to bloom is that of a Hindi-speaking vernacular boy, a small-town middle-class boy. For as soon as he steps into Delhi or Bombay, the English-speaking group, a certain mindset makes him feel so inferior and they never let his voice be heard... I have experienced that. When I had come to study at IIMC, there were 21 girls in my class and 4 boys. I was a young boy who studied in Bhopal, who didn't know English, who didn't have a pair of jeans, I felt very inferior. I have experienced that. I have understood that in this country there has been a copyright on intellectualism. The people who love their country, who love their hometown, who love their parents, who want to do something for this country despite its shortcomings, these people have never been given the status of "intellectuals" or "elites". The status of "intellectual" has been given to those people who speak of a utopia which is never possible. I remember my professor teaching us that India needs freedom from lots of evils and from a lot of things, I asked him, "But how?" and he never answered.

'I am looking for that answer for the past 30 years, I have still not found it. The freedom we speak of, how will we find it? And from what do we want this freedom? We don't want it from *Manuvaad*, I can guarantee you that no Indian student knows what *Manuvaad* is. *Manuvaad* doesn't speak of caste, it speaks of a world where Brahmins can become Shudras, Shudras can become Brahmins. We don't need freedom from *Brahmanvaad* because the country has benefited a lot from that too. We need freedom from this country's mediocrity... from inefficiency... from incompetence... we need freedom from those people who despite staying in the country don't let the country move forward. It's been 70 years since freedom, what is the reason that we have yet not been able to provide simple education for all? We need freedom from those people who have not allowed the middle class, who represent real India, to move forward. In all institutes, in all universities and all other places where a thought process could grow, it was curbed and controlled by the so-called elites, who have allowed only their ideology to grow, we need freedom from this narrative.

'This film has been made out of that anger and frustration. This film speaks of the freedom that India needs in 2016, it speaks of that revolution. Only one revolution has been spoken of in this country, never the other. The other revolution will only come from Indianness, from innovation, from creating capital, from creating wealth, it will come when you will send money to your home. No one can starve and revolt. There are some people who want a section of people to starve, so that the other revolution comes and their political shops keep running.

'This is the reason why this film has been made. This film doesn't agree with a certain thought process. Unfortunately, in India, all the literature festivals, film festivals are run by people with a fixed mindset and a fixed narrative, they are not run by people who love the country, their contribution to India's capital is zero but to India's chaos is hundred percent. They won't let this film show there. That's why we are here. To show you directly, like the film says, "without the middlemen".

'The only reason I am premiering this film here is because my faith in JNU is so high. I have a right here. Just under these trees, I have romanced my girlfriends. This is my land. When I heard Kanhaiya's speech, I felt that someone is cutting me out from here and I said to myself that at any cost nobody can cut me out from my country and my institute. And today you guys have decided to have this film shown here, this is the victory of the students, this is the victory of freedom of speech and lastly, I would like to say that this is the beginning of a new revolution. A constructive revolution.

'*Vande Mataram. Jai Hind.*'

The arena explodes with '*Vande Mataram*' and '*Bharat Mata ki Jai*'.

While watching the screening with the students, I am thinking about the people who are against this film. Why were some faculty members not letting it screen? Who are this faculty? I am amazed at their political power. Are they running these institutes at their whims? Are these educational institutions or political *madrasas*? Is the faculty Taliban and are the students *jihadis*? Why is it that the Barkha Dutts of the world did not even bother to cover this historic moment? Or have they taken an oath to cover only the anti-national news?

The politics, on which I had based my film, and which up until now I only believed and felt intellectually, was slowly revealing itself in actuality. Conviction of thought is stronger than any other power. I can see this as the students laugh, clap, cheer at the right moments, which the Bollywood friends of mine missed at the MAMI screening.

I text Pallavi, 'See, I told ya.'

'I knew that.' She texts back.

When the film ends, there is a huge roar of applause that makes a standing ovation redundant. For the next two hours, we are hounded by an unruly media and a selfie attack by our newfound fans and supporters.

As I head back to the hotel around midnight, some fifty-sixty students are taking out a victory march for Umar Khalid, who has just been released on bail.

Victory march? Really?

40. Gandhi vs Mao: IIT Gandhinagar

Soon after the JNU screening, we start getting invites from various universities and institutions for the screening of our film. Naireeta shows me the emails and is super excited.

'We have got an invite from IIT Gandhinagar, sir. Isn't that great?'

I am busy reading a text message on my phone.

'Why, aren't you happy, sir?' She asks me when she doesn't get any reaction from me. I don't want to spoil her mood by giving her the bad news that I have just received.

Just a few weeks before the JNU screening, I had met with an executive at PVR Cinemas, India's largest chain of multiplexes, because they run a project called 'Director's Rare' under which they support award-winning yet unreleased films on limited screens ranging between ten and twenty-five. To the producer it costs two to five lacs and his film gets a technical release for him to be able to sell satellite, overseas, digital, and other rights, and recover some of his costs. If one is really lucky, some indie lovers also come to see such films. I have been to some screenings and never found more than ten-fifteen people watching it, including the director and some actors. It's a tragic state of affairs but I wasn't complaining. The system brings down the maker of small indie films to such a level that even one screening feels like winning an Oscar.

I met PVR COO Deepak Sharma and showed him the screener. Deepak understands politics pretty well. When he saw the screener of the film, he got excited and told me that it's a very powerful film and asked me to go for a full nationwide release with hundred and fifty prints. A few meetings later, I realized that what Deepak had proposed would require nothing less than thirty-forty lacs for the digital prints. This is exactly hundred percent more than what we had. I did some quick mental math. I thought I would release it without any conventional TV or print advertising. Digital is free, which I can manage. I may need some money for travelling and print material. This would cost another ten lacs. I need fifty lacs. PVR charges fifty lacs to release a film and here they were offering to release my film for free. I didn't want such an opportunity to go away.

I called several people who finance films but they weren't interested in a non-starrer film and that too one which had been stuck for so long. Some people did not understand how a film could be released without publicity. The powerful people didn't want to touch it after the JNU screening. I requested Anurag Kashyap to see the film since he has major clout in distributing such films but he didn't respond. I even pleaded with Manish Mundra, founder of Drishyam Films, who has produced several small indie films, to invest any amount from five lacs to fifty but by and by I realized that it was going to be impossible to get film industry folks to invest in a controversial film. Also, it was impossible for anyone to understand how a film could create awareness without spending big bucks in conventional advertising. We don't have an innovation culture nor do we understand disruptive ideas. No wonder we are surrounded by mediocrity. After a lot of humiliation, disgust, and hyperacidity, I decided to meet Deepak and tell him my real situation. It's not easy to stand naked in front of people who put you on a pedestal.

As I was about to enter the swanky elevator of the PVR office in Andheri, someone called my name and he turned out to be an old friend and a trade consultant who had worked at Sony Pictures and is well connected with the distribution networks. He told me that he was looking for me as a childhood friend of his, Jay Merchant, wanted to contact me. Jay Merchant runs a theatre group in Vadodara and also teaches theatre. Jay was planning a play on the Naxal issue and while doing the research he read somewhere that I had made a film on Naxalism and since then he had been trying to find me. He made me speak to Jay on the phone. Jay wanted to see the film. I told Jay that I could show him the film in my office as I didn't see any hope of releasing it. On hearing this, he took a long pause.

'How much money do you need?' he asked me.

'Fifty maybe... but whatever I get would be fine...'

'I have a student in my theatre group who wants to invest small amounts in Hindi films. He wants to invest in a ready product. Would you be interested in meeting him?'

I felt like I was dying and someone had brought in my ventilator and asked me how long I would want to live.

In Vadodara, I met a wonderful couple, Sharad and Shreyanshi Patel. Sharad had invested some money in a Gujarati film which turned out to be a blockbuster. He wanted to invest small amounts in irregular cinema. He is apolitical and just by seeing the screener, he agreed to invest the required amount. I had reached his house at ten in the morning and by one PM, the deal was locked.

A tripartite contract was drawn up with PVR and all marketing plans and logistics were confirmed. It was decided that the film would release on May 6 on hundred and fifty-odd screens.

I was supposed to sign the contract today.

'What happened sir? Aren't you happy with the news?' Naireeta asked me again.

'No, I am happy with the news… it's just that we have the film, the audience, an investor but no distributor.'

'What do you mean no distributor? We have PVR, no?'

'No. They have backed out.'

'But why?'

'I don't know. And I think we will never know.'

Naireeta turned pale. First breakup, first news of someone's death and first rejection at work are the most painful feelings.

'I know… sir… I know… exactly…. Yes… I know…' she whispered as if she had understood the games this industry plays and then she added in the same breath, 'Should I cancel IIT Gandhinagar?'

'Not at all. There wasn't any PVR when we decided to make this movie. There was no PVR when we screened it at JNU. There will be no PVR when decades later people will refer to this film for understanding various shades of the Naxal movement. But the film will remain.'

The first thing the film industry does to a free-willed filmmaker is that it makes him believe that there is no life without the producers, distributors, and money. Actually, it's the other way around. There is no life for the middlemen without the creators.

Since the middlemen have the money, they have set the rules of the game which make them more powerful and rich and the filmmakers weaker. This is the reason filmmakers give in and start playing by their rules to fit in and survive, and in return, the truth and the creative quotient of the film become natural victims. I shall not give in to the middlemen.

The IIT Gandhinagar campus is new, the amphitheater-style indoor auditorium is big enough to take over a thousand people. The screening is at 6 PM. It's 5.50 PM and there isn't a soul except for the organizing students. My heart is pounding as, like any greedy filmmaker, I don't want to run the film in an empty hall after the blockbuster screening at JNU.

It's 5.55 PM and there isn't anyone in the hall.

'It's OK, we can't expect engineers to come and see a political drama,' I tell Naireeta who is very disheartened.

'Maybe they haven't informed students properly. Looks like a flop show.'

My phone rings. It's Akshay Rathi whose family owns the Rathi group of cinemas in the central province of India. He asks me if I would be interested in screening the film at SP Jain Institute of Management and Research in Mumbai. It's one of Asia's top management institutes and there is no reason why I shouldn't accept the invitation. They want to screen it the day after tomorrow as the students will be going on preparation leave.

I notice there are four missed calls from Naireeta. I call her back.

'Sir, where are you?' Naireeta is panicking. 'Please rush to the venue.'

It has to be some issue with the projection or sound. In India, there is bound to be some glitch at the eleventh hour. I rush to the auditorium. When I enter the hall from the rear door, I just cannot believe what I see. The hall is jam-packed with students. All eleven hundred of them.

'Where have they just come from?'

'Sir, they had a class until 5.45.' Naireeta informs me.

'This is the real test of our film,' I tell Naireeta, looking at a concentrated pool of India's top technological and scientific minds in a dark auditorium.

I introduce the film.

'How many of you know about Naxalism?'

Very few hands go up.

'Well, in that case, this film is for you.'

The film begins in complete darkness. In the first scene, we see the Adivasi cutting wood in 2000 BC, and as the shot changes to 2014 AD and we see the same Adivasi cutting wood without a thing changed around him except for the leaves of *mahua*, the students clap. Some laugh. Some whisper. Some smile. I know the film is making a connect. Students are reacting at the right moments. I am keen to see how they react to the climax.

When the climax comes, I go and stand near the exit door. From here, I can see everyone, in the flickering beam of the projector. As soon as Vikram Pundit takes out his iPad and says *'Yeh hai naye Bharat ki nai soch,* the new thinking of the new India', some students clap. Then more join in. And more. This applause is coming from the heart. As an emotional response. I never expected this reaction. A film which is made to intellectually stimulate the audience ends up stimulating them emotionally. Slowly, the applause starts echoing hard enough to break out of this newly-built auditorium and its high ceiling. I want them to stop clapping and concentrate on the dialogues. If I had the faintest idea that this dialogue would generate such an overwhelming reaction, I would have created some silence in the moment.

When the professor says 'Sorry, Papa' in the end, everyone laughs. This laughter isn't the same as the way one laughs upon hearing a joke. It's a laughter emanating from the satisfaction that evil has accepted defeat. This is the intended payoff of the film. And it has delivered.

The Q&A begins with some general questions related to the film, but slowly it becomes intense, shifting from Naxalism to caste issues and exploitation of the Dalit. A girl from Kerala asks me why I have not shown caste-based oppression as she is a victim of this social evil. She is angry and very tense. She tells me how Dalit power is rising and Naxalism is the only support that they have.

A very insightful discussion follows. What I gather from these small-town middle-class students is that they have a deep desire to rid India of its social evils, disparity, and inefficiency. They want to build India. They want change. Not by fighting the State but by fighting with ideas that do not let us grow. When I ask how many of them want to go abroad after graduation, very few hands go up. Student aspirations are changing. India is changing. The film has connected with them because it reaffirms this aspiration and the faith that the real revolution will come from ideas, and not war. While the students of JNU want to bring about transformation with a political fight, these students want to use innovation as a tool for social and financial justice. They are Buddhas.

Late at night, as I cross Gandhi*ji*'s *ashram* on Sabarmati river, I wonder what the first thing would be that Gandhi*ji* would say if he came back.

'Where is my India?'

Where is India in our education, arts, literature, films, media, market and national aspiration?

If we had followed Gandhi, we would have been a very different country. Kutir and Gram Udyog was built on a strong principle of entrepreneurship at the grassroots level. Native innovation is always more beneficial to the economy than imported technology. It's cheaper, more effective and useful to local needs. It took almost 65 years for us to package *amras*, *jaljeera* juices and market them nationally. But by this time, the market was already saturated with foreign brands. We made engineers but not builders. We made doctors but not medical scientists. Teachers but not educators. We had neither a blueprint for villages nor any urban planning. Our growth story has been haphazard. Every year, regional, social, economic and political disparities are increasing and creating new, unexplored and complex webs of caste and class conflicts.

Only time will tell us the real value of Gandhian economics, which does not distinguish between economics and ethics. Gandhi believed that an industry's worth shouldn't be gauged by the dividends its shareholders receive but by its effects on the bodies, souls, and spirits of its employees. In Gandhi's economic world, man is more important than the money. Means are more important than the ends. Gandhi believed in self-reliance, made a distinction between 'standard of living' and 'standard of life', and introduced the trusteeship principle. Gandhi believed that these principles would lead us to 'welfare of all' instead of 'welfare of few', which he called '*Sarvodaya*'.

Mao is the antithesis of Gandhi in that he believed war and armed conflict were necessary vehicles to drive a revolution forward. Gandhi explained that non-violence is crucial to a revolution. For Mao, political power comes from force and violence. For Gandhi, political power comes from cooperation and consent.

In independent India, much after Gandhi's death, two revolutions began almost at the same time and for the same purpose: redistribution of the landlord's land to poor peasants. While Mao's disciples were killing people to redistribute land, Gandhi's disciple Vinoba Bhave was walking all over India to request *zamindars* to donate their lands for the peasants and received over six lac acres for redistribution. One came to be known as Naxalism/Maoism and the other is known as *Bhoodan*. That we do not acknowledge *Bhoodan* but glorify Naxalism is a failure of our country's conscience.

A few journalists who have gathered ask me almost the same questions. The common theme is:

'Sir, would you say that your hero is like Kanhaiya?'

'Not at all. The Kanhaiya of my film wants to build India.'

As the Boeing 737 takes off from Ahmedabad, I see Sabarmati and remember the last time I had come here, as a student, for a national debate on Gandhi. But there was no water in the river. Today, there is water but Gandhi's Sabarmati doesn't flow here anymore.

I pick up *Sandesh*, the leading Gujarati newspaper, I read a headline 'My Kanhaiya is not anti-national, says controversial director Vivek Agnihotri.' Controversial? Anti-national? I never said this. Film reporting has become political reporting. And political reporting has become filmy. I know they are twisting my statement to score their political points. Media sells on negativity. As I read further, I realize that my fight is not going to be just with only the liberal or the left wing or the Leftist studios, but also with the media.

41. The Intolerance Debate: SPJIMR and IIT Bombay

Back in Mumbai, I show the film at SP Jain Institute of Management & Research and India's leading engineering institute, IIT Bombay. The film receives an overwhelming reception, followed by intense Q&A sessions.

At IIT Bombay, I meet Professor Bapat and his colleagues. This is the computer science department which most toppers of JEE (Joint Entrance Examination) opt for. These are some of the best professors in India with several innovations and patents in their bags. It's said that when these professors walk, instead of footprints they leave behind innovations. Despite such achievements and contribution to India's technological growth, the head of the department and his colleagues aren't happy people since Narendra Modi won the elections.

Professor Bapat tells me that all his life he has been attending the Indian Science Congress and various conferences to speak on Vedic science, but since Modi became PM, wherever he speaks on Vedic science, people start calling him Sanghi. He is worried about such intolerance. He has been able to overcome the biggest of the scientific challenges but sees himself failing in front of this emerging political intolerance of an idea that is rooted in Hindu traditions and history. He feels an organized campaign is being run to demoralize such citizens who take pride in Hindu civilization and its traditional knowledge systems.

IIT Bombay is not like any other institute. After a quiet screening, I am bombarded with questions ranging from Naxalism to Artificial Intelligence and Vedic knowledge. This, perhaps, is the only institute where research scholars have strong faith in ancient knowledge. This isn't a Q&A anymore, it has become an event to share ideas, aspirations, and concerns. I am observing that at each screening, the film intellectually stimulates the audience and engages them. Normally, Q&A sessions are mostly restricted to the film but in our case, students ask all kinds of political questions as if I have all the answers. In the end, all points of views merge and create one main flow of debate, a debate that every student, every professor is involved with: The Intolerance Debate.

I question myself. Where do I stand on this issue?

When you believe in something immensely, that belief works like an amulet. That belief protects you from the evilness of the world. That is why some people achieve what they want and most don't. Because they don't have the amulet of belief. Belief doesn't come on its own. There are many guiding forces which we meet on our path which drive it in an invisible manner.

Truth is simple. Everything else is complex. Realization is simple. Logic is complicated. Continuous self-scrutiny, analysis of one's own thoughts is a very lonely and cathartic process. It can take one towards wisdom and enlightenment or it can take you towards schizophrenia.

I believe that India, in being a polytheist society, has always welcomed, tolerated and accepted monotheist religions. We are one of those rare democracies where Communism, Marxism, Naxalism, and extreme religious and communal parties like Asadudidn Owaasi's MIM, Shiv Sena, Muslim League etc. are accepted in mainstream politics. Even with the plethora of religious beliefs, spiritual practices, rituals, customs, political ideologies, social hierarchies, traditions, and hundreds of cultural and linguistic divides, India has survived. It has survived invasions, loots, massacres, genocides, the Emergency, corruption, forced vasectomy, oppression, exploitation, social evils, abject poverty, and unemployment. With the gigantic disparity between inhuman living conditions on one side and unlimited wealth on the other, we have survived. The culture which has nurtured tolerance for centuries can't become intolerant in just one year.

A few months back, I had an opportunity to meet Prime Minister Modi at his residence at 7 Race Course Road, over an informal chat filled with humour, ideas, and positivity. And of course, there was *chai* along with *chaas*, *dhokla*, *idlis,* and veg *kathi* rolls which were literally forced on me and the rest by the Prime Minister himself.

It was a time when both the intolerance debate and award *wapsi* was at its peak and the media was loving to portray Modi as the root cause of the increasing intolerance. They wanted Modi's head but he kept silent. Munnawar Rana, a popular Urdu poet, was leading the attack on various channels.

I remember Prime Minister Modi sharing his belief that the cultural space shouldn't be '*rajya aashrit*', government-dependent, as it takes away the voice of reason but it should be '*rajya puraskarit*', awarded by the State. And without 'fearless cultural evolution', we would be a robotic society. He clarified that he never received any request from any '*kalakar*' to meet him. 'One day I saw on TV that Shri Munnawar Rana was saying that if PM invites us, we'll go and tell him about our concerns, so I immediately called my secretary and asked him to invite Shri Rana at his convenience but till date no one has come. As a PM, I can't go beyond this. Home Minister Rajnath Singh*ji* has publicly extended the invitation, twice, but no one has responded.'

On the murder of rationalist academic Kalburgi and the lynching of a Muslim man at Dadri, he said that no one has met the governors of the states and lodged their concerns in order to be channeled to him as he can't interfere in state issues. He had asked the Karnataka government to send him all the files on the Kalburgi murder but they had not sent them as yet.

PM Modi gave an example of administrative intolerance. During the last days of the Vajpayee government, it was decided to build six All India Institutes of Medical Sciences (AIIMS). The then health minister Sushma Swaraj named the Patna AIIMS Jaiprakash Narayan Institute, and similarly, the other five were also named after non-Congress national leaders. Vajpayee's government lost the elections and the Congress-led UPA came to power. The UPA passed a Bill in Parliament and 'banned' these names to be used for any government project. That was the level of intolerance, he said.

He was concerned about 'political concern vs national interest'. He told us that fifty-four heads of African countries were in India for the Indo-African summit. 'So many heads of state don't even attend a state funeral,' he said sarcastically. 'One-third of the world's population, its concerns, and aspirations were represented, yet in our media and public discourses, this event was absent.'

He said emphatically, 'If there is a loss to the country due to my mistake, please criticize me which you must... punish me... but just to oppose me or any other political rival, one shouldn't forget national interest. This much intolerance is not good.'

He quoted how Galileo was nearly killed for opposing a belief but in India, when Charvak, an atheist, challenged the *Vedas* with logic and rejected the idea of reincarnation, he was given the title of '*rishi*'. Indian thought isn't about tolerance, it's about acceptance. He reminded us that societies which champion the cause of human rights are the ones who started two world wars whereas India has been the most peace-generating country in the global context. He said, 'I have absolute faith that the *tapasya* of thousands of years can't be destroyed by you and me.'

Why is everyone talking about intolerance? Are we really intolerant?

How come we have so many political parties ruling so many different states? This means there is political tolerance. In industry, we have equal opportunities for all kinds of enterprise. Malls exist in the midst of local bazaars and street vendors. Sikhs have shops in the heart of Srinagar. Biharis have farms in Punjab. Which means there is no financial intolerance. In administration, education and health, we never question the religion or political alignment of the practitioner. If people can openly criticize the prime minister, ridicule religious leaders, question social taboos, debate issues ranging from FTII to bar dancers, return awards, make fun of regional leaders, it proves that there is no media or FoE intolerance.

I close my eyes and visualize the Indian map. I try to visualize each and every town, village and hamlet, focusing on how people live there. Are they at conflict? Are they killing each other? Are they wearing what they wish to wear? Do Hindus, Muslims, Christians and other minorities live, work, socialize together? We enjoy *kavi sammelans* and *mushairas* with the same enthusiasm. We hum our *geets* and our *ghazals* with the same joy. All young lovers fall back on Urdu *shayari* to express their love. Bollywood music will lose its sheen without Urdu lyrics. In movies, don't we cry and laugh together?

Generally speaking, people live in harmony, even though we may disagree with one another on many issues. The Supreme Court opening at midnight to reconsider Yakub Memon's death penalty on one side and some people celebrating Godse's anniversary on the other side. It indicates that there is extreme tolerance for polarized cultural and religious sensibilities. Writers are free to write on any subject, take, and then return their awards in protest. In art, in literature, in films and in almost all creative fields, there is tremendous tolerance for different ideas and creations. We don't buy a pot on the basis of the colour of its potter. Is this fear of intolerance built on a real threat or a perceived one? Does this exist in flesh or is it just a ghost?

Who is dividing our society? Who is communalizing issues? When a Dadri happens, why do TV channels invite Owaisi and Sadhvi Prachi? What is Owaisi's relevance to this theme when he has no *locus standi* in the politics of UP? How is Sadhvi Prachi relevant to cow slaughter? Is Sakshi Maharaj a spokesperson for Hindu aspirations? Is he the sole BJP MP to comment on every social issue? Why aren't sane, rational voices heard any more? If you invite sane voices, voices of reason, the lethal game of boutique activism stands exposed. Boutique Liberal Activism feeds on the misery of others. *Schadenfreude* is the oxygen of their business. That's why they show only the miserable side of our society. The evolved, enlightened and reasonable voice of India is absolutely absent from the national discourse. Who has divided us?

Our society is divided into 'overclass' (as described by Michael Find) and 'underclass'. Overclass has systematically siphoned off the national wealth, leaving the underclass to fight for two square meals. They either inherited or, in collusion with corrupt regimes, appointed themselves to positions of power and influence. With strong control over information, they kept the underclass in the dark. Their word was the final word. The biggest trick the overclass played on the underclass is keeping the hope alive that only they can get them out of this abject poverty. That we have problems and they have the solution. This is the same trick godmen and Satan play on us. This overclass with social, economic, and political clout has constantly shown disdain and contempt for the traditional social values and the underclass is now questioning their motives. If different ideologies, traditions and cultures co-exist and democracy finds popular favour, it's not due to this narrow but influential elite. It's due to the tolerance level of the underclass.

Two phenomena disturbed this *status quo*. One, the advent of social media, and second, the rise of Narendra Modi. With easy access to social and digital media, the underclass started questioning the authenticity of information provided by the overclass. Suddenly, their statements are scrutinized, their credibility is questioned, their sinister campaigns and lies are exposed. Their dilemma is that if they quit social media, they lose their relevance, and if they stay, they lose their credibility. This war of intolerance isn't between HDL (Hindu Defence League) and MDL (Muslim Defence league). This isn't between the left and the right. This is between the overclass and the underclass. The intellectual hierarchy has been demolished.

It's a sad commentary that in the world's largest democracy, writers' protest has become a subject of jokes. The power-hungry artists, writers, academics, and media-persons in India waste a huge amount of time making political statements to hide behind their lack of intellectual stands. Michel Houellebecq wrote *Submission*, a strong political statement; he didn't get press coverage for returning some award. The lustre is gone from our intellectual discourse. Secularism has lost its ideological currency. Artists, writers, activists are all suspect.

Media czars have lost their access to the corridors of power and to people's hearts. It's the overclass' space that has been taken over by the underclass. Their discomfort is with the new order where the *others* are also heard. Hence, the feeling of shrinking space. They are intolerant of this new phenomenon – the emergence of the underclass. They try to devalue this new, empowered underclass by associating it with Modi and, therefore, Hindutva, and that's a grave mistake. The universe that was full of their voice has expanded to accommodate this new voice. This is what they call an attack on FoE and growing intolerance.

They work exactly like religion. Most religious books are based on fear. If you do this, that will happen. Nobody knows what 'this' or 'that' is. Social justice, if it has to come, will come only from a free and fair market. Why didn't our liberals tell us this simple truth? When agendas, vote banks, and self-delusion take over, reasoning and sympathy are needed to keep up a common conversation. Without it, there is aggression, deafness, and an obsession with purification; hence the divisive politics of Boutique Liberalism. Boutique Liberalism is an Indian tragedy and a very damaging detour into the quicksand of communalism. Indian Liberalism has come to mean the colour opposite of saffron. That's their failure. In a desperate attempt, their new mantra is – 'We don't care if you are a murderer, we want to know whether you are a liberal or a Sanghi murderer?'

This is where the real intolerance lies.

42. Rohith Vemula and Dalit Politics: NALSAR and Osmania University

We are flooded with requests from top institutes to screen the film. Naireeta informs me that if we do two institutes a day, we will be able to finish all requests only in three months. We try to organize ourselves and select institutes which are on main trunk routes, easy to fly to and *are politically relevant to our film's theme.*_ We have to drop places like Bhubaneshwar, Coimbatore, Roorkee, Dehradun, Agra, Nagpur etc. We have to cover approximately forty institutes or universities in the next forty days. Everyone thinks it's a logistical nightmare. I wonder how politicians manage to give five to six speeches a day in scorching heat. Modi's politics aside, one can always be inspired by his relentless campaigning. We lock our schedule.

I land in Hyderabad. The city where this idea was fertilized. I am supposed to screen the movie at the prestigious National Academy of Legal Studies and Research (NALSAR) and at the Naxal nursery, Osmania University.

The NALSAR campus is world class. Bold, earthy architecture, stunning landscapes. It can pass off as a high-end luxury resort. It's got space, design, and vibes. I am taken to the vice-chancellor's office. It's a swanky office with lots of golden trophies on display. Faizan Mustafa, the vice-chancellor, receives me with utmost humility. Mr. Mustafa carries his minority card on his sleeve and wrongly assumes that I am close to Mr. Modi and the then HRD minister Smt. Smriti Irani, as I am anti-left in ideology.

My father was a vice-chancellor and I have met numerous vice-chancellors of that era – the pre-sycophancy era. They used to have wisdom, knowledge, integrity, and above all, fearlessness. They were the real intellectuals who shaped universities with value systems and because of their inspiring leadership, even governments feared them.

Then something changed. Indira Gandhi started appointing only loyalists in all major institutions. Slowly, almost all appointments became political and the institutions started behaving like extensions of the Congress (Indira) party. Sonia Gandhi knew that she was a weak leader and, therefore, she not just wanted loyalists but also weak people with no spine, no real qualifications. They wore their sycophancy as a medal on their blazers. Now with the advent of a new government under Modi's leadership, the entire ecosystem feels threatened. NALSAR is no different, as it's very obvious from Mr. Mustafa's unabated requests to give good feedback to the PM and the HRD minister of his leadership. In the last forty years, we have made our educational institutes hollow.

When we reach the auditorium, it's packed with future lawyers and lawmakers of India. I introduce the film and tell them why it's an important film for them to see. Because so far there has been one kind of argument and mostly in favour of Naxals. This film is the other side of the argument. I tell them that the real purpose of the film is to ignite a debate which presents a third side and eventually a constructive, fair and judicious argument which strengthens India rather than breaking it apart. I can see most of the students reacting to what I say but a few faces have an inscrutable expression; these students are more keen to grill me during the Q&A. They are sitting apart from one another yet connected by the same expression. I am getting trained in identifying interspersed Leftists in a crowd.

While the movie plays in the auditorium, Naireeta and I sit outside to fine-tune social media activities. Social media is all we have. It's quick and viral and, above all, free. Today, media picks up all news from social media, so we also save on PR cost. The success at JNU had made us realize the potential and power of social media but to what extent, maybe we have to yet learn.

I want to have tea but I can't see a soul anywhere on this sprawling campus. After an hour or so, I see a tall, lanky boy in a kurta and jeans with unkempt hair and uneven beard, walking towards the auditorium. I call him to ask where to find tea.

'Thanks. In case, you are going to see the film, you are already late by an hour,' I tell him.

'I don't want to see the film,' he replies. There is contempt in his body language. It intrigues me.

'Sorry, I didn't introduce myself. I am the director of the film – Viv...'

'I know you are Vivek Agnihotri,' he says with a cold look.

'Great. May I ask why you don't want to see the film?'

'Because I have already seen it.'

'Where?'

'On the net.'

'That's impossible.'

'Everything is possible on the net.'

'You mean the full film?'

'Yeah, we have seen the full film. Not just once, but several times. Last we saw it this morning.'

'And what did you think?'

'That we will tell you in the Q&A.'

I have never met anyone who can look into your eyes and offend you with his honesty.

'Since there is an hour for the Q&A to begin, why don't we sit down and chat? You tell me what doesn't work for you and if I can make you understand my reasons, maybe we can discover another truth.'

We sit on one of the concrete benches, overlooking the lush green garden.

'It's not about liking or disliking the film; this film is dangerous.'

I find him interesting. I want to indulge him. After all, that is the purpose of this journey, to debate and learn from a new perspective.

'The intention behind this film is to begin a debate,' I try to set the tone.

'You are not starting a debate; you are creating a narrative. And that's dangerous.'

'You sound like a logical young lawyer. Why would you say it's dangerous? It's just a film.'

'That's why. As a film, it will create a new narrative.'

'What's wrong with a new narrative? It's based on facts.'

'I don't care about your facts. We just don't need another narrative.'

'You hate the film so much?'

'I don't hate the film. In fact, the film is really good. Perhaps, one of the best. We just don't want the film to be released.'

'How can you even say that?'

'That's true. We have seen it several times and we have decided that we will rip it apart and ensure that it's not released.'

'We? Who are *we*?'

'We are everywhere. You will meet some of them in the Q&A. Today is going to be your worst day.'

'Why are you telling me all this? You could have just attacked me directly in the Q&A.'

'True. But when I met you, I wanted to hurt you. I want you to suffer.'

'Just because I have a point of view?'

'For the revolution to come, we must destroy any narrative which is against Naxalism. Including your film.'

'Why are you doing this?'

'Because we want an India which is free of Brahmins like you.'

I should feel offended. But I like his arrogance and upfront contempt for the truth. The Leftists' contempt for Brahmins is as dangerous as Brahmin discrimination against Dalits. India is facing reverse casteism. He isn't a Dalit. He is a Bengali. He is an educated, English-speaking Bengali training to be a lawyer – a lethal combination. Leftists always target such young boys and girls, who are angry with the system, as soon as they enter the campus because angry people are most vulnerable. These vulnerable students are then brainwashed with a false argument against Brahminism and gut-wrenching stories of oppression and class struggle. In a few months, they are trained to hate everything about Brahmins, upper class, the rich and successful, and money. All this anger is consolidated in one enemy: RSS. Since RSS' agenda is to create a Hindu nation, these young people end up hating everything related to Hinduism, including Hindus.

I see a lot of myself in him. As a student, I was as angry and as honest. But our dreams were different. This boy is not a hardcore Leftist yet. He is trying very hard to be one. He is a good boy. He has the sincerity, character, and passion. He has a dream for India and the energy and desire to accomplish it. These kinds of young men and women got us freedom. These are the kind of men and women, if used tactfully, can be instrumental in building a nation. Or breaking it.

Naireeta informs me that the film is about to get over. I know I am up for some serious opposition inside the auditorium. In public life, appreciation builds slowly but opposition builds exponentially.

A bright spotlight is turned on and its bright beam falls straight on my face. A few girls stand up and start clapping. Slowly, everyone stands up and claps. As the students give a standing ovation to the film, I try to identify those who are not clapping and these are the same students who had poker faces when I introduced the film.

The Q&A begins. There are some questions on the film, its theme, actors etc. but I am waiting for the real questions.

'What do you think about *Manu Smriti*?' a boy from the last row asks me. His body language is defensive but his eyes are aggressive.

I am not prepared for questions outside the scope of film's theme. I have to take a call whether to engage in a pre-decided strategy of the Leftist students or escape it with humour. I decide to counter–argue.

'I haven't read *Manu Smriti*. But I have read versions of it and I think maybe it had relevance in its time but in today's context it has no relevance,' I reply.

'Why are you avoiding the question?' he asks.

'No, I am not. I am not an expert on it and I feel it's irrelevant in my life so I don't care much.'

'That's because you are a Brahmin.'

I don't like it. I have never liked casteist discussions. If there is any one thing that is alien to my entire being, one thing that I detest, it is casteism. But I know where they want to lead me.

'The only time I was called Brahmin before this was when I went to study at Harvard. There we were called Boston Brahmins. But Brahmin there signified meritocracy. You are here in India's top institute, in a top profession, so in my eyes, you are also a Brahmin.'

'You are again running away from the issue.'

'I hope you realize that neither *Manu Smriti* nor Brahminism is within the scope of this film. The film is about Naxalism, about intellectual terrorism… feel free to ask anything around the theme.'

'So… you want me to shut up. OK, say so.'

Some whispering, some exchange of looks, some movement in the seats. It is an awkward moment. A French-bearded management professor, sitting next to the VC, asks the students to be quiet and he rises to speak.

'I think it's a democracy and we follow absolute freedom of speech, so I think students should be allowed to ask any question,' the management professor makes a point.

'OK. After seeing the film, you can't question my commitment to absolute freedom of speech. I just didn't want to digress.' I point at the VC and continue, 'Whatever VC *saheb* says.' I know I have put the VC in an awkward situation. He desperately wants to see the students corner me but he also wants me to give a good report card to his bosses. He has a tough job.

'I agree with Agnihotri *saab* that the questions should be around the film,' he turns to address me, 'But Agnihotri *saab*, you are not just a filmmaker. You write on politics, so it might be a good idea if you took some other questions from the students.' He smiles at me and then turns towards the students and smiles at them. Law schools teach you how to take a stand in favour of one of the arguments and here the VC wants to appease both sides.

They aren't interested in listening. They just want to attack. They throw questions on RSS, Godhra, Dadri, intolerance and of course on Rohith Vemula's suicide. For them, I represent the enemy. And now it seems, I am *the* enemy.

'What are your views on Rohith Vemula, Mr. Agnihotri?' a student with a long beard asks.

'It's very sad. Except for that, I have no views on Rohith Vemula.'

'Just sad. A Dalit student was forced to commit suicide and you have no views. Isn't that sad?'

'First of all, we don't know if he was forced or he did it of his own free will. We don't even know if he was a Dalit but his being Dalit doesn't make his death sadder. In my mind, a young bright boy lost his life. So, I feel as sad as I feel for any other young student.'

This makes them furious. In this mini-battle, their attempt is to corner me with personal attacks as they know film is my home ground and they can't win an argument there. Hence, this strategy to raise sensitive issues of Dalits, minorities, feminism, homosexuality, Ram Mandir etc. which have become sentimental issues. They want to cash in on the Dalit part of the story and put the blame on Hindu aspiration.

'What are your views on reservations?'

'I think reservations should be for FBC – Financially Backward Class.'

This makes the bearded guy furious.

'You know what is your problem? You are an oppressor. You have no right to make such a movie… you are a liar!' He starts using the most unparliamentary language.

I look at the VC and the professor. The VC avoids my eyes but the management professor keeps staring at me. He is keen to see my reaction. He wants to see me break. They let him speak his insulting language. I am in a very positive frame of mind. I don't want to get into an argument that leads nowhere. My film is my argument. I think I must navigate the session in a different direction.

'Why are you so angry, my friend? I empathize with your frustration as I have also been a student like you who has expressed his anger by burning government buses but as I grew up I realized that a little sense of humour helps,' I say, addressing the other group. The majority of the students agree.

'You want to see sense of humour?' He charges towards me.

All heads turn towards him. He charges through the aisles from the last row, yelling at me. I can feel an aura of violence around him. He is going to attack me. I prepare myself mentally. I look at Naireeta. She looks scared. I look at the VC and the professor who are not responding, as if waiting to see how the event unfolds. He picks up speed and comes running towards the podium. He climbs the podium. In the next four steps, he is going to catch my neck, or pounce on me, or spit on me. He takes the first step and the second…Naireeta jumps from somewhere and stands in front of me. The boy stops. Collective sigh.

He stares at me as if trying to do with his eyes what he couldn't do with his hands. He is gasping for air. His hands are trembling. He gives me a hateful look. Hate is very hurtful whether expressed by a physical attack, or words or just a look.

'How can you discuss money when so many people are dying? There is no point talking to you, Mr. Agnihotri,' and he walks out of the auditorium with the same speed, banging the door behind him.

After a long, suspended moment of awkward silence, the management professor raises his hand.

'I want to know your views on capitalism since your movie shows capitalism winning in the end,' says the professor.

'It depends on which side of capitalism we are looking at. Capitalism means innovation, excellence, wealth creation, empowerment, conveniences, quality of human life and so on. Capitalism also means greed, ambition, conflict, corruption, exploitation and so on. I believe in the former. I believe every facet of life has two sides: good and bad. I believe in balance. But if I have to make a choice, I'd always want to choose the good part.'

'So, you are pro-money?'

'I love money. I am sure you love money too. If not, then you should, because a great economist said, "Money is the most creative invention of humanity."'

'Who said this? Economics is my specialization but I have never heard this,' he says with arrogance.

'Kautilya,' I reply.

'Kautilya who?'

'Chanakya.'

There are murmurs interspersed with laughter in the audience. The VC looks at his professor and realizes that it's time to close the proceedings.

Later, as Mr. Mustafa comes to drop me off to my car, after a delicious Hyderabadi dinner, he requests me that if I meet the HRD minister I must tell her about his achievements and his desire to implement the vision of the new government.

Our car runs through a dark highway. We are late for our next screening at Osmania University. Naxalism has attracted many students of Osmania. It has always been a hotbed of radical politics. It was in Osmania in 1974-75 that fourteen students renounced family life and vowed never to marry with the purpose of devoting their entire lives to the revolution. 'Overground' organizations were formed. The first state-level conference of the newly formed Radical Students Union (RSU) was held in Hyderabad to formalize strategies to integrate the student movement with the armed revolution. It was attended by an overwhelming number of students whose enthusiasm and collective efforts gave impetus to the Naxal movement.

A huge screen has been put up in front of the main building under which many freedom fighters had found their resolve, many writers had written classic poetry, ideas of so many revolutions were seeded. If an orthodox politician Asaduddin Owaisi crossed this *sanctum sanctorum*, then the architect of liberalization, P.V. Narasimha Rao and the astronaut Rakesh Sharma also walked here.

When the first beam of the projector falls on the screen, it filters right through and lights up the main building. It's a magical sight to see the film play on these historic walls. There are so many stories hidden behind them. Today yet another story is getting inscribed. Ironically, the film is an antithesis of the revolution which was nurtured behind these walls. The screening gets a tremendous response. People laugh, clap and go silent like a statue. People clap very hard when the nexus between the professor, the NGO, and the Naxals is exposed towards the end of the film. After my experience at NALSAR, filled with negativity, pessimism, hatred and violence, this screening with its positivity, optimism, and hope feels spiritual.

The Leftists are too eager to latch on to anything that gives them an opportunity to publicly attack and defeat pro-India voices intellectually. Whereas these students at Osmania want to move away from the days of disturbance and conflict and are ready to latch on to any positive, optimistic and hopeful idea. At NALSAR, they had a plan, a strategy, and an agenda. When they saw themselves and their strategies getting exposed in the film in front of their ignorant colleagues, they got angry at me. They wanted to kill the messenger. That exactly is the reason they keep failing with their revolution. I will relish these contradictions all my life.

We have to catch a flight the next morning for Bengaluru. We have screenings at the National Law University and the Indian Institute of Science (IISc). We decide to leave at 9 AM. Sleep evades me. A mass of questions is whirling inside my head.

'Am I pro-money? Why is pro-money an accusation instead of a quality?'

But the question that has overshadowed all other questions.

'What if I am wrong in Rohith Vemula's case?'

Sun breaks. I call Naireeta's room.

'We will leave at 8,' I inform her.

'Aren't we supposed to leave at 9?'

'I have some work on our way.'

'What?'

'Don't waste time. Get ready, will tell you.'

I am standing in front of Hyderabad Central University, the university which, after Rohith Vemula's suicide, was at the centre of an emotional and social turmoil. The emotions behind a suicidal death, especially of a young student, defy all logic. Political masterminds never look at it as a loss of life. They look for political plugs like religion, caste, regionality, economic status etc. A Muslim death is always more beneficial than a Hindu death. A lower caste death, a farmer's death, a slum dweller's death always has the scope to be spun it into an emotional saga of the oppressed and thus maintain a fake narrative of class struggle.

As luck favoured the Leftists, Rohith Vemula wasn't an ordinary suicide. He was presented as a Scheduled Caste, a creative student who rose against oppressors and, therefore, he was forced to sacrifice his life for the cause of the oppressed.

I never knew him but I read his suicide note. Since then, I feel connected to him. The sensibility, sensitivity, curiosity, and honesty he displayed in his note sums up his state of mind. A young mind which sees the merits of all the arguments: the scientific, the political and the cosmic, and unable to decide what to choose, he goes into conflict mode. If he was an oppressed Dalit, I am sure he must have faced enough humiliation and would be immune to it. That couldn't have been the cause. He was too rational for that.

I take out my phone and google his suicide note. It reads like a literary piece, poetry to be precise. A poem of loss of trust, belief, innocence, search for truth and hope.

'I have no complaints on anyone. It was always with myself I had problems. I feel a growing gap between my soul and my body. And I have become a monster. I always wanted to be a writer.'

I see a man who sacrificed his passion, his talent for an ideology. But when he realized that he has, in turn, become a monster, he blamed himself.

'I loved Science, Stars, Nature, but then I loved people without knowing that people have long since divorced from nature. Our feelings are second handed. Our love is constructed. Our beliefs coloured.'

Here is a man who fell for a utopia and joined the Communist student body, the Students Federation of India (SFI). When he realized that the 'people's revolution' is a facade for the sinister and ruthless politics that is against every principle of humanity, his faith shattered.

'The value of a man was reduced to his immediate identity and nearest possibility. To a vote. To a number. To a thing. Never was a man treated as a mind.'

Instead of being led to social justice and people's empowerment, he found himself being exploited just as a political pawn in a dangerous, inhuman game.

'Maybe I was wrong, all the while, in understanding the world. In understanding love, pain, life, death. There was no urgency. But I always was rushing. I am not hurt at this moment. I am not sad. I am just empty. Unconcerned about myself. That's pathetic. And that's why I am doing this.'

He sounds like a young man who invested his physical, emotional, mental and spiritual energy in a concept which was antithetical to his own nature. He rushed into it in defiance of his nature. When the dreams started shattering and the rationality reappeared, when the ideologies of half-truths and white lies started crumbling, the truth glared in his eyes, and the realization came, he found himself exhausted. Spent up. Empty. Finished. I know that feeling.

Since Rohith hasn't mentioned any name, everything is an assumption. An interpretation of things we don't know. But two things are clear in my mind: 1) Whether he was a Dalit or not, only a fair inquiry will tell, but his suicide is not a function of his caste. 2) If such a cut-throat, competitive electoral politics is not stopped in our educational institutions soon, it will take suicidal shape.

43. The Science of Resistance: NLU, IISc

We are waiting at Bengaluru airport for our hosts, students of National Law University (NLU). My WhatsApp is full of Ram Navami greetings. While there is a holiday in the Northern states, in Karnataka, it's a working day.

After about half an hour, I finally see a boy come running. He starts pleading guilty until I ask him to introduce himself. He hesitantly tells us his name. Something is troubling him.

'Is everything OK?'

'Yes sir… yeah… I'll tell you everything.'

'What's the matter?'

'I have got the car for you.'

'I am asking what's the matter?'

'I'll tell you in the car.' He is panicky, nervous and jittery.

As we leave the airport, he starts crying.

'Saar, I am really sorry… I don't know how to tell you…' He turns towards Naireeta whom he seems more comfortable talking to, and continues, 'Madam, today is Ram Navami. We never have a holiday on Ram Navami…' He stops.

'Fine, but what has Ram Navami got to do with us?' I ask him.

'Saar, Ram Navami is never a holiday but our professor wasn't happy with the screening of your film… he asked me many times to cancel it… he can't cancel the permission for the auditorium because students will get angry… so last night he sent the mail to our network declaring today a holiday. Tomorrow and day after are Saturday and Sunday; so, as the students got a long weekend, all of them left. Saar, I was waiting to meet him, the professor, that's why I got delayed, sir.'

We take a deep breath and let it sink in. It's not easy to understand his accent and construction of sentences. I process whatever I understood.

'So, what's the status now?'

'Saar, if you want to show to ten fifteen students, it's fine but now he may not give the auditorium as he will say there are no students, why are you taking auditorium.'

'How do you know he declared a holiday just so that students don't attend the screening?'

'I know saar, he doesn't want screening.'

'But he hasn't seen the film.'

'Saar, but everybody has read about the film. Your film is very popular amongst the faculty.'

'You think it's a sabotage?'

'I am sure saar. Very positive, saar.'

'Why would he do that?'

'He doesn't want any alternate narrative saar.'

I don't have to ask him anything. I guess the rest.

'Can I tell the press? Will you stand by it?'

He looks at me as if I have pulled his tongue out. He starts crying.

'Saar, please don't tell anyone my name. He asked me to keep quiet. If they get to know I tell you saar, they will suspend me and my other colleagues in the organizing committee. I am very poor saar, my parents very poor, we can't go back home. We are research scholars… all our marks depend on professor saar. Please, saar.'

'I'll never say anything unless you agree. So, relax. But I am curious to know his name.'

'Sir he is Prof. Mathew. He is a very strong Leftist. He also contested the election on AAP ticket in 2014.'

I know we have lost the battle. There is no way we can question such a perfect and technically foolproof sabotage. I am not worried about our loss but I am worried what will happen if India ever loses this battle.

The Indian Institute of Science (IISc) ranks number one in India and it is one of the top ten specialized universities of the world. Once, the father of Indian industry, Jamshedji Tata, while travelling in a ship, had a chance meeting with Swami Vivekananda and they discussed various ideas, including Tata's plan to bring the steel industry to India and Vivekananda's quest for bringing scientific research to India. Many years later, Tata wrote a letter to Swami Vivekananda:

'I trust, you remember me as a fellow traveller on your voyage from Japan to Chicago. I very much recall your views on the growth of the ascetic spirit in India, in connection with my scheme of a research institute of science in India.' In the letter, he requested Vivekananda to guide him in this endeavour.

Jamshedji Tata conceived of a university in 1896 that would work for India's scientific development and at the behest of Vivekananda, the Maharaja of Mysore, Krishnaraja Wodeyar IV, donated three hundred and seventy acres of land in Bangalore. Since then, IISc has been headed by some of the best scientific brains of the world, such as Nobel Laureate CV Raman, Satish Dhawan, C.N.R. Rao, just to name a few. IISc's contribution in the fields of science, space technology, advanced computing and nuclear science is unparalleled.

After I failed to get into engineering, I tried to get admission in IISc but couldn't make it. Today I am being invited to screen my film there. This makes one wonder about the concepts of destiny, luck, and intent.

We reach half an hour before the screening. Students meet us outside the auditorium and inform us that the venue has changed and take us to a hall near the registrar's office. There isn't anyone here except for some workers trying to fix a generator for an uninterrupted screening. When I reach the hall, I just cannot believe that common sense is so scarce in one of the world's best science schools. The hall has long French windows everywhere without any curtain or blind cover. It's already very hot and the hall is not air-conditioned. The whirr of fans is very disturbing. There is an LED screen but the sound is pathetic. The noise of the generator can be heard easily inside the hall. A few people have come but they aren't enough to fill this ancient hall with lots of windows. I look for Naireeta who is crying in a corner. I am always chilled out but just can't take anyone tampering with my work. I lose my temper.

'What do you think we are doing here? Who organizes a screening in a hall with windows? Do you collect water in a sieve? Are you a science student?'

'Saar, we were allotted a screen in the main auditorium but some Leftist students raised serious objections and at the last minute we had to shift the venue.'

'Do you call this a venue? It's a godown with a hundred windows.'

'Saar, Dr. CV Raman used to conduct lectures here. It's of historical value.'

'Of course, I can see that in the last fifty years, since Raman, no one ever entered this hall.'

'Saar, we tried our best but we are small in number. We knew what happened at NLU and that's why we decided that whatever happens, we must do the screening. This is a victory for us, saar.'

I have no idea how to answer this. Naireeta advises me that it can't get worse. Let the screening go on and prepare better from now on by asking for all technical details in advance.

Why should a film suffer because of their politics? A film is not just some moving images with sound. A film is a complete experience. A film can deliver only when it gets a conducive environment. But if I can show it at JNU under an open sky and feel happy about it, then what stops me now? I can see the limitations of the human mind. Once we get comfortable, our capacity to struggle also diminishes. If we have decided to fight, to tell our story, to initiate a movement, then nothing should be difficult. I get up with positivity and a great learning. When I reach the 'hall with a hundred windows', to my surprise, it's jam-packed. People are sitting, standing, squeezing themselves and trying to fit into this extremely hot hall which is now stinking of sweat.

The front rows are taken by the professors who have come in large numbers. There are some outsiders from other institutes. I have no idea if they will be able to sit through this heat. I am felicitated and asked to speak.

'The only crime you can commit against a filmmaker is to show his film in a wrong atmosphere. This is that day. I was mad at the organizers but sitting outside, looking at Dr. CV Raman's statue, I thought about the hardships, struggles, pains, rejections, sabotages and failures that great men like Raman had to face. I thought about Gandhi and millions of his young followers wanting to free India. I thought about a poor student in tenth standard who is studying to get admission in IISc or IIT studying under a lamp-post. No fight is easy. Why did I expect my fight to be easy? I want to thank God, the students who didn't want this film to be screened in a dark air-conditioned hall and the students who didn't give up and ensured that the screening takes place, as screening the film is the real journey and not the paraphernalia attached to it.

'I know it's hot, noisy and uncomfortable. I have sacrificed a lot to be able to reach this far and I am ready to sacrifice more as this is the most important issue in my life, to be able to see a truly shining India and that isn't possible until we get rid of "invisible enemies" who want to break us. I would suggest that only those commit themselves to see the movie in bad projection, muffled sound and extreme heat who also share my dream and are willing to sacrifice something for it.'

Nobody moves. Then some students get up. More join and then some more. My heart sinks. Slowly, the entire gentry gets up and they scream together '*Vande Mataram*'. The film begins but the chant still echoes in this 'hall with a hundred windows'.

The student leader takes me around the institute. We sit under a tall statue of its founder Jamshedji Tata and chat about the politics.

'Saar, there is not much politics here. It's just some students who want to create a rift between Hindu and Dalit students. They don't want any work related to nationalism, culture or heritage to be discussed or displayed. Like for your screening, if the faculty and administration had helped us, we would have screened it in the main hall but sometimes the administration listens to them.'

'But why? You aren't doing anything wrong. It's your right to screen a film. You are also a research scholar like them. Then what is the basis for this discrimination?'

'Saar, they have created a perception that they are intellectuals and we are emotional buggers. They have convinced everyone that talking about our country or parents or *rakhi* for sisters or anything that is Hindu and Indian is regressive but talking about revolution, free sex, protest and Mao are progressive things. That's why, saar.'

The film ends amidst thunderous applause and chants of '*Vande Mataram*'. I speak.

'I am a bit emotional thinking about the hardships one has to go through in our country to excel, to innovate, and to express oneself. A lot of people choose to escape to foreign universities and jobs. A lot give up. Just two hours ago I was about to give up. I dedicate this evening to those who stay back, fight and dedicate their entire lives to make India a better, stronger place. Normally, we have a Q&A after the film but today I want to hear your experiences, after seeing the film, which you may want to share with me so that I can get more inspired, more determined to take this fight all across India and expose these invisible enemies.'

For the next hour and a half, I listen to lots of experiences, some scary, some painful. These are some of the most valuable insights. The common theme is intolerance of the Leftist community to accept them as intellectuals. It's true that most of the students from here go on to work for government institutions that work for India's development and scientific progress. It's clear that life is really hellish for a development-leaning, non-English-speaking, small-town student. He is considered to be a right-wing person. What can be a sadder commentary than this, where the world's top-class scientists, the real intellectuals, have no place in the national intellectual discourse. Today, I understand why. Because the entire Naxal/Left/Maoist movement in India is based on an illogical venom against the country and any kind of scientific and logical discourse works like an antidote to their destructive ideology.

44. The Technique of Sabotage: IIT Madras

We had a great screening and reception at the Maulana Azad National Institute of Technology at Bhopal. Bhopal is my hometown so it was natural for us to get such overwhelming affection, appreciation and applause. Now I am looking forward to a screening at one of the best institutes – IIT Madras.

As soon as we check in at Bhopal airport for Chennai, Naireeta shows me pictures of the Open-Air Theatre of IITM where the film is to be screened tonight. It's huge and accommodates around six thousand people. Naireeta tells me that the organizers are confident that it will fill more than the capacity. However, humble we try to become, numbers are always tempting. As we board the aircraft, Naireeta receives a call from Sumeet Roy, postgraduate student of IIT Madras, and the organizer of our screening. Naireeta's smile drops.

'No, you have to fight it out, Sumeet. How can they do this?' says an agitated Naireeta.

I can sense there is some hurdle on our way. Another sabotage?

'OK, send me quickly, we may take off anytime.'

Before I can ask Naireeta anything, she receives a screenshot of a tweet from Sumeet.

@Sumeetroy red elements at IITM tried their best to stop us. They removed our posters last night. However, we again kept posters today.

Sumeet belongs to a middle-class Bengali family, but he was born and brought up in the tribal-dominated district of Betul, Madhya Pradesh. He has seen Naxalism first hand. He has traveled extensively in sixteen states of India and has spent time on our international borders with China, Pakistan, Bangladesh, and Sri Lanka. Sumeet loves exploring new places, writing articles, and reading. He runs an organization called Vande Mataram at IIT Madras, an independent initiative by IIT Madras students. Along with other students, he created this Vande Mataram group with the vision of making the youth socially aware. To achieve this objective, they arrange talks, discussions, screenings and also do selfless service like teaching, tree plantation, cleanliness drives.

If you take out Vande Mataram from his resume, he is an ideal candidate to join the Leftists. But for his group, Vande Mataram is not just a name. When someone asks them, what is the difference between them and the Leftists, they say, '*Vande Mataram.*'

Vande Mataram invited us to screen our film because they felt *Buddha In a Traffic Jam* is the most relevant movie in recent times which reveals the nexus between NGOs, the Naxals, and the academia. IIT Madras is a fine example of it, where many professors and students of the humanities department openly support terrorists like Yakub Memon, Afzal Guru, Abdul Nasser Mahdani etc.

When we land at Chennai, the Vande Mataram team is waiting for us with flowers. Nobody speaks until the car picks up steady speed. Sumeet informs me that they had to face lots of problems for the screening of the film. 'First, they delayed the permission, without giving any reason, then they gave permission for the programme but not for the venue. Then just three days ago they gave permission for the Open-Air Theatre. Then they cancelled that yesterday. We were told by the Dean that the film secretary doesn't want to give Open Air Theatre for the screening of this movie.

'Whereas, we have a screening every weekend. Just a few days ago, *Aligarh* was shown because it's a film supported by the Leftists. But I know unofficially that the film secretary who is a Leftist got scared when he realized that the OAT will be jam-packed. When we protested, the Dean gave us permission for SAC (600 capacity). When more students signed up for the screening, they changed it at the last minute and finally, they gave permission for ICSR hall (capacity 300). Last night we put up posters of the movie but Leftists removed them overnight. Now the problem is that there are too many students, at least 800, who want to see the film, but the capacity is only 300.'

'Ask the rest of them to sit or stand in the aisles. That's how it has been wherever we screened,' I try to find a solution.

'No sir, we can't do that. They aren't allowing anyone to sit or stand in the aisles, whereas last week there was a talk and we were all standing in the aisles, shoulder to shoulder.'

'Is that a new rule?' I ask.

'No sir. New tactic.'

A pattern is emerging. The Urban Naxals are installed in top institutes. Institutes which matter, which engineer the narrative. They are using these campuses as 'intellectual training zones'. Like in the military, no point of view other than the combat is allowed to enter a soldier's mind; in these campuses, no narrative other than theirs is allowed to pass through the minds of their intellectual soldiers.

I am taken to their professor's home for high tea before the screening. A few more professors have come for an informal interaction. The professor's wife has made lots of Maharashtrian snacks. Their families turn out to be big fans of Pallavi. As we relish these delicacies, I discuss the problems students faced for the screening and how it is possible in one of the world's most respected institutes. All of them express their regret and helplessness. They admit that the institute is indeed infested with left ideology. They sound like they have given up and that's why they are so eager to see this film.

It's a compact auditorium filled with students and their enthusiasm. After I introduce the film, the lights go off. Slowly, the future engineers, innovators, researchers and scientific thought leaders immerse themselves in the film and its characters.

'Because of our name, our ideology, we face lots of problems from the IIT administration and faculty, which is mostly captured by the Leftists. Most of the top management of IIT Madras openly favour Leftists. Leftists are allowed to distribute hateful pamphlets and anti-India substance whereas the voices of common students, who love the country, are being suppressed.' Sumeet is explaining the politics of IITM as we sip our tea in small glasses, sitting under a lamp-post.

'During Independence Day in 2015, the Dean didn't allow the '*Vande Mataram*' song. Can you believe it?' He laughs at the irony of it. 'The slogan which has given independence to India?'

This is what I call intellectual terrorism. In the Kashmir Valley, they do not let anyone raise slogans like '*Vande Mataram*' or '*Bharat Mata Ki Jai*'. In the rest of India, the Leftists take extreme steps to curb such sentiments. He tells me how during March-April 2016, the IIT administration blocked all the venues when Vande Mataram tried to organize a programme and pressured their volunteers to eventually cancel it.

'In almost every instance, they deliberately delay the permission to the last minute leaving us with hardly any time to organize the programme. Many times, they give permission for the programme *per se*, but don't give permission for the venue. This is their standard strategy. Never give in fully to your needs. Create hurdles. Change venues at the last minute. Make your life so miserable that you finally give up. They kill you without using arms.'

Sumeet narrates many incidents which are a sad commentary on our education management. He sounds very perturbed with Dalit politics.

'Leftists present themselves as rational, liberal and supporters of equality; however, they support irrational things like caste reservation and Muslim Personal Law Board. Leftists mostly use the fraud Aryan-Dravidian theory to divide the people on the basis of region and skin colour. Leftists refer to Ambedkar and Periyar to justify hatred against upper castes and Indic religions.'

'In an engineering college, how do students get attracted to an unscientific and irrational narrative? By temperament, shouldn't they be apolitical?' I inquire.

'Many Leftist activists, mostly from Kerala, have taken admission in the Humanities department. Many of them are associated with SFI, DYFI, CPI. Most of them are from non-engineering backgrounds and have taken admissions through tests and interviews conducted by department faculties. The admission process is highly questionable as it is mostly based on department faculty recommendations rather than any open competitive exam score. They haven't taken admission through JEE, GATE, CAT or any other tough competitive exam.'

One of the observations he makes is that the faculty members, who are also alumni of JNU, are trying to divide the students in the name of caste and religion. Distribution of pamphlets and sticking posters of hate speeches and anti-India substance are now becoming common on the IIT campus.

'You know sir; this is a very successful strategy. Leftists always try to spread their message through educational institutes which are the best places to brainwash young minds. That's the reason the Leftists captured all the influential posts in educational institutions. It is a long conspiracy which was started in the 1970s when Leftists demanded influential posts in universities in return for their support to the Indira Gandhi government,' he explains.

'Why do you oppose the Left?'

'Because Leftists don't believe in borders. This campus has a border. States they fight for have borders. Their houses have borders. But they don't believe in national borders. They are violent in nature and want to take control with the use of arms. I am against violence. Leftists always play the victim card, cry in the name of human rights, minority, lower caste etc. I am against identity politics. Leftists have a common agenda all over the world. They want to overthrow the democratic set-up and want to take over the control of the country. For this, they use the principle of divide and rule, where they try to spread hatred among the people in the name of caste, religion, community, region. They want to prepare a chain of anti–democracy and anti-national forces to overthrow the system. I am against any kind of polarization.

'Leftists have great sympathy for *jihadis*, which is a part of their international agenda. India is not the only country, US universities like the University of California are also affected by Leftists. Many student bodies are working there to reveal the nexus between Leftists and *jihadis*. I am dead against terrorism. I want a strong, successful India, and they want to break India. They believe in *Lal Salaam* and I believe in *Vande Mataram*.' He pauses and then adds, 'I am rational. I have reasons. But they call me *bhakt* as if I am blind to reason.'

'What kind of students join them?'

'Students belonging to SC/ST are attracted to Leftist propaganda because of the fraud theory of Aryan-Dravidian divide. Leftists have also misrepresented Indian epics like *Manu Smriti* and manipulated Indian history books to brainwash students. Students from Kashmir with a *jihadi* mentality easily get attracted towards Leftists as they both have a common agenda of weakening India.'

'If you are right, you must follow your conviction. Never give up.'

'That's what we are doing. We don't fight. We just do the right things. But unfortunately, in India, "what is right" is decided by Leftist ideology. All debate is decided by the Leftists, there is very little space for an alternate narrative. The greatest gift of India to the world is the capacity to debate. India has given shelter to people of all religions including Jews and Zoroastrians. India is the country of Lord Buddha, where '*Ahimsa Paramo Dharma– non-violence is the greatest* dharma)' is preached. It is the country of Lord Rama which believes in *Janani Janma-bhoomischa Swargadapi Gariyasi–* mother and motherland are dearer than Heaven. He starts getting emotional.

I don't want to intrude into his emotional moment. I just put my hand on his shoulder.

'Sir, the real tragedy is that the moment we start talking about *Vedas*, Ram, Krishna, Vivekananda or quote anything in Sanskrit, we are labeled Sanghis. Which means regressive Hindu fundamentalist. I am doing my masters in analytics sir; do you think I can ever be regressive or fundamentalist?'

Indian campuses are going through turmoil. Cracks are becoming visible. Unfortunately, nobody is trying to cement these cracks. Everyone is busy widening them.

The screening is a great success. These students understand the politics of the film very well. The professors give me an IITM trophy as a memento. Holding this trophy, I remember how miserably I had failed in the entrance exam of IIT. My office is filled with awards that the film has won and I know where am I going to keep this one: right in front.

We have come for dinner to a friend's house, whose wife is in a very senior position at Ford Motors and is in Chennai on a three-year off-shore term to set up their Asia-Pacific network. They live in a posh bungalow and talk and behave like typical NRIs. Unhappy with Indian slowness, lack of professionalism and wanting to do something for India without compromising on American comforts. The discussions here are so different that it has taken me some time to make the transition. Here the concerns are related to trade, money, technology, competition, and market. The market is the universe. There is no religion, caste or colour. There is no gender. The only goal is profit.

Both the worlds are so polarized. So different and contradictory. Yet, they have some things in common. Complexity, chaos, and conflict. And there is no place for any other narrative.

I open the newspapers but there is no news about the sabotage. It would have been national news backed up with protests if I were a Dalit or a Muslim or a Leftist or a liberal.

Indian media, especially the metro-based English media, is the most dishonest institution of India. They are always in a hurry, their questions are statements, they have no courtesy, they are arrogant, rude and humiliating. They are always running late for something and, therefore, have no concentration. I am not talking about those hundreds and thousands of hard-working young girls and boys who are running from one breaking news to another. I am talking about those who instruct them to twist the news. Or who twist it themselves to further their or someone else's agenda.

And it's no rocket science to understand the design of this parallel politics. They have become victims of their own agenda. For the last 70 years, English media has loved to paint any rightist organization, especially RSS, as regressive, uncivilized, aggressive and fundamentalist. Any organization connected with RSS e.g. ABVP is considered a party of goons. Whereas the student members of left-wing parties are considered rebels, revolutionaries, progressive and intellectuals. It's more like a perception battle. The media has created a 'group of somebodies' and a 'group of nobodies'. Those raising slogans against the State of India are painted as The Superiors and the ones singing '*Vande Mataram*' as The Inferiors. This is the reason why people like to associate themselves with the left – The Superiors.

Some people like to believe they are liberals. Liberals are those who do liberal things, not the ones who are against the right. If you look at the reporting of the Jadavpur University crisis after the seditious JNU incident, they always wrote 'left-wing students' and ABVP goons or outsiders. I realized this when a journalist asked me at JU, 'What do you have to say about the presence of some outsiders, ABVP goons?' I wondered, 'Aren't they students here?

Aren't they called Akhil Bhartiya VIDYARTHI Parishad? *Vidyarthi* means student.' She was taken aback and said 'But…no… yeah… But…' I knew she had no answer, only biases. I again asked her, 'Aren't they students of the same university? What do they need to do to be recognized as students? Raise anti-India slogans?' She got upset and left me to cover the protesting students – the real students, according to her.

Another problem with our media, intellectuals, elites and posh class is that they are always negative. Desperate. Insecure. All signs of a weak institution. They are scared that if the hungry masses get empowered, they will destroy their empires built on the blood and sweat of the same people. That's why they constantly try to keep the masses deprived, and their very existence in fear. They never let the masses forget who is Superior and who is Inferior.

Their strategy is very well summed up in a highly acclaimed film, *Silver Linings Playbook*, where Jennifer Lawrence's character says:

'You love it when I have problems. You love it because then you can be the good one…'

45. Two Indias: Allahabad and Benares

Allahabad airport is the worst airport I have ever landed in. It's like a small government office with unnecessary grills between a small check-in hall and security, reminding me of Nazi camps.

A young, tall boy with a fixed smile, Manish Tiwari, is our escort. He has a saffron *gamcha* around his neck.

'Do you work for BJP? I ask him.

'No, *bhaiya*.'

'RSS?'

'No, *bhaiya*.'

'Then why do you have this *gamcha*?'

He looks at his neck, feels the scarf and looks at me as if I have asked him why he wears clothes.

'*Kabhi socha nahi, bhaiya* I presume, everyone wears,' he says, simply.

I look around and see almost everyone wearing a saffron scarf. Some are spitting *paan* and tobacco. The walls are red with *paan* spits. I am back in UP after a long time. It's a culture shock.

We have to go directly to Allahabad University. I am excited and a bit nostalgic. I had come here with my father. He had to attend a vice-chancellors' conference and I tagged along. As a young boy, I had loved the university. If one takes out Allahabad University from India's history, we will lose some of our best freedom fighters, politicians, writers, thinkers, teachers, reformers, historians, scientists, civil servants, lawyers, and judges. Allahabad University is not just one of the oldest universities, it's a monument of Indian history. The city of Triveni, the meeting point of three rivers, Ganga, Jamuna and Saraswati, the invisible river. The university is the meeting point of Ganga Jamuna *tehzeeb* and Saraswati, the invisible conscience of India. For me, to be invited to screen the film in the main building is a matter of great pride and joy.

Allahabad, like any other city of Uttar Pradesh, is crowded, chaotic, noisy, and filthy. Most Indian cities today are a mix of the new and the old. One can see heritage and development in a single canvas, whereas cities of UP are *just* old.

We enter the university through its main gate which is plastered with umpteen layers of political posters. When we stop in front of the main building, I see a great architecture ravaged by political enthusiasts. To add some colour, *paan* spitters have contributed generously. Some students are roaming around with saffron scarfs, some with green.

A few boys come running to receive us. They are enthusiastic and eager to welcome with flowers, selfies, and broad smiles. There is press waiting. Some students with black flags are opposing my screening. Some ruckus is going on between the organizers and the opposing boys. I can't see any girls anywhere. Conflict is in the vibes. It seems like a workshop of Indian parliamentary politics.

Naireeta who had gone to check the arrangements comes back panicking.

'Why have you put two screens?' she asks Manisha.

'So, people on both left and right can see it,' he replies with a smile.

'You can't show a film on two screens.'

'*Didi*, there is a 58' LED TV also in the centre. So, we will have three-dimensional screening which nobody has ever done before. '*Yeh hamara idea tha*,' he says with pride while adjusting his saffron *gamcha*.

I know there is no point in making him understand. He hasn't seen anything beyond this well of ignorance and decay.

'Naireeta, just shut one screen and show it only on one.'

'Sir, I checked but we can't do it as they have connected both through one output and the change will take at least a couple of hours.'

When I enter the hall, I can't believe the atmosphere. People are screaming at the top of their voices, some are laughing, some are running around as if tackling an emergency, some are fighting with the protesting boys. It's chaos everywhere. There is a stage where already six-seven people are sitting and all of them are busy with their smartphones. As soon as I enter, an announcement is made which is appropriate for a singer making an entry into a Durga Puja pandal. Seven people give speeches. Provocative speeches. Long speeches. The super energetic students are loving every moment of it. I want to run away. I have a screening tomorrow at BHU (Benaras Hindu University). I leave as soon as the screening begins without waiting for the Q&A. There is no point. I can't relate to them.

We were supposed to leave at five. It's 6 AM now and Manish is nowhere in sight. His phone is unreachable and I am getting impatient to get out of Allahabad. I am feeling suffocated. The last time I had this feeling was after meeting a huge star. I had fantasized about meeting him all my life. All of us carry images of some memories, some dreams, some fantasies and when they shatter with the onslaught of reality, you just want to run away from the horrifying reality. When Manish reaches at six thirty, he has a big smile and a big bundle of newspapers.

'*Bhaiya*, sorry I am late because I had gone to get all the newspapers from their offices. If I had waited for the vendors, we wouldn't have been able to leave before seven,' he says with an infectious smile. According to his understanding, he has saved us half an hour even after coming one and a half hour late.

As we approach the Allahabad-Benaras highway, I go through all the papers. The news is on the front page with a common theme 'Vivek Agnihotri exposes Naxals'. As I go through the other news I start to realize I have not been exposed to this kind of journalism in a long long time. The papers are full of news that concerns the common man. Common themes, good news, constructive articles, and a lot of local events. There are no semi-nude girls and no Bollywood. The writing quality is exceptionally good. Unlike a manipulative and isolating English national media.

Manish can sense that I am not very happy with the headlines.

'Why *bhaiya*, it's a very good coverage. Even Prashant Bhushan didn't get such coverage.'

'But it sounds political. I am not part of Naxal/Communist politics. Why put so much focus on one thing? I also spoke about innovation.'

'Because *bhaiya*, Allahabad and Patna University are the nerve centres of Communism in North India.'

He is right. Communism was seeded in the Allahabad University campus somewhere between 1940 and 1945. Communist ideology flourished unchallenged until in 1964, its sister ideology socialism emerged to complement it. At the same time, nationalism also started showing its signs but it didn't really get adopted by the students, until 2013, when for the first time in the student's union election, ABVP emerged as a serious contender. Communism also lost its sheen due to the Communist Party's unconditional support to Indira Gandhi's Emergency.

I want to utilize this drive to Benaras to understand their politics. I just want to listen without judging.

'Tell me what is your understanding about this politics,' I ask him and adjust my front seat and get in a comfortable position to concentrate on what he has to say.

'To understand Communism in Allahabad University, one has to understand its influence in the entire eastern belt. Here, Communists work at two levels – one, with the poor labour, landless farmers, and second, in the university,' he begins.

'Marx believed that society is divided between the financially empowered and the financially deprived. One has everything and the other has nothing. One is the oppressor and the other the oppressed. That's why Marx talked about a revolution when these two forces would clash and that day everything would end. This is called class struggle. But Marx didn't realize that between these two there is a vast middle class which works as a cushion between them and prevents a direct clash. That's why Communists don't want a middle class because they are not programmed or equipped to deal with the middle class and that is the reason they don't work with the middle class.

'Now, the rural Communist is closer to socialist ideology. You will never find a rural Communist criticizing rural culture or their gods and deities because they know that for a rural person, the gods and the deities are the masters of his livelihood. He will never agree for a revolution at the cost of his gods or culture. That is the reason that, in villages, Communists talk only about poverty, exploitation, atrocities of the system and their rights,' Manish speaks with passion.

'But as soon as you enter a university, we witness a radical and communal face of Communism. Here, they propagate the weaknesses and evils of Hindu culture. They manipulate and twist ancient books to misrepresent them and provoke students. For example, they use Tulsidas' *chaupai*, without mentioning the rest of the *Ramcharitmanas*, which is the real context.

"ढोल गंवार शूद्र पशु नारी, सकल ताडना के अधिकारी."

Dhol ganvar shudra pashu nari, sakal tadana ke adhikari.

'The above lines are spoken by the Sea Deity Samudra to Ram. When Lord Ram got angry and took out his weapon in order to evaporate the whole sea, the deity appeared and said the above lines in the context of boundaries that are created by God himself in order to hold his creations.

'What Leftists do is that they very cleverly translate it literally in Hindi, ignoring the fact that *Ramcharitmanas* is written in Awadhi and the same word means one thing in Hindi and another in Awadhi. While the literal meaning of the line in Hindi is 'Drums, the illiterate, lower caste, animals and women deserve a beating to straighten up and get the acts together', its real meaning in Awadhi is different. In Awadhi, *tadna* means to take care, to protect. Whereas, in Hindi, the same word means punishment, torture, oppression. Samudra meant that like drums, the illiterate, Shudra, animals and women need special care and need to be protected in the boundary of a social safety net. In the same way, the sea also needs to reside within the boundaries created by God. And hence, Samudra gave the suggestion to create the iconic Ram Setu.

'Here, Shudra doesn't mean lower caste or today's Dalit. It meant people employed in cottage industries.'

I remember there is a book by R.C. Dutta, *Economic Interpretation of History*, in which he has said that when the Indian economy was based on the principles of *Varna*, handicrafts accounted for over twenty-five percent of the economy. Artisans and labour who were involved in the handicraft business were called 'Shudra'. If there was so much caste-based discrimination, why would Brahmins use their produce? Both Dutta and Dadabhai Naoroji have written that the terminology of 'caste discrimination' was used by the British to divide Indian society on those lines.

Manish continues, 'Like the British, they provoke young students to believe that Hindu scriptures are against Dalits and women and want them to suffer torture. Young students are emotional and passionate. They come here with the dream of changing the world. The concept of "revolution" attracts them and they get swayed by an illogical logic.'

I am enjoying the ride. We stop at a *dhaba* for breakfast. While we relish *tandoori aloo* and *gobi parathas* with the typical *aloo ki subzi* of UP, I ask Manish to tell me about their *modus operandi* in the university.

'Communists spread lots of unfounded theories which provoke students against the system. They exploit women on the pretext of women empowerment and propagate free sex. I am not against free sex but it should be out of free will and not a condition to be part of their revolution. Most of them come from orthodox backgrounds and sex works as an incentive and a bond. That's how they create a large intellectual ecosystem.

'*Bhaiya*, I have a friend, Neeraj Singh. His grandfather was a loyal Communist and even when he was bedridden in his old age, he used to say my vote will only go to *laal,* meaning Communist party. He was a very religious person and used to read *Ramayana* and *Gita* regularly. He wasn't anti-religion like today's Communists. When Neeraj *ji* came to Allahabad University, he met members of CPI(ML) and told them about his grandfather's Communist background. They invited him for their meeting but to his utter shock, he found that the entire meeting was centred around only anti-national and anti-Hindu discussions. That day, Neeraj Bhai quit CPI-ML and joined ABVP.

'Though Communists say they don't spend any money to attract the poor, in reality, they organize seminars very frequently. They put up posters everywhere. Now, if one poster costs nine to ten rupees, for five hundred posters it costs five thousand rupees. Where do they get it from when if you ask an individual worker to buy you a cup of tea he will start telling you how poor he is? And what are the themes of their seminars? "The Economics of Riots", "We are also Kalburgi", "Understanding Naxalism for a Bright India". They deliberately organize them in the open spaces because at any time at least five to six hundred freshers roam around. These freshers start listening to these speakers and when they find someone listening curiously, they target those students and introduce them to senior research scholars who introduce them to senior professors who further influence the student.

'Concepts of free sex and free drugs also attract freshers who have never seen such freedom. The fresher thinks that if intellectuals are supporting them, then they must be right. Slowly, they start attending all their seminars and private meetings where they are further brainwashed. Is there anybody *bhaiya*, in this world, who thinks that injustice has not been done to him? Slowly, the fresher becomes their loyalist and he starts brainwashing others. Most people don't really want the truth. They just want constant reassurance that what they believe is the truth. They choose comforting lies over unpleasant truth.'

When Manish speaks about these things, he comes across as very different from his appearance. He has things sorted out in his head. He talks more like an observer and I am happy that he is not hateful and bitter.

'What stops you from exposing them, debate with them?' I ask.

'Prashant Bhushan came to our university in 2015-16. He was invited by the president of the Student's Union, Richa Singh, who is elected under the coalition of socialist and Communist parties. The topic of Bhushan's seminar was "Employment for the youth", but he used the occasion to abuse and ridicule Hindu culture and nationalism. We asked him if lawyers would force courts to open their gates at three in the morning, to free a terrorist, how is one supposed to feel safe amongst them? At this, Bhushan got really angry and there was big chaos and we were forced to leave the hall. They never reply, never answer. Theirs is a one-sided communication, like in the army. Army kills enemies outside our borders but these people want to kill their own brothers and sisters.

'Then there was a programme after Kalburgi's murder: "I am also Kaburgi". One speaker said, "What can happen if I piss on a Shiva *lingam*?" He compared Bharat Mata with a witch. The students who felt hurt at such provocations started questioning their theories. Soon, everything converted into mayhem. They started beating up those students who were questioning them. Police came. They have a very smart tactic. Whenever a clash happens between them and ABVP students, their girls start saying that they were molested. *Bhaiya*, you read reports about any incident, you google, in every single fight between them, the Communist girls always accuse ABVP students of molestation. Now even the police know it. One journalist even told me that you don't have to tell me what happened because the headline is ready that girls were molested by ABVP students.

'But in the last couple of years, their hold is becoming weaker. Maybe, due to social media, now they are not as strong. This has rattled them and they have become active differently. At this moment, all I know is that these students work as underground agents of CPIM and Naxals. They secretly go to Shankargadh, a nearby area which is declared Naxal-infested. I have a feeling they are up to something. Something is going to happen. Because there is silence, and their silence means danger.' Manish takes a deep breath. I can feel he is exhausted.

As we approach Benaras Hindu University (BHU), I ask the driver to stop at the entrance, next to Pandit Madan Mohan Malviya's statue, the founder of BHU, which is the largest residential university in Asia and one of the largest in the world. I get out of the car to salute the man.

The huge Swatantra Bhavan in the campus seats over a thousand people each in its two levels. Professor Mishra informs me that there are over two thousand students inside. As I enter, struggling to find a way in between the tightly squeezed students sitting on each step, the entire hall fills up with the chants of '*Har har Mahadev*'. They felicitate me and give me Pandit Madan Mohan Malviya's books. I am going to read them as soon as I am done here. I am forced to give a speech. I ask the audience a question.

'India has given some of the finest political brains to the world. Not just political thinkers but also political innovators. A country which gave Krishna, Chanakya, Ashoka, Gandhi, Ambedkar to the world, I fail to understand what Mao is doing in India?'

The hall fills up with '*Har har Mahadev*' and '*Vande Mataram*'. I sit through the screening as with their reactions I am seeing my own film in a new light. Some nuances which even I had ignored come alive and fills my eyes with tears.

In Varanasi, Ganga *Aarti* is a daily ritual, and for the visitors a must. Sitting on the stairs of Assi Ghat, watching the flames against a serene Ganga, slowly, I get lost in my own world and the mesmerizing sounds of the chanting and the manjiras become the barrier between my thoughts and the world. I am somewhere between the meditative state and tranquility. The many sides of India are appearing in my mind, in slow motion. There are many realities of India hidden in one large Nation.

India is an apt example of social contradictions. India is Ram. India is Ravana. India is Buddha. India is Aurangzeb. India is Gandhi. India is Godse. India is a prophet and a pusher. India is partly truth, partly fiction.

We are an inexplicable, undefinable and incomprehensible nation. We can't be understood on the semantics of tolerance and intolerance. In India, wisdom (Saraswati), wealth (Lakshmi) and power (Durga) are manifested as goddesses while globally, we rank extremely low on women empowerment. One wouldn't be surprised to hear of a *khap panchayat* ordering the killing of a young girl for loving a boy of a different *gotra* while celebrating woman as Shakti.

In one part of India, a Hindu mob lynches a Muslim and in another part, Hindus empty a road to facilitate the Friday *namaz* for Muslims. We can witness a Sikh *langar*, Muslim *namaz*, Hindu *kirtan* and a Christian mass in a radius of 500 metres, and within the same radius, Hindus will refuse to rent their houses to Muslims and vice versa. Muslim classical singers start their performances with *Saraswati vandana*, whereas, in movies, a Hindu couple breaks into a Sufi song devoted to *Allah, Maula* or a *Khwaja*.

We are the world's least innovative country, yet we made the cheapest journey to Mars. We are world leaders in unorganized recycling and repairing. We are champions of multi-purpose usage of devices. We call it *jugaad*. The best example is how we use our railway tracks for mass sanitation and use the excreta as fertilizer for growing vegetables. We are the world's oldest country with the world's first planned cities in Mohenjo Daro and Harappa. Paradoxically, we have the worst planned cities with appalling quality of sanitation, drinking water and hygiene today. We built the world's first global university at Nalanda and today, we have a pathetic education system. We have given holistic wellness sciences such as Yoga and Ayurveda to the world but have high rates of malnutrition in our society. We are the world's second most populated country and ironically also have a history of forced sterilizations.

We are a country of the world's oldest texts in the *Vedas* but don't have an authentic written history. We are also a country of the Emergency, of literary and creative bans. We kill people who try to rationalize popular ideas. We do not just tolerate cows sitting in the middle of the road; we accept them as part of our urban landscape. In a lot of Indian cities, monkeys live freely. Tourists find them menacing and throw stones at them while locals live with them with an inexplicable understanding and reverence, treating them like descendants of Lord Hanuman.

We don't question men who urinate under '*Yahan Peshab Karna Mana Hai*' signs forbidding urination and those men who enjoy their bus/train rides sitting on '*Women Only*' seats. We love our malls and five-star hotels for their cleanliness but spit out our *gutka* the moment we are out on the street. If you want to see our civic sense, just take the staircase of any building in any part of India and look at the corners; if they aren't painted red with *paan* spits, you aren't in India. We pick up filth from private properties and throw them on public properties.

We have Muthaliks who beat up pub-going girls (with 'loose character') and we have girls who send him thousands of 'pink *chaddis*'. We want every anti-national kicked out of India while wanting our children to settle abroad after receiving subsidized education in India. We want the government to bring social justice but look for a *gori*, convent-educated, cultured, adept-at-household-chores bride with a good dowry, for our sons. We want the government to shower us with '*achchhe din*' while we evade taxes.

We have not just given Satyajit Ray, Raj Kapoor, and Guru Dutt to the world, we have invented film genres like 'mindless comedies', '*masala* films', 'family films' and 'story-less films'. We take pride in Bollywood as our best-known brand in the world and yet we love to censor our films. We aspire to be like Hollywood but refuse to pay our writers and love to fake box office figures.

We love to hate the rich but don't hesitate to be corrupt to become rich. We take pride in our simplicity but do vulgar displays of wealth at our children's weddings. We believe in reincarnation, but our funerals are very melodramatic. Our Constitution specifies our rights and their extent, yet we believe everything is our right: from unnecessary honking to spitting in public places, to eve-teasing a girl, to ragging juniors. Many people believe it's their right to hurt others, to make it difficult for others and if need be, even kill others. As a country, we still spend years debating the reasons for massacres and riots but never hold anyone accountable. It's okay for us to steal, to bribe, to lie, to be a hypocrite and to be perpetually late. Nobody has a clear view of whether not standing for our national anthem is our right or throwing the defiant viewer out of the cinema hall is our right.

In some states, people suffer from police atrocities and in some, people throw stones at the police. We are victims of intense terrorism, yet we take decades to convict a terrorist and then fight for his right to live. We hang terrorists and also mourn them as martyrs. Liberalism is defined by attacking and ridiculing the majority while secularism is practiced by appeasing the minority.

We make gods out of our cricketers but hurl water bottles and abuses at them when they fail to score runs. We curse God for killing people in the Chennai rains and pray to the same God for their safety. We can be blind worshippers and passionate agnostics of the same God. Our philosophy begins with '*Tatvam asi*' but mediocrity is our national culture. We have millions of gods, but we live in a hell.

If you travel the length and breadth of India crossing its metropolises, *kasbahs,* and *gaons*, at the end of your journey, you would feel as if India is a concentrated display of the entire world's problems. Abject poverty, hunger, unemployment, inflation, insurgency, political unrest, lack of basic amenities like drinking water and electricity, housing, epidemics, droughts, floods, dying rivers, terrorism, social exploitation, women's safety, corruption, unethical media, partisan politics, unreported crimes, racism, sexism, female infanticide, child labour, regional, social and financial disparity, inefficient systems, unproductive public sector, lopsided education, coal mafia, water mafia, religious crimes, hate crimes, cybercrimes – you name a problem, it exists here. A new problem is invented almost every day. To top it all, people have to constantly deal with mosquitos, infections, dengue, dug-up roads, heat, noise, and delays in almost everything, ranging from trains to court cases. Yet, we live. Together.

We are a loud noisy, melodramatic, and over-the-top society. Be it a wedding or a funeral, an election or a selection, traffic or TV, everything in India is larger than life. Amidst all this, people travel here to find peace.

India isn't an either/or society. She is an amalgamation of all these things. India can irritate you with its filth, stench, and bugs, or it can give you an orgasmic flash of enlightenment. India is perhaps the world's most liberal society, being the birthplace of major peaceful religions, yet she is ridden with religious clichés.

For a visitor, India is a mess. For an inhabitant, India is the cosmic truth. When foreigners arrive, India is a question. When they leave, India is the answer. They come to discover India but end up discovering themselves.

India is '*Vasudaiva Kutumbakam*' – one world family. It's a home. Home is not a building. It's a feeling. Our roots are in the joint family system. Joint families don't run on tolerance. They run on understanding and acceptance. This kind of coexistence doesn't come from tolerating. It comes from understanding the reality of our world, our potential, and our limitations and by accepting them. We believe in universal acceptance and unconditional surrender to cosmic reality. It's in our nature. It's our DNA. This is the real 'Idea of India'.

Sitting on the steps of Ganga, in the world's oldest city of *moksha*, as I probe India, I also discover my own reality and the purpose of my life.

46. Roses and Thorns: Panjab University

In the next four days, we have to screen the film at some of the best universities like Panjab University, Chandigarh; Himachal University, Shimla; Delhi University and IIT Kanpur. We have to fly, take trains and cabs to be able to accomplish such an ambitious schedule.

When we land at Chandigarh's new swanky airport, Harmanjot Singh Gill receives us with a huge bouquet of flowers. Looking at the size of the bouquet, his smile, and the car, I know we are in Punjab – the land of big-hearted people. He wears an immaculately tied turban in psychedelic pink matching with the piping on his shirt. Punjab is an ALL CAPS state.

'Sir, I must thank you for exposing Leftists. I have been following you on Twitter and I RT all your tweets,' Harman opens the conversation.

Harman is from Bhusla, a small village in Kaithal district of Haryana. He is passionate about reading books on various subjects and is an ace tennis player. He supports ABVP over AISA and SFI as he believes that ABVP is the only organization among students which is constructive, positive, and dedicated to nationalist causes.

'The Leftists have a habit of spreading false propaganda. First, they tried to label me as anti-Sikh and failed. But after the suicide of Rohith Vemula, a lot changed. When I questioned Rohith's caste and motivation for his suicide, they tried to frame me as anti-Dalit. They know it's a very sensitive issue and whatever you say, it is bound to be used against you,' Harman describes the local politics with fervour. 'I am very passionate about India and I just don't like it when someone wants to weaken it.'

'Someone?'

'I mean parties like SFI, AISA. That's why we invited your movie because we wanted to expose these Leftist organizations. But they tried their best to cancel the screening. Because I am involved, they even said the movie is anti-Sikh and anti-Dalit but this time I had decided to fight. They tore up our posters, I made new ones and pasted them again, at night. They tried to influence the faculty to cancel the screening, but I fought with the faculty. Sir, I am a Sardar. We can give our lives for what we believe in and I believe in One United India, not its divisions, which Leftists want to do.'

He gets a call and speaks in Punjabi.

'Sir, we have information that there are going to be some unruly elements from the Left. They will try to ridicule and humiliate you. I have to rush to ensure they don't come at all.'

'Please don't stop them. This film becomes relevant only when someone challenges it,' I tell him honestly. 'And I like to engage with most opposing views.'

'Sir, you don't know them. They are dangerous. They get Dalit students with them and start asking Dalit-related questions and whatever you say they counter question and finally start raising slogans, labeling you as an anti-Dalit. I must stop them.'

'No. Don't. I know I am not anti-Dalit, so I have nothing to be afraid of. Please let them come.'

'No sir, I'll have to go. You don't understand, this politics its very dangerous.'

He drops us at the hotel and leaves in a jiffy.

Two senior journalists want to have a long chat with me. I invite them for the screening. One of them is Vandana Shukla, associate editor of the arts section of *The Tribune*. I am very impressed with their line of questioning. These are the real journalists of India. While they work their ass off to maintain high standards of journalism, fearlessly and honestly, a few corrupt journalists of Lutyens Delhi have brought such shame to the entire profession that even honest journalists are called 'presstitutes'. The brokers of journalism have created a perception that the entire media is corrupt.

'They must rot in the hell of democracy for such disservice to the noble profession,' one of them tells me.

The film finds a new meaning in the context of local politics. Dalit students of this university aren't as poor, backward or oppressed as in other parts of the country. Here, the Leftists have strong ties with Khalistan activists. In the rest of the country, they are trying to unite the radical Islamists and Dalits to create a bloc, here they are trying to connect Dalits with the separatists of the Khalistan movement.

As the movie progresses, the jam-packed auditorium starts getting divided. I can see a set of students have slowly stopped responding to the film, unlike their counterparts. There is tension in their body language. When the film ends, I am called on the stage for the Q&A amidst thunderous applause and scattered booing, I know in my bones that I am up for some surprises other than the serious grilling by the Leftist students.

'Dear friends, I have flown thousands of kilometres, not because I want to hear your applause. I am here to understand what is bothering you, what are your concerns, aspirations and whether this film portrays them rightly. I am here to discuss, debate and learn. So, all those who don't agree with the film raise their hands.'

Two hands go up. They ask me questions on 'intolerance', cow slaughter, Hindutva and slowly a few more hands come up and the line of questioning shifts to its intended issue: Rohith Vemula and Dalits.

'If you are talking about Dalits because of Rohith's suicide, then I must say you are not doing your job well,' I reply, which irks some. 'I am against using Rohith's suicide as a crutch to win an argument. I believe your politics should be such that it helps empower Dalits rather than using them as a bait to settle scores with your political opponents.'

By and by, more sensitive questions are hurled at me but my outspokenness and fearlessness come in really handy. The biggest weakness of the Leftists is that they lack facts and logic. I use facts and logic. When the angry students who have come with the purpose of not letting me succeed, start getting entangled in their own hate and violent ideology, some professors come to their rescue. A professor rises up and starts giving me a lecture on the language of the film.

'I am very upset and ashamed to have seen this film. You have characters abusing and speaking all kinds of filthy language which is not appropriate for the students and especially in such an esteemed University of Punjab. If I had known, I would have never let this screening take place.'

'Sir, I thought this is a University and not Aastha Channel. When I came here, I thought I am coming to a University which has led the fight for freedom of expression. A University which has given us radical thinkers and leaders like Khushwant Singh, Manmohan Singh, Kalpana Chawla, Balraj Sahni, Romila Thapar, Kiran Bedi, Sushma Swaraj, and Shankardayal Sharma. And of course, Hargobind Khurana and Prem Dutt, Bhagat Singh's comrade. But if that is the thought process, then I am afraid soon we will bring a lot of shame to the legacy of this University.'

'I take very strong objection to what you say.'

'Sir, even I take strong objection to your views of censoring reality, for interfering with my freedom of speech. What the film shows is the reality and if the University wants to isolate its students from the reality, then I think it's for the students to decide whether they want to fight for freedom of speech or not.'

This starts a cross-argument between the student groups. Another professor gets on stage and orders to shut the event. Harman says he has the permissions and asks him the reason for stopping it, to which he says he has the right to shut anything if he fears indiscipline or any kind of conflict.

'But it's a debate of ideologies, sir.'

'There is no place for such films on our campus.'

'Is that the reason?' I butt in.

'Yes.'

He snatches the mike from Harman and announces that the show is over, asks everyone to leave instantly and orders to shut the lights. The Leftist students leave like a victorious team leaves the field. The other students who are in the majority, protest for some time and then leave, saying 'nothing is going to change here'.

Vandana Shukla is stunned and surprised by the professor's behaviour.

'Aren't universities supposed to be nurseries of ideas? Shouldn't debate and disagreement be the very foundation of our campuses? How can he stop the function? Is this a primary school? Why doesn't anyone protest?' the journalist in Vandana raises some tough questions.

'Madam, protests will not change anything but films like these will. The problem with India is that our wise men, good men, the knowledgeable men don't speak. Our media never speaks in favour of students who want to build India. In a deaf and dumb society, you don't need protests, you need awareness, education of poor unaware Dalits and Muslims who are being used as pawns by the Leftists. We need films like these. And we showed it successfully… it's a victory,' Harman tells Vandana.

Later, while dropping me back to the hotel, Harman shows me a WhatsApp message, from an article by Professor Chaman Lal, a retired professor from JNU, New Delhi, and Fellow of Punjab University Chandigarh.

'… Sadly, Punjab University, Chandigarh, has not even put any plaques in the university in memory of Prof. M G Singh, Prof. Brij Narain, who became victims of Partition-induced hatred and were assassinated in their offices in PU, Lahore, nor about Bhagat Singh's comrade Prem Dutt Verma, who taught in Punjab University, Chandigarh, after his release from jail. Whereas, the Lahore website of the university proudly claims Pakistani scientist Abdus Salam and Indian scientist Hargobind Khurana as its alumni, Nobel laureates of 1968 and 1979 with photographs and brief biographies, the Chandigarh website does not even mention Hargobind Khurana.'

I get up at 5 AM and go for a run in the famous rose garden of Chandigarh, before leaving for Shimla. My mind is spinning with a web of questions as to why there is so much bitterness. Why is there so much hatred, violence in our behaviour? Can Indians ever stop working at cross-purposes? I have only questions, no answers. Why do we have two Indias instead of one? After all, our Constitution, our flag promises one India. In times like these, people go to a guru. I have nowhere to go.

When I look at my watch, I realize I have been jogging for an hour. In Mumbai, I hardly do three kilometres and think I can never do more. I can feel a new energy in abundance. I can run more but I have to leave for Shimla soon. I feel my body is expanding to accommodate this newfound energy. I feel infinite. Does it happen when one finds a cause? A purpose? Is this that moment?

As I start to walk slowly to cool down, I start becoming aware of the fresh scent of roses mixed with the fragrance of the grass, wet with dew. As the rays of the morning sun, filtering through thick trees, fall on my body, every pore opens up. Perhaps for more energy to get in. I start noticing beds of roses and slowly my focus shifts below, at thorns, and I notice that the bigger the rose, the thicker the thorns. More beautiful the rose, sharper the thorns. When our heart truly seeks, Mother Nature provides the answers. Mother Nature is the real guru.

I take a picture of a rose and its thorns and tweet with the caption 'Roses don't come without thorns'.

47. The New Politics: DU, IITK, IIM Indore

It's after some twenty years that I am travelling by train. The Shatabdi Express to Kanpur is a fantastic train. Wide seats with a work table and plug points, efficient service, delicious ethnic food and noiseless.

We screened the film last night at Delhi University. They had fixed an LED screen at the main arena of the Arts Faculty, under the statue of Swami Vivekananda. The vast arena was filled with students who watched the film with concentration. The Q&A was loaded with ideas to improve our democracy. These are serious students who take their roles very seriously. They understand politics, society, and the economy. They have an 'idea of India'. It's very different from the 'idea of India' I saw in JNU. They are hardly 20 km apart from each other but poles apart in vision.

'Sir, have you shown your film to Kejriwal?' an IAS aspirant asked me.

'No. Never thought about it. Also, why would he see this film?'

'Sir, he will definitely see it. He is a regular Bollywood critic. He sees every movie and writes about it. If you can get a critic for free, and that too a chief minister, then why not?'

In the last few weeks, a lot of people have asked me to show the film to Arvind Kejriwal but I never took the suggestion seriously. During the Anna Hazare movement, I left all my work, travelled to Delhi and invested my hopes, emotions, thoughts and money in Kejriwal's campaign against corruption. Slowly, a lot of myths shattered and I found him utterly selfish, shallow, and pretentious. He became hungry for votes. The end became more important than the means, so he started using all sorts of unethical means.

But I feel that a lot of youth with contrarian views listen to Kejriwal. His tweets reviewing Bollywood movies go viral, so if he reviews the film, it will benefit the movie. I write a mail to him quoting 15 reasons why he must see the film:

Monday, April 25, 2016

Dear Shri Arvind Kejriwal *Ji*,

I am the writer/director and producer of a small, revolutionary film *Buddha In A Traffic Jam*. It's one of the boldest political dramas ever made in India. The film releases on May 13th.

I believe if any politician who must see this film it is you and instead of writing a template–based invite I'll tell you why you must watch this film.

- Where most of the political films raise questions, this film gives a solution – how we can find real '*Azaadi*' from the middlemen and hence corruption. This is exactly what your '*Swarajya*' campaign seeks.
- The film probes and exposes Naxal-NGO-Academia nexus and delves deep into the theme of 'intellectual terrorism' which I believe is a developing threat to our great country.
- You were India's first disruptive politician. This is India's first disruptive film.
- Since you had no resources you used it to your advantage with political innovation. We have no resources and we have relied on marketing innovation.
- You started your fight against crony-capitalism and corruption, which became a movement. I started this fight against crony-socialism and this film has become a movement.
- Yours was a movement of the common man, by the common man and for the common man. Ours is a movement of the students, by the students and for the students. (Just to mention, this film was initiated by the students of Indian School of Business, Hyderabad).
- AAP was a political start-up in true sense. This film is a start-up in true sense.
- You found opposition in a rigid political system and the corrupt politicians. We are finding opposition by a rigid academia and the corrupt faculty.
- People who associated with you for immediate gains left you

one by one. People who associated with us for Box Office returns left us one by one.

- Your functions were sabotaged and disrupted by vested interests that didn't agree with you. Our screenings have been sabotaged and disrupted by vested interests that do not agree with the film.
- You didn't have money but '*junta*' made it possible for you. We don't have money but 'students' are making it possible for us.
- Your politics is based on truth and evidences where you exposed so many nexuses. This film is based on truth and evidences and exposes Naxal-NGO-Academia nexus.
- You are a champion of student's cause and freedom of expression. This film champions students' cause and seeks its right to expression.
- You were alone in your fight. I am alone in my fight.
- Last but not the least, you are a man on a mission. I am also a man on a mission – to help build India.

We are releasing the film on the 13th of May. Please let us know a good time so that we can screen the film for you.

Jai Hind!

Vivek Agnihotri

I never got a reply to the mail but when *Buddha in a Traffic Jam* released, the AAP would take note. Negatively. But more of that later.

Nothing has changed in Kanpur. If someone threw a cigarette packet on the road many years ago, there are chances that he may still find it there. But it's my hometown and I love it the way it is. The moment we step out of the train, I feel a certain belonging. For me, it's some sort of a milestone to screen the film at IIT Kanpur, which as kids we only dreamt of as the highest body of knowledge.

The screening is at 10 PM in their Open-Air Theatre. It's been deliberately kept late so that students can finish their dinner before the mess closes at ten. Some three thousand students are expected. The Director has invited me to be the chief guest at their annual cultural evening where the faculty and the staff present various acts on stage and students are the audience. Senior professors and their wives perform skits, songs, dances, stand-up comedy and it's obvious that they are enjoying their performances. There is a sense of openness and maturity in the atmosphere.

I reach the venue fifteen minutes early to check the arrangements and am surprised to see it's one of the most hi-tech, state-of-the-art setups. The screen is huge, the sound system exceptional and the seating is like a large amphitheater. Students have started coming in in small groups. Around 9.55, the groups become larger and slowly the entire theatre converts into an overpowering sight of thousands of heads over one another, rising above the ground like a sea wave in a storm.

The film gets a long-standing ovation. Here too I see some students still sitting and not clapping. They have a frown and their eyes are cold. Taking a bow in all humility and gratitude, I am also preparing myself for the storm. Not the one I saw before the screening but the real storm.

As expected, after a few questions from the happy students, the angry students raise their hands.

'Who is the professor based on?'

'My professor.'

'Tell us the name.'

'I can't.'

'Why? Are you scared?'

'No. It's unethical.'

'So there is no professor.'

'That's what you are saying. I never said that.'

Happy students start booing him. Angry student stands up.

'Did you live with Adivasis? Or with the Naxals?'

'No. But I have interacted with them.'

'So, you never lived with them but you find yourself competent to make a film on their problems.'

'I am sure most scientists never went to the moon but they created machines that sent man to the moon.'

Happy students boo. Angry students start abusing them. Slowly, tens of students who were raising their hands start coming on stage and a group of about twenty students *gherao* me and start pushing and heckling me. Naireeta tries to disperse them along with the organizers who are too hesitant to intervene. One boy takes my arm and starts twisting it. I decide to stay cool. I know they need a reaction and I am not going to give them that pleasure. I also want to see the extent to which they can go.

'What you have shown is not true,' one young man screams.

'I don't know the truth but whatever I have shown is absolutely real,' I stand my ground.

'No. It's not real.'

He is furious. The veins on his forehead are on the threshold of exploding. He starts screaming at the top of his voice.

'You have no shit idea about Adivasis. You have no right to make a film about Adivasis. Naxals are right. You are wrong. Your film is a lie!' He is running short of breath. He starts pushing me, twisting my arm. If there was any background sound it would be people screaming 'Kill Agnihotri, kill Agnihotri!' From somewhere a girl screams and enters inside the cordon.

'Talk to me. I have lived with Adivasis in Bastar. Every single thing shown in this film is true. If anyone of you has ever lived the way I did, then challenge me, otherwise shut up.' And she starts crying. Naireeta holds her.

The guy who was twisting my hand, stops, stares me in the eye, gasps for air, pushes me and leaves. With him, all the others leave.

Students apologize to me and one by one start telling me their stories of discrimination by some of the faculty. Naireeta uses her presence of mind and starts shooting all those testimonials on her phone. I know we have captured invaluable sights and evidences to support the film's theme. I am looking for the girl who came to my rescue. She is nowhere to be seen. Sometimes God sends messengers to help you at moments when you are helpless and least expect them.

As we start to leave at 2 AM, a few boys chase our car, calling for Naireeta. Car stops. I roll down the window. Two boys literally touch my feet and start pleading.

'Sir, please ask madam to delete our video recordings. We told you all that in emotion. We can't antagonize our professors.'

'But we will never show it to anyone. It's only for our eyes,' Naireeta tries to take them in confidence.

'Sir, we trust you fully but please delete it…sir, please… if our professors ever get to know about it, they will ruin our life.'

I keep looking at their terrified faces as Naireeta deletes the recordings. Where fear ends, terror begins.

The sun is rising and we are speeding towards Lucknow airport. We have to be in Indore this evening, for the screening at IIM Indore. I open my phone and go through all the messages and mails. I stop at a mail which is written to Naiteeta and a CC to me. It reads:

'Hi Naireeta,

I just saw *Buddha In A Traffic Jam* today at IIT Kanpur and wanted to appreciate the whole team who made such a realistic movie.

First of all, I would like to make it clear that I am not an Adivasi…I was born and brought up in Jagdalpur which is a city in Bastar. I always wondered why national media seriously never reported the atrocities done by Naxals on the tribe of this region. This movie had clearly depicted the dilemma of a tribal who is stuck between the government and Naxals. I understand how difficult it is to convince people from the other parts of the country to and make them believe that the situations shown in this movie are real. This is because nobody else has ever brought up this issue before. The condition of Bastar is fairly complex and it's really difficult to put whole scenario in single movie. There are both, bright sides and dark sides. This movie highlights the dark part of Bastar which has been ignored for a long time.

I occasionally visited village in Bastar and I always felt sad that the people who live in the interiors are fighting for basic amenities. Moreover, the Naxalites are destroying schools and other public and private facilities in villages and this made me even more sad because this way they ensured that the tribals do not get educated and empower themselves. There are various incidents which are really disturbing.

I had no intentions to watch this movie because it would bring back many sad memories but after watching this movie it gives me a hope that the situation could be changed. I strongly believe that technology and education is the key to development in any part of the world. There are numerous ways in which technology can improve the situation in the Naxal affected regions. I really appreciate that this movie is being shown at prominent educational institutes to catch the attention of the new generation and give them a message that there are some parts in our country which are in immediate need of technologists and entrepreneurs.

Looking forward to see more such fantastic movies from your team.

Best regards.

(Name withheld on request)

(I have not made any changes in the email. Exactly as received)

IIM Indore is located on a height. Some places have vibes. When I am asked to speak to students, I tell them what my heart is feeling at this moment.

'Hello everybody. Good evening.

'I love talking to B-school students because you are the guys who love money and I love money too. I am going to tell you the reason why I love money and why you should love money too. Chanakya, the great political thinker, the great economist of India, said, "Money is the most creative invention of human beings." Unfortunately, in our country, we never celebrated money. We always celebrate mediocrity. I have always seen in Hindi movies that a rich man's son is always a rapist or a bad boy. A rich man's daughter has to necessarily be a bad girl. We have always shown that it is good to be poor and it is bad to be rich.

'If you travel to UK, US or any of the developed countries, you ask a young boy, "What do you want to be in life?" and nine out of ten will say, "I want to be rich." Unlike us, they do not feel guilty about money. It's not a moral issue. And why should it be a moral issue? Can we imagine life without money? I am deliberately using the word money here because whichever institute I go to, wherever I talk about money, people think here comes a capitalist bastard. In fact, one student came to hit me at NALSAR. This is the reason I am discussing money.

'This is the reason this film was made...because we have been told in a very clever political narrative that it's not good to celebrate success. This has been done systematically to cover up the government's own failure in delivery. Mediocrity has become the central narrative, the central theme of this country. And this is the reason why despite being number one in *jugaad*...like, if anything goes wrong, a tap is not working, a bulb is not working, there is a traffic jam, the kind of traffic jams we have in this country, imagine if this kind of traffic jam happens in London or New York, trust me people will be on the streets for 30 days.

'It happened in London when there was a heat wave which led to a traffic jam and people were on a highway for several days, a lot of people died. *Jugaad* means how effectively and quickly we solve our problems with minimal resources and expenditure. We are smart people. We are a country of young, struggling, middle class people. And this is our asset. Struggle gives you a lot of ideas. If we are so smart in solving problems with *jugaad*, any problem of any magnitude, be it a Mars mission, or expeditions to the Antarctic, having the largest number of IT professionals, and yet we are not the innovation hub of this world, it's because we do not let merit succeed.

'We do not celebrate merit. Whenever somebody talks about business, people think he is a bad guy as he trying to earn money. I believe if you want to change something, obviously you have to have new plans, new strategies, new systems in place, you have to have a different kind of systems thinking. Also, what you need is to change the conversation from a poverty mindset to a rich mindset; from scarcity to abundance. Once you change the conversation, in favour of innovation, the country will automatically start making money.

'The intellectual space of this country has always supported the Naxal movement which is why they are anti-rich, anti-success. If Tendulkar, with his merit, becomes rich, you find the same people starting to criticize and belittle him. They want to confuse people and want to blur the difference between people with talent, who work hard and have ideas and innovation to make money and people who became successful by corruption.

'This film is a start-up in the true sense. After our film was made, people who were financing it backed out. Whoever saw this film, ran away; they ran away because a lot of people didn't understand it. They said how is it possible that academia is brainwashing our students and converting them into intellectual terrorists. The second kind of people who ran away said we understand but it is so bloody controversial that you know it's not good for us, and the third set of people obviously were against the film because the film exposes those very people. A lot ran away because they wondered how can we show a capitalistic idea as a solution. How can we celebrate private enterprise, profits and money?

'So, we were stuck with a product which we believed is one of the best products because it not just exposes the truth, it also shows the might of Indian students that they are capable of telling a story which has not been allowed to be told in the last 70 years because of a corrupt system, corrupt administration, corrupt government who kept blaming rich people, successful people and criticizing money.

'We were alone. We tried to show it in some universities but unfortunately there also the faculty was hand in glove with a lot of anti-national activities and they also rejected our film. Then some students said we want to show this film outside on the street. On 18th March, in JNU, some five thousand students watched this film sitting on the ground, on the street actually, on trees, on terraces and on rooftops. Since then we have not stopped for a moment. This is the first time in the history of world cinema that a film has been shown to so many students and people before the release. Does any manufacturer go out sampling his product, free, before the formal launch of the product? People are generally scared...What happens if my film gets badmouthed, what if people criticize it on social media, then I am doomed. The biggest of the stars will never do that. Second thing, any filmmaker worth his salt will never allow his film to be screened in halls, auditoriums, in amphitheatres, outdoors on streets with thousands of mobile phones ready for piracy. We've had screenings with bad sound systems, we've shown it right on the wall of a university because there was a lot of wind and the screen was flying like a kite. We have shown this film in places where one channel had conked off.

'Why are we doing this? Why are we showing this film to whoever that invites us? In every institute, university? Because it's not about the box office, trust me, I am not lying, the mathematics is not on our side. Even if every single person watches this film, this film cannot make the kind of money big films make. Then why are we doing this? The purpose to show this film is to make people realize, to make young students realize that the time has come to work in the direction of innovation. You have to work in a direction where this country can be an innovation hub of the world and that must happen now because we have a golden opportunity.

'We have brought this film thus far without spending a penny. Have you ever seen any film in your lifetime which has been marketed without any TV spots, press ads, hoardings, radio spots etc.? We have not spent any money. Because nobody is giving money. But slowly it is finding its own audience. It is making people discuss, debate. If you go to social media, you will find angry comments saying, "Kill these people", "Destroy this movie", but you won't find anybody saying bad things about this movie. Nobody will say it's away from reality. And this is success. This is the success of an idea. Of marketing. Of disruption. I have learnt a lot from this and three learnings I want to share with you are:

'a) Believe in the power of collective conviction of thought. If four or five of you think of an idea, an innovative idea, you can make it work.

'Sometimes the dips which come, the failures which come, they are just the testing times, of how strongly you feel and believe in the idea. Sometimes you have an idea before its time has come, like we made this film four years ago. Nobody understood; if the Kanhaiya episode had not happened, nobody would have understood the film. I lost money and my sleep but never the belief. If you have belief, the time will surely come.

'b) Every product and service which you create has to contribute to people's lives so that people are emotionally invested in it and that, I think, is the key to success. Be it an Apple, be it a Google or Ola, or any product or service, if it does not genuinely satisfy or gratify some human needs and doesn't connect with them emotionally, it's very difficult to make that work. This is the reason why this film is working today, without any marketing, without any stars. This is happening because somewhere we have been honest, we have really been struggling to be heard and people can see that. The film must be contributing to their lives and connecting with their concerns. The film has given them hope.

'c) There is nothing wrong in marketing your ideas. Be ruthless. Because ultimately the purpose of our lives is to communicate our ideas to as many people as possible. Marketing is not a bad word, like money, if you are honest about it. If you really believe in something, go ahead and market it shamelessly. Don't care whether people are listening to you or not. A time will come when people will listen to you. Like you are listening to me now. (Laughter).

'So, here's a film which we have marketed without marketing it. In marketing, there is a push factor and a pull factor. This film has worked with the pull factor which you know is better than a push factor. Push involves lots of money. Pull builds on quality and word of mouth. Consumer reviews. Consumer satisfaction.

'The last thing I want to share with you is that very often you may find your professors or leaders asking you to think out of the box. I have been trying to think out of the box all my life, and I have been failing. Honestly. I felt that everybody was thinking out of the box, and I was one of them. So, I said, what do I do? I demolished the box. I just demolished the box. I said there is no box and then I got freedom and liberation. You should try it too. Imagine you are box–less, become a bubble.

'You know the difference between a box and a bubble. A box is always opaque, a box has sharp edges and a box never changes. But a bubble is always transparent and because a bubble is round, it doesn't hurt anybody. And when a bubble meets another bubble, it becomes a bigger bubble. So, these are all the insights I can share with you and I believe tonight my bubble will meet yours and we will have a bigger bubble. And if we truly want a revolution, we will have to meet more bubbles and keep growing into a huge bubble which can change the destiny of India forever. So, here is a film made of the students, for the students, and marketed by the students. So, I am presenting your film to you.'

After the screening, in an extremely passionate interaction, we formed bubbles of some great ideas with a promise to take them forward. I believe only such Buddha moments can transform India.

48. The Left and the Right of Struggle: FTII, Pune University

The attempts to cancel our screenings have reached a figure where now I feel there is a conspiracy behind this pattern. Verbal attacks, ridicule, heckling, resistance, sabotage have been the attractions of this journey. A friend from the US called after reading some FB posts on the attack at Kanpur IIT.

'What are they are fighting?' he asked me.

'A film,' I replied, to his utter shock.

I am on the last leg of the campaign. The film is releasing in one week. The last week has been extremely hectic. We have been to so many institutes that I have lost count. After Ahmedabad, Jaipur, Mumbai and many other universities, I am in Pune, before I fly the entire night to be in Kolkata tomorrow for a screening at Jadavpur University (JU). I have some time before the screening and I want to visit FTII. I always do so whenever I am in Pune, as it never fails to give me a new perspective. The film was supposed to be screened at FTII but as expected, Leftist groups did not allow it.

The last few months have kept India engaged in ruthless campus politics in institutes like IIT Madras, JNU, Osmania University, JU, DU, Bhagalpur University, HCU, and FTII. The fire was ignited at FTII and it led to all the other agitations. These agitations were centred around an argument that the new government is crushing the constitutional rights of free speech and dissent. In reality, no constitutional right was ever curbed or can ever be curbed. But the losers of the 2014 elections created a fact–less story, amplified by the media. The political masters, in order to embarrass Modi, made these students mouth anti-India slogans. This left the entire world wondering 'What went wrong with these institutes that they have started churning out anti-national students?'

Pallavi was elected to the FTII board of directors along with Raju Hirani, Santosh Sivan, Jahnu Barua, and Vidya Balan, but

Pallavi doesn't like to be involved in political bodies, so she resigned. The Left parties tried to make her their voice but she refused. I took a very strong stand against the government's decision to make Gajendra Chauhan the chairman of the board.

It's not because of my film background that I fell in love with FTII. There is an old connection. When we were in college and figuring out what to do next, most of us were secretly aspiring to join FTII. But we couldn't. We ended up doing secure courses with job assurance. Like our parents wanted.

For small-town middle-class kids, Bollywood is a secret dream but most of them don't have the liberty to express their ambition. Bollywood is perceived as a closed-door castle where family and friends keep making movies. Which door does the kid knock on, for an entry? For an outsider, FTII is that door. He knows that a lot of small-town middle-class unemployed graduates made it big in films because FTII trained them. There are several IITs, IIMs, AIIMSs. But there is only one FTII.

When an aspiring graduate fills the FTII form, he does not have much money in his pocket, not much support from family, not much understanding of the world of cinema, no idea about the functioning of an industry he is being trained for and, very often than not, not much fluency in English. All this guy has is a dream to become a part of this magical world called Cinema. To be able to tell stories, in his unique style.

Most of them don't even know what specialization they would want to go for. I don't think anyone specifically wants to join Sound Design or Production Design. How many have even held a camera before joining Cinematography? So, a lot of aspiring actors get into direction, directors into cinematography or editing. For, their dream is to become a filmmaker.

Then these minds are cultivated. They get a perspective, a context and a deep understanding of the art and science of filmmaking. FTII has had a tradition of being headed by some excellent filmmakers. The people who come out of that FTII gate are exceptionally trained, passionate and determined filmmakers. My crew always has a majority of FTII graduates.

When a student graduates from IIT, he becomes an engineer.

When a student graduates from AIIMS, he is a doctor. When a student graduates from any IIM, he is the future CEO. But when a student graduates from FTII, he becomes a struggler. A struggling actor, struggling director, struggling cinematographer and so on. Which other government-funded premier institute produces strugglers? Have you ever heard of a struggling IITian? At FTII, the struggle begins from day one. Struggle to be in sync with modern filmmaking. Struggle to finish the course– some students have to spend four to five years to finish a three-year course. Struggle to join the film industry, struggle to make movies, struggle to financially sustain themselves in '*Mahanagri* Mumbai'.

Times have changed. The world of films has changed. Technology is changing every six months. Trends, narrative, logistics, and marketing strategies are changing constantly. Audience tastes are changing every minute. Stories are changing. Aspirations are changing. Ethos and social realities are changing. Unlike a privately-run film institute, FTII is not being able to cope with the changing times. FTII isn't aligned with the industry. If you are doing an MBA, your institute is aligned with industry, which does campus interviews and picks up students according to its requirements. A catering college is aligned to the food and beverages industry. A travel course or a fashion course is aligned to their respective industries. But FTII? You finish your course and then become a struggler.

Why doesn't the government utilize the same subsidy as a soft, long-term loan? Why can't FTII become the avenue for film business? Why can't FTII be in a position to negotiate best career options for its alumni and be like a lighthouse to this never–ending ocean of film business?

Cinema is all about aspiration. It's about dreaming. It's about vision. When a young boy, with hope in his eyes, fills the admission form of FTII, he is aspiring to be a Naseeruddin Shah, a Raju Hirani, a Renu Saluja, an Anil Mehta, a Resul Pookutty, He comes with very high standards of aspiration. He wants to surpass these masters. If he is failing to see that vision in Gajendra Chauhan, how will he aspire to surpass the masters? He is beginning his course with a compromise. In life, we don't get what we deserve. We get what we negotiate. And Gajendra Chauhan is not what FTII students negotiated for, while filling the admission form. This is cheating. And I think government should not cheat.

In Pune, I meet two wonderful people, Nikhil Karampuri, the organizer from Think India and our host, and the disruptive blogger Shefali Vaidya, the chief guest. Nikhil isn't a stereotyped *bhagwa* flag holder or temple goer. He is an atheist who questions everything, besides being an Apple freak who loves his gadgets more than anything, a person who watches TV series like *Suits* and *The Blacklist* and enjoys reading the RSS' Hindi magazine *Panchajanya* as well.

Nikhil is from Ahmednagar and studies at MIT, Pune, the Oxford of the East. He comes from a family which is religious, rooted in Hindu ideology and sympathetic to RSS. Despite this background, Nikhil, at an early age, worked with some left-leaning NGOs, and found himself in alien territory. So, he joined Think India.

Think India was set up in 2007 to inculcate the value of thinking that could nurture the growth of India. With its maiden national convention in Bengaluru, Think India started its work in premier national institutes like IIT, IIM, AIIMS, NIT etc. Since then, Think India has spread across all the national institutions to bring the youth together to collaborate for realizing the dream of National Reconstruction.

'At some point, I was disillusioned with the left and their inhuman ideologies, and I was planning to quit both my studies and my job when Think India gave me the courage and confidence to do both at the same time,' Nikhil tells me.

Nikhil neither looks political nor has a tone that indicates any political inclination. I let him talk as I want to learn this unique perspective.

'Humans fear change. Everyone wants a perfect life, a perfect society, but no one takes the steps for making it happen. The authorities fear the younger generation and see them as a threat. Whenever we stand up to raise our issues, they threaten to shut us up. The educational institutes today have been turned into graduate-producing machines rather than places where the students are encouraged to think rationally and question wrongdoings. Apart from this, there is a careless attitude among the students where they feel no responsibility of giving back to society. On top of that, the Leftists never let anyone do any good social work. So overall, the path to change has not been a cakewalk for us but we fight our battles every day and tackle the challenges head-on.'

He cites many examples where injustice was done to their group just because they talk about national integration and development. What catches my attention is one of their recent issues with the Leftist students at FTII.

'Think India activists were eager to interact with the protesting students but were denied initially by the student association of FTII,' says Nikhil. 'Finally, after a long dialogue with the authorities and the student association, our activists were allowed to interact with the student community which didn't want the strike and they outnumbered the protestors. When we started speaking to students who wanted the institute to function, the Leftist students stopped our interaction and booed us out. I was shocked at the muzzling of our voice in a flagship institute for freedom of expression. The students who wanted to study were threatened and boycotted by their seniors and were forcefully dragged into the whole lockdown of the institute. These students were openly working on the instructions of Leftist and AAP leaders.

'The film industry has always portrayed only one side of the story, creating an illusion about Naxalism. As they say, "It's better to debate a question without settling it than to settle a question without debating it." We wanted the students to know both sides of the intellectual discourse. In *Buddha In A Traffic Jam*, we see the dawn of a different narrative and we decided to screen it at FTII. More for symbolic reasons. What could be a better place for a filmmaker, who faced resistance everywhere, to screen his film in one of the world's best film institutes? But to my surprise, FTII denied an open screening of the film, just because it portrayed a perspective that was contrary to a few students' ideological belief. We pursued the administration but even then, the permission to screen this movie was denied, citing some petty and baseless reasons.

'With no option left, we then decided to screen it at Savitribai Phule Pune University. When the event was finally organized, the authorities demanded a pre-screening for censoring the movie. The movie was subjected to scrutiny, unlike any other movie or documentary that has been previously screened on the campus. A movie carrying a new narrative of Naxalism in India as never portrayed before was seen as a threat for reasons that are still unknown to us.

'The left in India is just an NGO, which only seeks grants for doing nothing. We all know about the problems that we are faced with and the Indian public is interested now to find solutions rather than indulging themselves in cribbing. The leftists are supposed to be the champions of the oppressed classes and Dalits, but there is no representation of Dalits in any of the Communist politburos of India. The worshippers of non-violence have been known to indulge in extreme violence in Kerala and West Bengal. A very interesting term was introduced a decade ago by a few investigative journalists – The Golden Corridor. This acts as a furnisher of the Naxalites' monetary requirements. These forces act as middlemen between Naxalites and Maoist supporters spread across the world.

'There needs to be clarity on the concepts of modernization, Westernization, globalization and liberalization. But Leftists oppose everything without any logical reasoning. A lot of them are pure vegetarians but they want the cow to be slaughtered because the right wing wants to ban it. They even try to convert basic tenets of social and cultural life into an "intellectual fight". The world today is dominantly run on capitalist and socialist/ Communist models. India has created a very intriguing model by amalgamating the two models and extracting the best from both to serve its citizens. What India has done is the most amazing example of setting up an alternate narrative to these pre-recognized models. Another indigenous example of an alternate narrative was presented by Deen Dayal Upadhyay in form of Integral Humanism which he has described perfectly in the book with the same title. Integral Humanism has human development at the core of it.'

On similar lines, my 'ideal' Idea of India resembles a strong chemical compound which comprises various elements of opposite properties, yet converging into something valuable. India is not divided by her various parameters, instead, she is tied together by the individual identities of the many communities spread across the nation. Conservation of our history and culture brings us together but also reminds us of the mistakes that have divided us over centuries, leaving us vulnerable to foreign rulers and being used for their benefits. National reconstruction is a collaborative effort to carry out what has been forgotten for decades. This nation has been founded on very strong ideals and values, which is why it hasn't perished like many other civilizations around the globe.

The India that we are talking about here is not the India that won her independence from the British in 1947 but the one that has existed for thousands of years. Be it Chandragupta Maurya who along with Chanakya tried to form a unified India or Chhatrapati Shivaji Maharaj who did the same against a different resisting force. India is not a modern concept but an age-old belief that has been passed on to us over the generations. It is not merely an idea but a reality that has existed well before any other civilization. I dream of an India which is the 'Guru' for the world, a role model that the world looks up to for setting all wrongs right, a teacher that teaches them to create a harmonious co-existence of thousands of communities under a single unified belief.

India has been a habitat to a spectrum of ideologies for centuries and it can continue to remain so but the crux of them all should hold the Nation-first attitude.

Nikhil quotes an apt line from our beloved Prime Minister Shri Atal Bihari Vajpayee in his own words,

भारत जमीन का टुकडा नही, जीता जागता राष्ट्र पुरुष है।

India is not a piece of land, but a living entity.

It's been an enriching interaction and I am so glad that finally, India is arriving.

49. The Politics of Struggle: Jadavpur University

We travel overnight from Pune to reach Kolkata. Naireeta is very sick. As soon as we reach the hotel at 5 AM, I call for a doctor only to learn that Naireeta has chicken pox. I feel handicapped without her. She has been my navigator through this struggle. Moreover, it's her city. As I am making arrangements for her to go to her parents' house, she receives a mail from Pritam Duttagupta, the head of the student body which invited us. Some mornings start with a bundle of bad news. This is that morning.

From: Pritam Duttagupta <dr.prit87@gmail.com>
Date: Friday 6 May 2016
Subject: Screening of Buddha In A Traffic Jam in Jadavpur University
To: naireetadasgupta@gmail.com

'We want to inform you with sadness that the Jadavpur University authority has cancelled the screening of the film in the Dr. Triguna Sen auditorium at the eleventh hour. It is a deep shame, they invoked that the screening of the film violates the model code of conduct of Election commission. It is the deepest blow to the Freedom of Speech in the country… It has been proved again and again that the dominant intellectual hegemony of the Jadavpur University is silent on this regard and even passively or actively supports the decision of the authorities, much for their great talk on dissent and the Freedom of Speech. It is established that we have not violated any rules. Political slogans and posters are regularly put on in the campus by the left political parties without being censored. So how can a non-political platform be denied entry into an auditorium at the last minute for screening a film passed by the censor board? We have also consulted the legal experts and they have also agreed with us that this doesn't violate any code of conduct because this is a cultural event.

The events as narrated today are...

The JU students who got inspired by the previous successful screening of the film in different campuses are willing to screen the film in the campus of JU. But the dean orally transmitted that the film needs to be censored by an internal board. The students dissented and due to the shortage of time for the whole process to get completed devised other ways.

Some of the students being part of 'Think India' took the matter and approached the university through their platform and booked the auditorium for the screening. But the authorities at the last minute has cancelled the booking and left the students in dismay.

It is to be noted that the VC has equivocally said that he stands for freedom of speech and even allowed the anti-national posters to remain. There has been much protest on the campus without even informing the authorities.

But we, fortunately, maintained all due process but unfortunately were ruthlessly suppressed because we don't confront to the intellectual paradigm of the university nor we have' comrades in the faculty'.

But lastly, we stand by our freedom and our right to dissent and peacefully agreed to oppose the authoritarian fascist attitude of the authorities.

We also are surprised about the staring silence of the intellectuals and it proves their intolerance towards dissent.

We finally are peacefully organizing the screening in the campus in the open and will always stand by our fundamental right to our last breath.

N.B JU intelligentsia always speaks of critical thinking but it doesn't give the right to be a critic of their critical thinking. It's time to change it.'

Pritam Duttagupta

The censoring and banning of and resistance to right-wing material in our educational institutions has been going on for a long time. Unchallenged. The right-wing has assumed that it's impossible to fight the Leftists on their home turf. That's why it had given up on institutes like JNU, HCU, JU etc. But somebody had to challenge this myth. I did it by making *Buddha In A Traffic Jam*. I did it by taking the film directly to students and that too in Naxal citadels like JNU, IITM, NALSAR, and now at Jadavpur. They hate my guts, my conviction and my fearlessness. I exposed the shallowness of their arguments on *Manuvaad se Azadi, Brahmanvaad se Azadi*. I explained to them how one has to innovate, make profits, create capital in order to find *bhukmari se azadi,* freedom from hunger. Challenged them in their idiom and with sound logic.

They hate logic because logic destroys their mythical world. They have been showing the poor masses and gullible students an 'invisible end' of suffering, exactly like the *tantriks*, fake *babas* and godmen or magicians do, and they protect this illusion by not allowing debates, dissent, and rationality to exist in their fortresses. And if one still challenges them with facts and logic, they collectively attack you in collusion with the media to destroy you. I have come to this conclusion only after visiting the top institutes of India and with over hundred hours of intense Q&A sessions, debates, and discussions, especially with Leftist students. Wherever the faculty and administration are left-leaning, attempts were made to cancel the screening or just sabotage it by creating inane hurdles.

As Pritam explained on the phone, they kept making the rounds of the Administration Office without any movement on their application. They were sent from one desk to another. Then the administration started citing absurd reasons that many students don't want this anti-Naxal film to be screened, though nobody had seen the film in this part of the country. The organizing students asked them why they allowed anti-India sloganeering, marches and graffiti when most pro-India students didn't like it, and when the admin couldn't win the argument, they put another condition – that film could be screened only after their 'internal censor committee' saw and approved it.

Really? The students argued that the film is already censored by CBFC and they have no right to re-censor it. They told the registrar that when the decision of the 'internal censor committee' is already known, why didn't they straightaway refuse to show it? This fight went on for over two weeks without any party relenting on the censorship issue. Finally, the students gave up and went to book

Triguna Sen Auditorium which is managed by the alumni association and can be booked for a certain sum. They contributed money and booked the hall.

Pritam told me that it happens to them all the time, therefore this time they decided to not give up and go ahead with the screening even if it had to be done in a hostel room. There was genuineness in his voice. With anguish, he told me that there is a systematic 'institutional minoritization' of their voice. Simply put, nobody hears them. They are labeled 'Sanghi' and aren't considered intellectual because they speak against Naxalism. BTW, he is a research scholar in Physics. Yet, he is 'The Inferior'.

At 4.15, I leave the hotel in an Innova driven by a Bihari driver named Prabhu, hoping to reach JU at 5, to screen the film in an open ground. Only if we can manage to. We enter JU from Gate no 8. There are hundreds of students smoking, chatting and preparing placards and black flags. This is when some students see me and in less than a second, the car is *gheraoed* by an unruly and violent mob of students. They start raising slogans, hitting the car and trying to pull me out. A mob of journalists runs towards the car. We hear a big crash and realize that they have broken the windscreen of Prabhu's taxi.

Prabhu is really scared. He looks at me and then at the students. He wants to protect me. And his car too. The car, he can't. Me, he can, perhaps. I don't know what to do. I am not prepared for a political ambush. It's getting claustrophobic. They are banging on the car. They are abusing me in Bengali. And then a girl spits on my window and screams: 'Agnihotri, you bloody, fascist Brahmin… go back.'

A student slides his hand inside and calls me the murderer of Rohith Vemula.

'You killed Rohith Vemula, you murdered him.'

'Rohith wasn't murdered. He committed suicide,' I reply coolly.

'You… you fucking liar. He was murdered. And you guys murdered him.'

'I have stronger reasons to believe Rohith than you,' I tell him.

He is angry. He tries to pull me out of the car. Anticipating violence Prabhu rolls up the window and in that jiffy my hand gets stuck in the window. This boy doesn't leave my hand. He is pulling my hand out. My hand is stuck. I pull it hard and give up as I feel a shooting pain in my shoulder. Some students jump in front of the car. Like highway thugs. Some of them start kicking the car. I can see some major dents on the bonnet. I don't want to think about other dents all over. One skinny student comes running and jumps on the bonnet. A few girls start throwing sticks on the car. Some start attacking the car with the wooden handles of placards. One boy kicks the side mirrors. A mirror falls down, crumbling on the hot tar.

I see a bunch of students running towards the car. They have badges on. Looks like they are the organizing students. Yes, they are. They are fighting with the protestors. A fight breaks out. Girls are hitting boys. After some time, some organizers find their way in by pushing the protestors away from the car. They form a human chain around the car. In this half-hour, there has been no security, administration or police. It was a free-for-all.

The car moves slowly, inside a human chain of over a hundred students. We are guided to the playground which is full of students who want to see the film. Behind them are hundreds of students with black flags and posters abusing me, Anupam Kher, and Modi. The car stops.

'They could have killed us,' Prabhu tells me before I get down.

There is a projection system and sound system but I can't see any screen.

'Sir, they tore apart our screen. We asked for a new one but they are not letting it enter the gates. I have no idea what to do.'

The force that brings a crisis on us also shows us the light. I am not going to give up.

'Does anyone in your hostel have a white bedsheet?' I ask.

'Yes.'

'Run and get it.'

'Sir, it will take ten minutes. The students are very restless and there can be a fight. So why don't you address them for ten minutes?' he pleads.

I have given speeches in closed auditoriums and in front of controlled audiences but never spoken extempore to volatile students, surrounded by violent protestors. On top of that, the shooting pain in my broken shoulder is killing me. Do I have a choice?

I take the mike. The protestors raise their volume and start sloganeering, '*Brahmanvaad se Azadi... bhukmari se Azadi...*' and so on. I look at them for some time and when I realize they won't give me space to speak, I address them at an equally high pitch and ask them:

'OK brothers and sisters, I agree with your call for *Azadi*, but this time you tell me how will we attain this freedom? Your biggest misunderstanding is that I am speaking against you. You love India and I love India too. You want to change India and I want to change India too. You want India's name to rise so much that the entire world says "*Bharat Mata ki Jai*", I too want the same. The only difference is that you carry black placards, whereas here some boys are carrying white ones. The difference between black and white is that black is the colour of death, whereas white is the colour of peace. You want India's betterment with the colour black, we want it with the colour white.'

Their protest starts slowing down. Students with white flags start chanting '*Vande Mataram*'.

'Friends, for the past forty-five days non-stop, I have been visiting universities across India, where I have continuously been with students. and I have decided that the battle which started from JNU must end at Jadavpur University.

'This fight is not between the left and the right, neither is it a fight between Sanghis and *Laal Salaam*; this fight is between those who want to make India better and those who want to break India. The past forty-five days that I have interacted with students have convinced me that if a revolution is to happen, it will be brought by those students who want to make India shine with their ideas.'

Protesting students again raise their slogans of '*Azadi*'.

'Brothers and sisters, the question is from whom will you attain this freedom? Freedom is attained when you are a slave to someone. You are not a slave. Who are you seeking this *Azadi* from? Before asking for freedom, for once, question yourself and think about your parents who have sent you here after investing their blood and sweat for your education.

'Your fight should be with those people who are not efficient, who are unproductive, who are corrupt and dishonest. But if you will fight with your brothers and brainwash the gullible to hate other brothers, then this country will never change.

'I cannot stand by the thought process of people who celebrate a terrorist, who speak about the destruction of India. And nowadays, there is a new fashion, a weird new attitude that is developing that the road to fame is through abusing the country. But this is wrong. On Barkha Dutt and Rajdeep Sardesai's channels, the ones who are called intellectuals are actually not intellectuals. Have you ever heard the names of those people in the list of intellectuals who sent a mission to Mars? What is the reason that only those people make the list of intellectuals who abuse all the traditions and festivals of India, who abuse everything related to India and speak about breaking India? Real intellectuals are those who quietly work hard, who want to study, innovate and take this country forward.

'Friends, I have lived in the freest country in this world, America, I have studied there too. In any American university, if ten boys stand up and shout slogans promoting Osama Bin Laden, within three minutes they will be sent to an undisclosed location. India is the only country in the world that gives us so much freedom. We must make good use of it. By expressing new ideas and not by breaking windows of a taxi.

'If you want freedom from starvation, then I will tell you how we can achieve that. Freedom will be attained because of your thoughts, because of your creativity. The next war will not be fought with guns but will be fought by entering the minds of students. And let me remind you that numbers don't matter, quantity doesn't matter, quality does. The Kauravas were a hundred. The Pandavas were just five. Today at Jadavpur University, the boys who speak in favour of building the country may be less in number. But they can. And they must.

'In the end, I want to say just one thing. If you will free Kashmir, free Meghalaya, free Bastar, free every place of the country, then who will be left to give freedom? You know that in China it is not possible to become a citizen, so you will not be able to go there. Then what happens? So now the time has come, no matter what your thought process is, to see a collective dream. Together we dream that by 2025 (by which time you will have graduated and started working someplace), India becomes the world's "idea capital"! A global innovation hub! There is no country in the world where this kind of *jugaad* is possible. You need a lot of brains for *jugaad* and that is why our students are so highly respected wherever they go in the world. So, can we not decide that in the next ten to fifteen years, we make India the innovation and idea hub? This will happen with our ideas and not slogans, because slogans have no science.

'I would like to thank you all for inviting me here. It was very courageous of you to call me, I really liked it. When I was sitting in the car, someone asked me if I was feeling scared. I said, now I feel more determined. After coming to Jadavpur University, my courage has risen more, now nobody can stop this film, it will release on May 13, this is my faith. This is my truth. This is my Buddha.

'Thank you, thank you very much.'

While I speak, a few students have got a bedsheet and have tied it on the grill of the playground. The projector turns on and the beam falls on the bedsheet… the screen. I can see the power of collective thought. Even the protestors have learnt that it's never about the numbers; it's about the conviction of ideas. As the projection falls on the bedsheet, a record of sorts is being created as no film has been ever been screened on a bedsheet, prior to its release. I take a picture. This is the mother of all dissent images. An alternative narrative has begun. History is being created.

As the movie reaches its mid-point, amidst the sloganeering, I hear someone screaming. I get up to see and find that a short man is yelling at Pritam and his friends in Bengali. Someone tells me he is the registrar. I can make out he wants the screening to stop instantly. I run towards the screening spot and ask the boys not to stop it until the registrar speaks to me. Students don't give up. Two masses of students are threatening each other. With abuses, hatred, and violence. The registrar senses that the situation is getting out of hand so he threatens the organizing students with dire consequences and leaves.

It feels like I am in a war zone. Jadavpur, it feels like, has everything, barring education. This isn't political activism. It's *goondagardi*, hooliganism – supported by the administration and faculty. It's an extremely sad commentary on the state of our education system. These poor students don't even realize that they aren't anti-establishment anymore. Slowly, they have become anti-India. What can I say about the students when our media also writes headlines like 'Them vs Us' (*Indian Express* headline on Yaqub hanging).

Well, the film ends. I have to say it with deep anguish that Jadavpur is the only university where I didn't have a Q&A session. Because they believe in only raising questions. Not willing to listen to the answers.

Lights shut down. It is pitch dark. My driver Prabhu is trying to fix the bumper of his car. Students are shaking hands with me, congratulating me, hugging me, taking selfies with me. For them, it is a victory. For me, it is a shameful commentary on seventy years of democracy.

After an hour and half, while I am having dinner at the hotel, I get a call from one of the students and he tells me that they are being beaten up very badly by the Leftist students.

I switch the TV on and the news is everywhere. On all the channels, I am the centre of the news. The fight started with a boy called Sandeep Das. He is a Dalit. Leftist boys asked him why he watched the film despite being a Dalit. He said he liked the movie and liked my speech as it made sense to him and opened his eyes. So, they started beating him up saying this was how he would learn to support them. Then riots broke out and the entire thing became political. The political sharks have hijacked the issue. BJP and Left are furthering their agenda. I am advised by the security to stay in my room and not tweet until I leave Kolkata. I obey.

Before Prabhu dropped me at the hotel, he had asked me:

'Why are they against you?'

'Because I talk about working hard, making money and being successful.'

'What's wrong with that?' He paused and then added, 'What are they fighting for?'

'They are fighting for the poor.'

'But I am poor. Why did they have to break my car?'

I put my hand on his shoulder and told him, 'Even I am trying to figure that out. Let's have a deal. Whoever figures it out first will call the other.'

I knew pretty well that I will never have to call him because I'll never have the answer.

Epilogue – The Victory of Buddha

Mumbai has never been this cold. The preparations for the New Year eve party tonight are in full swing. Holi, Diwali, and New Year parties are rituals in our house. This year we have good reason to celebrate. It's been over seven months since May 13, 2016, the release of *Buddha In A Traffic Jam*. This was the first time I released a film on my own and I learnt that the night before the D-day feels exactly like your daughter's *bidaai*. Once the film hits the theatre, the maker loses all control over it. You conceive, deliver, nurture, protect, give form, shape and a soul and finally it goes away to where it belongs: the audience. Normally, the release day is the most important day in a filmmaker's life. But in my case, the journey after the release has been the most important experience of my life.

I am so grateful to the invisible power, viewers, supporters, politicians, activists, critics, media, trolls, and the intellectuals for richly contributing to my life-changing experience. I am not the same person anymore. Today, I do not fear losing anything. I fear no one. Not out of arrogance but because of my complete surrender and understanding of the principle that eventually, only truth wins: *Satyameva Jayate*. Because of my realization that no sacrifice is as valuable as the discovery of truth. No opposition is as strong as the truth. For, the truth is the real enlightenment, the real Buddha. The created became so strong that it changed the creator. A film became so powerful that it changed the beliefs of its maker. This is the victory of Buddha.

It was just a film. A small film, initiated by a bunch of students. It would have gone unnoticed. But they converted it into a political fight. In this fight, everyone left me. They were huge in number, might, and control. I walked alone. They tried everything to stop it but, eventually, it reached the audience and, in the end, the film won. The truth won. Buddha won.

When the Jadavpur University incident happened and the media started building up the news, bringing the film to the forefront, a lot of Urban Naxals were rattled. It was easy for them to restrict the film on university campuses but to curb its spread into households was beyond their might. They had broken the legs of the movie and never expected it to release but they had forgotten to break its spirit.

The drama began on May 7th, a night after the Jadavpur incident caught fire. A group of people in Lutyens Delhi, led by AAP–supporter scribe Abhinandan Sekhri of newslaundry.com and other journalist accomplices started a campaign to ridicule the film. Sekhri tweeted:

'@vivekagnihotri and while I think no matter how silly or mediocre your film, it must be screened, that doesn't take away from your buffoonery.'

This was nasty and unnecessary. He was commenting on the film without even seeing it. But he was not alone. The cocktail circuit of Lutyens intellectuals started attacking me on social media, columns, blogs and all available public forums. A few days after the film released and found massive appreciation, and once the public opinion started building in favour of the film, Sekhri was forced to call me for an interview. When he came to my office with his camera team, I asked him if he had seen the film which he ridiculed so much. He admitted that he had not. I made him sit in my office and watch the entire film on my computer. After watching the film, he hugged me and said he was wrong in pre-judging me and apologized for the longest time. During the interview, he confessed at least three times to the camera about running a dirty campaign against me, apologized and praised the film extensively, and asked others to see it. Later, he tweeted:

'Thanks for that (interview and screening of the film) & I owe u an apology. I was disparaging about your film without seeing it I then watched it & enjoyed it'

This was Buddha's victory.

Well, how can Bollywood be left behind? Lyricist and stand-up comedian Varun Grover led the attack with a number of tweets:

'Many versions of who got violent 1st at JU screening of VA's film. But bottom-line – stopping a film from being screened is plain Talibanism.'

He didn't stop at this sarcasm and in a series of tweets, puked a lot of venom at the film.

'So yeah, good for the film that some noobs (JU admin or students or whoever) considered it worth stopping. *Shaheed*i *ka tamga*, best *tamga*! (Martyr's label, best label)'

An ex-critic of *The Hindu*, Sudhish Kamath wrote several pieces, tweets on the film, ridiculing it, bashing it, ripping it apart, and raping it, trying to prove that the film is worse than *Gunday*, a film supposed to be the worst ever. This came from a man who has himself made a film. Ironically, these people take pride in calling themselves reformists, liberals, progressive. So far, they had opposition only from vernacular, *sanskari* people in kurta pyjamas, who they could label as regressive or Hindu fundamentalist. For the first time, one of them was exposing them in their own idiom, style, and manner. Nobody from their own community had called them 'Urban Naxals'. I did.

They started debating if my shoulder was actually broken or not. How could I hold the mike if it was broken? One journalist even wondered how I was alive without the backing of the ruling party. Not all, but some of them wanted me dead. Some wondered why my dad didn't use a condom, besides hurling abuses at my mother, wife, and daughter. They sent me life threatening messages. I still sometimes revisit some messages from a pimp of a large corporation asking me to withdraw my film from the release. 'You don't know our power,' he had threatened. By this time, a filmmaker should have chickened out. But I didn't and this made them angrier and they employed all their weaponry to destroy me.

On May 13th, when the movie released, it found two distinct responses. One from Mumbai and Delhi-based critics and another from the rest of the world. The Mumbai/Delhi critics club was led by Raja Sen of *Rediff* and Suprateek Chaterjee of *Huffington Post*. If you were to read the reviews from *Rediff* to *Huffington Post* to *Scroll.in*, the movie is 'a propaganda film'. *Scroll.in*'s Nadini Ramnath says 'warnings about the "red menace" sound like direct quotes from the speeches of Baba Ramdev and Mohan Bhagwat.'

Suprateek Chaterjee called it a 'right-wing propaganda piece', Raja Sen said *Buddha in a Traffic Jam* made him 'feel sorry for Indian right-wingers' because it was apparently not good enough propaganda. Sarit Ray, writing in *Hindustan Times*, called it 'propaganda disguised as cinema'. It was a mere coincidence that all of them are Bengalis and they wrote exactly the same reviews as if out of a pre-decided template. Be it tweets, FB posts, reviews or blogs, all the paragraphs were in the same order with the same content with the word 'propaganda' spread out evenly.

I had always believed that *Huffington Post* was a responsible publication and would never entertain personal grudges to become part of its editorial. Raja Sen refused to give the film any star. This was the first time in my memory when I saw a critic refusing to give any star to a film. How bad can a film be which won so many awards and was selected by MAMI under Shyam Benegal's chairmanship as one of India's best five films?

These people didn't write reviews. They wrote hate pieces. In some time, it came out that most of them had written those hate pieces without even watching the film.

Slowly, other reviews started coming from other, non-agenda parts of India and abroad where genuine critics, who saw the film in the theatre, and not just wrote reviews but essays on the politics of Naxalism and the points the film made. Those who live outside competitive and ambitious Mumbai and Delhi are more socially and politically conscious. While metro critics start with finding negatives, the non-metro and rooted critics try to find positives. One critic, Mayuresh, wrote:

'To truly appreciate the scale of the attack on Freedom of Expression (FoE) that the Jadavpur incident represents, you have to see *Buddha in a Traffic Jam*. I think most of the social media discourse about the movie is misleading as it refers the movie as anti-Naxal or anti-left, and hence the battle for its screening as a battle between red and saffron in a manner of speaking. Actually, the movie is neither of these. It is a microscopic, almost anthropological, look at how the poorest people of India are hard done to by evil corporates on one side and the militants on the other. As the movie cuts back and forth between the metro where college professors talk revolution, and the harsh, arid landscapes of rural India, we realize there are no heroes, only victims. That, argues Vivek, is the true tragedy of this conflict.

'The first strike against Vivek is, of course, his refusal to drink the Leftist concoction of 'intolerance' and 'award *wapsi*'. Vivek was always going to be a target after that. *Buddha* shows the poor people in nothing but sympathetic light, it is the gun-toting maniacs that Vivek has problems with. The Jadavpur gang does not care for the poor people, or they would have allowed a movie proposing a solution for the poor to be screened. In this dispute, the Jadavpur gang is acting as bouncers of the armed militants. They are the bullies, trying to crush Vivek's voice so that the armed militants can continue exploiting some of the poorest people on the earth.

'The second strike is his balanced portrayal of the problem at the root of the Naxal terrorism, and his temerity to suggest that technology and trade may be the answer to the problem. For people who are used to terming modern business and modern technology as the villains of the episode, Vivek's solution is damn near blasphemous.'

Slowly but steadily, the film started finding its cult. This is the victory of Buddha.

Today, at the end of the year, *Huffington Post* has released a list of the ten best films of the year and they have rated *Buddha In A Traffic Jam* as the second best, only after *Dangal*. Many other prominent listings have rated the film among the three best films of the year. *Huffington Post* writes in honour of our film, of course after watching it and understanding it:

'*Buddha in a Traffic Jam* is a powerful film about morality, corruption, and social injustice that forces us to think about things which we don't usually pay heed to. The film was panned by the Indian left-wing lobby at the time of its release. The issue at the heart of *Buddha in a Traffic Jam* is the Naxalite crisis. But the film dares to show us a different side to the Naxalite movement – not as a struggle in the jungle but driven according to a sophisticated business model designed by high-thinking masterminds. Directed by Vivek Agnihotri, *Buddha in a Traffic Jam* is well-researched and extremely well made. It is a real pity that the film was unjustly censured for leaning towards the right at the time of its release when in actuality it is equally critical of both the extremes. Here is an important film that hopefully will find a cult following in times to come.'

This is the victory of Buddha.

On the release day, some three hundred troll handles were opened with zero followers to troll the film. This was led by Arvind Kejriwal's fans and the group of trolls was led by the queens of trolls – @Rajyashree and Swati Chaturvedi @Bainjal, who later wrote a book on trolls. The best part is that none of them had seen the film. Like they share articles without reading them only on the basis of the headline, they started writing pre-determined reviews and comments. One anonymous guy/girl with the handle @GabbbarSingh trolled the film and called it a shitty film. Reading the comments, I knew that he/she had not seen the film so I deliberately asked which chapter he/she hated the most, which was never replied to. This person had not seen the film but was either paid or motivated to write against the film, otherwise, how can anybody be so stupid?

These were testing times for me. On any other day, I would have gone into depression or would have quit this dirty world of politics and Bollywood but I had nothing to lose. Any more Anymore. Instead, I focused on the positive side. Slowly, the appreciation started pouring in on social media. Support came from everywhere, from students, housewives, ex-Naxals, social workers, scientists, economists, sociologists, writers, painters, editors, religious gurus, soldiers, NRIs, and by and by, it became a people's film. I can guarantee no other small film in recent times has received so much of appreciation, support and fan following like *Buddha in a Traffic Jam*.

We started getting invitations from Oxford and Cambridge, Australia, Singapore and many American universities and associations. Random people started exposing the lies of people like Raja Sen and Sekhri. Slowly, an army of thousands of *Buddha* believers started protecting the film from Urban Naxals and started promoting it through unconventional channels. The film found its market, its audience and created an ecosystem. The film got sold to all major digital platforms. It got over a million organic views on YouTube in no time. This is the victory of Buddha.

Today, if one has to follow my social media handles, he will find that almost every tenth minute someone writes something great about the film. A lot of handles which were trashing the film earlier are now my followers, friends, and admirers. The trolls became brand ambassadors of the film. One of them sent me a mail:

'Hello sir,

Before I go all out in praise for your film let me take this opportunity to congratulate you on your movie "Buddha in A Traffic Jam".

Initially, I had been observing you in the public space for quite some time and in all fairness, must say that I was very sceptical about you, the movie and your entire movement. And that, in fact, was the reason why I held back and persuaded myself not to go for the movie. It's been quite some time now that your movie has released and I happened to see it very recently and, I must say the skepticism which was there is completely gone in fact yes, it was a reality check for me that, one should have the ability to hear the counter-narrative too. I happen to be a student of Political Science and such topics are part of our discourse but I never expected that actually a script such as this would ever come up in Bollywood. Although this is not the genre I really go for, but this movie has been an exceptional case for me. This movie is a perfect response to the current situation and now I realize why there was this great opposition you faced on different campuses. Once again, congratulations to you and your entire team sir. Also, good luck for your upcoming project.

Best wishes,
Nikunj Chaudhari

(I have not made any changes to the email)

This is the victory of Buddha.

The same media which tried every trick in their bag to discredit me has been requesting me to write articles for them, which I do now on a regular basis. *NDTV* and *India Today*, which I had come to believe would never call me to their studios, have been regularly inviting me to their debates. This is the victory of Buddha.

The Leftists, liberals and intellectuals and their sympathizers had panned the film as my fantasy. Journalist Saba Naqvi, in a TV debate, even went to the extent of saying that I oppose Naxals because I have no intellect and radical activists like Kavita Krishnan and Shehla Rashid called the film my fantasy. But once the film started getting ground support, their own organizations, forums started inviting me to their seminars, conventions as the main speaker. The doors of literature festivals opened up for me. Academic forums started inviting me to present my views on Urban Naxalism and Intellectual Terrorism. Since the release of the film, I have been travelling the length and breadth of the country for almost 15-20 days a month to give lectures at various prestigious forums.

I was invited by TedX. I have been commissioned by the Forum for Integrated National Security (FINS) to make a documentary on Naxalism and the shooting is on in Bastar. Arvind Kejriwal's left-hand man, Ashish Khetan of AAP, was forced on national TV to invite my film for a screening at Delhi's secretariat. There hasn't been a day when the national media hasn't called me for a byte on national issues. They can condemn me but not the voice of Buddha. This is the victory of Buddha.

Suresh Chukappali, the producer who had abandoned the film midway to die, called me to his house after the release. Not only that, he requested me to send the awards and the trophies to him to be displayed at the reception of his new swanky office. This is the victory of Buddha.

The hangover of New Year hasn't subsided and as I start work on my next film, trying to discover yet another political mystery, there is news that has brought the film back in the limelight. Professor G.N. Saibaba of Delhi University has been sentenced to life imprisonment for colluding with the Naxals and working against national security. Along with him, the students whom he brainwashed and mentored to pick up guns and become Naxals were also arrested. The Inspector General of Police of the Nagpur Range, Ravindra Kadam, said that a few students of the university had joined the underground Maoist cadre at the behest of the professor. The students who joined the Naxal movement were members of the Democratic Students' Union (DSU). It's the same students' body whose member Umar Khalid was arrested by the Delhi police, in relation to the Afzal Guru sloganeering case at JNU.

'Professor Saibaba had been active with Left-leaning students of both JNU and DU and had been indoctrinating and recruiting them for the Maoist movement. In course of time, Saibaba had prepared and recruited four students as Maoist cadre,' Kadam said.

'Either these people followed your script in real life, or you are a clairvoyant who read their future script. Whatever it is, your effort to show the truth is worthy of a salute,' anti-Naxal hero Inspector General Kalluri told me. *This is the victory of Buddha.*

Earlier, in November 2016, a Delhi University professor Nalini Sunder was booked along with other Naxals on charges of murder of an Adivasi villager in the insurgency-hit Sukma district of Chattisgarh. The government has identified hundreds of NGOs who have been working illegally and are suspected of helping anti-national elements. Many ex-Naxal women have reported sexual abuse, rape and oppression of women exactly like the film depicted.

A few days ago, Naxals shot down twenty-five CRPF soldiers in a dastardly act of violence. In a quick operation, police nabbed some Naxals and some surrendered. One of the surrendered Naxals, Podium Panda, confessed to the police and later in the court that he was the link between Nalini Sunder, activist Bela Bhatia, and the Naxals. He used to drive them on his motorbike to the Naxal bastion.

It's been established beyond doubt that some members of academia have been helping Naxals in attaining their objective of toppling the democratic system of India with an armed revolution. Exactly like the film.

Today, unanimously, the film is recognized as a prophetic film of our times. Even by its opponents. *This is the victory of Buddha.*

I was invited for a town hall at Facebook's headquarter at Menlo park in Silicon Valley and this is where I realized that most of the Indians in the audience have been discussing 'Urban Naxalism' after seeing the film. I spent the entire evening with them discussing this red terror and almost all of them felt that they have been victims of Urban Naxalism while in college. One young IT engineer who has just joined Facebook hugged me and held my hand tightly and said,

"Sir, your film is my story. I was also influenced by my professors to turn leftist and before I could realize I had started hating India. It's only after watching our movie I realized how I was brainwashed and now I believe in India and will do anything to build a New India. Thanks for speaking up." This is the *victory of Buddha.*

They tried to shut me up by painting me as a part of the Hindutva campaign. But it was never about Hindutva. It's neither about freedom of speech or intolerance. This is a tactic employed to protect their castles. They confuse the issue by bringing in lots of counter news and views. They quote laws. They try to make it look like an anti-RSS, anti-BJP issue. This isn't about any of the above. It's about a war against India. In 2010, there was an intelligence report that terror groups were making inroads in Indian universities. Everyone ignored it exactly like when intelligence said Ishrat Jahan was a suicide bomber. They believe in intelligence reports only when it suits them. This is India's real threat.

The myth that sustains the Naxalite movement is that the 'Indian State' and the 'government' are outright evil entities, and every instrument of the State is, therefore, a justifiable target for violence and that the Naxalites themselves, in turn, are the only protectors of the people against the evil State. Far from Charu Majumdar and Kanu Sanyal's class war, today's Naxalites are 'guns for hire', and exploit and oppress the very people they claim to be fighting for. Even schools in rural areas, which could help them break out of the poverty trap, have been blown up by Naxals, for whom every educated child represents the potential loss of a blinkered recruit.

The people who work as their mouthpieces also know very well but they succeed in spreading the lie as they have been controlling the narrative. We broke into it, challenged it and tried to introduce a new narrative. In the last six months, we have travelled in deep Bastar and recorded umpteen stories of Naxal barbarity and exploitation of Adivasis. The awareness the film created has given a lot of confidence to ex-Naxals who have been secretly wanting to share their stories with me. *This is the victory of Buddha.*

Today, I am at the nerve centre of the Naxal movement: Chhattisgarh. I have been invited by a group of ex-Naxals and anti-

Naxal groups. There is a flood of innocent Adivasis who can't even speak properly but they are here to acknowledge the dent the film has made to Naxalism. I am overwhelmed with their love. They have made me feel like a hero, a crusader.

A couple meets me. Their story can make any sane person puke with disgust. They are ex-Naxals. While fighting the 'revolution', they fell in love but couldn't marry as the Naxal law dictates that every man gets a vasectomy operation done before marrying a Naxal woman cadre. One day, after their colleagues killed an innocent villager, opened his chest, gouged out his eyes and mutilated the corpse with an axe, both of them fled and took protection in Jagdalpur. They married and now have children. They are crying. Not because of the suffering but out of the joy of meeting and sharing their pain with me.

'Sir, whatever you have shown in the film is absolutely true. Everything. We have come here to pay our gratitude to you for showing the truth behind the barbarity of savages like Naxals. Somebody had to do it. Thanks.'

I have tears in my eyes. This is the victory of Buddha. *The truth.*

There may not be a place for the alternate narrative in Naxal-infested jungles, campuses, media and minds but in the world of real, rational and sane people, there is always a place for truth – the only narrative one needs to know.

Satyameva Jayate.

❑❑❑

THE MAKING OF

BUDDHA IN A TRAFFIC JAM

Vivek is an award-winning filmmaker and writer. An ex-advertising man, Vivek is a very popular public speaker on socio-political issues and lectures on 'Creative Thinking' and 'Innovation' in top global institutes.

His prophetic film, *'Buddha In A Traffic Jam'* dealt with the theme of Urban Naxalism and exposed the sinister nexus between the Naxals, Media, NGOs and academia. The film faced extreme resistance from the Left and was stuck for five years before Vivek travelled all across India to show his film, facing violent attempts to curb his freedom of speech.

Vivek is an avid traveler, columnist and a social media influencer. He is married to national award-winning actor Pallavi Joshi and has two children.

Vivek Agnihotri

garudabooks.com/urbannaxals

Made in the USA
San Bernardino, CA
24 June 2018